Artificial Intelligence Techniques for Solar Irradiance and PV Modeling and Forecasting

Artificial Intelligence Techniques for Solar Irradiance and PV Modeling and Forecasting

Editors

Fouzi Harrou
Ying Sun
Bilal Taghezouit
Abdelkader Dairi

Basel • Beijing • Wuhan • Barcelona • Belgrade • Novi Sad • Cluj • Manchester

Editors
Fouzi Harrou
King Abdullah University of
Science and Technology
(KAUST)
Thuwal
Saudi Arabia

Ying Sun
King Abdullah University of
Science and Technology
(KAUST)
Thuwal
Saudi Arabia

Bilal Taghezouit
Renewable Energy
Development Center (CDER)
Algiers
Algeria

Abdelkader Dairi
Oran University of Science
and Technology-Mohamed
Boudiaf
Oran
Algeria

Editorial Office
MDPI
St. Alban-Anlage 66
4052 Basel, Switzerland

This is a reprint of articles from the Special Issue published online in the open access journal *Energies* (ISSN 1996-1073) (available at: https://www.mdpi.com/journal/energies/special_issues/AI_Solar_Irradiance_PV).

For citation purposes, cite each article independently as indicated on the article page online and as indicated below:

Lastname, A.A.; Lastname, B.B. Article Title. *Journal Name* **Year**, *Volume Number*, Page Range.

ISBN 978-3-7258-0067-4 (Hbk)
ISBN 978-3-7258-0068-1 (PDF)
doi.org/10.3390/books978-3-7258-0068-1

© 2024 by the authors. Articles in this book are Open Access and distributed under the Creative Commons Attribution (CC BY) license. The book as a whole is distributed by MDPI under the terms and conditions of the Creative Commons Attribution-NonCommercial-NoDerivs (CC BY-NC-ND) license.

Contents

Fouzi Harrou, Ying Sun, Bilal Taghezouit and Abdelkader Dairi
Artificial Intelligence Techniques for Solar Irradiance and PV Modeling and Forecasting
Reprinted from: *Energies* **2023**, *16*, 6731, doi:10.3390/en16186731 1

Fouzi Harrou, Bilal Taghezouit, Sofiane Khadraoui, Abdelkader Dairi, Ying Sun and Amar Hadj Arab
Ensemble Learning Techniques-Based Monitoring Charts for Fault Detection in Photovoltaic Systems
Reprinted from: *Energies* **2022**, *15*, 6716, doi:10.3390/en15186716 6

Amor Hamied, Adel Mellit, Mohamed Benghanem and Sahbi Boubaker
IoT-Based Low-Cost Photovoltaic Monitoring for a Greenhouse Farm in an Arid Region
Reprinted from: *Energies* **2023**, *16*, 3860, doi:10.3390/en16093860 34

Wilson Castillo-Rojas, Fernando Medina Quispe and César Hernández
Photovoltaic Energy Forecast Using Weather Data through a Hybrid Model of Recurrent and Shallow Neural Networks
Reprinted from: *Energies* **2023**, *16*, 5093, doi:10.3390/en16135093 55

Jesús Polo, Nuria Martín-Chivelet, Miguel Alonso-Abella, Carlos Sanz-Saiz, José Cuenca and Marina de la Cruz
Exploring the PV Power Forecasting at Building Façades Using Gradient Boosting Methods
Reprinted from: *Energies* **2023**, *16*, 1495, doi:10.3390/en16031495 80

Miguel López Santos, Xela García-Santiago, Fernando Echevarría Camarero, Gonzalo Blázquez Gil and Pablo Carrasco Ortega
Application of Temporal Fusion Transformer for Day-Ahead PV Power Forecasting
Reprinted from: *Energies* **2022**, *15*, 5232, doi:10.3390/en15145232 92

Elmamoune Halassa, Lakhdar Mazouz, Abdellatif Seghiour, Aissa Chouder and Santiago Silvestre
Revolutionizing Photovoltaic Systems: An Innovative Approach to Maximum Power Point Tracking Using Enhanced Dandelion Optimizer in Partial Shading Conditions
Reprinted from: *Energies* **2023**, *16*, 3617, doi:10.3390/en16093617 114

Faris E. Alfaris
A Sensorless Intelligent System to Detect Dust on PV Panels for Optimized Cleaning Units
Reprinted from: *Energies* **2023**, *16*, 1287, doi:10.3390/en16031287 137

Mahmoud Dhimish and Pavlos I. Lazaridis
Approximating Shading Ratio Using the Total-Sky Imaging System: An Application for Photovoltaic Systems
Reprinted from: *Energies* **2022**, *15*, 8201, doi:10.3390/en15218201 154

Jingwei Zhang, Zenan Yang, Kun Ding, Li Feng, Frank Hamelmann, Xihui Chen, et al.
Modeling of Photovoltaic Array Based on Multi-Agent Deep Reinforcement Learning Using Residuals of I–V Characteristics
Reprinted from: *Energies* **2022**, *15*, 6567, doi:10.3390/en15186567 170

Sajid Sarwar, Muhammad Annas Hafeez, Muhammad Yaqoob Javed, Aamer Bilal Asghar and Krzysztof Ejsmont
A Horse Herd Optimization Algorithm (HOA)-Based MPPT Technique under Partial and Complex Partial Shading Conditions
Reprinted from: *Energies* **2022**, *15*, 1880, doi:10.3390/en15051880 187

Chao-Ming Huang, Shin-Ju Chen and Sung-Pei Yang
A Parameter Estimation Method for a Photovoltaic Power Generation System Based on a
Two-Diode Model
Reprinted from: *Energies* **2022**, *15*, 1460, doi:10.3390/en15041460 . . . . **209**

Editorial

Artificial Intelligence Techniques for Solar Irradiance and PV Modeling and Forecasting

Fouzi Harrou [1,*], Ying Sun [1], Bilal Taghezouit [2] and Abdelkader Dairi [3]

1. Computer, Electrical and Mathematical Sciences and Engineering (CEMSE) Division, King Abdullah University of Science and Technology (KAUST), Thuwal 23955-6900, Saudi Arabia
2. Centre de Développement des Energies Renouvelables, CDER, B.P. 62, Route de l'Observatoire, Algiers 16340, Algeria; bi.taghezouit@cder.dz
3. Computer Science Department, University of Science and Technology of Oran-Mohamed Boudiaf, USTO-MB, BP 1505, El Mnaouar, Bir El Djir 10587, Algeria
* Correspondence: fouzi.harrou@kaust.edu.sa

Citation: Harrou, F.; Sun, Y.; Taghezouit, B.; Dairi, A. Artificial Intelligence Techniques for Solar Irradiance and PV Modeling and Forecasting. *Energies* 2023, *16*, 6731. https://doi.org/10.3390/en16186731

Received: 6 September 2023
Accepted: 19 September 2023
Published: 21 September 2023

Copyright: © 2023 by the authors. Licensee MDPI, Basel, Switzerland. This article is an open access article distributed under the terms and conditions of the Creative Commons Attribution (CC BY) license (https://creativecommons.org/licenses/by/4.0/).

Solar Photovoltaic (PV) systems represent key and transformative technology at the forefront of the global shift towards sustainable energy solutions. These systems harness the renewable radiation of the sun, converting it into clean electricity. Their importance cannot be overstated as they play a fundamental role in mitigating climate change, reducing dependence on finite fossil fuels, and providing access to clean energy sources for both developed and developing regions. Solar PV systems are not only a key component of the renewable energy portfolio, but also a symbol of our commitment to a greener and more sustainable future for generations to come.

The main difficulty in solar energy production is the volatility and intermittency of photovoltaic system power generation, primarily stemming from unpredictable weather conditions. Variations in irradiance and temperature can have a profound impact on the quality and reliability of electricity production from solar PV systems. Since solar irradiance is intricately linked to the efficiency of solar power harvesting, its accurate prediction serves as a crucial indicator of power production potential. For large-scale solar plants, any power imbalance within the PV system can lead to significant economic losses. Therefore, precise solar irradiance prediction, coupled with the appropriate modeling of PV system behavior, has emerged as a vital necessity to mitigate the impact of uncertainty and control energy costs. Furthermore, it facilitates the seamless integration of PV systems into smart grids, a growing trend driven by the increasing adoption of PV technology.

Numerous studies were undertaken to develop models and algorithms that predict solar irradiance based on various routinely measured meteorological parameters, such as temperature and humidity, to address these challenges. These advancements in accurate solar irradiance forecasting and the sophisticated modeling of PV systems have now become the cornerstone of modern smart grid development, supporting the expansion of Renewable Energy Sources (RESs).

The importance of Artificial Intelligence (AI) methods in predicting, modeling, and fault detection in PV systems cannot be overstated in today's energy landscape. AI has emerged as a transformative force in addressing the inherent challenges associated with solar energy production. Through the utilization of advanced machine learning algorithms and data analytics, AI techniques can ingest vast datasets, including historical weather patterns, system performance data, and real-time measured parameters, to provide highly accurate solar irradiance predictions. This precision in forecasting enables PV systems to optimize their energy capture, adapt to changing weather conditions, and maximize their overall efficiency. Moreover, the AI-driven modeling of PV systems goes beyond mere prediction by providing a comprehensive understanding of how these systems behave under various operating conditions. These models allow for the fine-tuning of PV system parameters, such as PV array orientation and tracking mechanisms, to achieve ultimate performance. Additionally, AI-based modeling helps to identify potential issues and areas of improvement, contributing to system longevity and reducing maintenance costs. In fault detection, AI technologies offer real-time monitoring and anomaly detection capabilities. By continuously analyzing the performance data from PV systems, AI algorithms can swiftly identify deviations from expected behavior, such as PV module failures, inverter malfunctions, or shading issues. The early detection and identification of these anomalies is crucial in preventing downtime, reducing energy losses, and ensuring the overall reliability of the PV system. Furthermore, AI-driven insights are indispensable for the integration of PV systems into smart grids. These systems require precise forecasting, adaptive control mechanisms, and seamless coordination with other energy sources to ensure grid stability and reliability. AI plays a pivotal role in enabling this integration by providing real-time information on the expected power output from PV systems, allowing for grid operators to make informed decisions about load balancing and energy distribution.

After an exhaustive and thorough review process, eleven high-quality articles were finally accepted for their contributions to the topic.

In [1], Castillo-Rojas et al. presented forecast models for PV energy generation based on a hybrid architecture that combines Recurrent Neural Networks (RNNs) and shallow neural networks. Two categories of models are developed, the first utilizing records of exported active energy and meteorological variables as inputs, and the second relying solely on meteorological variables. The models are rigorously evaluated using real data from a solar plant, and the best-performing model from each category is selected. The selected model from the first category achieves impressive accuracy metrics, including a root mean square error (RMSE) of 0.19, mean square error (MSE) of 0.03, mean absolute error (MAE) of 0.09, correlation coefficient of 0.96, and determination coefficient of 0.93, demonstrating its robust forecasting capabilities. Although the second category model exhibits slightly lower accuracy, with metrics such as RMSE = 0.24 and MAE = 0.10, it still performs well, with a correlation coefficient of 0.95 and determination coefficient of 0.90. Both models exhibit good performance in forecasting weekly PV energy generation, offering valuable insights for efficient solar energy management.

In [2], Hamied et al. proposed a cost-effective monitoring system designed for an off-grid PV system located in the Sahara region of South Algeria, serving a small-scale greenhouse farm. The system incorporates a simple, yet accurate, fault diagnosis algorithm integrated into a low-cost microcontroller for real-time validation. Leveraging the Internet of Things (IoT) technology, the system remotely monitors critical data such as PV currents, PV voltages, solar irradiance, and cell temperature. Additionally, a user-friendly web interface is developed to visualize the data and remotely check the PV system's status, with the capability to notify users via phone SMS. The results of the study demonstrate the system's effectiveness under specific climate conditions, confirming its ability to supply the greenhouse farm. Moreover, the integrated algorithm exhibits good accuracy in detecting and identifying various defects. Impressively, the total cost of this IoT-based monitoring system is approximately EUR 73, with an average daily energy consumption of around 13.5 Wh, making it a viable and economical solution for PV system monitoring and management in arid regions.

In [3], Halassa et al. considered the challenges of partial shading (PS) on PV installations, where an uneven solar irradiance distribution can lead to multiple peaks in PV cell power–voltage characteristics. They propose a novel technique for achieving the global maximum power point (GMPP) based on the Dandelion Optimizer (DO) algorithm, inspired by dandelion seed movements in the wind. This innovative approach aims to enhance power generation efficiency in PV systems, particularly under PS conditions. The paper conducts a comprehensive comparison with various advanced Maximum Power Point Tracker (MPPT) algorithms, including Particle Swarm Optimization (PSO), Grey Wolf Optimization (GWO), Artificial Bee Colony (ABC), Cuckoo Search Algorithm (CSA), and Bat Algorithm (BA). The simulation results affirm the DO-based MPPT's superiority in terms of tracking efficiency, speed, robustness, and simplicity of implementation. Notably, the DO algorithm exhibits exceptional performance with an RMSE of 1.09 watts, a rapid convergence time of 2.3 milliseconds, and a MAE of 0.13 watts, positioning it as a highly efficient and reliable solution for MPPT in PV systems, especially in the presence of partial shading conditions.

In [4], Polo et al. investigated power forecasting for Building Integrated PV (BIPV) systems integrated into vertical façades. They employ machine learning algorithms based on decision trees, utilizing the skforecast library within the Python environment to facilitate various deterministic and probabilistic forecasting approaches. In the deterministic forecasting phase, hourly BIPV power predictions are made using the XGBoost and Random Forest algorithms across different scenarios. Notably, incorporating exogenous variables enhances forecasting accuracy. Subsequently, the study delves into probabilistic forecasting, employing XGBoost in conjunction with the Bootstrap method. The results underscore the effectiveness of Random Forest and gradient-boosting algorithms, particularly XGBoost, as regressors for the time-series forecasting of BIPV power. The deterministic forecast results reveal mean absolute errors around 40% and slightly below 30% for south- and east-facing arrays, showcasing the potential of these machine learning techniques for BIPV power forecasting.

In [5], Faris E. Alfaris investigated a significant challenge in deploying PV systems, particularly in desert regions, where dust accumulation on PV panels can hinder their performance. Unlike traditional methods involving cameras, sensors, and power datasets, this study proposes an intelligent, sensorless approach to detect dust levels on PV panels, optimizing attached Dust Cleaning Units (DCUs). The approach leverages comprehensive data on solar irradiation, PV-generated power, and forecasted ambient temperatures. An expert AI computational system, implemented using MATLAB, is employed to enhance data prediction and processing. This AI system estimates missing information, emulates provided measurements, and accommodates additional input/output data. The study demonstrates the feasibility of this innovative system using real-world field data collected under various weather conditions, presenting a promising solution to the dust-related challenges faced by PV installations.

In [6], Dhimish and Lazaridis introduced an innovative approach to estimating the shading ratio of PV systems, a critical parameter for identifying potential PV faults and degradation mechanisms. This technique utilizes an all-sky imaging system and follows a structured process: Firstly, four all-sky imagers are deployed across a 25 km^2 region. Next, cloud images are computed using a new Color-Adjusted (CA) model. Subsequently, the shading ratio is calculated, and Global Horizontal Irradiance (GHI) is estimated, allowing for the prediction of PV system output power. The accuracy of the GHI estimation is empirically evaluated against data from two different weather stations, demonstrating an average accuracy within a maximum ±12.7% error rate. Furthermore, this study highlights the PV output power approximation's accuracy, reaching as high as 97.5% under shading-free conditions and decreasing to a minimum of 83% when the PV system is affected by overcasting conditions.

In [7], Harrou et al. proposed a robust method for accurately detecting anomalies in photovoltaic (PV) systems. With the growing adoption of solar energy worldwide, protecting PV plants from anomalies is crucial. This approach combines ensemble learning techniques, including boosting and bagging, with the Double Exponentially Weighted Moving Average (DEWMA) chart, enhancing modeling accuracy and sensitivity for anomaly detection. By employing Bayesian optimization for parameter selection and employing kernel density estimation to set decision thresholds, the method effectively identifies various anomalies, such as circuit breaker faults, inverter disconnections, and short-circuit faults. The results, based on measurements from a 9.54 kW PV small plant, demonstrate superior detection performance compared to traditional methods, underlining the effectiveness of this ensemble learning-based approach in PV plant management.

In [8], Zhang et al. proposed a novel approach based on multi-agent deep Reinforcement Learning (RL) that utilizes residuals of I–V characteristics. The RL agents are designed to operate in an environment defined by the high-dimensional residuals of I–V characteristics, with cooperative rewards. Actions for each agent, considering damping amplitude, are specified. The study shows the complete framework for modeling a PV array using multi-agent deep RL and demonstrates its feasibility and accuracy using one year of measured data from a PV array. The results indicate improved modeling accuracy compared to conventional meta-heuristic algorithms and analytical methods, with a daily RMSE starting at approximately 0.5015 A on the first day and converging to 0.1448 A on the last training day. The proposed multi-agent deep RL framework simplifies the design of states and rewards for parameter extraction, offering promising prospects for enhancing PV array modeling accuracy.

In [9], Santos et al. introduced the Temporal Fusion Transformer (TFT), an attention-based architecture that offers interpretability of temporal dynamics and high-performance forecasting across multiple horizons. To evaluate the proposed forecasting model, they use data from six different PV facilities located in Germany and Australia and compare the results with several other algorithms, including Auto-Regressive Integrated Moving Average (ARIMA), Long Short-Term Memory (LSTM), Multi-Layer Perceptron (MLP), and Extreme Gradient Boosting (XGBoost), using statistical error indicators. The findings indicate that TFT outperforms the other algorithms in terms of accuracy when predicting PV generation for the mentioned facilities, showcasing its potential for improving day-ahead PV power forecasting and contributing to enhanced grid stability and an energy supply–demand balance.

In [10], Sarwar et al. introduced a novel population-based optimization approach called the Horse Herd Optimization Algorithm (HOA) for maximizing power output from PV systems, especially under partial or complex partial shading conditions. The HOA is inspired by the natural behavior of a horse herd, particularly their surprise pounce-chasing style. This intelligent optimization strategy demonstrates superior performance compared to conventional techniques like "Perturb and Observe" (P&O), bio-inspired Adaptive Cuckoo Search (ACS) optimization, Particle Swarm Optimization (PSO), and the Dragonfly Algorithm (DA). The HOA stands out due to its ability to efficiently track the maximum power point even in challenging and varying weather conditions, its minimal computational time requirements, fast convergence, and its capacity to maintain stability and reduce oscillations once the maximum power point is reached, making it a promising technique for enhancing PV system performance under partial and complex shading scenarios.

In [11], Huang et al. presented an effective parameter estimation method for optimizing parameters in a two-diode PV power generation system. The proposed method comprises three stages. Firstly, it converts the original seven parameters of the two-diode model into seventeen parameters to account for varying environmental conditions, thus enabling a more precise parameter estimation for the PV model. Subsequently, a PV power generation model is established to capture the nonlinear relationship between inputs and outputs. The second stage involves a parameter sensitivity analysis using the overall effect method to identify and retain only the parameters that significantly impact the output. In the final stage, an Enhanced Gray Wolf Optimizer (EGWO) is applied in conjunction with measurement data to optimize the selected parameters from the second stage. After parameter estimation, the method calculates the predicted PV power output for specific solar irradiation and module temperature values. The effectiveness of this approach is demonstrated on a 200 kWp PV power generation system by comparing parameter estimation results before and after optimization and benchmarking them against other optimization algorithms, as well as a single-diode PV model, confirming its feasibility and potential advantages.

Author Contributions: F.H. writing—review and editing. Y.S. supervision, and writing—review and editing. B.T. writing—review and editing. A.D. review and editing. All authors have read and agreed to the published version of the manuscript.

Funding: This publication is based upon work supported by King Abdullah University of Science and Technology (KAUST) Research Funding (KRF) from the Climate and Livability Initiative (CLI) under Award No. ORA-2022-5339.

Data Availability Statement: Not applicable.

Conflicts of Interest: The authors declare no conflict of interest.

References

1. Castillo-Rojas, W.; Medina Quispe, F.M.; Hernández, C. Photovoltaic Energy Forecast Using Weather Data through a Hybrid Model of Recurrent and Shallow Neural Networks. *Energies* **2023**, *16*, 5093. [CrossRef]
2. Hamied, A.; Mellit, A.; Benghanem, M.; Boubaker, S. IoT-Based Low-Cost Photovoltaic Monitoring for a Greenhouse Farm in an Arid Region. *Energies* **2023**, *16*, 3860. [CrossRef]
3. Halassa, E.; Mazouz, L.; Seghiour, A.; Chouder, A.; Silvestre, S. Revolutionizing Photovoltaic Systems: An Innovative Approach to Maximum Power Point Tracking Using Enhanced Dandelion Optimizer in Partial Shading Conditions. *Energies* **2023**, *16*, 3617. [CrossRef]
4. Polo, J.; Martín-Chivelet, N.; Alonso-Abella, M.; Sanz-Saiz, C.; Cuenca, J.; de la Cruz, M. Exploring the PV Power Forecasting at Building Façades Using Gradient Boosting Methods. *Energies* **2023**, *16*, 1495. [CrossRef]
5. Alfaris, F.E. A Sensorless Intelligent System to Detect Dust on PV Panels for Optimized Cleaning Units. *Energies* **2023**, *16*, 1287. [CrossRef]
6. Dhimish, M.; Lazaridis, P.I. Approximating Shading Ratio Using the Total-Sky Imaging System: An Application for Photovoltaic Systems. *Energies* **2022**, *15*, 18201. [CrossRef]
7. Harrou, F.; Taghezouit, B.; Khadraoui, S.; Dairi, A.; Sun, Y.; Hadj Arab, A. Ensemble Learning Techniques-Based Monitoring Charts for Fault Detection in Photovoltaic Systems. *Energies* **2022**, *15*, 5716. [CrossRef]
8. Zhang, J.; Yang, Z.; Ding, K.; Feng, L.; Hamelmann, F.; Chen, X.; Liu, Y.; Chen, L. Modeling of Photovoltaic Array Based on Multi-Agent Deep Reinforcement Learning Using Residuals of I–V Characteristics. *Energies* **2022**, *15*, 6567. [CrossRef]
9. López Santos, M.; Ortega, P.C.; Echevarr, F.; Bl, G. Power Forecasting. *Energies* **2022**, *15*, 1–22.
10. Sarwar, S.; Hafeez, M.A.; Javed, M.Y.; Asghar, A.B.; Ejsmont, K. A Horse Herd Optimization Algorithm (HOA)-Based MPPT Technique under Partial and Complex Partial Shading Conditions. *Energies* **2022**, *15*, 1880. [CrossRef]
11. Huang, C.M.; Chen, S.J.; Yang, S.P. A Parameter Estimation Method for a Photovoltaic Power Generation System Based on a Two-Diode Model. *Energies* **2022**, *15*, 1460. [CrossRef]

Disclaimer/Publisher's Note: The statements, opinions and data contained in all publications are solely those of the individual author(s) and contributor(s) and not of MDPI and/or the editor(s). MDPI and/or the editor(s) disclaim responsibility for any injury to people or property resulting from any ideas, methods, instructions or products referred to in the content.

Article

Ensemble Learning Techniques-Based Monitoring Charts for Fault Detection in Photovoltaic Systems

Fouzi Harrou [1,*,†], Bilal Taghezouit [2,3,†], Sofiane Khadraoui [4,†], Abdelkader Dairi [5,6,†], Ying Sun [1,†] and Amar Hadj Arab [2,†]

1. Computer, Electrical and Mathematical Sciences and Engineering (CEMSE) Division, King Abdullah University of Science and Technology (KAUST), Thuwal 23955-6900, Saudi Arabia
2. Centre de Développement des Energies Renouvelables, CDER, B.P. 62, Route de l'Observatoire, Algiers 16340, Algeria
3. Laboratoire de Dispositifs de Communication et de Conversion Photovoltaique, Ecole Nationale Polytechnique Alger, Algiers 16200, Algeria
4. Department of Electrical Engineering, University of Sharjah, Sharjah 27272, United Arab Emirates
5. Laboratoire des Technologies de l'Environnement LTE, BP 1523 Al M'naouar ENP Oran, Oran 31000, Algeria
6. Computer Science Department Signal, Image and Speech (SIMPA) Laboratory, University of Science and Technology of Oran-Mohamed Boudiaf (USTO-MB), El Mnaouar, BP 1505, Bir El Djir 31000, Algeria
* Correspondence: fouzi.harrou@kaust.edu.sa
† These authors contributed equally to this work.

Abstract: Over the past few years, there has been a significant increase in the interest in and adoption of solar energy all over the world. However, despite ongoing efforts to protect photovoltaic (PV) plants, they are continuously exposed to numerous anomalies. If not detected accurately and in a timely manner, anomalies in PV plants may degrade the desired performance and result in severe consequences. Hence, developing effective and flexible methods capable of early detection of anomalies in PV plants is essential for enhancing their management. This paper proposes flexible data-driven techniques to accurately detect anomalies in the DC side of the PV plants. Essentially, this approach amalgamates the desirable characteristics of ensemble learning approaches (i.e., the boosting (BS) and bagging (BG)) and the sensitivity of the Double Exponentially Weighted Moving Average (DEWMA) chart. Here, we employ ensemble learning techniques to exploit their capability to enhance the modeling accuracy and the sensitivity of the DEWMA monitoring chart to uncover potential anomalies. In the ensemble models, the values of parameters are selected with the assistance of the Bayesian optimization algorithm. Here, BS and BG are adopted to obtain residuals, which are then monitored by the DEWMA chart. Kernel density estimation is utilized to define the decision thresholds of the proposed ensemble learning-based charts. The proposed monitoring schemes are illustrated via actual measurements from a 9.54 kW PV plant. Results showed the superior detection performance of the BS and BG-based DEWMA charts with non-parametric threshold in uncovering different types of anomalies, including circuit breaker faults, inverter disconnections, and short-circuit faults. In addition, the performance of the proposed schemes is compared to that of BG and BS-based DEWMA and EWMA charts with parametric thresholds.

Keywords: photovoltaic systems; ensemble bagged trees; anomaly detection; shading; electrical faults; statistical control charts

1. Introduction

Even with the COVID-19-induced economic slowdown, the renewable power sector is continuously experiencing high growth in installed capacity, with more than 260 Gigawatts (GW) in 2021, mostly by solar photovoltaic (PV). This fact led to a total installed capacity of 3064 GW [1]. The highest increase ever is due in large part to political support and cost reductions. In most countries, producing electricity from solar PV and wind is becoming increasingly more cost-effective than generating it from coal and gas power plants [2].

The solar PV market increased in 2021 to a record 175 GWdc, for a total power capacity of 942 GWdc [3]. A recent investigation by the BloombergNEF company shows that the global benchmark levelized cost of electricity (LCOE) [4] for fixed-axis utility-scale PV is $46 per megawatt-hour (MWh) in the first half of 2022, while some of the cheapest PV projects were able to achieve an LCOE of $21/MWh for tracking PV farms in Chile with very competitive returns. In 2022, the solar PV market experienced strong competitiveness between PV module manufacturers with new yields of up to 22.8% [5]. Despite this progress, numerous challenges remain to be solved before solar PV can become a significant source of power generation worldwide, leading to a sustainable energy future [6].

Like all electricity production systems, solar PV systems are often subject to various faults and failures that significantly affect their components, such as PV modules, cables, protection circuits, inverters, etc. [7]. The most general effect of faults is the loss of energy, which is caused by one or more independent anomalies and failures. Some electrical faults cause total shutdowns of PV plants, and other faults such as electric arcs can cause fires, which leads to shortfalls and loss of income. Early detection of such faults is crucial to prevent critical PV system failures and increase their reliability with a high quality of performance. Over the past few years, the Fault Detection and Diagnosis (FDD) of solar PV systems has become a topical research topic for many researchers [8,9]. Generally, anomalies or faults occurring in grid-connected PV systems can be classified primarily according to the side of the fault in the PV installation, either the DC side before the inverter or the AC side at the output of the inverter up to the point of injection [8]. Faults in the DC side of PV systems, which are principally located in the PV array, include; temporary and permanent mismatches, hotspot, degradation, short circuit, open circuit, electrical arc, line–line, and line–ground faults, as well as the DC/DC converter fault inside the PV grid-tie inverter. On the AC side, total blackout and grid abnormalities (unbalanced voltage and lightning) are the types of faults commonly found in PV systems [10]. A statistical study of the power loss evaluation and clustering of faults affecting PV systems installed in different climate zones in the world helps to decrease the number of faults in the new PV installations [11]. The experimental data from PV installed systems show that a better operation and maintenance (O&M) service significantly improves the average performance ratio from 88% to 94%, and as a result, profits and environmental benefits are increased. Indeed, improvements of the PV O&M include the following: (1) increasing efficiency and energy production, (2) extending the lifetime of PV systems (25 to 40 years), (3) decreasing system downtime, (4) reducing the possible risks and ensuring safety and (5) reducing the cost of O&M [12,13].

Continuous and real-time monitoring of PV systems is essential during their working cycle to ensure the rapid detection of faults, reduce downtime, maintain long-term profitability, and exploit their full power. The key point of reliable monitoring and FDD strategy is related to the quality of measurement accuracy of both meteorological and electrical data of the PV system. Without a reliable monitoring system, the PV system is often expected to operate with poor performance for a limited time period before the fault is detected and identified. This fact generally results in a major loss of income [13].

An FDD tool based on the Artificial Neural Network (ANN) algorithm using Laterally Primed Adaptive Resonance Theory (LAPART) was developed in [14] in order to detect module-level faults with minimal error. The results showed that the LAPART algorithm can quickly learn PV performance data (only 4 days of one-minute data) and provide an accurate multi-level FDD tool. Other FDD methods include the k-Nearest Neighbors (kNN) algorithm, which is a non-parametric method used for regression models and fault classification [15]. In [16], four approaches made by EWMA (Exponentially Weighted Moving Average) schemes and kNN-based Shewhart with parametric and non-parametric models were used to detect faults. The results obtained showed a high capability for detecting short-circuit faults, open-circuit faults, and temporary shading, whereas this algorithm does not have the ability to distinguish the partial shading among faults occurring on the DC side of the PV array. A real-time detection and classification technique based on the clustering kNN rule was proposed in [15]. This technique does not require any predefined threshold to classify the faults; the threshold values are unknown and difficult to choose for each PV system due to the strong dependence of the output power on the climatic conditions. In [17], a C4.5 decision tree (DT) approach is proposed to detect and diagnose the faults in a Grid-Connected PV system (GCPV) using a non-parametric model by learning the task. In this work, a semi-empirical model by Sandia National Laboratories (SNL) was used to predict the power produced from the PV array under normal operation conditions (fault-free). Then, the supervised decision tree algorithm was exploited to classify four cases: (1) fault-free, (2) string fault, (3) short-circuit fault, and (4) line-line fault. The results obtained showed a high accuracy of around 99.86% for detection and 99.80% for diagnosis. This supervised learning method requires data from several sets of training examples to build a good classifier that can distinguish between different faults. The authors in [18] used the ANN technique and FL (Fuzzy Logic) system interface to develop a PV FDD algorithm that has been tested to detect ten faults cases, such as a combination of four cases of faulty PV modules and two cases of low and high partial shading. In such a PV FDD algorithm, the voltage and power variations of the studied PV system were used as input for both the ANN technique and the FL system. An unsupervised monitoring approach for detecting anomalies and faults in PV installations using a one-class SVM technique is proposed in [19], where the one-diode model is used under PSIMTM to simulate the normal operation of the PV array, while the one-class SVM technique is applied to calculate residuals between measured and simulation data for FDD. The use of machine learning techniques (MLT) is advantageous in the sense that they have rapid detection response, they allow distinguishing among faults of the same signature and classifying faults with high accuracy, and setting threshold limits is not required. Nevertheless, the FDD accuracy depends proportionally on the trained PV model to estimate the expected energy yield. Moreover, these techniques require more advanced skills for real-time hardware and software implementation, and obtaining a training dataset of all possible faults scenarios could be difficult.

Accurate monitoring of PV plants is necessary to meet the desired specifications regarding power production and safety and help avoid serious incidents. Machine learning techniques have demonstrated themselves as a prominent field of study within a data-driven framework over the last decade by addressing numerous challenging and complex real-world problems [20–24]. Thus, this study aims to design a semi-supervised data-driven detector for anomaly detection in PV plants that do not require labeled data. Unlike supervised methods, semi-supervised anomaly detection methods aim to train the detection model using a normal event dataset only, which make them more attractive for detecting anomalies in PV plants, since it is not always easy to obtain accurately labeled data. Until now, very few research papers have investigated integrating machine learning models and statistical control charts for fault detection in multivariate data. The contribution of this work is threefold as summarized below.

- This paper aims to develop flexible and efficient semi-supervised machine learning-driven methodologies to improve the operation and performance of PV plants. These semi-supervised approaches only employ normal events data without labeling to train the detection models, making them more attractive for detecting faults in practice. This study presents a semi-supervised monitoring approach for anomaly detection in PV plants by combining the advantages of the ensemble learning models and the Double Exponentially Weighted Moving Average (DEWMA) chart. In the last decade, ensemble learning-driven methods (e.g., boosting and bagging models), which combine several single models, have demonstrated a promising solution compared to traditional machine learning methods. Notably, ensemble models are characterized by their ability to reduce the model's variance while achieving a low bias, making them appealing to improve prediction quality [25]. Overall, an efficient monitoring strategy relies principally on the accuracy of the adopted modeling method and the sensitivity of the anomaly detection technique. Here, we employed ensemble learning methods to exploit their capability to enhance the modeling precision of the PV monitored system. On the other hand, the key characteristic of the DEWMA scheme resides in its capacity to enclose all of the information from past and actual samples in the detection statistic, which makes it sensitive for uncovering anomalies with small magnitudes. In the proposed approach, ensemble learning models are used for residual generation. Essentially, residuals are close to zero in the absence of anomalies, while residuals diverge from zero in the presence of anomalies. The DEWMA detector is employed to check the generated residuals to uncover possible anomalies in the inspected PV array.

- Additionally, in this work, Bayesian optimization (BO) has been adopted to optimally tune hyperparameters of the boosted trees (BS) and bagged trees (BG) models. Specifically, the BO is used to find the optimal parameters of the ensemble models based on training data (anomaly-free data). This enables obtaining more accurate prediction models and improves the detection performance.
- Note that the detection threshold in the DEWMA chart is computed based on the Gaussian assumption of data. Here, to extend further the flexibility of the proposed fault detection method, we employed kernel density estimation (KDE) to compute the detection threshold in a non-parametric way. We assessed the effectiveness of the considered fault detection approaches on real data from a 9.54 kWp photovoltaic system. The detection capacity of the proposed approaches is investigated in the presence of different types of faults. Six statistical scores are computed to judge the fault detection quality. Results revealed the promising performance of the proposed approaches in detecting various types of anomalies in a PV system.

This paper is structured as follows. The studied PV system is briefed in Section 2. Then, the BS and BG models are introduced in Section 3. In Section 4, after presenting the DEWMA scheme, we introduce the proposed approach. The experimental results are provided In Section 5. Lastly, conclusions are offered in Section 6.

2. PV System Description

This section is devoted to presenting briefly the grid-tied PV system used in this study. Indeed, the proposed algorithm for fault detection in this work will be verified using the meteorological and electrical data measurement collected from a 9.54 kWp PV system at the Renewable Energy Development Center (CDER) in Algeria. This PV system contains 90 PV modules with a total power of 9.54 kWdc in operation since 2004; it is composed of three identical single-phase PV sub-systems (Figure 1).

The entire produced PV energy is injected into the low-voltage electrical grid. As shown in Figure 1, each PV sub-system consists of a 3.18 kW sub-array, grid-tie inverter, and electrical cabinets for protection. The sub-array contains two parallel strings of 15 PV modules (PVM) in a series.

Tables 1 and 2 display, respectively, the main technical specifications of the PV sub-array and the PV inverter.

Here, the STC refers to Standard Test Conditions (irradiance =1000 W/m^2, cell temperature =25 °C, air mass = 1.5) and MPP denotes Maximum Power Point. G is the received irradiance by the PV module during the flash test, TC is the temperature of the PV cell, and AM is the air mass. VOC is the open circuit voltage, ISC is the short circuit current, VMPP is the voltage at MPP, IMPP is the current at MPP, and PM is the maximum power.

The meteorological and electrical measured data used in this work are recovered by an external monitoring system composed essentially of sensors, data acquisition unit Agilent 34970A, and software under PC (Figure 2).

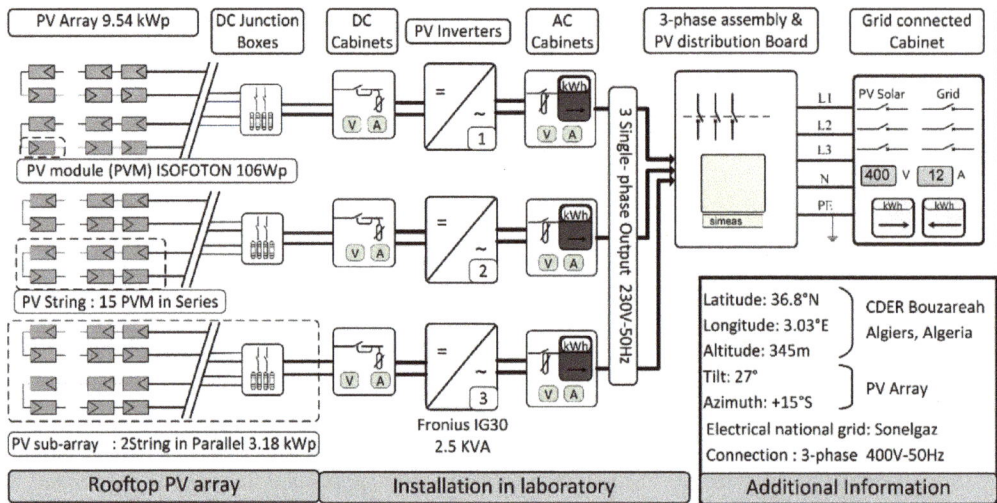

Figure 1. Main electrical specifications of the PV module and sub-array at STC.

Table 1. Main electrical specifications of the PV module and PV sub-array at STC.

Parameters	V_{OC} (V)	I_{SC} (A)	V_{MPP} (V)	I_{MPP} (A)	P_M (W)
PV Module	21.6	6.54	17.4	6.1	106
PV sub-array	324	13.08	261	12.2	3180

Table 2. Main specifications of the PV inverters Fronuis IG 30 under nominal operating conditions.

Parameters	Nominal AC Power (W)	DC Voltage Range (V)	AC Voltage Range (V)	Inverter Efficiency (%)	Frequency Range (Hz)
Value	2500	150–400	195–253	92.7–94.3	49.8–50.2

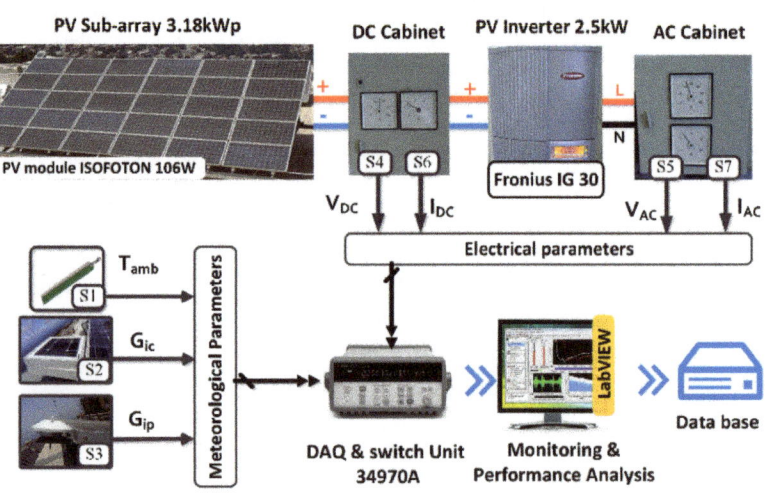

Figure 2. Synoptic diagram of the PV monitoring system.

For the measure of tilted irradiance at 27 °C, a pyranometer and a reference cell are used, and a thermocouple measures the ambient temperature. The DC voltage at the

MPP of the PV sub-array is measured by a simple voltage divider circuit, while a voltage transformer measures the AC voltage at the inverter output. A hall-effect sensor was used to measure the current on both the DC and AC sides of the PV inverter. Table 3 reviews the measured parameters with the main sensor information. Agilent 34970A provides the conditioning and the measure of the signal at the sensor's output. While the monitoring user interface is designed under LabVIEW software, this interface can recover, display, record, and analyze the measured data. According to IEC 61724 standard, the sampling time was chosen at 1 min, which gives 1440 samples per 24 h.

Table 3. Measured parameters of the PV inverters Fronuis IG 30 under nominal operating conditions.

Measured Parameters	Sensor N°	Symbol	Sensor Type & Reference	Accuracy
Ambient Temperature (°C)	S1	T_{amb}	Thermocouple K	0.5 °C
Tilted Global Irradiance for 27° (W/m^2)	S2	G_{ic}	Isofoton PV Reference Cell	±5%
	S3	G_{ip}	CM 11 Pyranometer	±2%
PV array DC Voltage (V)	S4	V_{DC}	Voltage Divider	±0.9%
Grid AC Voltage (V)	S5	V_{AC}	Voltage Transformer	1.5%
PV array DC Current (A)	S6	I_{DC}	Hall Effect Sensor	±0.5%
Inverter AC Current (A)	S7	I_{AC}	F.W. BELL CLSM-50S	

3. Ensemble Learning Methods

This section briefly presents the two considered ensemble learning models: boosting and bagging methods.

3.1. Boosted Trees

The boosting approach, which belongs to ensemble learning models, tries to enhance the prediction accurateness of learning methods by boosting weak learners to strong learners [26–31]. This work employs the boosting technique for prediction problems with base learners as regression trees. To introduce the boosting algorithm, regression trees are first briefly described. Let $y \in \mathbb{R}$ and $\mathbf{X} \in \mathcal{D} \subset \mathbb{R}^d$ denote, respectively, the wind power and the input features used in the wind power prediction, where $\mathcal{D}$ is the feature space and d is the number of input features.

Regression trees typically are based on the the partition of the feature space $\mathcal{D}$ into different and non-overlapping areas, which are known as leaves. The leaves of the regression trees are denoted here by $\mathcal{D}_1, \ldots, \mathcal{D}_T$, where T denotes the number of leaves. Each leaf $\mathcal{D}_i$ is associated with a weight w_i. For predictions via a given tree, the response is predicted as the weights w_i for the input feature $\mathbf{X} \in \mathcal{D}_i$. The leaves $\mathcal{D}_i$ and the weights w_i are learned from the training set.

In the process of regression tree training for a given data set $\{(\mathbf{X}_1, \mathbf{y}_1), \ldots, (\mathbf{X}_n, \mathbf{y}_n)\}$, the feature space $\mathcal{D}$ is recursively partitioned into sub-regions such that the objective function defined by the residual sum of squares (RSS) is minimized until a certain stopping criterion is achieved. The stopping criterion frequently used in the boosting algorithm is a fixed number of leaves. For instance, if only two leaves are considered in a regression tree training, then the feature space $\mathcal{D}$ should be split once, and the resulting tree is known as a stump [32]. Indeed, the first step is based on selecting a cut-point $s \in \mathbb{R}$ and an input feature X_j from the feature set $\mathbf{X} = \{X_1, \ldots, X_d\}$ so that the RSS objective function is minimized. Then, the second step aims at defining the sub-regions $\mathcal{D}_1(j,s) = \{\mathbf{X} \in \mathcal{D} | X_j \leq s\}$ and $\mathcal{D}_2(j,s) = \{\mathbf{X} \in \mathcal{D} | X_j > s\}$.

$$\sum_{i:\mathbf{X}_i \in \mathcal{D}_1(j,s)} (\mathbf{y}_i - \bar{\mathbf{y}}_{\mathcal{D}_1(j,s)})^2 + \sum_{i:\mathbf{X}_i \in \mathcal{D}_2(j,s)} (\mathbf{y}_i - \bar{\mathbf{y}}_{\mathcal{D}_2(j,s)})^2, \quad (1)$$

such that $\bar{y}_{\mathcal{D}_1(j,s)} = \sum_{i:\mathbf{X}_i \in \mathcal{D}_1(j,s)} \mathbf{y}_i/n_1$, and n_1 stands for the number of samples for which the input feature $\mathbf{X}_i \in \mathcal{D}_1(j,s)$. $\bar{y}_{\mathcal{D}_2(j,s)}$ is defined analogously. If a two-leaves tree is trained, then the weight w_1 (resp. w_2) corresponding to $\mathcal{D}_1(j,s)$ (resp. $\mathcal{D}_2(j,s)$) is $\bar{y}_{\mathcal{D}_1(j,s)}$ (resp. $\bar{y}_{\mathcal{D}_2(j,s)}$). The algorithm splits both regression trees $\mathcal{D}_1(j,s)$ and $\mathcal{D}_2(j,s)$ (same idea of partitioning $\mathcal{D}$) until the stopping criterion is achieved. Quite often, the weight w_i is used as the mean of the response variable in the training data with the corresponding input features $\mathcal{D}_i$. More details about regression trees can be found in [33].

To illustrate the boosting algorithm for wind power prediction, let us consider the problem of predicting the wind power $\mathbf{y}$ by a function $f^*(\mathbf{X})$ of input features $\mathbf{X}$ so that the risk is minimized,

$$f^*(\mathbf{X}) = \arg\min_{f(.)} \mathbb{E}[\rho(\mathbf{y} - f(\mathbf{X}))], \qquad (2)$$

where $\rho(.)$ denotes a loss function ($\rho(e) = e^2$ is the squared error loss) and arg min stands for the argument of the minimum, that is the function $f^*(\mathbf{X})$ that minimizes the risk index function over all possible functions under consideration. The boosting algorithm is based on the idea of approximating $f^*(\mathbf{X})$ by an additive function of the following form

$$f(\mathbf{X}) = \sum_{i=1}^{M} f_i(\mathbf{X}), \qquad (3)$$

where $f_i(\mathbf{X}), i = 1, \ldots, M$ are regression trees.

3.2. Bagged Regression Trees

Breiman introduced the concept of bootstrap aggregating (bagging) trees by constructing multiple similar but independent predictors, and the final prediction is obtained by averaging the outputs of these predictors [34]. This allows the reduction of the variance error, as pointed out in [35]. In bagging trees/ensembles of decision trees methods, a large number of individual models (trees) are combined with each other (see Figure 3) to improve the quality of prediction of the model. The use of the BGs predictive model is of great importance due to the fact that it allows a reduction of the regression trees' variance and addressing the over-fitting problem in the regression progress with a single tree.

Figure 3 presents the main idea of a bagging trees predictive model. Such a figure shows that N new training datasets of size n are first created from the original data through the selection of n out of n samples uniformly with replacement from the original training set of data. Then, a training process starts by training individually each tree on the corresponding training new sets. In the present work, the bagging trees models are based on 30 trees. Lastly, the final prediction is obtained by averaging all output predictions. The prediction of the bagging trees model has the following form:

$$\hat{y} = \frac{1}{N}\sum_{i=1}^{N} f_i(\mathbf{X}), \qquad (4)$$

where the ith tree model f_i is trained on the ith bootstrap data.

Theoretically, it is clear that the variance of prediction using n learners can be reduced to $1/n$ of the original variance (single learner). Thus, the use of a large number of learners is advantageous in the sense that a reduced variance is obtained compared to the prediction with a small numbers of learners. To understand how the bagging process significantly reduces the mean squared error of the prediction, the following regression problem with base regressors $b_1(x), \ldots, b_n(x)$ is considered. Additional details on BG models can be found in [23].

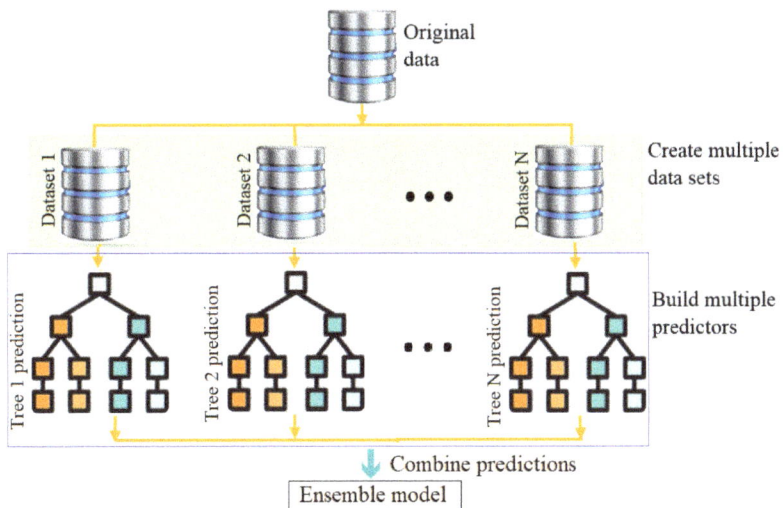

Figure 3. Schematic drawing of the concept of the BG model.

Algorithm 1 below summarizes the main steps to calculate the bagging trees prediction.

Algorithm 1: Bagging trees approach

Input: Training and testing datasets, $\mathcal{D}$
Output: Prediction output
for $i = 1 : N$ in *TrainingDataset* **do**
- Take a bootstrapped replica $\mathcal{D}_i$, from $\mathcal{D}$
- Call Decision Tree with $\mathcal{D}_i$ and receive prediction $\hat{y}_i$
- Add $\hat{y}_i$ to the ensemble $\hat{Y}$
- Compute the final prediction: $\hat{\mathbf{y}} = \frac{1}{N}\sum_{i=1}^{N}\hat{y}_i$.

end
$Prediction_{BaggestTrees} \leftarrow \hat{\mathbf{y}}$;
return $Prediction_{BaggestTrees}$
---

4. PV System Modeling and Validation

4.1. Data Analysis

In this study, we used one month of data collected every ten minutes under normal operating conditions to construct the studied machine learning models. The first three weeks are used to train the models, and the last week is testing data to verify the prediction performance of the constructed models. The collected data contain nine variables: solar irradiance, ambient temperature, cell temperature, maximum dynamic DC power, DC current, DC voltage, AC power, AC current, and AC voltage. Figure 4 shows the probability density function of the KDE fit to the nine recorded variables in training data, which indicates that these datasets are non-Gaussian distributed. Table 4 summarizes the descriptive statistics of each variable, which confirm the non-Gaussian distribution of data. It would be challenging for traditional monitoring charts, such as DEWMA and EWMA, that are constructed based on the Gaussian assumption of data.

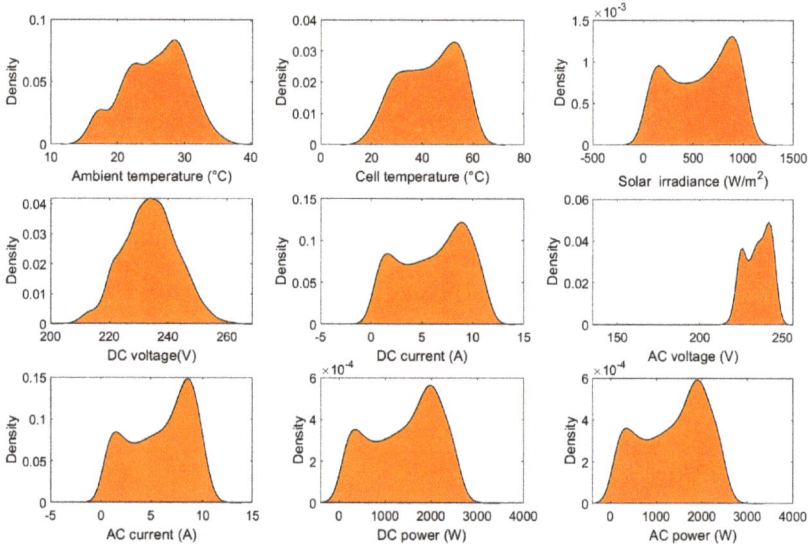

Figure 4. Distribution of the investigated time-series data.

Table 4. Descriptive statistics of the training data.

	Min	Max	STD	Q 0.25	Q 0.5	Q 0.75	Skewness	Kurtosis
Ambient Temp	14.51	37.22	4.61	22.26	26.04	29.14	−0.22	2.36
Cell Temp	16.12	64.47	11.21	33.43	44.07	52.49	−0.25	1.98
Irradiance	42.67	1085.10	312.30	277.07	614.26	862.42	−0.21	1.65
DC voltage	205.56	263.19	9.24	227.58	233.76	240.11	0.01	2.78
DC current	0.50	11.78	3.22	3.22	6.57	8.96	−0.22	1.76
AC voltage	140.72	250.67	7.68	227.89	235.52	241.27	−0.64	7.28
AC current	0.38	11.83	3.00	3.24	6.45	8.49	−0.33	1.81
DC power	104.10	2969.84	733.36	784.03	1551.90	2034.70	−0.28	1.83
AC power	92.73	2857.53	703.93	764.18	1502.86	1961.53	−0.29	1.84

To quantify the self-similarity in the given time-series data over different delay times, we computed the autocorrelation function (ACF). It is a time-domain measure of the stochastic process memory. Importantly, the ACF for a time-series, x_t is expressed as [36],

$$\rho_k = \frac{\text{cov}(x_t, x_{t-k})}{\sqrt{\text{var}(x_t)\text{var}(x_{t-k})}} \tag{5}$$

where $\text{cov}(x_t, x_{t-k})$ denotes is the covariance between x_t and x_{t-k}, and var(x) refers to the variance of x. Figure 5 depicts the ACF of the training data. Visually, we clearly observe the presence of an apparent periodicity of 24 h. The time-series periodicity can be identified by measuring the distance between two successive extremum points in the ACF. We suspect this periodicity is caused mainly by the diurnal solar irradiance cycle.

It is important to note that the traditional monitoring charts are designed under the assumption that the data are normally distributed and uncorrelated. However, in many real applications, the normal distribution assumption is violated. In addition, it has been shown in the literature that the performance of the traditional charts is significantly impacted by the presence of autocorrelation [37,38]. Here, we observe from Figures 4 and 5 that the collected data from the inspected PV system are non-Gaussian and correlated. Accordingly, developing advanced monitoring charts based on machine learning is essential.

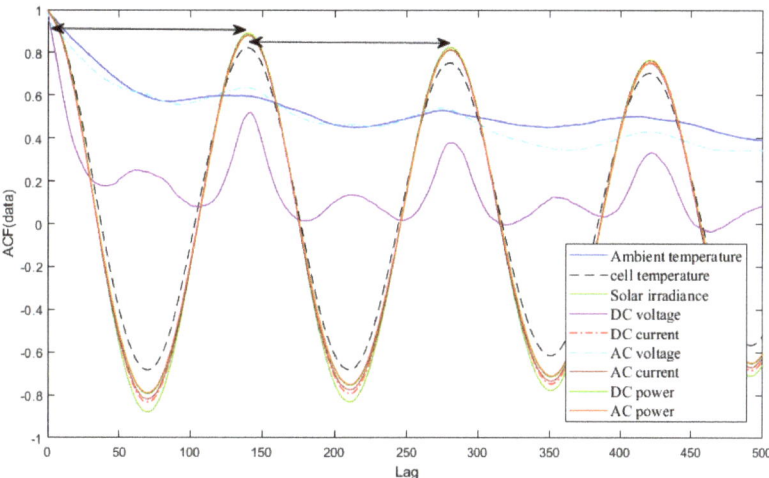

Figure 5. Sample ACF of the training data.

Figure 6 depicts a Pearson correlation heatmap to highlight correlations between measured variables. We can see from Figure 6 the presence of a strong relationship between the following variables: irradiance, DC current, DC power, AC current, and AC power. The DC current generated by the PV cell, PV module, or PV array is proportional to the tilted irradiance. In the literature, there are many mathematical relationships that explain this high correlation (i.e., more than 0.98) [39,40].

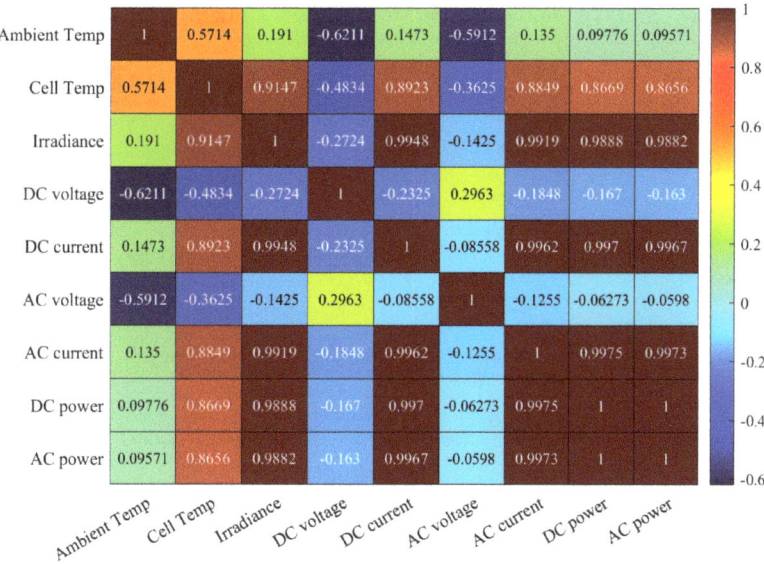

Figure 6. A Pearson correlation heatmap of data.

Since the cell temperature is proportional to the irradiance [41–43], there is a high positive correlation (i.e., above 0.86) between cell temperature and the following parameters: irradiance, DC current, DC power, AC current, and AC power. Furthermore, the cell temperature is also influenced by variations in the ambient temperature.

The DC voltage of the PV module is the sum of the cell's voltages in series. It is generally almost stable but decreases when the cell temperature increases [39–41], which explains the presence of this negative correlation (i.e., around -0.59). Because the DC voltage is almost stable, the DC power is directly proportional to variations of the DC current.

We observe from Figure 6 the absence of correlation between inverter AC voltage and other variables. Indeed, the PV inverter converts DC energy to AC energy with typical efficiency from 95% to 99% in recent inverters [44,45]. When driving power to the grid, the PV inverter must provide a stable sinusoidal AC waveform that matches grid voltage and frequency according to utility standards to obtain good synchronization.

Figure 6 shows clearly a high correlation between the irradiance, cell temperature, current DC, AC current, power DC and power AC. The data of such a figure show positive and negative correlations as well as low correlation between the DC voltage and the ambient cell temperature, the DC current, AC current, DC power, and AC power. AC voltage does not show a negative weak correlation with other parameters.

4.2. PV Array Modeling Using Ensemble Learning Models

In this study, we used one month of data collected every ten minutes under normal operating conditions to construct the studied machine learning models. The first three weeks are used to train the models, and the last week is testing data to evaluate the prediction accurateness of the constructed models. Here, a fivefold cross-validation procedure is adopted during the training to avoid the over-fitting problem. At first, we used the default parameters for the BT and BST models: 30 learners with a minimum leaf size of 8, and a learning rate of 0.1. We also considered hyperparameter optimization in this study by investigating the performance of the optimized ensemble learning models (OBT and OBST).

Note that one of the most important steps in machine learning-based prediction is hyperparameter tuning or optimization. Optimized ensemble models with tuned hyperparameters are characterized by the highest accuracy and least prediction error based on the training dataset. Broadly speaking, hyperparameters can be computed via the minimization of the loss function (e.g., mean squared error (MSE)) or via the maximization of the prediction accuracy. Of course, the selection of the hyperparameters certainly plays a crucial role in constructing accurate machine learning models, as the efficacy of the model greatly relies on them. In this study, Bayesian optimization (BO) is applied to determine the values of hyperparameters in the two investigated ensemble learning models [23,46]. The main advantage of the BO consists in its capability to select the optimal parameters in an informed manner. More specifically, the BO accounts for the past evaluations when selecting the hyperparameters set to consider next [47], making it less time-consuming compared to both grid search and random search [48,49]. Table 5 lists the calculated values of the hyperparameters of both BT and BST models using the BO procedure.

Table 5. The optimum hyperparameters using Bayesian hyperparameter optimization.

Model	Hyperparameter Search Range	Optimized Hyperparameters
Bagged	-Number of learners: 10–500 -Minimum leaf size: 1–1684 -Number of predictors to sample: 1–7	-Number of learners: 10 -Minimum leaf size: 2 -Number of predictors to sample: 7
Boosted	-Number of learners: 10–500 -Minimum leaf size: 1–1684 -Number of predictors to sample: 1–7	-Number of learners: 46 -Minimum leaf size: 89 -Number of predictors to sample: 7

Figure 7 depicts the actual and the predicted DC power from both the optimized and non-optimized BT and BST models. From Figure 7, it is clear that the ensemble models can catch the trend in the DC power data.

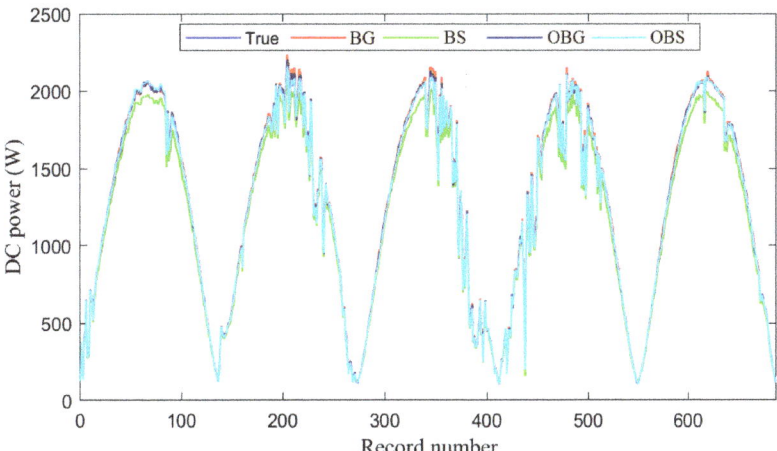

Figure 7. Power prediction using BG, BS, OBG, and OBS models based on training data.

To visually show the prediction accuracy of the four investigated models, Figure 8 contains the boxplots of the prediction errors of each model. It confirms that the optimized models can reach better performance compared to the non-optimized models in predicting DC power. Specifically, we can see that the prediction errors of the optimized BG and BS models fluctuate around zero, indicating that the models can capture the variation and follow the trend in the DC power data. Hence, these boxplots affirm the promising prediction capacity of the two optimized models. Figure 9 illustrates the empirical cumulative distribution function of the prediction errors from the four models; similar conclusions hold true. Figure 9 indicates the superior prediction performance of the OBG model, which is followed by the OBS model.

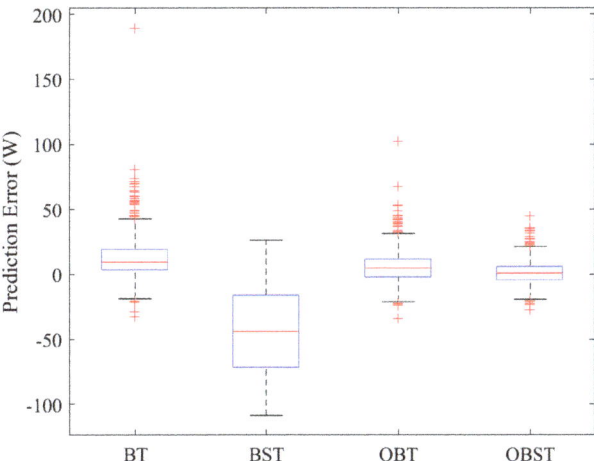

Figure 8. Boxplot of residual errors of bagged tree, boosted tree, optimized BG, and optimized BS models.

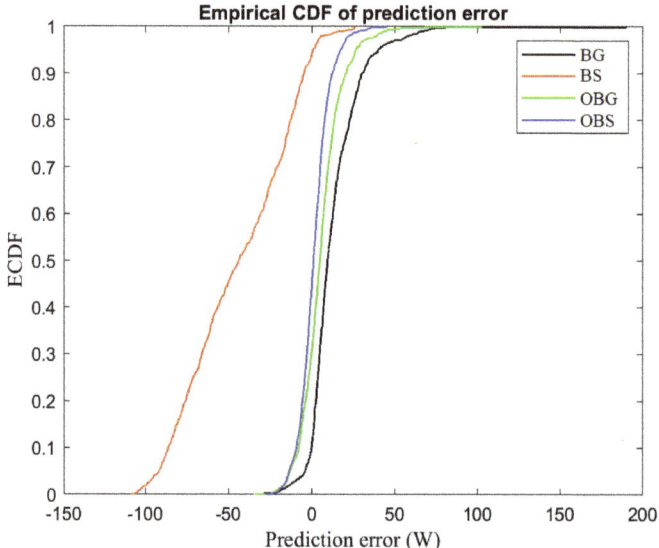

Figure 9. Empirical CDF of the prediction errors for the invstigated models.

We also assessed the deviation of the prediction from each model ($\hat{y}$) and the testing data (y_t) in quantitative way by computing the three most commonly used statistical metrics: root mean square error (RMSE), mean absolute error (MAE), coefficient of determination (R^2), and mean absolute percentage error (MAPE).

$$\text{RMSE} = \sqrt{\frac{1}{n}\sum_{t=1}^{n}(y_t - \hat{y}_t)^2}, \tag{6}$$

$$\text{MAE} = \frac{\sum_{t=1}^{n}|y_t - \hat{y}_t|}{n}, \tag{7}$$

$$R^2 = \frac{\sum_{i=1}^{n}[(y_{i,} - \bar{y}) \cdot (\hat{y}_i - \bar{\hat{y}})]^2}{\sqrt{\sum_{i=1}^{n}(y_i - \bar{y})^2} \cdot \sqrt{\sum_{i=1}^{n}(\hat{y}_i - \bar{\hat{y}})^2}}, \tag{8}$$

$$\text{MAPE} = \frac{100}{n}\sum_{t=1}^{n}\left|\frac{y_t - \hat{y}_t}{y_t}\right|, \tag{9}$$

where n denotes the length of the testing data. From Table 6, the results indicate that the optimized models (i.e., OBT and OBST) achieved better prediction accuracy compared to their unoptimized counterparts. This confirms that considering hyperparameter tuning using Bayesian optimization is a very important step to reduce prediction errors and construct more effective models. In addition, results show that the OBST achieved the best performance with an RMSE of 11.36, which is followed by the OBT model with an RMSE of 14.65. Prediction results have been significantly improved by optimizing the prediction models (Table 6).

Table 6. Evaluation scores of the prediction using testing data.

Methods	RMSE	R2	MSE	MAPE (%)
BG	20.03	1	401.07	13.88
BS	53.98	0.99	2914.1	44.94
OBG	11.36	1	129.11	8.31
OBS	14.65	1	214.59	11.53

5. EWMA and DEWMA Monitoring Schemes

This subsection presents the basic idea behind the EWMA and the DEWMA monitoring charts. Unlike Shewhart charts employing only the value of the actual measurement, the EWMA and DEWMA charts, as control charts with memory, are not very sensitive in detecting small and moderate changes. Thus, they are better than Shewhart charts in uncovering changes with small magnitude in the process mean.

5.1. EWMA Monitoring Scheme

Roberts introduced the EWMA chart as a memory chart to bypass the limitations of the Shewhart chart in detecting small changes [50]. In short, the EWMA chart is characterized by its use of information from the past and actual data points, making it sensitive to small changes [51]. Lucas et al. investigated the statistical properties of the EWMA scheme and showed it has similar performance to the CUmulative SUM (CUSUM) scheme in sensing small changes. It is more straightforward to implement and use in practice than the CUSUM chart [52–54]. The EWMA statistic is derived as a weighted linear combination of current and past data.

$$s_t = \nu x_t + (1-\nu)s_{t-1}; \quad s_0 = \mu_0, \tag{10}$$

where ν denotes the smoothing parameter such that $0 < \nu \leq 1$, and μ_0 is usually selected to be equal to the mean of fault-free data. Using small values of ν provides less weight to the most recent data points and larger weight to the past observations. In other words, ν regulates the memory depth of the EWMA chart. Crucially, the use of small values of ν enables a more significant influence of the past observations, enabling the EWMA chart to be more capable of sensing small changes [52,55,56]. In practice, ν is usually chosen within the interval [0.15 0.3] for detecting anomalies with small or medium magnitude. We observe that the EWMA chart becomes similar to the Shewhart chart if $\nu = 1$.

From (10), we obtain the following formula by recursively substituting s_t,

$$s_t = \nu \sum_{j=0}^{t-1}(1-\nu)^t x_{t-j} + (1-\nu)^t s_0. \tag{11}$$

We observe from (11) that the weights $\nu(1-\nu)^t$ are decreasing exponentially with time, and the sum of these weights is unity because:

$$\nu \sum_{j=0}^{t-1}(1-\nu)^t x_{t-j} = \nu \left[\frac{1-(1-\nu)^t}{1-(1-\nu)}\right] = 1-(1-\nu)^t. \tag{12}$$

The upper and lower detection thresholds of the EWMA scheme are computed using the following equation.

$$UCL, LCL = \mu_0 \pm L\sigma_0\sqrt{(\tfrac{\nu}{(2-\nu)}[1-(1-\nu)^{2t}]}, \tag{13}$$

where the factor L represents the width of the decision thresholds. From (13), the asymptotic thresholds are expressed as:

$$UCL, LCL = \mu_0 \pm L\sigma_0\sqrt{\tfrac{\nu}{(2-\nu)}}. \tag{14}$$

As it can be noticed, the $[1-(1-\nu)^{2t}]$ in (13) becomes closer to unity in case of larger t. The EWMA chart signals a potential fault if the EWMA statistic exceeds the decision thresholds. Here, we used the one-sided EWMA chart by using the absolute value of the EWMA charting statistic and only an upper detection threshold. More details on the EWMA chart can be found in [57].

DEWMA Monitoring Approach

The DEWMA chart was introduced in [58,59] to improve the capability of the conventional EWMA approach to sense small changes in the process mean. The basic concept of the DEWMA is founded on the double exponentially weighted moving average, which is a common forecasting technique in time-series analysis. Several authors investigated the performance of the DEWMA in the litterature [60–63]. It has been shown in [64] that the DEWMA outperformed the EWMA scheme in the detection fault with small and moderate magnitude. The two charts deliver relatively similar results in the case of large and moderate changes [65]. The DEWMA charting statistic, w_t is derived as follows,

$$\begin{cases} w_0 = s_0 = \mu_0, \\ w_t = \nu s_t + (1-\nu) w_{t-1}, \\ s_t = \nu x_t + (1-\nu) s_{t-1}, \quad t = 1, 2, \ldots, n. \end{cases} \quad (15)$$

As it can be noticed, in the DEWMA chart, the exponential smoothing is carried out two times, and the w_t values are extra smoothed (compared to the s_t). Here, we use DEWMA with equal smoothing constant when computing s_t and w_t as recommended in [64]. We can compute the variance of w_t as,

$$Var(w_t) = \nu^4 \frac{1 + (1-\nu)^2 - (1-\nu)^{2t}((t+1)^2 - (2t^2 + 2t - 1)(1-\nu)^2 + t^2(1-\nu)^4)}{(1-(1-\nu)^2)^3} \sigma^2. \quad (16)$$

The asymptotic variance when t is large is computed as follows,

$$Var_{\text{asymptotic}}(w_t) = \frac{\nu(2 - 2\nu + \nu^2)}{(2-\nu)^3} \sigma^2. \quad (17)$$

The DEWMA scheme declares an anomaly if the charting statistic w_t overpasses the decision thresholds, UCL, and LCL.

$$UCL, LCL = \mu_0 \pm k\sigma \sqrt{\frac{\nu(2-2\nu+\nu^2)}{(2-\nu)^3}}. \quad (18)$$

5.2. Monitoring PV Systems Using Ensemble Learning Techniques Based DEWMA Chart

As discussed above, there are several motivations for utilizing ensemble learning methods with monitoring charts for fault detection purposes. The main motivation consists in the capacity of ensemble learning methods to model multivariate input–output data, and they outperform their alternative single models in many practical situations. It is known that using ensemble models reduces the prediction error compared to single models. Furthermore, monitoring charts, such as the EWMA and DEWMA, assume that data are uncorrelated. Therefore, there is a consequent need for some ensemble-driven models for generating uncorrelated residuals to enable successful fault detection using monitoring charts. In addition, these integrated ensemble learning techniques-based monitoring charts only employ the data of normal events to train the detection model, making them more attractive for detecting faults in PV systems, since it is not always easy to obtain accurately labeled data.

The proposed ensemble learning (BS and BG)-based DEWMA chart to detect anomalies in PV systems is briefly explained in this section and depicted in Figure 10. Specifically, this approach is implemented in two main stages: model construction using training data and fault detection. At first, the ensemble learning models are trained using training data. Here, Bayesian optimization is used to optimally find values of the hyperparameters of the BS and BG models based on training data. In addition, in this step, the detection threshold of the DEWMA and EWMA charts are computed when applied to the residuals obtained from the ensemble learning models. Residuals represent the deviation separating the real output measurements and the predicted values from the ensemble learning model. Under normal operating conditions of the inspected PV systems, the residuals are around zero due to noise measurements and model errors; however, in the case of faulty conditions, the residuals deviate significantly from zero. Here, the ensemble learning models (BS and BG) are trained using fault-free data and then employed for monitoring new data. Then, in the second stage, the constructed models are used for residuals generation, and the DEWMA chart with the previously computed detection threshold is applied to detect potential anomalies in the monitored PV systems.

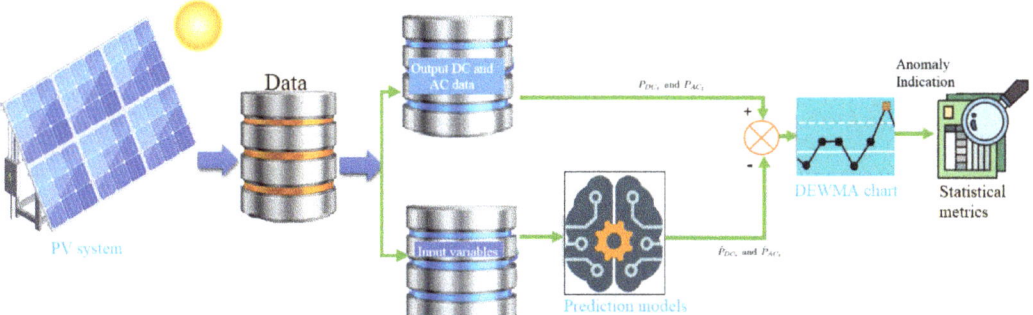

Figure 10. The framework of the proposed ensemble learning-driven fault detection technique.

Note that the decision threshold of the DEWMA and EWMA charts is derived based on the Gaussian distribution of data. However, often in practice, the underlying distribution of data deviates from Gaussianity or is unknown. In such cases, the monitoring results would be unsuitable. To bypass this limitation, in this paper, a non-parametric kernel density estimation (KDE) method was used to set a detection threshold of the DEWMA and EWMA for fault detection. For more details about KDE, refer to [66]. Importantly, it has been shown that the use of KDE to set up the detection threshold does not need to assume that the data follow a Gaussian distribution [67,68], which extends the flexibility of the monitoring charts. Thus, KDE-based detection thresholds are widely employed for process monitoring. A non-parametric detection threshold of the DEWMA chart using KDE is carried out as follows. First, we used KDE to estimate the distribution of the DEWMA statistic based on fault-free data. Given the DEWMA statistic w, the PDF through the KDE is computed as follows.

$$\hat{f}(\mathbf{w}) = \frac{1}{nh} \sum_{i=1}^{n} K\left(\frac{\mathbf{w} - \mathbf{w}_i}{h}\right), \quad (19)$$

where $K(\cdot)$ is the kernel function, and h is the kernel bandwidth parameter and refers to the number of samples. It is mentioned that the Gaussian kernel function is commonly used.

$$K(\mathbf{w}) = \frac{1}{\sqrt{2\pi}} \exp\left(-\frac{\mathbf{w}^2}{2}\right). \quad (20)$$

Now, the threshold of the distribution-free DEWMA chart is derived as the $(1 - \alpha)$-th quantile of the estimated distribution of the DEWMA statistic computed via the KDE. We signal the presence of a potential anomaly if the DEWMA charting statistic exceeds the KDE-based threshold.

The DEWMA with a non-parametric detection threshold is performed as follows:
- Step 1: Computing the DEWMA charting statistic (Equation (18)) for each observation.
- Step 2: Estimating the probability density function for given DEWMA measurements via KDE.
- Step 3: Setting up the detection threshold based on the previously estimated distribution of DEWMA in a non-parametric way as the $(1 - \alpha)$-th quantile.
- Step4: Flagging out a fault if the DEWMA statistic is above the detection threshold.

To assess the efficiency of the studied ensemble learning-based monitoring charts, we used six most commonly used performance measures: true positive rate (TPR), false positive rate (FPR), accuracy, recall, F1-score, and area under curve (AUC), and EER (equal error rate) [69]. For a binary detection problem, the number of true positives (TP), false positives (FP), false negatives (FN), and true negatives (TN) is utilized to calculate the performance measures. The 2 × 2 confusion matrix is depicted in Figure 11. The six performance measures are computed as the following.

$$\text{TPR} = \frac{TP}{TP + FN}. \tag{21}$$

$$\text{FPR} = \frac{FP}{TN + FP}. \tag{22}$$

$$\text{Accuracy} = \frac{TP + TN}{TP + TN + FP + FN}. \tag{23}$$

$$\text{F1-score} = 2\frac{\text{Precision} \cdot \text{Recall}}{\text{Precision} + \text{Recall}} = \frac{2TP}{2TP + FP + FN}. \tag{24}$$

$$EER = \frac{FP + FN}{NF}. \tag{25}$$

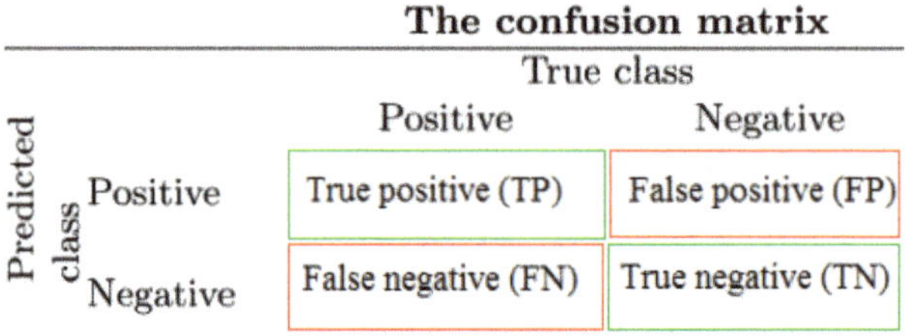

The confusion matrix

		True class	
		Positive	Negative
Predicted class	Positive	True positive (TP)	False positive (FP)
	Negative	False negative (FN)	True negative (TN)

Figure 11. Performance indices used in fault detection.

6. Results and Discussion

As discussed above, ensemble learning-based monitoring charts enable automatically flagging anomalies in the inspected PV system while avoiding false alarms during normal operating conditions. In this section, the ability of the proposed ensemble learning-based DEWMA schemes to detect anomalies in the DC side of a PV system is assessed. Here, the experimental data were collected from an actual PV system described in Section 2. This study considered five kinds of anomalies: PV string fault (F1), inverter disconnection (F2), circuit breaker faults (F3), partial shading of two pylons (F4), and two PV modules (PVM) short-circuited (F5), as they are represented in Figure 12. For an effective fault detection approach, the TPR, accuracy, F1-score, and AUC values should be close to 1 so that all faulty data are detected. On the other hand, the FPR and EER values should be close to zero to avoid false alarms. For a fair comparison between the competing fault detection methods, in what follows, we used the optimized BG and BS models for each monitoring chart.

6.1. Scenarios with String Faults

The aim of the first experiment is to study the efficiency of the proposed methods in detecting open-circuit faults in the monitored PV system. Broadly speaking, open-circuit faults could be caused by the deterioration of DC protection or the disconnection between PV modules in series. In this case, a string fault is intentionally generated by switching off the circuit breaker of the PV system. More specifically, we disconnect one string from the PV array. The results of the optimized ensemble models (BG)-based DEWMA and EWMA charts are provided in Figure 13 and show the presence of energy losses in terms of DC power. The results based on BS-based schemes are omitted because they all provide relatively similar results. We observe that the considered monitoring charts with parametric and non-parametric thresholds perform similarly for detecting this severe fault that resulted in a decrease of relatively 50% of the rated power, making it easy to detect by the investigated models.

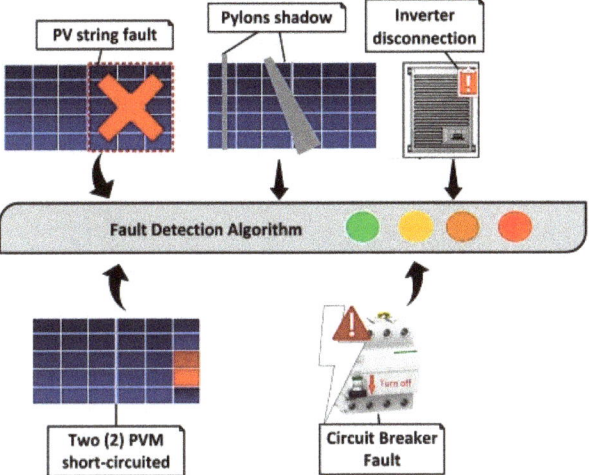

Figure 12. Considered anomalies in this study.

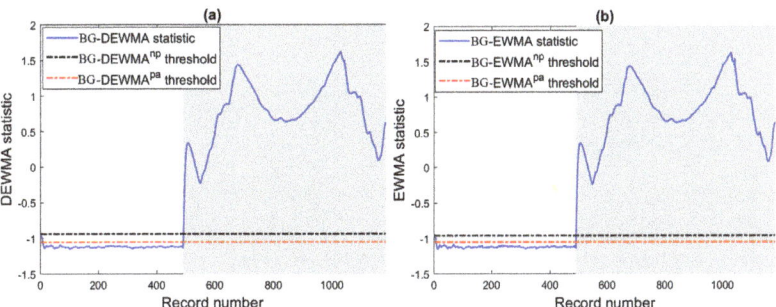

Figure 13. Results of the BG-based schemes in monitoring a string fault: (**a**) BG-DEWMA scheme, and (**b**) BG-DEWMA scheme.

6.2. Scenarios with Inverter Disconnections

In the next experiments, the efficiency of the BG and BS-based DEWMA charts and the competing charts using both parametric and non-parametric thresholds have been investigated in the case of inverter disconnections. Broadly speaking, inverter disconnections are caused if the electrical characteristics exceed the operational limits of the inverter, which are usually given in the datasheet. Note that if inverter disconnections occur, the PV system will shut down until the re-connection of the inverter. In this case study, to verify the detection efficiency of the considered methods, we selected one day of data with inverter disconnection faults. Here, the inverter disconnections are caused by grid instability. More specifically, the voltage and frequency of the grid overpassed the inverter operating limits. Inverter disconnections can be recognized by their very short period and look like spikes, making them easy to discriminate from temporary shading and string faults.

The monitoring results of the investigated ensemble learning-based fault detection charts are depicted in Figure 14. Visually, Figure 14 indicates that these inverter disconnections have been recognized by the considered charts. In addition, we observe that residuals of DC power from the BG and BS models deviate significantly from zero (Figure 14). This means that the constructed models describe well the fault-free data and diverge in the presence of faults. Table 7 lists the detection performance of the considered charts in terms of the five commonly used evaluation scores. As the magnitude of this fault is large, Table 7 clearly indicates that the considered charts easily detect this fault. The results in this table also revealed that the BG and BS-based DEWMA charts with non-parametric thresholds achieved the best performance compared to the other charts. Here, the BS-DEWMA obtained the best detection with an AUC of 0.99, which was followed by the BG-DEWMA chart with an AUC of 0.9881. This could be due to the use of non-parametric thresholds, allowing the DEWMA to be more sensitive than other considered charts. Note that for this fault with a large magnitude, the two types of DEWMA charts (parametric and non-parametric) have slightly similar performance.

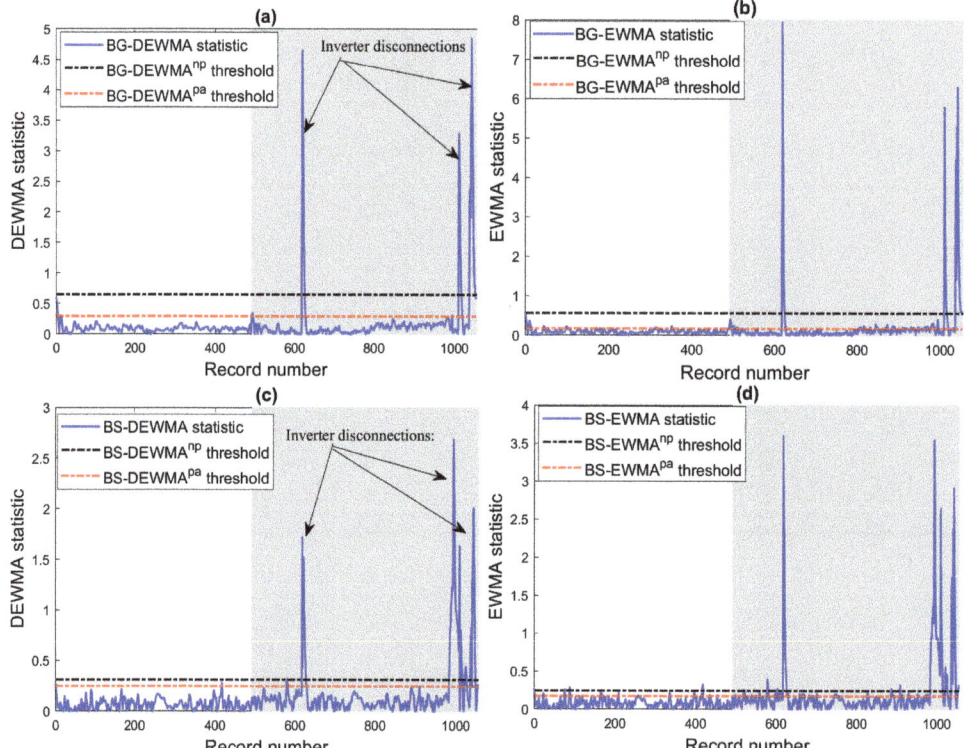

Figure 14. Results of the BG and BS-based schemes in monitoring inverter disconnections: (**a**) BG-DEWMA, (**b**) BG-EWMA, (**c**) BS-DEWMA, and (**d**) BS-EWMA schemes.

Table 7. Detection results by procedure when inverter disconnections occurred.

Method	TPR	FPR	Accuracy	AUC	EER
BS-EWMA^{pa}	1	0.0779	0.9223	0.9610	0.0777
BS-EWMA^{np}	1	0.0304	0.9697	0.9848	0.0303
BS-DEWMA^{pa}	1	0.0276	0.9725	0.9862	0.0275
BS-DEWMA^{np}	1	0.0200	0.9801	0.9900	0.0199
BG-EWMA^{pa}	1	0.1511	0.8494	0.9244	0.1506
BG-EWMA^{np}	1	0.0257	0.9744	0.9872	0.0256
BG-DEWMA^{pa}	1	0.0437	0.9564	0.9781	0.0436
BG-DEWMA^{np}	1	0.0238	0.9763	0.9881	0.0237

6.3. Scenario with Circuit Breaker Faults

The third experiment aimed to assess the ability of the proposed monitoring schemes in detecting circuit breaker fault failures. Crucially, the use of a residual current circuit breaker (RCCB) with a miniature circuit breaker (MCB) is necessary for ensuring the desired performance and protecting PV systems from sudden shock or electrical anomalies. The key role of RCCB is the protection of people from electric shock, and the principal MCB function consists of protecting a PV system against short circuits or overloads. More specifically, the RCCB immediately turns off the power in the presence of a potential electrical fault in the inspected PV system. In this scenario, we generate an RCCB fault within one hour using the collected data. Figure 15 shows the detection performance of the eight investigated ensemble learning-based EWMA and DEWMA charts. We observe that this large fault has been recognized by all the studied charts (Figure 15). We can also see that the BG-DEWMA chart can clearly uncover this fault with reduced false alarms compared to the other charts.

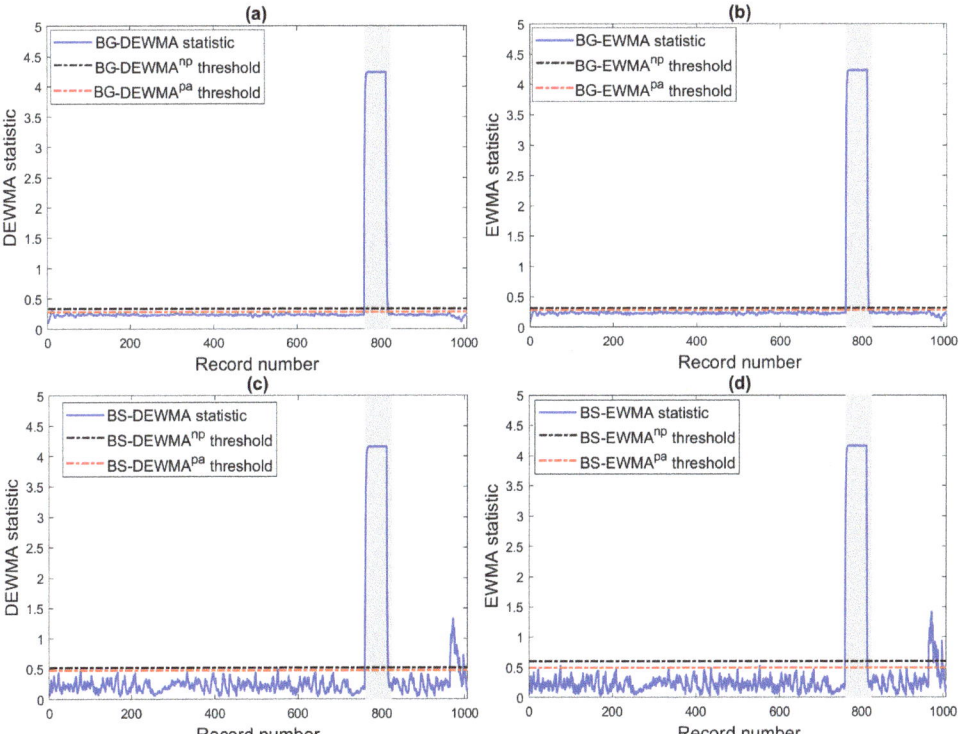

Figure 15. Results of the BG and BS-based schemes in monitoring a circuit breaker fault: (**a**) BG-DEWMA, (**b**) BG-EWMA, (**c**) BS-DEWMA, and (**d**) BS-EWMA schemes.

Table 8 presents the performance of the studied BS and BT-based monitoring schemes. From Table 8, it can be clearly seen that BT-based schemes perform slightly better than BS-based schemes. Here, BG-based schemes achieved an AUC of around 0.98, and BS-based schemes obtained an AUC of around 0.97. This means that the considered schemes can efficiently detect this RCCB fault. Results showed that the BG-based EWMA and DEWMA schemes with non-parametric thresholds models reached the highest detection performance in terms of the five evaluation metrics. As the magnitude of the occurred RCCB fault is large, we can see that the BG-based EWMA and DEWMA schemes perform similarly.

Table 8. Detection results by procedure when a circuit breaker fault occurred.

Method	TPR	FPR	Accuracy	AUC	EER
BS-EWMA^{pa}	0.9815	0.0315	0.9692	0.9750	0.0308
BS-EWMA^{np}	0.9815	0.0241	0.9762	0.9787	0.0238
BS-DEWMA^{pa}	0.9815	0.0346	0.9662	0.9734	0.0338
BS-DEWMA^{np}	0.9815	0.0304	0.9702	0.9755	0.0298
BG-EWMA^{pa}	0.9815	0.0063	0.9930	0.9876	0.0070
BG-EWMA^{np}	0.9815	0.0042	0.9950	0.9886	0.0050
BG-DEWMA^{pa}	0.9815	0.0084	0.9911	0.9865	0.0089
BG-DEWMA^{np}	0.9815	0.0042	0.9950	0.9886	0.0050

6.4. Scenario with Shaded Modules

Next, the capability of the ensemble learning-based techniques in detecting partial shading is demonstrated. Broadly speaking, different factors can cause shading losses, such as the installation of the PV system close to pylons and trees [8]. Crucially, the production of a PV system exposed to partial shading will decrease from the desired production. Here, the monitored system is exposed to two communication pylons (Figure 16), which can decrease the power output. The data are collected within a period of the day in the presence of partial shading.

Figure 16. (**Top**) PV array with shaded modules due to two communication pylons installed in front of this PV array. (**Bottom**) Shading of pylon 2 on PV sub-array 2.

The results of the BG and BS-based techniques are depicted in Figure 17. From the plots in Figure 17, we observe that the partial shading of the two pylons resulted in a significant power. It is observed from Figure 17 that the considered charts can sense the presence of this partial shading. So, the proposed ensemble learning-based detection methods effectively flagged out this partial shading. Furthermore, we notice that the BS-based EWMA and DWEMA schemes detect this shading partially, i.e., with some missed detections. On the other hand, all BG-based schemes provide good detection results of this partial shading.

Hence, we conclude that the BG model catches most of the variability in the data compared to the BS model, facilitating obtaining more sensitive residuals.

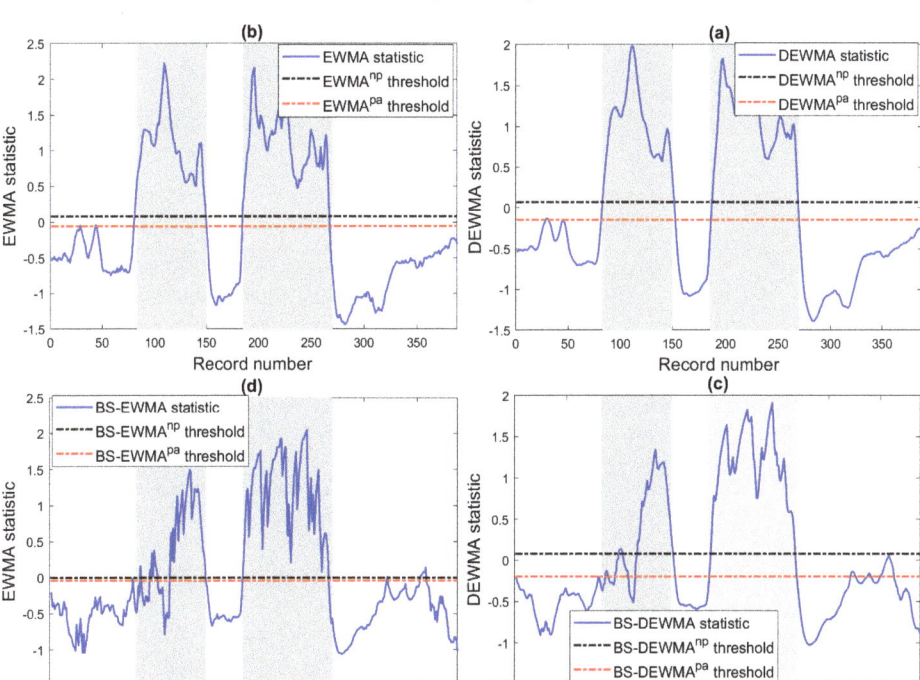

Figure 17. Results of the BG and BS-based schemes in monitoring partial shading: (**a**) BG-DEWMA, (**b**) BG-EWMA, (**c**) BS-DEWMA, and (**d**) BS-EWMA schemes.

Table 9 shows that the non-parametric DEWMA performed better than the conventional DEWMA and single EWMA schemes with lower FPR and the highest TPR, accuracy, and precision. The non-parametric DEWMA reaches an AUC of 0.984, and the conventional DEWMA and EWMA schemes reached, respectively, AUC values of 0.932 and 0.65. The conventional schemes flag this shading but with some false alarms and missed detection. Such results may indicate the non-parametric DEWMA rather than the conventional DEWMA and EWMA charts for appropriately revealing partial shading in a PV array.

Table 9 lists the detection results of the BG and BS-based techniques in terms of the five evaluation scores. From Table 9, it can be inferred that the BG-based EWMA and DEWMA schemes with non-parametric thresholds outperformed all other methods by providing the best detection performance with a TPR of 0.9805 and very few false alarms (FPR = 0.9869), and an accuracy of 0.9869. This highlights the capacity of these BG-based EWMA and DEWMA schemes in accurately detecting partial shading. Furthermore, it is worth observing that the BG-based schemes with non-parametric thresholds dominate the parametric BG-based schemes' counterparts. In the parametric schemes, the detection thresholds are determined based on the assumption of the Gaussian distribution of data, which is not often valid. However, in the non-parametric counterparts, the threshold is automatically determined using the KDE approach, making them more effective and flexible. As expected for anomalies with a large magnitude as in this case of partial shading, the DEWMA and the EWMA perform similarly. In contrast, the BS-based monitoring schemes can sense the presence of power loss but with some missed detections. Here, the BS-based DEWMA and EWMA schemes are showing comparable performance with an AUC around 0.89 but with several missed detection (TPR around 0.8).

Table 9. Detection results when shading has occurred.

Method	TPR	FPR	Accuracy	AUC	EER
BS-EWMA^{pa}	0.8182	0.0342	0.9072	0.8920	0.0928
BS-EWMA^{np}	0.8052	0.0299	0.9046	0.8876	0.0954
BS-DEWMA^{pa}	0.8831	0.0983	0.8943	0.8924	0.1057
BS-DEWMA^{np}	0.7727	0	0.9098	0.8864	0.0902
BG-EWMA^{pa}	0.9740	0.0214	0.9768	0.9763	0.0232
BG-EWMA^{np}	0.9675	0.0128	0.9794	0.9774	0.0206
BG-DEWMA^{pa}	0.9935	0.0256	0.9820	0.9839	0.0180
BG-DEWMA^{np}	0.9805	0.0043	0.9869	0.9881	0.0103

6.5. Short-Circuit Fault

In this last investigation, we examine the performance of the proposed monitoring schemes in the presence of short-circuit faults. Short-circuit faults if not detected can induce degradation of the PV modules' performance [70]. In this scenario, the BG and BS-based monitoring schemes are verified in the case of two PV modules short-circuited. The monitoring results of BG and BS-based strategies are presented in Figure 18. Here, the EWMA and DEWMa charts are applied to residual of DC power obtained from the already constructed ensemble learning models (i.e., BG and BT). We observe that the studied monitoring schemes can recognize this short-circuit fault (Figure 18). The BS-based DEWMA and EWMA schemes flag this fault, but with several missed detection. In contrast, BG-based charts detect the fault with minimum false alarms and missed detection.

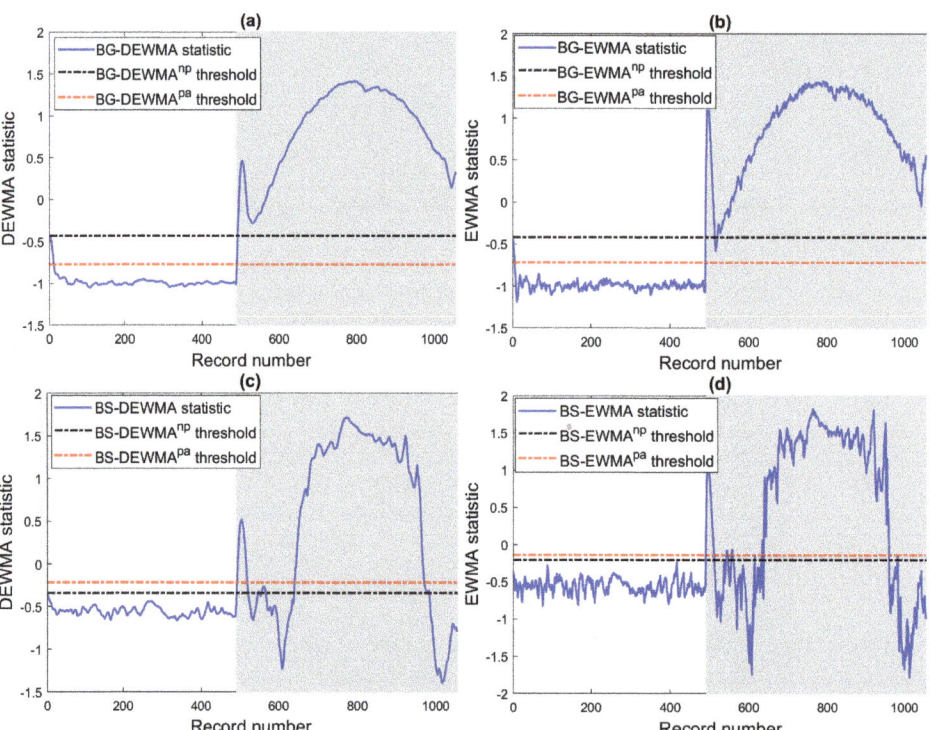

Figure 18. Results of the BG-based schemes in the presence of two short-circuited modules: (**a**) BG-DEWMA, (**b**) BG-EWMA, (**c**) BS-DEWMA, and (**d**) BS-EWMA schemes.

Table 10 quantitively summarizes the results of BG and BS-based monitoring techniques. From Table 10, the results confirm that the BS-based schemes dominate the BG-based monitoring schemes. In addition, results revealed that the proposed BG-based

DEWMA scheme with a non-parametric threshold provides the best results in this case study. It is followed by its parametric counterpart.

Table 10. Detection results by procedure when two modules are short-circuited.

Method	TPR	FPR	Accuracy	AUC	EER
BS-EWMA^{pa}	0.6230	0	0.7983	0.8115	0.2017
BS-EWMA^{np}	0.6407	0	0.8078	0.8204	0.1922
BS-DEWMA^{pa}	0.6319	0	0.8030	0.8159	0.1970
BS-DEWMA^{np}	0.6832	0	0.8305	0.8416	0.1695
BG-EWMA^{pa}	1	0.0122	0.9943	0.9939	0.0057
BG-EWMA^{np}	0.9876	0	0.9934	0.9938	0.0066
BG-DEWMA^{pa}	0.9965	0.0244	0.9867	0.9860	0.0133
BG-DEWMA^{np}	0.9929	0.0041	0.9943	0.9944	0.0057

In summary, this work shows that merging ensemble learning models to capture describe DC power with the good detection capability of DEWMA enables an efficient detection of anomalies on the DC side of a PV system. The ensemble learning-based fault detection schemes presented in this paper can effectively detect the presence of potential anomalies on the DC sides of the PV system, but they do not identify the types of detected anomaly. Anomaly identification can be performed by the analysis of the DC current and DC voltage. Table 11 lists the influence of the considered anomalies on DC current and DC voltage. Overall, anomaly identification could be conducted by employing semi-supervised anomaly detection methods, such as one-class SVM and isolation forest, to monitor DC current and DC voltage.

Table 11. Considered faults with their indicators.

	Duration	DC Current Indicator (A)	DC Voltage Indicator
PV string Faults (open-circuit)	Permanent	−50%	No change
Circuit breaker fault	Permanent	Zero energy	Voc (280–300)
Inverter disconnection	Temporary (1–5 min)	Zero energy	Voc (280–300)
Partial shading (pylons)	Temporary (0.5–2 h)	−15/35%	220–260
2 PV modules short-circuited	Permanent	No change	−10%

7. Conclusions

Accurate fault detection is essential to photovoltaic systems' efficiency and continuous operation while maintaining the desired performance level. In this work, we developed and studied ensemble learning-based EWMA and DEWMA control charts that are suitable for detecting different anomalies in the AC and DC sides of the PV system. This is mainly motivated by the ensemble learning-driven models' capability to enhance the performance of machine learning models by merging numerous learners versus single regressors. Specifically, the boosted trees (BST) and bagged trees (BT) models are considered in this study. To enhance the detection performance, we employed Bayesian optimization to find the optimal parameter values of the ensemble learning models based on training data. In addition, kernel density estimation is adopted to non-parametrically determine the detection threshold of the DEWMA chart, which makes it more flexible in dealing with both Gaussian and non-Gaussian data. In order to evaluate the accuracy and performance of the proposed techniques, different electrical faults and environmental anomalies, generally occurring in PV systems, were considered The obtained results showed that the detection and the identification of faults were successfully achieved.

Despite the encouraging obtained results, future research works on PV systems monitoring could be undertaken in several directions:

- It would be useful to incorporate more data inputs such as open circuit voltage, short circuit current, and fill factor to further enhance the fault detection and diagnosis

capabilities of the proposed approach. Moreover, electrical sensors on the AC side of the PV system at the connection point could be added to monitor the energy flow.
- We also plan to develop deep learning-driven monitoring charts by merging the extended capacity of deep learning models (e.g., long short-term memory (LSTM) and gated recurrent unit (GRU) [71,72]) in automatically extracting important features from multivariate data with statistical monitoring charts such as the generalized likelihood ratio test [73,74] to improve fault detection in PV systems.
- We plan also to construct parsimonious ensemble learning models by selecting only the important variables for the prediction by the random forest algorithm. Then, the reduced models can be employed for residuals generation to detect faults.
- Since the DEWMA chart assumes a fixed threshold [75], which may not be suitable to deal with non-stationary (or time-varying) data, adaptive ensemble learning-based DEWMA techniques will be developed in future work by allowing the thresholds of these methods to varying online to account for the changing nature of the data.
- Data from PV systems are usually tainted with noise measurements, which can degrade the performance of the designed fault detection methods by increasing the number of false alarms and masking pertinent features in data. Future works will improve the robustness of the ensemble learning-based-DEWMA model to noisy measurements by developing a wavelet-based DEWMA detector. Noise effects will be reduced using wavelet-based multiscale denoising; hence, the fault detection performance will significantly be improved.
- In addition, it will be interesting to investigate the detection capability of the proposed data-driven anomaly detection methodology in other renewable energy systems, such as wind turbine monitoring.

Author Contributions: F.H.: Conceptualization, formal analysis, investigation, methodology, software, supervision, writing—original draft, and writing—review and editing. B.T.: Conceptualization, formal analysis, investigation, methodology, writing—original draft, and writing—review and editing. S.K.: Writing—original draft, and writing—review and editing. A.D.: Formal analysis, methodology, writing—review, and editing. Y.S.: Investigation, conceptualization, formal analysis, methodology, writing—review and editing, funding acquisition, and supervision. A.H.A.: Formal analysis, investigation, review, and editing. All authors have read and agreed to the published version of the manuscript.

Funding: This work was supported by funding from the King Abdullah University of Science and Technology (KAUST), Office of Sponsored Research (OSR), under Award No: OSR-2019-CRG7-3800.

Institutional Review Board Statement: Not applicable.

Informed Consent Statement: Not applicable.

Data Availability Statement: Not applicable.

Conflicts of Interest: The authors declare no conflict of interest.

References

1. IRENA. *Renewable Capacity Statistics 2022*; IRENA: Abu Dhabi, United Arab Emirates, 2022.
2. BloombergNEF Cost of New Renewables Temporarily Rises as Inflation Starts to Bite. Available online: https://about.bnef.com/blog/cost-of-new-renewables-temporarily-rises-as-inflation-starts-to-bite/ (accessed on 18 August 2022).
3. *REN21 Renewable Energy Policy, Renewables 2022 Global Status Report*; UN Environment Programme: Nairobi, Kenya, 2022.
4. Caroline, T.; David, M.; Ulrike, J.; Matthias, A.; Ioannis Thomas, T.; Máté, H. *Solar Bankability PV Investment Technical Risk Management 2017*; Solar Bankability: Brussels, Belgium, 2017.
5. Clean Energy Reviews Most Efficient Solar Panels 2022. 2022. Available online: https://www.cleanenergyreviews.info/blog/most-efficient-solar-panels (accessed on 11 August 2022).
6. Obeidat, F. A comprehensive review of future photovoltaic systems. *Sol. Energy* **2018**, *163*, 545–551. [CrossRef]
7. Richter, M.; Tjengdrawira, C.; Vedde, J.; Green, M.; Frearson, L.; Herteleer, B.; Jahn, U.; Herz, M.; Köntges, M. *Technical Assumptions Used in PV Financial Models Review of Current Practices and Recommendations: International Energy Agency Photovoltaic Power Systems Programme: IEA PVPS Task 13, Subtask 1: Report IEA-PVPS T13-08: 2017*; International Energy Agency: Paris, France, 2017.

8. Pillai, D.S.; Rajasekar, N. A comprehensive review on protection challenges and fault diagnosis in PV systems. *Renew. Sustain. Energy Rev.* **2018**, *91*, 18–40. [CrossRef]
9. Madeti, S.R.; Singh, S. A comprehensive study on different types of faults and detection techniques for solar photovoltaic system. *Sol. Energy* **2017**, *158*, 161–185. [CrossRef]
10. Livera, A.; Theristis, M.; Makrides, G.; Georghiou, G.E. Recent advances in failure diagnosis techniques based on performance data analysis for grid-connected photovoltaic systems. *Renew. Energy* **2019**, *133*, 126–143. [CrossRef]
11. Halwachs, M.; Neumaier, L.; Vollert, N.; Maul, L.; Dimitriadis, S.; Voronko, Y.; Eder, G.; Omazic, A.; Mühleisen, W.; Hirschl, C.; et al. Statistical evaluation of PV system performance and failure data among different climate zones. *Renew. Energy* **2019**, *139*, 1040–1060. [CrossRef]
12. Walker, H. *Best Practices for Operation and Maintenance of Photovoltaic and Energy Storage Systems*; Technical Report; National Renewable Energy Lab. (NREL): Golden, CO, USA, 2018.
13. Lumby, B. *Utility-Scale Solar Photovoltaic Power Plants: A Project Developer's Guide*; Technical Report; The World Bank: Washington, DC, USA, 2015.
14. Jones, C.B.; Stein, J.S.; Gonzalez, S.; King, B.H. Photovoltaic system fault detection and diagnostics using Laterally Primed Adaptive Resonance Theory neural network. In Proceedings of the 2015 IEEE 42nd Photovoltaic Specialist Conference (PVSC), New Orleans, LA, USA, 14–19 June 2015; pp. 1–6.
15. Madeti, S.R.; Singh, S. Modeling of PV system based on experimental data for fault detection using kNN method. *Sol. Energy* **2018**, *173*, 139–151. [CrossRef]
16. Harrou, F.; Taghezouit, B.; Sun, Y. Improved kNN-based monitoring schemes for detecting faults in PV systems. *IEEE J. Photovolt.* **2019**, *9*, 811–821. [CrossRef]
17. Benkercha, R.; Moulahoum, S. Fault detection and diagnosis based on C4. 5 decision tree algorithm for grid connected PV system. *Sol. Energy* **2018**, *173*, 610–634. [CrossRef]
18. Dhimish, M.; Holmes, V.; Mehrdadi, B.; Dales, M. Comparing Mamdani Sugeno fuzzy logic and RBF ANN network for PV fault detection. *Renew. Energy* **2018**, *117*, 257–274. [CrossRef]
19. Harrou, F.; Dairi, A.; Taghezouit, B.; Sun, Y. An unsupervised monitoring procedure for detecting anomalies in photovoltaic systems using a one-class support vector machine. *Sol. Energy* **2019**, *179*, 48–58. [CrossRef]
20. Harrou, F.; Saidi, A.; Sun, Y.; Khadraoui, S. Monitoring of photovoltaic systems using improved kernel-based learning schemes. *IEEE J. Photovolt.* **2021**, *11*, 806–818. [CrossRef]
21. Khaldi, B.; Harrou, F.; Benslimane, S.M.; Sun, Y. A data-driven soft sensor for swarm motion speed prediction using ensemble learning methods. *IEEE Sens. J.* **2021**, *21*, 19025–19037. [CrossRef]
22. Toubeau, J.F.; Pardoen, L.; Hubert, L.; Marenne, N.; Sprooten, J.; De Grève, Z.; Vallée, F. Machine learning-assisted outage planning for maintenance activities in power systems with renewables. *Energy* **2022**, *238*, 121993. [CrossRef]
23. Alkesaiberi, A.; Harrou, F.; Sun, Y. Efficient wind power prediction using machine learning methods: A comparative study. *Energies* **2022**, *15*, 2327. [CrossRef]
24. Wang, W.; Harrou, F.; Bouyeddou, B.; Senouci, S.M.; Sun, Y. Cyber-attacks detection in industrial systems using artificial intelligence-driven methods. *Int. J. Crit. Infrastruct. Prot.* **2022**, *38*, 100542. [CrossRef]
25. Lee, J.; Wang, W.; Harrou, F.; Sun, Y. Reliable solar irradiance prediction using ensemble learning-based models: A comparative study. *Energy Convers. Manag.* **2020**, *208*, 112582. [CrossRef]
26. Freund, Y.; Schapire, R.E. A decision-theoretic generalization of on-line learning and an application to boosting. *J. Comput. Syst. Sci.* **1997**, *55*, 119–139. [CrossRef]
27. Bartlett, P.; Freund, Y.; Lee, W.S.; Schapire, R.E. Boosting the margin: A new explanation for the effectiveness of voting methods. *Ann. Stat.* **1998**, *26*, 1651–1686. [CrossRef]
28. Schapire, R.E. The boosting approach to machine learning: An overview. In *Nonlinear Estimation and Classification*; Springer: Berlin/Heidelberg, Germany, 2003; pp. 149–171.
29. Bühlmann, P.; Hothorn, T. Boosting algorithms: Regularization, prediction and model fitting. *Stat. Sci.* **2007**, *22*, 477–505.
30. Chen, T.; Guestrin, C. Xgboost: A scalable tree boosting system. In Proceedings of the 22nd acm Sigkdd International Conference on Knowledge Discovery and Data Mining, San Francisco, CA, USA, 13–17 August 2016; pp. 785–794.
31. Bibi, N.; Shah, I.; Alsubie, A.; Ali, S.; Lone, S.A. Electricity Spot Prices Forecasting Based on Ensemble Learning. *IEEE Access* **2021**, *9*, 150984–150992. [CrossRef]
32. Friedman, J.; Hastie, T.; Tibshirani, R. Additive logistic regression: A statistical view of boosting (with discussion and a rejoinder by the authors). *Ann. Stat.* **2000**, *28*, 337–407. [CrossRef]
33. Breiman, L.; Friedman, J.; Olshen, R.; Stone, C. *Classification and Regression Trees*; Chapman & Hall: London, UK, 1984.
34. Breiman, L. Bagging predictors. *Mach. Learn.* **1996**, *24*, 123–140. [CrossRef]
35. Sutton, C.D. Classification and regression trees, bagging, and boosting. *Handb. Stat.* **2005**, *24*, 303–329.
36. Box, G.E.; Jenkins, G.M.; Reinsel, G.C.; Ljung, G.M. *Time Series Analysis: Forecasting and Control*; John Wiley & Sons: Hoboken, NJ, USA, 2015.
37. Alwan, L.C. Effects of autocorrelation on control chart performance. *Commun. Stat.-Theory Methods* **1992**, *21*, 1025–1049. [CrossRef]
38. Leoni, R.C.; Costa, A.F.B.; Machado, M.A.G. The effect of the autocorrelation on the performance of the T2 chart. *Eur. J. Oper. Res.* **2015**, *247*, 155–165. [CrossRef]

39. Stein, J.S.; Klise, G.T. *Models Used to Assess the Performance of Photovoltaic Systems*; Technical Report; Sandia National Laboratories (SNL): Albuquerque, NM, USA; Livermore, CA, USA, 2009.
40. King, D.L.; Kratochvil, J.A.; Boyson, W.E. Photovoltaic Array Performance Model. 2004. Available online: http://www.mauisolarsoftware.com/MSESC/xPerfModel2003.pdf (accessed on 18 August 2022).
41. Rawat, R.; Kaushik, S.; Lamba, R. A review on modeling, design methodology and size optimization of photovoltaic based water pumping, standalone and grid connected system. *Renew. Sustain. Energy Rev.* **2016**, *57*, 1506–1519. [CrossRef]
42. Mora Segado, P.; Carretero, J.; Sidrach-de Cardona, M. Models to predict the operating temperature of different photovoltaic modules in outdoor conditions. *Prog. Photovolt. Res. Appl.* **2015**, *23*, 1267–1282. [CrossRef]
43. Nguyen, D.P.N.; Neyts, K.; Lauwaert, J. Proposed Models to Improve Predicting the Operating Temperature of Different Photovoltaic Module Technologies under Various Climatic Conditions. *Appl. Sci.* **2021**, *11*, 7064. [CrossRef]
44. Boyson, W.E.; Galbraith, G.M.; King, D.L.; Gonzalez, S. *Performance Model for Grid-Connected Photovoltaic Inverters*; Technical Report; Sandia National Laboratories (SNL): Albuquerque, NM, USA; Livermore, CA, USA, 2007.
45. Driesse, A.; Jain, P.; Harrison, S. Beyond the curves: Modeling the electrical efficiency of photovoltaic inverters. In Proceedings of the 2008 33rd IEEE Photovoltaic Specialists Conference, San Diego, CA, USA, 11–16 May 2008; pp. 1–6.
46. Protopapadakis, E.; Voulodimos, A.; Doulamis, N. An investigation on multi-objective optimization of feedforward neural network topology. In Proceedings of the 2017 8th International Conference on Information, Intelligence, Systems & Applications (IISA), Larnaca, Cyprus, 27–30 August 2017; pp. 1–6.
47. Shahriari, B.; Swersky, K.; Wang, Z.; Adams, R.P.; De Freitas, N. Taking the human out of the loop: A review of Bayesian optimization. *Proc. IEEE* **2015**, *104*, 148–175. [CrossRef]
48. Snoek, J.; Larochelle, H.; Adams, R.P. Practical bayesian optimization of machine learning algorithms. *Adv. Neural Inf. Process. Syst.* **2012**, *25*. Available online: https://proceedings.neurips.cc/paper/2012/hash/05311655a15b75fab86956663e1819cd-Abstract.html (accessed on 8 September 2022).
49. Nguyen, V.H.; Le, T.T.; Truong, H.S.; Le, M.V.; Ngo, V.L.; Nguyen, A.T.; Nguyen, H.Q. Applying Bayesian Optimization for Machine Learning Models in Predicting the Surface Roughness in Single-Point Diamond Turning Polycarbonate. *Math. Probl. Eng.* **2021**, *2021*, 6815802. [CrossRef]
50. Roberts, S. Control chart tests based on geometric moving averages. *Technometrics* **2000**, *42*, 97–101. [CrossRef]
51. Hunter, J.S. The exponentially weighted moving average. *J. Qual. Technol.* **1986**, *18*, 203–210. [CrossRef]
52. Montgomery, D.C. *Introduction to Statistical Quality Control*; John Wiley & Sons: Hoboken, NJ, USA, 2020.
53. Khaldi, B.; Harrou, F.; Cherif, F.; Sun, Y. Monitoring a robot swarm using a data-driven fault detection approach. *Robot. Auton. Syst.* **2017**, *97*, 193–203. [CrossRef]
54. Harrou, F.; Nounou, M.; Nounou, H. A statistical fault detection strategy using PCA based EWMA control schemes. In Proceedings of the 2013 9th Asian Control Conference (ASCC), Istanbul, Turkey, 23–26 June 2013; pp. 1–4.
55. Zeroual, A.; Harrou, F.; Sun, Y.; Messai, N. Integrating model-based observer and Kullback–Leibler metric for estimating and detecting road traffic congestion. *IEEE Sens. J.* **2018**, *18*, 8605–8616. [CrossRef]
56. Harrou, F.; Sun, Y.; Madakyaru, M.; Bouyedou, B. An improved multivariate chart using partial least squares with continuous ranked probability score. *IEEE Sens. J.* **2018**, *18*, 6715–6726. [CrossRef]
57. Lucas, J.; Saccucci, M. Exponentially weighted moving average control schemes: Properties and enhancements. *Technometrics* **1990**, *32*, 1–12. [CrossRef]
58. Shamma, S.E.; Shamma, A.K. Development and evaluation of control charts using double exponentially weighted moving averages. *Int. J. Qual. Reliab. Manag.* **1992**, *9*. [CrossRef]
59. Shamma, S.E.; Amin, R.W.; Shamma, A.K. A double exponentially weigiited moving average control procedure with variable sampling intervals. *Commun. Stat.-Simul. Comput.* **1991**, *20*, 511–528. [CrossRef]
60. Mahmoud, M.A.; Woodall, W.H. An evaluation of the double exponentially weighted moving average control chart. *Commun. Stat. Comput.* **2010**, *39*, 933–949. [CrossRef]
61. Khoo, M.B.; Teh, S.; Wu, Z. Monitoring process mean and variability with one double EWMA chart. *Commun. Stat. Methods* **2010**, *39*, 3678–3694. [CrossRef]
62. Adeoti, O.A.; Malela-Majika, J.C. Double exponentially weighted moving average control chart with supplementary runs-rules. *Qual. Technol. Quant. Manag.* **2020**, *17*, 149–172. [CrossRef]
63. Raza, M.A.; Nawaz, T.; Aslam, M.; Bhatti, S.H.; Sherwani, R.A.K. A new nonparametric double exponentially weighted moving average control chart. *Qual. Reliab. Eng. Int.* **2020**, *36*, 68–87. [CrossRef]
64. Zhang, L.; Chen, G. An extended EWMA mean chart. *Qual. Technol. Quant. Manag.* **2005**, *2*, 39–52. [CrossRef]
65. Taghezouit, B.; Harrou, F.; Sun, Y.; Arab, A.H.; Larbes, C. A simple and effective detection strategy using double exponential scheme for photovoltaic systems monitoring. *Sol. Energy* **2021**, *214*, 337–354. [CrossRef]
66. Rosenblatt, M. Curve estimates. *Ann. Math. Stat.* **1971**, *42*, 1815–1842. [CrossRef]
67. Chen, Q.; Wynne, R.; Goulding, P.; Sandoz, D. The application of principal component analysis and kernel density estimation to enhance process monitoring. *Control Eng. Pract.* **2000**, *8*, 531–543. [CrossRef]
68. Taghezouit, B.; Harrou, F.; Sun, Y.; Arab, A.H.; Larbes, C. Multivariate statistical monitoring of photovoltaic plant operation. *Energy Convers. Manag.* **2020**, *205*, 112317. [CrossRef]
69. Harrou, F.; Khaldi, B.; Sun, Y.; Cherif, F. An efficient statistical strategy to monitor a robot swarm. *IEEE Sens. J.* **2019**, *20*, 2214–2223. [CrossRef]

70. Pei, T.; Hao, X. A Fault Detection Method for Photovoltaic Systems Based on Voltage and Current Observation and Evaluation. *Energies* **2019**, *12*, 1712. [CrossRef]
71. Harrou, F.; Kadri, F.; Sun, Y. Forecasting of photovoltaic solar power production using LSTM approach. *Adv. Stat. Model. Forecast. Fault Detect. Renew. Energy Syst.* **2020**, *3*. Available online: https://library.oapen.org/bitstream/handle/20.500.12657/43847/external_content.pdf?sequence=1#page=17 (accessed on 18 August 2022).
72. Harrou, F.; Sun, Y.; Hering, A.S.; Madakyaru, M. *Statistical Process Monitoring Using Advanced Data-Driven and Deep Learning Approaches: Theory and Practical Applications*; Elsevier: Amsterdam, The Netherlands, 2020.
73. Harrou, F.; Zeroual, A.; Sun, Y. Traffic congestion detection based on hybrid observer and GLR test. In Proceedings of the 2018 Annual American Control Conference (ACC), Milwaukee, WI, USA, 27–29 June 2018; pp. 604–609.
74. Madakyaru, M.; Harrou, F.; Sun, Y. Improved anomaly detection using multi-scale PLS and generalized likelihood ratio test. In Proceedings of the 2016 IEEE Symposium Series on Computational Intelligence (SSCI), Athens, Greece, 6–9 December 2016; pp. 1–6.
75. Knoth, S.; Saleh, N.A.; Mahmoud, M.A.; Woodall, W.H.; Tercero-Gómez, V.G. A critique of a variety of "memory-based" process monitoring methods. *J. Qual. Technol.* **2022**, 1–27. [CrossRef]

Article

IoT-Based Low-Cost Photovoltaic Monitoring for a Greenhouse Farm in an Arid Region

Amor Hamied [1], Adel Mellit [1], Mohamed Benghanem [2,*] and Sahbi Boubaker [3]

1. Renewable Energy Laboratory, Faculty of Sciences and Technology, Departement of Electronics, University of Jijel, Jijel 18000, Algeria
2. Department of Physics, Faculty of Science, Islamic University of Madinah, Madinah 42351, Saudi Arabia
3. Department of Computer and Network Engineering, College of Computer Science and Engineering, University of Jeddah, Jeddah 21959, Saudi Arabia
* Correspondence: mbenghanem@iu.edu.sa

Abstract: In this paper, a low-cost monitoring system for an off-grid photovoltaic (PV) system, installed at an isolated location (Sahara region, south of Algeria), is designed. The PV system is used to supply a small-scale greenhouse farm. A simple and accurate fault diagnosis algorithm was developed and integrated into a low-cost microcontroller for real time validation. The monitoring system, including the fault diagnosis procedure, was evaluated under specific climate conditions. The Internet of Things (IoT) technique is used to remotely monitor the data, such as PV currents, PV voltages, solar irradiance, and cell temperature. A friendly web page was also developed to visualize the data and check the state of the PV system remotely. The users could be notified about the state of the PV system via phone SMS. Results showed that the system performs better under this climate conditions and that it can supply the considered greenhouse farm. It was also shown that the integrated algorithm is able to detect and identify some examined defects with a good accuracy. The total cost of the designed IoT-based monitoring system is around 73 euros and its average energy consumed per day is around 13.5 Wh.

Keywords: photovoltaic; monitoring system; fault diagnosis; internet of things

Citation: Hamied, A.; Mellit, A.; Benghanem, M.; Boubaker, S. IoT-Based Low-Cost Photovoltaic Monitoring for a Greenhouse Farm in an Arid Region. *Energies* **2023**, *16*, 3860. https://doi.org/10.3390/en16093860

Academic Editor: Jesús Polo

Received: 19 March 2023
Revised: 26 April 2023
Accepted: 28 April 2023
Published: 30 April 2023

Copyright: © 2023 by the authors. Licensee MDPI, Basel, Switzerland. This article is an open access article distributed under the terms and conditions of the Creative Commons Attribution (CC BY) license (https://creativecommons.org/licenses/by/4.0/).

1. Introduction

Nowadays, as reported by the international energy agency (IEA), some isolated and rural areas are experiencing a large shortage in the supply of electric power [1]. Around 770 million people are still living without access to electricity, particularly in Africa and Asia [1]. Sub-Saharan Africa's share of the global population without access to electricity has risen from 74% before the COVID-19 pandemic to 77% after [1]. Due to the increase in energy demand, the challenge has shifted from saving classical fuel-based energy sources to creating and efficiently managing renewable energy sources mainly composed of solar and wind.

Starting a few years ago, investment in solar photovoltaic (PV) energy has become a common trend in developed and developing countries. This new orientation is mainly empowered by a relative decrease in solar module cost. Thus, a large number of PV plants were installed around the world. According to IEA [2], about 940 GW of PV were installed at the end of 2021. The African Energy Outlook 2022 report estimates that between 2021 and 2030, more than 40% of total capacity additions will come from solar PV [3].

There are various applications of PV systems around the globe where PV sources may provide appropriate solutions for remote sites without access to electricity. As this source of power is free and does not require hard maintenance, most sectors are attracted by the application of PV systems (e.g., telecommunication, water pumping, rural electrification, building, health, transportation, street lights, electric vehicles, agriculture, etc.). For the above-cited reasons, the current research work is devoted to investigate the performance of a PV system used to supply a small-scale greenhouse farm in a remote site located in the south of Algeria.

Monitoring PV installations in order to detect probable defects is a real challenge that should be faced by PV systems designers and end-users. The main objective of a monitoring PV system is to maintain a high level of reliability, effectiveness of operation and availability of the system to provide electricity in the best conditions. The defects that may occur in a PV installation may significantly decrease the power yield and may exhibit a high risk of fire [4,5]. As per the reference [6], the annual energy loss due to defects in PV systems is estimated to be around 18.9%.

From research and engineering design perspectives, various kinds of PV monitoring systems have been designed, deployed and studied. Among the recent automatic monitoring systems developed worldwide, the system developed in [7] was based on the European Solar Test Installation sensor. Despite the advanced technologies and novelties of the developed system, the high sampling period (8 min) is a big drawback. In addition, the storage capacity, limited to 16,300 measurements (observations), may represent a challenging limitation. Another recent work dedicated to a universal data acquisition system (DAQ) for PV performance monitoring is designed based on a microcontroller (68B09). The collected data can be easily accessed through a server, which can help users to perform the diagnosis and analysis of the PV system under various operating conditions [8]. In [9], the authors developed another data logging system using a 12-bit precision Analog to Digital Converter (ADC). Despite the improvements embedded to the designed monitoring system, the number of acquired variables remains small, which may limit the deployment of the device. However, this system has the advantage of not requiring the physical connection of the monitored system to the data collection server [10]. In [11], the authors designed an improved Data Acquisition (DAQ) system for which the number of variables to be acquired has reached 20 analog inputs, which seems to be acceptable, particularly for small-scale applications.

Recently, with advancements in the field of embedded microcontrollers and telecommunication technologies such as wireless sensor networks (WSNs), many researchers were attracted by the application of the internet of things (IoT) to remotely monitor their PV systems. For instance, the authors in [12] designed a monitoring system (IoT-DAS) for grid-connected PV systems. Among the features of such a system, we can cite its ability to identify non-ideal (faulty or degenerated) operating conditions. The obtained results are reported to show compliance with the International Electrotechnical Commission (IEC) standard. Moreover, the developed system is found to be efficient in monitoring all necessary parameters with low power consumption and high accuracy. Additionally, a smart solar still prototype for water desalination was designed using a remote monitoring system, based on the IoT technique [13]. The monitoring system is developed and integrated into the hybrid solar still in order to control its evolution online, as well the quality of the freshwater.

A monitoring system for smart greenhouses using IoT and deep convolutional neural networks has been designed [14]. The controlled parameters such as air temperature, relative humidity, capacitive soil moisture, light intensity, and CO_2 concentration were measured and uploaded to a designed webpage using appropriate sensors with a low-cost Wi-Fi module (NodeMCU V3). The same Wi-Fi module, NodeMCU V3 ESP8266, was used in [15] to monitor PV parameters such as current, voltage, and other data (air temperature and relative humidity). In [16], the authors also used the same Wi-Fi-module (NodeMCU V3) to monitor data of a 3.6 kWp On-grid PV system. The hardware cost of the designed prototype is affordable. A low-cost monitoring system based on the internet as a prototype was designed to measure solar PV generation of an off-grid system. The system cost was around 33 USD [17] and an html page was used to upload the measured data.

A wireless low-cost solution based on long-range (LoRa) technology was used to develop a PV monitoring system applied to an installation of 5 kW [18]. It allows for the correct display of electrical and meteorological data in real tim, while the main limitation is its restricted duty cycle (1%). In [19], a new technique for fault diagnosis of PV systems based on independent component analysis (ICA) is proposed. It can mainly diagnose defects related to electrical failures. The system was evaluated based on simulation and experimental data. A DAQ system based on open-access software and cloud service is proposed in [20]. A comparative study against other IoT-based monitoring systems was also presented and the result showed that this system could save energy up to 58%. In [21], a novel strategy for monitoring a PV junction box based on LoRa for a PV residential application is designed. The designed DAQ system is able to collect various parameters and achieve excellent characteristics. The use of low-cost LoRa for designing an IoT-based monitoring system was evaluated for a large-scale PV system in Istanbul [22]. The main advantage of such a system is its low-cost. A Supervisory Control and Data Acquisition (SCADA) system was also implemented through a DAQ. Extensive tests have shown this system to have the lowest cost when applied for a PV plant with local data logging [23]. The total cost of the designed monitoring system was around 761 USD, which is competitive compared to the available SCADA systems. An intelligent monitoring system for automatically monitoring PV plants was described and developed in [24]. To design this monitoring system, the authors used software and cost-efficient hardware. Another option included in this monitoring system is its ability to detect defective PV modules. For more details about various configurations of data-acquisition systems based IoT, a good systematic review can be found in [25].

A large share of future solar energy plants are going to be located in desert environments [26]. Dust build-up is the greatest technical challenge facing a viable desert solar industry. Desertic regions (such as Sahara of Algeria) are more influenced by sandstorms, and this has a negative impact of the PV plants installed in such regions. 60% energy yield losses during and after sand storms are widely reported [27]. Various works were carried out to study the performances of PV plants installed in similar regions [28–31]; however, few works related to the development of smart PV monitoring systems were found in the literature [32].

In one of our previous works [33], a DAQ system based on an Arduino board (a low-cost microcontroller) and an ESP8266 Wi-Fi module, for PV parameters monitoring, was developed. Although the designed DAQ system is inexpensive and can display the collected data remotely via a website, some of the sensorsused are not sufficiently accurate, such as the LM335 for temperature. In addition, this monitoring system is not able to detect anomalies. To improve the system performance, in [34], we presented a similar work as the one in [35], but in this work, the developed monitoring system is equipped with a simple fault detection procedure. We also used more accurate sensors to measure solar irradiance and cell temperature. The PV monitoring system was tested and evaluated at a location in the north of Algeria (Jijel region) characterized by a Mediterranean climate. The idea consists of integrating a fault detection algorithm inside a low-cost microcontroller in order to detect faults in real-time. The system showed its ability to detect defective PV modules with acceptable accuracy. The same monitoring system was tested and evaluated in another location (Amiens, France, characterized by typical oceanic climate) with a little improvement. In fact, we used the Matlab/Simulink environment with DSpace to examine the accuracy of the designed monitoring system [35]. Three defects were studied and the system showed a good ability to detect and identify the origin of the fault [35].

In Table 1 below, a summary of previous systems designed for monitoring PV solar systems covering the period between 2018 and 2023 is provided. The focus of this comparative study was mainly the location, used equipment/devices, cost, and power consumption. Later in this paper, the performance of the system designed in this work will be provided and compared to the systems provided in Table 1.

Table 1. IoT-based PV monitoring systems.

Ref./Year	System/Monitored Parameters	The Used Devices	Platform/Type of Network	Cost or Complexity	Power Consumed Wh/Day	Region
[33] 2018	PV module Air temperature, DC current, DC voltage and light intensity	Arduino Mega	Webpage locally hosted Wi-Fi module 8266	€ 75 Easy	N/A	North of Algeria
[18] 2019	Grid-connected PV Air temperature, DC current, DC voltage, solar irradiance and DC power	Raspberry PI	- LoRa	39.26 EUR easy	N/A	South of Spain
[36] 2019	PV module Current and voltage at the maximum power	Arduino Uno	ThingSpeak IoT Wi-Fi module 8266	Easy and low-cost	N/A	North of India
[34] 2020	PV module Air temperature, cell temperature, DC current, DC voltage and solar irradiance	Arduino Mega	ThingSpeak IoT Wi-Fi module 8266	80 EUR Relatively easy	N/A	North of Algeria
[37] 2020	Grid-connected PV DC power	N/A	Web visual interface in HTML ZigBee module 4G getway	N/A	N/A	East of China
[20] 2021	PV module Air temperature, relative humidity, dust density, wind speed and solar irradiance	N/A	Blynk App NodMCU ESP8266	300 USD	N/A	North of India
[22] 2022	PV module Air temperature, DC current, DC voltage and solar irradiance	Arduino Nano	LoRa	Low power and low cost 18.72 USD	6.11	North of Turkey
[38] 2023	PV string Air temperature, intensity light, DC current and DC voltage	Arduino Mega	NodMCU ESP8266	Low-cost Relatively complex	N/A	North pf Pakistan

From the above Table 1 the following points can be highlighted:
- Wi-Fi module 8266 is the most used device to upload and visualize data into a platform
- The main collected data are DC current, DC voltage, module temperature, and solar irradiance
- Most developed IoT-based monitoring systems are cost effective, where the cost ranges between 39–300 USD.
- Arduino is the most employed microcontroller to develop the monitoring code.
- Based on the previous literature review, the research gaps can be summarized as follows:
- Most available IoT-based PV monitoring systems lack of fault detection and diagnosis procedure and mainly used to only monitor data.
- Existing IoT-based monitoring systems are not evaluated under climatic conditions characterized by severe sandstorms.
- The mostly used communication technology are the Wi-Fi, Zigbee, and GPS. Each of them has a different performance in power consumption, distance covering, and cost.

The objective of the present study is to develop a low-cost IoT-based PV monitoring system equipped with an effective fault diagnosis procedure. The system is evaluated under specific climatic conditions (arid climate, Sahara of Algeria) with sandstorms. Additionally, other improvements are added to the system such as using suitable and low-cost components. The PV system is used to supply a small-scale greenhouse farm installed in this region. The greenhouse is considered as a load of the stand-alone PV system. Thus, the novelty is to evaluate the developed system (PV monitoring with fault detection procedure) under an arid-region with specific climatic conditions. To the best of the authors' knowledge, this kind of monitoring system was not evaluated under such arid areas.

The main contributions of this work are summarized as follows:

- Develop a low-cost, portable IoT-based PV monitoring system that can be easily extended to other applications in control and PV systems characterization.
- Integrate a PV fault diagnosis procedure in order to detect failures that may occur in the PV module.
- Study and verify the feasibility of providing electricity to a mini greenhouse farm at isolated arid area (Sahara of Algeria) under high temperature in summer and sandstorms phenomena.

The rest of this paper is organized as follows: Materials and methods are given in Section 2, including PV system and greenhouse prototype description, as well as the designed IoT-based monitoring system description. Results and discussion are provided in Section 3. Concluding remarks and perspectives are reported in the final section.

2. Materials and Methods

2.1. Photovoltaic System Description

The considered stand-alone PV system is installed in a desert region of Algeria (Ouargla city), which is characterized by an arid climate. The system consists of two photovoltaic panels connected in parallel, a charge regulator and a battery (See Figure 1). The climate of Ouargla is subtropical desert, with mild winters (during which, it can be cold at night) and very hot sunny summers. The PV system is designed to supply a small-scale greenhouse farm (prototype).

Figure 1. The PV system under consideration and the considered location (Ouargla city: 31.9527° N, 5.3335° E).

The PV module specifications and the corresponding I-V curve are shown in Table 2 and Figure 2, respectively.

Since the objective of the present study is to develop a PV monitoring system to analyze the behavior of the PV module under different operating conditions, including different deficiencies, different kinds of faults were created intentionally. Figure 3 shows photos taken onsite of the created/investigated faults.

The studied faults are, respectively, shading effect, short-circuited PV module, open-circuited PV module, sand accumulated on PV modules, and covered PV module. As can be seen in this figure, PV modules are subject to sandstorms, which decrease their output power significantly, in addition to the high temperature, which may reach 55 °C in the summer at the study location.

Table 2. PV module specifications.

Module type	100 P (36)
Maximal power	100 W
Tolerance	±3%
Voltage at Pmax (Vmp)	17.45 V
Current at Pmax (Imp)	5.73 A
Open-circuit voltage (Voc)	21.87 V
Short-circuit current (Isc)	5.98 A

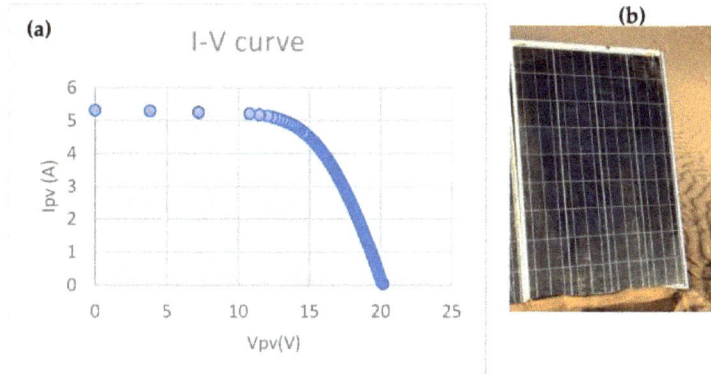

Figure 2. (a) The I-V curve of the PV module at Standard Test Conditions (STC) (b) the used PV module.

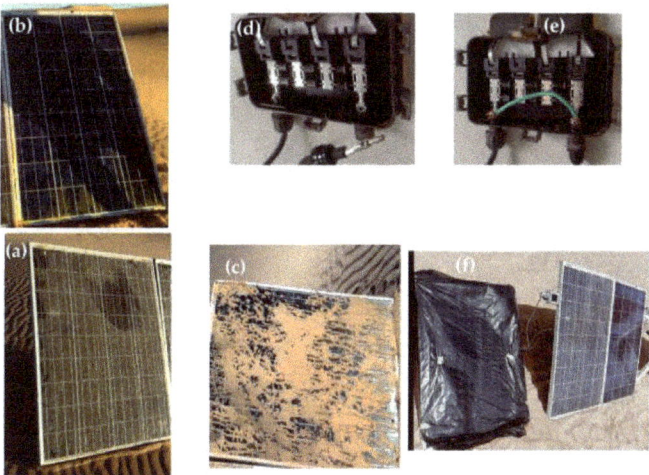

Figure 3. Illustration of the investigated defects: (**a**) dirty PV module, (**b**) shading effect, (**c**) sand accumulated on the surface, (**d**) open circuit, (**e**) short-circuit, and (**f**) covered PV module.

2.2. Greenhouse System Description

Due to severe climatic conditions in the study location, keeping suitable environmental conditions for plants is a big challenge. Plant watering and providing adequate air conditioning need energy, which is not sufficiently available in such remote regions. Figure 4 shows a real photo of the designed greenhouse prototype. The greenhouse is equipped with a watering system, light, and fans to keep adequate environmental conditions inside the greenhouse. A simple controller is developed to monitor the operational parameters such as temperature, humidity, water, and lighting inside the greenhouse. For that purpose, three sensors were used; namely, soil moisture, Light Dependent Resistor (LDR), and air temperature.

Figure 4. Photo of the designed greenhouse farm (prototype) with sensors.

To measure the temperature and the relative humidity, an AM2302 sensor (See Figure 4) was used. Through this sensor, both the temperature and humidity can be measured simultaneously. Cooling and heating are performed by using a Peltier cooling piece circuit (Plate module 12706) (See Figure 4). Soil moisture is measured via the Soil Moisture Detector Sensor (See Figure 4). Figure 5 shows the developed system during the testing phase. The direction of the cooling or heating circuit is controlled by a 180° motor. It rotates in two directions, according to the demand, through special electrical circuits (see illustration in Figure 5, below).

Once the temperature is measured and compared to the reference temperature (T_{ref}, stored into the microcontroller), Algorithm 1 is run to set a suitable temperature.

Algorithm 1: Setting a suitable temperature

Step #1: Measure air temperature (T_m)
Step #2: Compare the measured (T_m) with the reference temperature (T_{ref}), $\Delta T = T_m - T_{ref}$
    If not ($-2\ °C < \Delta T < 2\ °C$) **then**
        If T > 2 **then** Open relay #1, open heating system with a delay of 3 min
        else open relay #2, open cooling system with a delay of 5 min
        endif
    endif
Step #3: Display the results

Once the instantaneous value of humidity is measured using the previously mentioned sensor, it is possible to control the increase or decrease in the humidity through a similar algorithm used for the control of temperature. When the humidity level is slightly increased, the fan installed at the top of the greenhouse is turned on until it returns to the reference percentage. A door could be also opened for fresh air. To measure the illumination intensity, we used an LDR sensor. When the illumination value decreases, a LED light turns on immediately. A watering pump is turned on based on the measured value of soil moisture.

Currently, for operating actuators, the implemented algorithms compare the measured value with the reference value and make a decision. Table 3 shows the used components, their specifications, and cost. The total estimated cost is also provided in this table.

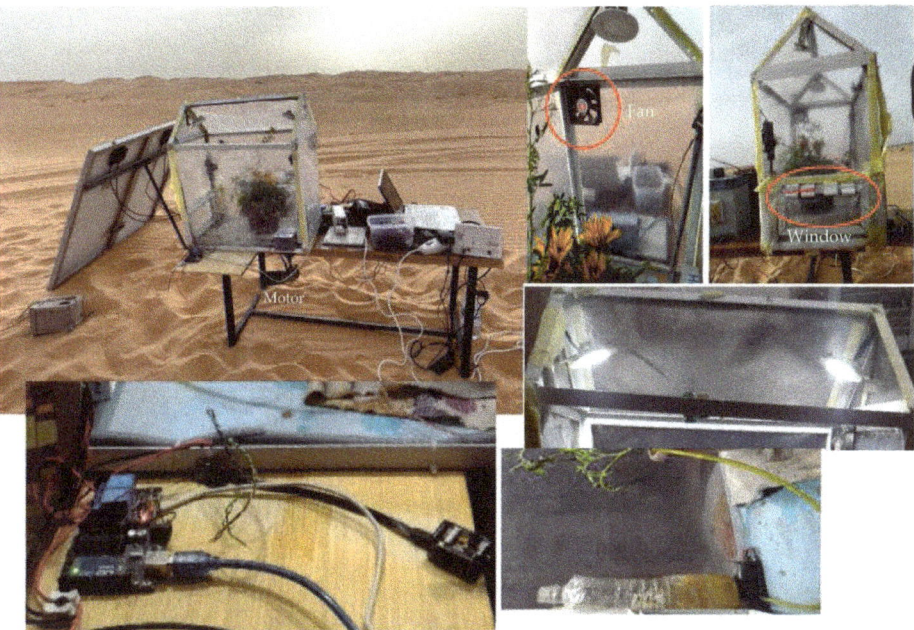

Figure 5. Illustration of the whole system during testing phase.

Table 3. The used components, specification and cost (Greenhouse farm).

Components	Specifications	Cost (€)
Cooling and heating circuit	Peltier Plate Module 12706 Thermoelectric Cooler	5
Half-cycle electric motor	Motor 180° 12 VDC	10
Exhaust fan	Fan 12 VDC	4
Linear drive	Motor 12 VDC	5
Aluminum angle tube	Tube 10*10*600	6
Total		30

2.3. IoT-Based PV Monitoring System Description

A block diagram of a general PV monitoring system based on IoT technique is shown in Figure 6 [32]. It consists of a PV array, sensors for measuring electrical and climatic parameters (DC current, voltage, air temperature, and solar irradiance), a data-acquisition unit based on a low-cost microcontroller (e.g., Arduino Mega), a combiner box, an inverter with other sensors (AC current and voltage), a Wi-Fi module (network), and display devices (computer or phone) posting the collected data.

The used ESP8266 Wi-Fi module is a self-contained SOC with integrated TCP/IP protocol stack that can give any microcontroller access to a Wi-Fi network. The ESP8266 is capable of either hosting an application or offloading all Wi-Fi networking functions from another application processor.

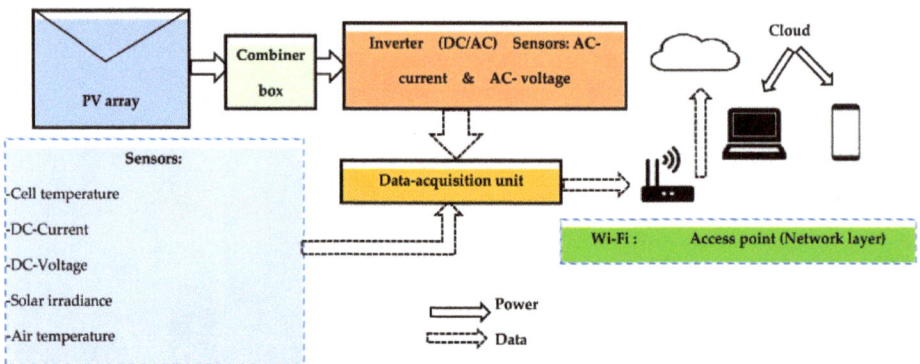

Figure 6. Block diagram of a PV monitoring system based on IoT technique.

Wi-Fi (based on IEEE standard 802.11) is a mature networking technology and is appropriate for medium distances (100 m—few kms) with medium power consumption, while Zigbee (based on IEEE standard 802.15.4) has low power consumption and cost, but it is suitable only for small distances (up to 100 m). LoRa network is much appropriate for large distances, up to 15 km, with low power consumption [32].

The electronic components of the developed monitoring system as well as the cost of each item are included in Table A1 (See Appendix A).

To measure the PV current and voltage, an ACS712 sensor with a maximum current of 30 A, and a voltage sensor with a maximum voltage of 25 V are used. Both sensors are calibrated using the following expressions:

$$A = \left(5\frac{I_r}{1024} - 2.5\right) \quad (1)$$

where, I_r is the measured real value of current.

$$V = \left(5\frac{V_r}{1024}\right) \quad (2)$$

where, V_r is the measured real value of voltage, R1 and R2 series resistors (tension divider)

Solar irradiance was measured by using a reference solar cells and calibrated with a pyranometer (the calibration coefficient is $K = 1000$), so

$$G_r = kV_m \quad (3)$$

where, V_m is the produced voltage by the reference solar cell

The estimated total cost is around 73 EUR. As compared to other monitoring systems such as those, respectively, in [33–35], this cost can be considered as low with acceptable performance.

2.4. Fault Detection Procedure

The developed fault detection and diagnosis procedure is summarized in Algorithm 2.

Thp and Thv were estimated empirically after several experiments. Additionally, the value limits of Isc (0.45 A and 0.55 A) were estimated experimentally (based on several tests). It should be noted that these parameters are related to this PV configuration. K1 and K2 denote the used relays allowing the measurement of two physical parameters (Isc and Voc). These later help the estimation of the nature of the defect, which may occur in the PV module.

Algorithm 2: The developed fault detection and diagnosis procedure

Step #1: Read solar irradiance, cell temperature, Ipv, and Vpv
Step #2: Compare the measured power Pm= Ipv*Vpv with the one estimated based on one diode model Pe, (ΔP = Pm-Pe),
    if ΔP > = Thp **then** move to step #3
    else move to step #1.
    endif
Step #3: Open relay K2 and measure the Voc_m
Step #4: Compare the measured Voc_m with the one calculated Voc_e,
    if (ΔVoc > Th_v) **then**
        if ΔVoc = Thv **then** send SMS (Shading effect: dust or sand accumulate),
        else send SMS (Short-circuited or all PV modules are disconnected)
        endif
    else
        open relay K1 and measure Isc_m
        calculated ΔIsc = Iscm-Isce
        if 0.45 < ΔIsc < 0.55 **then** send SMS (PV module disconnected)
        else send SMS (short circuited)
        endif
    endif

Figure 7a,b show the operation of the electronic circuits related to the two relays during the measurement of I_{sc} and V_{oc}.

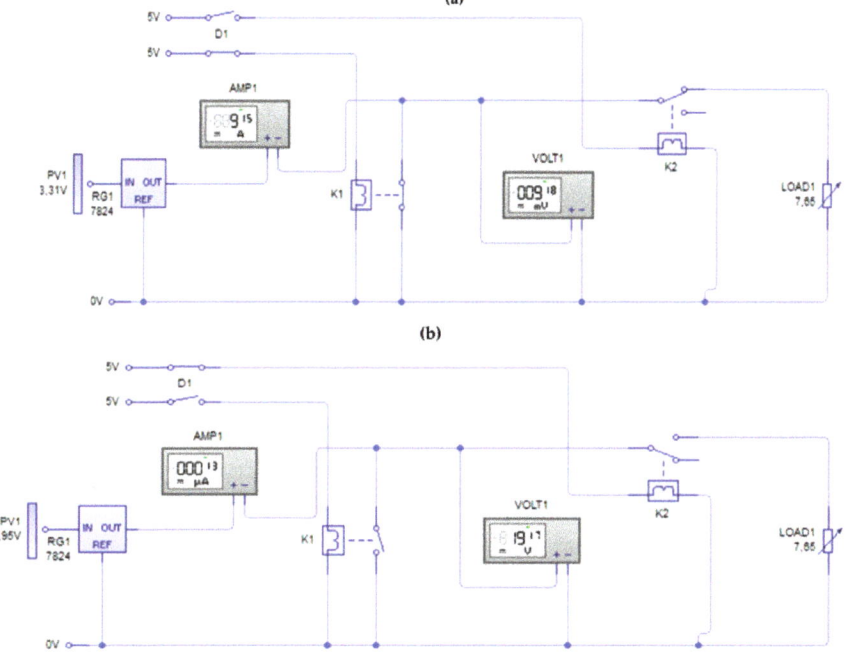

Figure 7. (**a**) Electronic circuit for measuring Isc (relays position) (**b**) Electronic circuit for measuring V_{oc} (relays position).

This procedure was written and integrated into an Arduino Mega board for a real-time application. The algorithms built into the circuit were designed through the Matlab program to determine the state of the system, normal or faulty, and then classify the type of the defect.

3. Results and Discussion
3.1. Experimental Results

Figure 8a shows the designed PV monitoring system based on the IoT technology. It consists of voltage and current sensors, air temperature sensors, reference solar cell, a DC-DC MPPT converter, a 16 × 4 LCD display for local results, and an electronic circuit based mainly on an Arduino Mega2560 board and ESP8266 Wi-Fi module. Figure 8b depicts the PV modules used to test the monitoring system under normal and abnormal conditions.

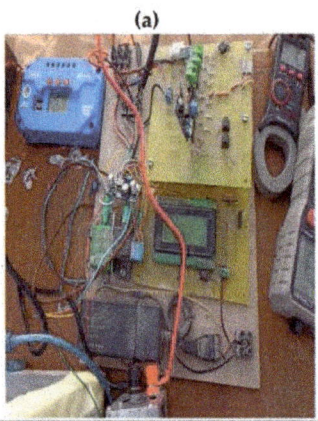

Figure 8. (a) The developed PV monitoring system based on the IoT technology and (b) the PV modules used to test the monitoring system.

In order to display the results online (measured data), a webpage was designed. For example, Figure 9a shows the collected data, such as the PV current, PV voltage, air temperature, and solar irradiance (morning at 8 o'clock, 3 December 2022). Figure 9b shows the measured data of the greenhouse.

Table 4 summarizes the power consumed by each used component of the monitoring system. The power consumed by the designed IoT-based monitoring system is estimated to be around 13.5 Wh/day.

Table 4. Power consumption of the used sensors and components.

Sensors/Component	Current Drawn (mA)	Time of Use	Consumed Energy per Hour (Wh)	Consumed Energy per Day Wh/day
Voltage sensor	8	10 h	0.048	0.48
Current sensor	10	10 h	0.050	0.50

Table 4. Cont.

Sensors/Component	Current Drawn (mA)	Time of Use	Consumed Energy per Hour (Wh)	Consumed Energy per Day Wh/day
Temperature sensor	2.5	10 h	0.085	0.85
Wi-Fi module ESP8266	80	10 s per min	0.25	3.75
Arduino Mega	79	10 h	0.45	4.50
Solar irradiance	-	-	-	-
GSM module sim800l	80	One per 10 h	0.50	0.50
LCD4 × 16	20	10 s per min	0.15	2.25
Relay	90	twice per 10 h	0.65	0.65
Total				13.48

Figure 9. (**a**) Collected data of the PV system: Solar irradiance, air temperature, PV voltage and PV current. (**b**) Collected data of the greenhouse farm: Temperature, Humidity, soil moisture, solar irradiance and water level.

Figure 10 displays an example of the measured data (DC current and DC voltage) of a PV module for a short period of a configuration of three PV modules connected in parallel by the developed monitoring system.

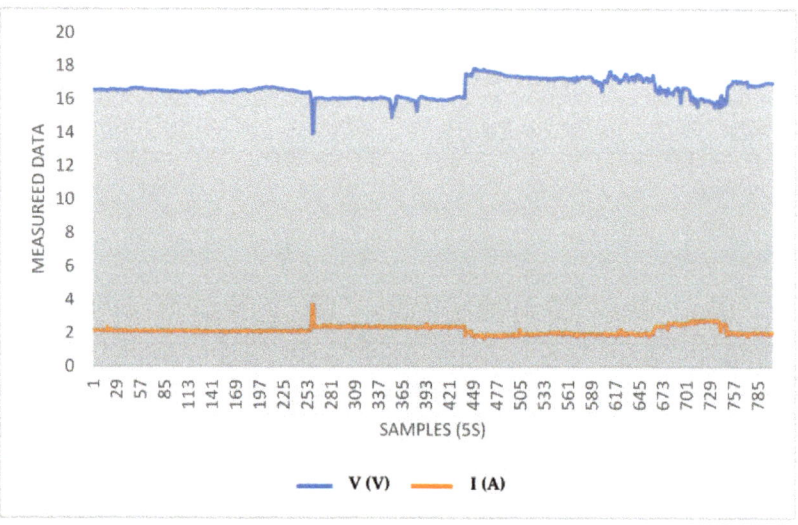

Figure 10. Measured DC current and DC voltage of a PV module.

3.2. Discussion

Figure 11 reports the collected curves under normal and abnormal operating conditions. To check the effectiveness of the developed PV data-acquisition system, we compared the measured (See Figure 11a) with the simulated under the Matlab environment (See Figure 11b). As can be seen, a good agreement is obtained.

To check the effectiveness of the designed system, faulty scenarios were created. As shown in Figure 11b, the measurement intervals were divided into 9 time periods (Z1, Z2, ... Z9) and each experiment lasted approximately 20 min. To test the circuit's ability to detect the fault, each period was compared with the corresponding one extracted from the result obtained by the Matlab program.

For example, in region 2 (Z2), we notice that an error occurred (anomaly in the output power). The error was detected based on the following detection Algorithm 3. The idea consists of comparing the measured power with the estimated power.

Algorithm 3: The errors detection procedure

ΔP = Pmax_m − Pmax_e
  If ΔP > Thp **then** default = true
  else default = false
  endif

Where Pmax_m is the measured power, Pmax_e is the estimated power based on an explicit model [39]. The threshold Thp ≅ 3 was estimated empirically throughout the experiments.

Then the next step aims to find the fault type based on the proposed procedure. In this case, a single PV module is disconnected from the system. More details are listed in Table 5.

For example, in zone Z6, after measuring the module temperature and solar radiation values, G = 802 W/m^2, T = 20 °C, it was expected that the maximum power value should be 182 W. However, the value of the current and voltage in the MPP were 2 A and 14 V, respectively, and the estimated power was 28 W. Thus, the threshold Thp = 182-28 = 154 W. The fault detection algorithm detects an anomaly in the system, and by tracking the value of V_{oc} and I_{sc}, it was estimated that the defect corresponds to a covered solar panel.

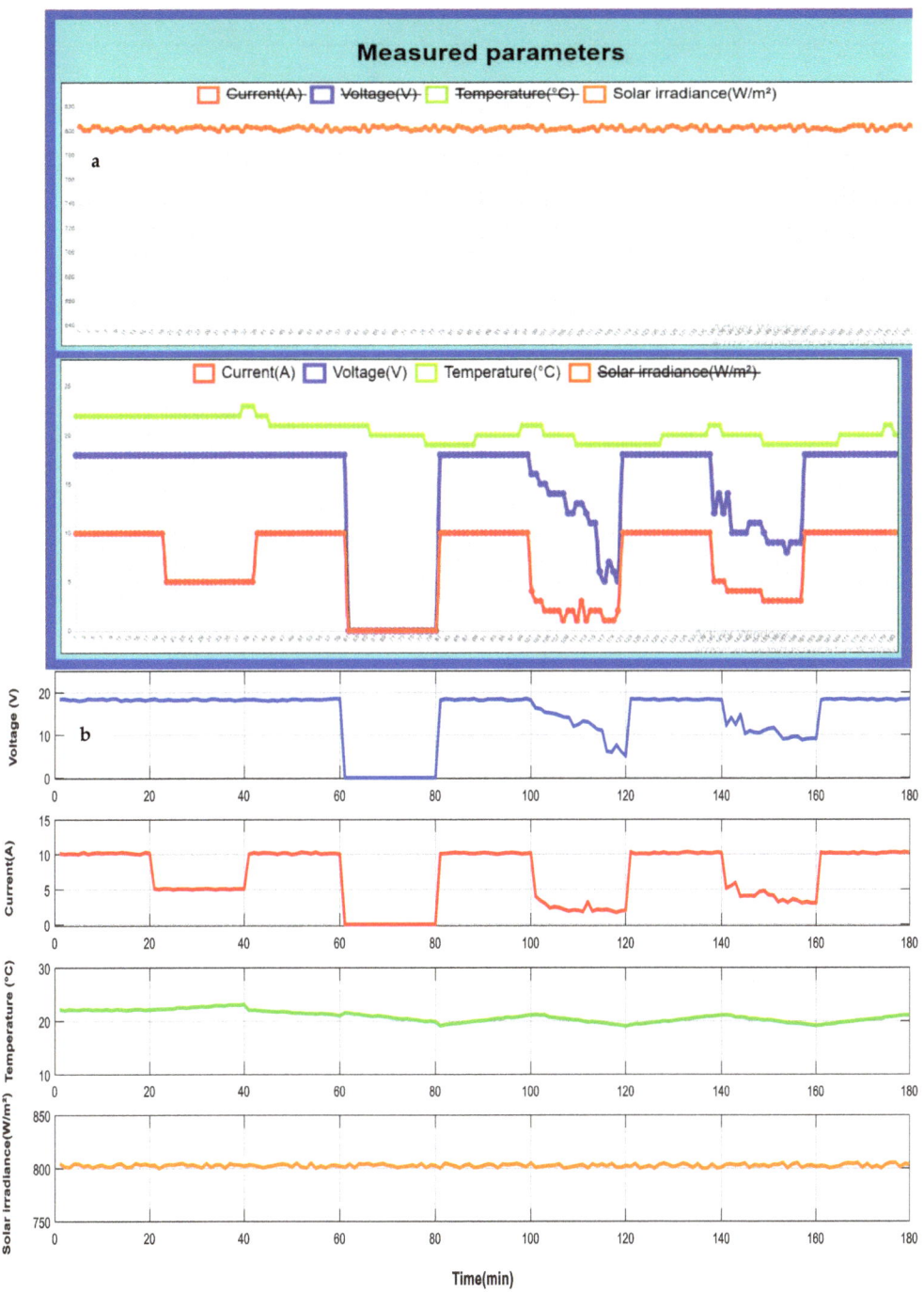

Figure 11. Electrical and changes in the faulty system. (**a**) The curve extracted from our website. (**b**) The simulated curve under Matlab.

Table 5. The state of the PV system over the time periods.

Zone	Time (min)	System Status
Z1	0–20	It works normally
Z2	20–40	Defective system (a single PV module separated)
Z3	40–60	It works normally
Z4	60–80	Defective system (total separation of PV panels)
Z5	80–100	It works normally
Z6	100–120	Faulty system (a significant part of the PV panels is covered, despite the clear weather)
Z7	120–140	It works normally
Z8	140–160	Faulty system (sand deposit on the surface of the PV panels)
Z9	160–180	It works normally

Figure 12 shows other tests developed under IoT-ThingSpeak application in the same region. As can be seen from 12:55 to 13:00, the system works normally without any fault (stable DC voltage and DC current). In a very short period of 1 min, we observe a remarkable decrease in solar irradiance, DC voltage, and DC current. This is not a fault, rather, the reason is that the clouds moved. However, during the period from 13:03 to 13:06, we can clearly observe a decrease in DC voltage and DC current due to the artificially covered PV module. In the period from 13:07 to 13:08, the system is also faulty, due to an accumulation of dust on the PV module. Then, when we removed the sand from the PV module, the DC voltage and current increased again (time period 13:10).

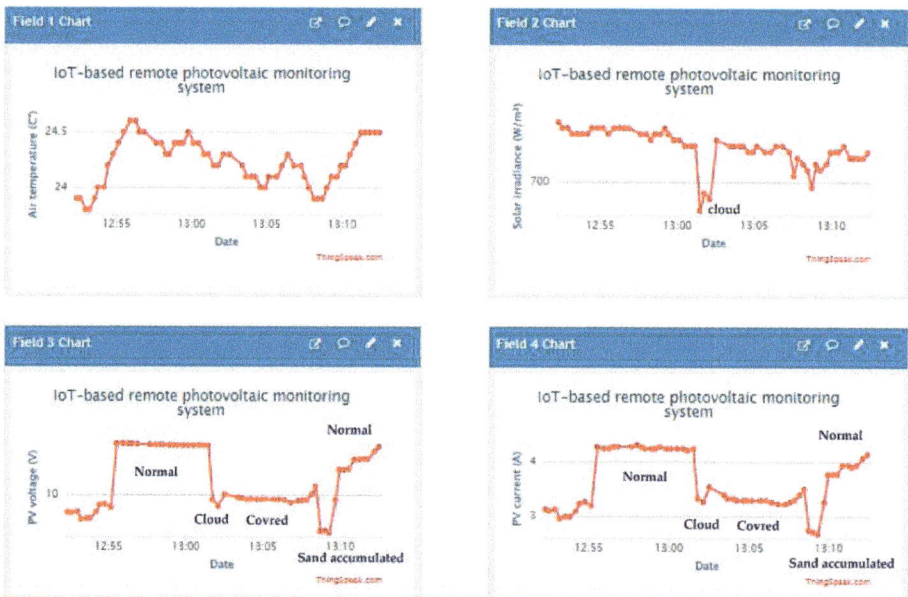

Figure 12. Monitored data (air temperature, solar irradiance, DC voltage, and DC current) based on ThingSpeak application.

Once the fault is detected and the nature of the defect estimated, an SMS is sent to notify the user about the state of the system using a SIM8001 module (See Figure 13).

Figure 13. Notifications of faults: Sending SMS messages to notify the user by phone about the state of the PV system.

The designed system is equipped with an interactive webpage. This can help users check the state of the PV system remotely. As an example, Figure 14 shows the notification on the website. Additionally, the designed webpage is able to display the state of the PV system, indicating the type of the defect online. As shown in Figure 14, all investigated faults are reported clearly on the website (Faults: open circuit 1 PV module, open circuit 2PV module, short circuit, and other faults).

Our IoT-based monitoring system is equipped with a fault detection procedure and can notify users about the system. In other presented systems, this option is not available. This is the main difference between our study and those published that are only used to monitor data.

3.3. Advantages and Limits of the Designed IoT-Based Monitoring System

Some advantages and limits of the proposed monitoring system are listed in Table 6.

Table 6. Advantages and limits of the proposed IoT-based monitoring system.

Advantages	Limits
✓ Low cost and lower power monitoring system	✓ The system was tested and evaluated for a small-scale PV system
✓ Easy to implement	✓ Security of the collected data
✓ Interactive webpage can help users monitor their system remotely	✓ Limited distance of the used Wi-Fi module
✓ The integrated code can be reprogramed and updated at any time	✓ The fault diagnosis procedure is developed for only three types of faults
✓ Other types of defects could be easily integrated into the microcontroller	✓ The system is not able to detect multiple faults
✓ Users can be notified by an SMS regarding the state of their PV system	
✓ The used Wi-Fi module ESP8266 module is an extremely cost-effective board	

The benefits of the PV monitoring system-based IoT technique compared to classical monitoring systems are: (1) cost effective, as we use a low-cost Wi-Fi module, (2) higher productivity and efficiency, is easily realized, and increases mobility.

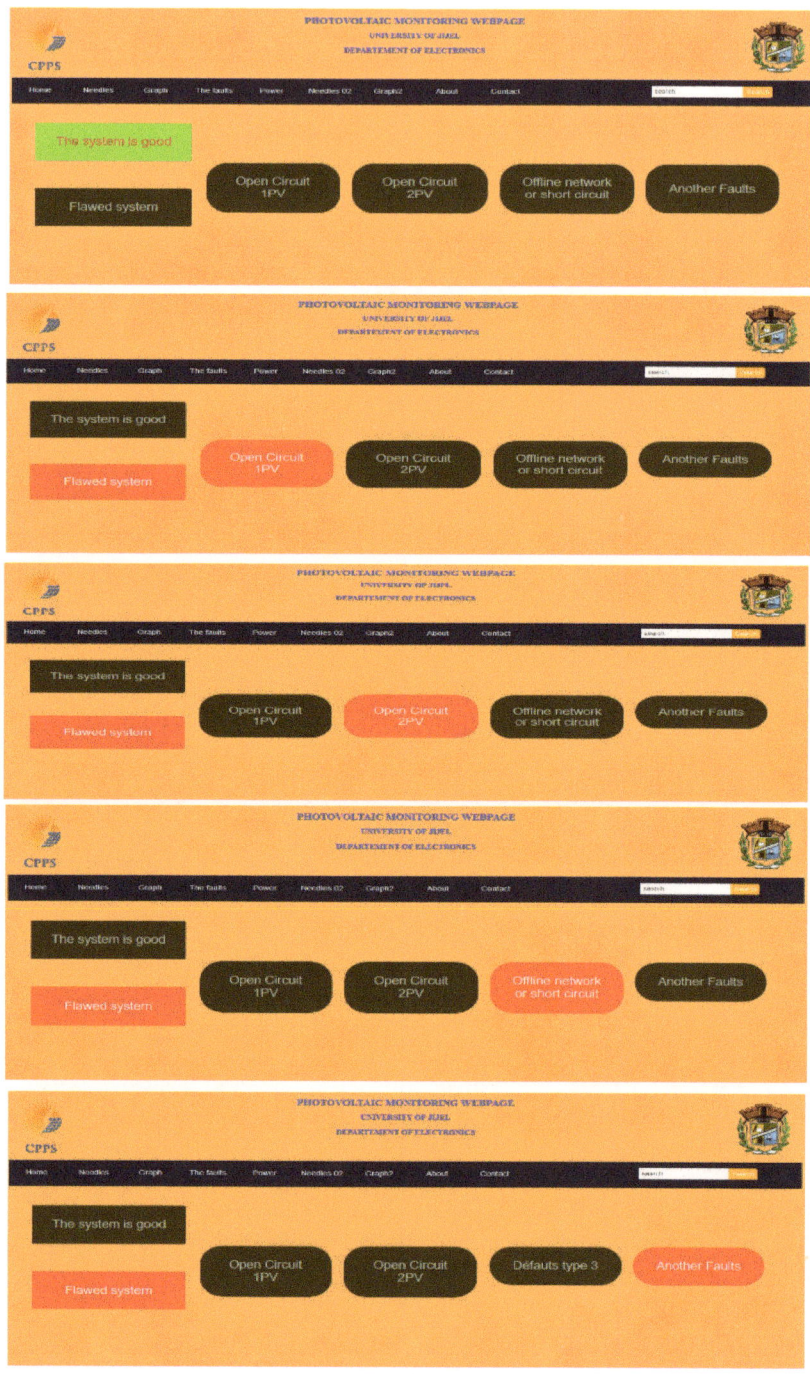

Figure 14. Notification of the state on the PV system displayed on the website.

The major drawback of the IoT is to ensure the security of application in its large database. In addition, a non-smart IoT system will have limited capability and will be unable to evolve with big data. No security protocol is associated with the system to secure the uploaded data on the website. Another limit is the short distance of the used Wi-Fi module. A cost-effective embedded solution including IoT and fault detection techniques seems to be an important technology that should be further improved for large scale photovoltaic applications.

IoT technology will continue to play a major role in increasing the quality of the monitoring and diagnosis of PV plants installed in remote locations. This can help users to check their PV systems online, predict possible faults, visualize the evolution of different parameters, and analyze the data [32].

4. Conclusions and Perspectives

In this paper, a low-cost PV monitoring system with a fault detection procedure was designed. The system was simulated and verified experimentally in a specific desertic region with a hot climatic condition and sandstorms (south of Algeria). The obtained results show the designed system to be effective, particularly in its data-acquisition component and real-time monitoring, specifically in fault detection and isolation. To collect data remotely, a webpage was developed and activated. The investigated types of defects were, respectively, disconnection of one or more panels, sand accumulated on a PV module, and short circuit in a PV module. The IoT is a good platform for the development of a cost-effective smart monitoring system, assuming the final application successfully complies with the relevant technical standards. The developed system can help O&M make correct decisions about the cleaning or changing of the PV modules.

This system was used to supply a small greenhouse farm (prototype) with consistent environmental conditions. Experimentation investigation showed the capability of this system to feed the used components by the greenhouse prototype, such as sensors, fans, lamps, and a water pump.

IoT technology is strongly recommended for designing smart monitoring systems with fault detection techniques for PV plants installed in desert regions. Furthermore, a smart scheme is highly recommended for the fast isolation and immediate protection of the plants.

The main limits of the developed PV monitoring system are: (1) it is suitable only for very small-scale off-grid PV systems (PV string), (2) the Wi-Fi module used is limited in terms of distance (up to 100 m), (3) only three major faults can be detected, and (4) the uploaded data on the developed webpage are not secured.

To address the above issues, we plan to test the system for a large PV array by using other suitable sensors (current and voltage). Additionally, other type of defects related to the PV modules will be investigated, such as browning, bubbles, snail trails, and others. We will use another long-range data transfer technology, such as LoRa, as LoRaWAn works on a lower radio frequency band than Wi-Fi.

Author Contributions: Conceptualization, A.H. and A.M.; methodology, M.B. and S.B.; software, A.H.; validation, A.H., A.M., M.B. and S.B.; writing—original draft preparation, M.B. and S.B.; writing—review and editing, A.M.; visualization, A.H.; supervision, M.B. and S.B. All authors have read and agreed to the published version of the manuscript.

Funding: Deanship of Scientific Research at the Islamic University of Madinah for the support provided to the Post-Publishing Program.

Data Availability Statement: Not applicable.

Acknowledgments: The researchers wish to extend their sincere gratitude to the Deanship of Scientific Research at the Islamic University of Madinah for the support provided to the Post-Publishing Program.

Conflicts of Interest: The authors declare no conflict of interest.

Appendix A

Table A1. The used components, specification and cost.

Components	Specifications	Cost (€)
Current sensor (ACS 711)	• Supply Voltage: 5 Vdc Nominal. • Measurement Range: −30 to +30 Amps. • Voltage at 0 A: VCC/2 (nominally 2.5 VDC). • Scale Factor: 66 mV per Amp. • 5 µs output rise time in response to step input current. • 80 kHz bandwidth. • Total output error 1.5% at TA = 25 °C. • 1.2 mΩ internal conductor resistance.	5
Voltage sensor	• Voltage input range: DC 0–25 V • Voltage detection range: DC 0.02440–25 V • Output signal type: Analog • Voltage Analog Resolution: 0.00489 V.	3
Temperature sensor (AM2302)	• Power supply 3.3–5 V • Response time of less than 0.5 s • Measurement range—40 °C to 80 °C • Accuracy ±0.5 °C	3
Reference solar cell Si-V-1.5TC	• Solar cell: Monocrystalline Silicon (50 mm × 33 mm) • Operating temperature: −35 °C to 80 °C • Electrical connection via shielded cable, length 3 m standard, or IP 67 rated connector • Case, protection mode: Powder-coated aluminum, IP 65 • Dimension, Weight: 155 mm × 85 mm × 39 mm, Approximately 350–470 g • Irradiance ±5 W/sqm ±2.5% from value; with temperature compensation, vertical light beam, and AM 1.5	15
Microcontroller Atmega2560	• Program Memory Size (KB) 256 • CPU Speed (MIPS/DMIPS) 16 • Data EEPROM (bytes) 4096 • Timers 2 × 8-bit—4 × 16-bit • Stand alone PWM 15 • Number of ADCs 0 • Diff ADC Inputs 14 • ADC Channels 16 • Max ADC Resolution (bits) 10 • Number of Comparators 1 • Temp. Range Min. −40 • Temp. Range Max. 85 • Operation Voltage Max.(V) 5.5 • Operation Voltage Min.(V) 1.8 • I2C 1–I2C	12
Wi-Fi module Esp8266	• Operating Voltage 3.0~3.6 V. • Operating Current Average value: 80 mA. • Operating Temperature Range −40°~125°. • Wi-Fi Protocols 802.11 b/g/n. • Frequency Range 2.4–2.5 G (2400–2483.5 M). • Types of Antenna PCB Trace, External, IPEX Connector, Ceramic Chip • Distance 20 m.	6

Table A1. *Cont.*

Components	Specifications	Cost (€)
GSM Module sim800l	• GSM: 850, 900, 1800 and 1900 MHz. • FLASH: 16 Mbit. • RAM: 32 Mbit. • Power supply 3.4~4.4 V. • Power saving. Typical power consumption in sleep mode is 1.04 mA. • Quad-band: GSM 850, EGSM 900, DCS 1800, PCS 1900. Frequency bands: can search the four frequency bands automatically.	10
Relay	Maxtor (30 A;12 V), Module 4 relay 5 V, 10 A	7
LCD	LCD16 × 4	6
Electronics components	Diode, resistor, capacitor, transistor	5
Total		73

References

1. Available online: https://www.iea.org/reports/sdg7-data-and-projections/access-to-electricity (accessed on 15 May 2022).
2. Available online: https://iea-pvps.org/snapshot-reports/snapshot-2022/ (accessed on 22 April 2022).
3. Available online: https://www.iea.org/reports/africa-energy-outlook-2022 (accessed on 15 June 2022).
4. Zhao, Y.; De Palma, J.F.; Mosesian, J.; Lyons, R.; Lehman, B. Line–line fault analysis and protection challenges in solar photovoltaic arrays. *IEEE Trans. Ind. Electron.* **2012**, *60*, 3784–3795. [CrossRef]
5. Cancelliere, P. PV electrical plants fire risk assessment and mitigation according to the Italian national fire services guidelines. *Fire Mater.* **2016**, *40*, 355–367. [CrossRef]
6. Firth, S.K.; Lomas, K.J.; Rees, S.J. A simple model of PV system performance and its use in fault detection. *Solar Energy* **2010**, *84*, 624–635. [CrossRef]
7. Lundqvist, M.; Helmke, C.; Ossenbrink, H.A. ESTI-LOG PV plant monitoring system. *Sol. Energy Mater. Sol. Cells* **1997**, *47*, 289–294. [CrossRef]
8. Benghanem, M.; Maafi, A. Data acquisition system for photovoltaic systems performance monitoring. *IEEE Trans. Instrum. Meas.* **1998**, *47*, 30–33. [CrossRef]
9. Koutroulis, E.; Kalaitzakis, K. Development of an integrated data-acquisition system for renewable energy sources systems monitoring. *Renew. Energy* **2003**, *28*, 139–152. [CrossRef]
10. Kalaitzakis, K.; Koutroulis, E.; Vlachos, V. Development of a data acquisition system for remote monitoring of renewable energy systems. *Measurement* **2003**, *34*, 75–83. [CrossRef]
11. Tina, G.M.; Grasso, A.D. Remote monitoring system for stand-alone photovoltaic power plants: The case study of a PV-powered outdoor refrigerator. *Energy Convers. Manag.* **2014**, *78*, 862–871. [CrossRef]
12. López-Vargas, A.; Fuentes, M.; García, M.V.; Muñoz-Rodríguez, F.J. Low-Cost datalogger intended for remote monitoring of solar photovoltaic standalone systems based on Arduino™. *IEEE Sens. J.* **2019**, *19*, 4308–4320. [CrossRef]
13. Benghanem, M.; Mellit, A.; Emad, M.; Aljohani, A. Monitoring of Solar Still Desalination System Using the Internet of Things Technique. *Energies* **2021**, *14*, 6892. [CrossRef]
14. Mellit, A.; Benghanem, M.; Herrak, O.; Messalaoui, A. Design of a Novel Remote Monitoring System for Smart Greenhouses Using the Internet of Things and Deep Convolutional Neural Networks. *Energies* **2021**, *14*, 5045. [CrossRef]
15. Sutikno, T.; Purnama, H.S.; Pamungkas, A.; Fadlil, A.; Alsofyani, I.M.; Jopri, M.H. Internet of things-based photovoltaics parameter monitoring system using NodeMCU ESP8266. *Int. J. Electr. Comput. Eng.* **2021**, *11*, 62088–68708. [CrossRef]
16. Prasetyo, H. On-grid photovoltaic system power monitoring based on open source and low-cost internet of things platform. *J. Nov. Carbon Resour. Sci. Green Asia Strategy* **2021**, *8*, 98–106. [CrossRef]
17. Zago, R.M.; Fruett, F. A low-cost solar generation monitoring system suitable for internet of things. In Proceedings of the 2017 2nd International Symposium on Instrumentation Systems, Circuits and Transducers (INSCIT), Fortaleza, Brazil, 28 August–1 September 2017; pp. 1–6. [CrossRef]
18. Paredes-Parra, J.M.; García-Sánchez, A.J.; Mateo-Aroca, A.; Molina-García, Á. An alternative internet-of-things solution based on LoRa for PV power plants: Data monitoring and management. *Energies* **2019**, *12*, 881. [CrossRef]
19. Qureshi, F.A.; Uddin, Z.; Satti, M.B.; Ali, M. ICA-based solar photovoltaic fault diagnosis. *Int. Trans. Electr. Energy Syst.* **2020**, *30*, 12456. [CrossRef]
20. Gupta, V.; Sharma, M.; Pachauri, R.K.; Babu, K.D. A low-cost real-time IoT enabled data acquisition system for monitoring of PV system. *Energy Sources Part A: Recovery Util. Environ. Eff.* **2021**, *43*, 2529–2543. [CrossRef]
21. Kim, M.S.; Kim, D.H.; Kim, H.J.; Prabakar, K. A Novel Strategy for Monitoring a PV Junction Box Based on LoRa in a 3 kW Residential PV System. *Electronics* **2022**, *11*, 709. [CrossRef]

22. Kaly, M.S.; Kilic, B.; Mellit, A.; Oral, B.; Saglam, S. IoT-based data acquisition and remote monitoring system for large-scale photovoltaic plants. In Proceedings of the IoT-Based Data Acquisition and Remote Monitoring System for Large-Scale Photovoltaic Plants, Saidia, Mrorocco, 20–22 May 2022.
23. Ahsan, L.; Baig, M.J.; Iqbal, M.T. Low-Cost, Open-Source, Emoncms-Based SCADA System for a Large Grid-Connected PV System. *Sensors* **2022**, *22*, 6733. [CrossRef]
24. Emamian, M.; Eskandari, A.; Aghaei, M.; Nedaei, A.; Sizkouhi, A.M.; Milimonfared, J. Cloud Computing and IoT Based Intelligent Monitoring System for Photovoltaic Plants Using Machine Learning Techniques. *Energies* **2022**, *15*, 3014. [CrossRef]
25. Kalay, M.Ş.; Kılıç, B.; Sağlam, Ş. Systematic review of the data acquisition and monitoring systems of photovoltaic panels and arrays. *Solar Energy* **2022**, *244*, 47–64. [CrossRef]
26. Wiesinger, F.; Sutter, F.; Fernández-García, A.; Wette, J.; Hanrieder, N. Sandstorm erosion on solar reflectors: A field study on height and orientation dependence. *Energy* **2021**, *217*, 119351. [CrossRef]
27. Alshawaf, M.; Poudineh, R.; Alhajeri, N.S. Solar PV in Kuwait: The effect of ambient temperature and sandstorms on output variability and uncertainty. *Renew. Sustain. Energy Rev.* **2020**, *134*, 110346. [CrossRef]
28. Available online: https://www.nomaddesertsolar.com/the-desert-solar-challenge.html (accessed on 22 April 2022).
29. Zaghba, L.; Khennane, M.; Fezzani, A.; Borni, A.; Mahammed, I.H. Experimental outdoor performance evaluation of photovoltaic plant in a Sahara environment (Algerian desert). *Int. J. Ambient. Energy* **2022**, *43*, 314–324. [CrossRef]
30. Alghamdi, A.S.; Bahaj, A.S.; Blunden, L.S.; Wu, Y. Dust removal from solar PV modules by automated cleaning systems. *Energies* **2019**, *12*, 2923. [CrossRef]
31. Mostefaoui, M.; Ziane, A.; Bouraiou, A.; Khelifi, S. Effect of sand dust accumulation on photovoltaic performance in the Saharan environment: Southern Algeria (Adrar). *Environ. Sci. Pollut. Res.* **2019**, *26*, 259–268. [CrossRef] [PubMed]
32. Mellit, A.; Kalogirou, S. Artificial intelligence and internet of things to improve efficacy of diagnosis and remote sensing of solar photovoltaic systems: Challenges, recommendations and future directions. *Renew. Sustain. Energy Rev.* **2021**, *143*, 110889. [CrossRef]
33. Hamied, A.; Mellit, A.; Zoulid, M.A.; Birouk, R. IoT-based experimental prototype for monitoring of photovoltaic arrays. In Proceedings of the International Conference on Applied Smart Systems (ICASS), Medea, Algeria, 24–25 November 2018; Volume 24, pp. 1–5. [CrossRef]
34. Mellit, A.; Hamied, A.; Lughi, V.; Pavan, A.M. A low-cost monitoring and fault detection system for stand-alone photovoltaic systems using IoT technique. In *ELECTRIMACS*; Springer: Cham, Switzerland, 2020; pp. 349–358. [CrossRef]
35. Hamied, A.; Boubidi, A.; Rouibah, N.; Chine, W.; Mellit, A. IoT-based smart photovoltaic arrays for remote sensing and fault identification. In *International Conference in Artificial Intelligence in Renewable Energetic Systems*; Springer: Cham, Switzerland, 2019; pp. 478–486. [CrossRef]
36. Khan, M.S.; Sharma, H.; Haque, A. IoT enabled real-time energy monitoring for photovoltaic systems. In Proceedings of the 2019 International Conference on Machine Learning, Big Data, Cloud and Parallel Computing (COMITCon), Greater Noida, India, 18–19 October 2019; Volume 14, pp. 323–327.
37. Xia, K.; Ni, J.; Ye, Y.; Xu, P.; Wang, Y. A real-time monitoring system based on ZigBee and 4G communications for photovoltaic generation. *CSEE J. Power Energy Syst.* **2020**, *6*, 52–63.
38. Ul Mehmood, M.; Ulasyar, A.; Ali, W.; Zeb, K.; Zad, H.S.; Uddin, W.; Kim, H.J. A New Cloud-Based IoT Solution for Soiling Ratio Measurement of PV Systems Using Artificial Neural Network. *Energies* **2023**, *16*, 996. [CrossRef]
39. Pavan, A.M.; Vergura, S.; Mellit, A.; Lughi, V. Explicit empirical model for photovoltaic devices. Experimental validation. *Solar Energy* **2017**, *155*, 647–653. [CrossRef]

Disclaimer/Publisher's Note: The statements, opinions and data contained in all publications are solely those of the individual author(s) and contributor(s) and not of MDPI and/or the editor(s). MDPI and/or the editor(s) disclaim responsibility for any injury to people or property resulting from any ideas, methods, instructions or products referred to in the content.

Article

Photovoltaic Energy Forecast Using Weather Data through a Hybrid Model of Recurrent and Shallow Neural Networks

Wilson Castillo-Rojas [1,*], Fernando Medina Quispe [2] and César Hernández [1]

1. Departamento de Ingeniería Informática y Cs. de la Computación, Universidad de Atacama, Av. Copayapu 485, Copiapó 1530000, Chile; chdez293@gmail.com
2. Facultad de Ingeniería y Arquitectura, Universidad Arturo Prat, Av. Arturo Prat 2120, Iquique 1100000, Chile; femedina@unap.cl
* Correspondence: wilson.castillo@uda.cl

Abstract: In this article, forecast models based on a hybrid architecture that combines recurrent neural networks and shallow neural networks are presented. Two types of models were developed to make predictions. The first type consisted of six models that used records of exported active energy and meteorological variables as inputs. The second type consisted of eight models that used meteorological variables. Different metrics were applied to assess the performance of these models. The best model of each type was selected. Finally, a comparison of the performance between the selected models of both types was presented. The models were validated using real data provided by a solar plant, achieving acceptable levels of accuracy. The selected model of the first type had a root mean square error (RMSE) of 0.19, a mean square error (MSE) of 0.03, a mean absolute error (MAE) of 0.09, a correlation coefficient of 0.96, and a determination coefficient of 0.93. The other selected model of the second type showed lower accuracy in the metrics: RMSE = 0.24, MSE = 0.06, MAE = 0.10, correlation coefficient = 0.95, and determination coefficient = 0.90. Both models demonstrated good performance and acceptable accuracy in forecasting the weekly photovoltaic energy generation of the solar plant.

Keywords: shallow neural networks; recurrent neural networks; predictive hybrid model; photovoltaic energy; photovoltaic energy prediction

1. Introduction

Photovoltaic energy has experienced remarkable growth worldwide due to increasing energy demand and the imperative to reduce greenhouse gas emissions. In both the industrial and residential sectors, this renewable energy source meets the needs of large consumers and promotes decentralized electricity production in homes, thereby reducing reliance on non-renewable sources and fostering a sustainable energy model. Photovoltaic energy generation stands out for its capacity to mitigate CO_2 emissions, positioning it as an effective and expanding solution in the fight against climate change and the transition towards a cleaner and more sustainable energy future [1,2].

The proliferation of photovoltaics has brought forth a range of challenges that necessitate attention and innovative solutions. One pertinent issue is associated with the intermittent and volatile nature of energy generation in photovoltaic systems, which is directly influenced by weather conditions such as solar radiation, cloud cover, and seasonal variations. The availability and intensity of sun radiation significantly impact photovoltaic energy generation. Although solar panels convert sun radiation into electrical energy during the day, this generation can fluctuate considerably due to climatic changes [3].

This volatility can lead to imbalances in the photovoltaic system, and they impact the stability of the integrated electrical grid. In large-scale solar plants, particularly those connected to the power grid, these unforeseen fluctuations can cause significant swings in power generation, resulting in power quality issues and supply disruptions [4]. Apart from the technical and system stability challenges, the volatility of photovoltaic generation also carries economic implications. Large solar plants typically operate based on long-term power supply contracts, and any unanticipated variation in generation can lead to contract violations and substantial financial losses [5].

To tackle this issue, several solutions have been developed. One of these solutions involves the utilization of short-term forecast models. These models enable the monitoring and forecast of photovoltaic energy generation based on weather conditions and other pertinent factors. By employing machine learning techniques, these models provide more precise forecasts, thereby aiding in the optimization of solar plant operations and mitigating the adverse effects of generation volatility. The pursuit of technological solutions is pivotal in alleviating the negative impacts associated with such volatility, ensuring the efficient integration of photovoltaic energy into the power grid and fostering the sustainable development of this significant renewable energy source [6].

Solar plants regularly measure and record the daily exported active energy (EAE) generated by their photovoltaic panels. These plants typically have weather stations that capture important climatic variables. By combining these data, solar plants can monitor their production and examine the relationship between the generated EAE and local weather conditions. However, meteorological variables inherently exhibit volatility and uncertainty, which means that unexpected fluctuations in these parameters can lead to variations in the power output of photovoltaic systems.

Despite the research efforts made in recent years to develop innovative models that can predict meteorological variables relevant to photovoltaic generation, an essential step is often overlooked: the exploratory analysis of the data before its utilization. This analysis provides a comprehensive understanding of the data's characteristics and patterns, yielding valuable insights to enhance forecast models and attain more accurate and dependable results.

Accurate forecasting of photovoltaic power generation is essential for ensuring efficient operation of solar plants. Enhancing the precision of short-term forecasts has significant benefits, including supporting the quality of operational schedules, providing guidance for photovoltaic maintenance, and enabling effective response to emergency situations. Typically, the data sources used for such forecasts include weather records, numerical weather forecasts, and historical records of EAE generated by the solar plant [6].

In recent literature, comparative studies have been conducted on recurrent neural networks (RNN) with various structural configurations, input hyperparameters, and prediction horizons [7]. Additionally, there are research efforts focused on generating forecast models for photovoltaic energy, which can be broadly categorized into three groups:

- Machine learning techniques: use artificial neural networks (ANN), RNN, support vector machines (SVM), and genetic algorithm (GA) techniques.
- Statistical techniques: includes forecast models based on statistical techniques such as regression analysis, Bayesian networks, time series analysis, autoregressive integrated moving average (ARIMA), and autoregressive moving average (ARMA) models.
- Hybrid approaches: hybrid models combine elements of statistical methods, machine learning techniques, and physical models.

While many studies in the field of photovoltaic energy forecasting primarily utilize machine learning techniques, particularly RNNs, due to their effectiveness in processing time series data, it is worth highlighting the significance of initiatives that explore the development and utilization of hybrid models for predicting photovoltaic energy production.

In terms of model validation techniques, the majority of reviewed works tend to focus on a single metric, such as the root mean square error (RMSE). There are other important metrics that are often considered secondary. These metrics include mean square error (MSE), mean absolute error (MAE), mean absolute percentage error (MAPE), and Pearson's correlation coefficient. Additionally, these studies typically do not utilize large volumes of data for training and validating their models [7–9].

Extreme weather conditions pose a challenge for accurate photovoltaic energy forecasts, as they can result in intermittent and unpredictable volatility in photovoltaic systems.

While RNN models are effective for forecasting time-series data, they may encounter difficulties when confronted with abrupt long-term climate changes. These changes can cause the gradient to vanish during the training process of an RNN, leading to suboptimal forecasts.

In such situations, it is crucial to carefully consider the limitations and potential drawbacks of RNN models. Alternative approaches or modifications to the traditional RNN architecture, such as long short-term memory (LSTM) or gated recurrent unit (GRU) models, may offer better performance and more robust forecasts in the face of extreme weather events and long-term climate changes [9,10].

In this article, the focus is on the development of forecast models for the generation of photovoltaic energy. It uses a base architecture described in a previous research work, referred to as [11]. This hybrid architecture combines RNN and ANN components in two hidden layers:

- The first layer contains neurons with LSTM or GRU recurrent units.
- The second layer is composed of shallow neurons with a multilayer perceptron (MLP) structure.

Although this hybrid RNN–ANN architecture had already been used in the aforementioned work, it only generated forecast models with a single input variable. However, in this paper, multiple input variables are utilized in the models, and different hyperparameter configurations are explored. The input variables consist of historical EAE records and measurements of weather variables, including solar radiation, temperature, and wind speed, taken throughout one year. The hyperparameters are associated with the internal components of the model, including the activation function and the loss function, among others.

Two types of models are configured. First, six models are developed that receive the EAE records along with the weather variables as input. Second, eight models are created that only use weather variables as input. Both types of models achieve good accuracy in forecasting photovoltaic energy generation. The models with the best performance indicators of each type are selected by analyzing five metrics: RMSE, MSE, MAE, correlation coefficient, and determination coefficient. This process is accomplished through controlled experiments and the optimization of various hyperparameter configurations. Finally, the two models with the best performance of each type are compared. The results show that the models using the EAE records along with the weather variables as input exhibit better performance in most of the metrics.

The contributions of the results of this work are as follows:

- By using multiple variables as input in the generated models, the validation of the efficient performance of the RNN–ANN hybrid architecture allows us to project the improvement of the forecast models. This is because we can incorporate new variables related to internal factors of the photovoltaic panels and other physical features in subsequent works.
- The implementation, configuration, and generation of a wide variety of photovoltaic energy forecast models through the RNN–ANN hybrid architecture.
- The general implementation of models based on the RNN–ANN hybrid architecture stands out for its simplicity, flexibility, and applicability in various contexts, such as wind energy forecasting or others, provided that the data sets are prepared as input sequences for time series.

In relation to the primary studies reviewed in the related works section, this work distinguishes itself through the following contributions:

- It provides a hybrid approach for generating forecast models, utilizing both univariable and multivariable inputs. This approach can be further discussed to improve its performance or combined with other RNN structures.
- It evaluates the performance of forecast models using five metrics. This allows for an analysis of the models' performances from different perspectives, thereby strengthening the evaluation stage.

The article is structured as follows: the "Related Works" section provides a literature review of the past five years, focusing on studies directly related to this work. This review allows us to corroborate the innovation of the work carried out and the use of appropriate techniques and metrics. The "Materials and Methods" section describes the data source, the methodology used, the preliminary analysis of the data, as well as its preparation and transformation. Additionally, the tool built and used to automate the entire process of design and generation of predictive models is explained. The "RNN–ANN Models" section presents the model design, hyperparameter configuration, and metrics used for their assessment. Subsequently, the "Analysis of Experimental Results" section provides a discussion of the results obtained through the selected models and performs a comparative analysis. Finally, the article ends by stating the respective conclusions obtained from the work carried out, as well as projections for future work. Table 1 below presents the list of abbreviations used in this work.

Table 1. Abbreviation list.

Abbreviation	Meaning	Abbreviation	Meaning
ANN	Artificial neural network	CO_2	Carbon dioxide
RNN	Recurrent neural network	EAE	Active energy exported
CNN	Convolutional neural network	SVM	Support vector machine
LSTM	Long short-term memory	GA	Genetic algorithm
GRU	Gated recurrent units	IRRAD	Radiation
MLP	Multi-layer perceptron	TEMP	Temperature
BiLSTM	Bidirectional long short-term memory	WS1	Wind speed
RMSE	Root mean square error	WANG	Wind angle
MSE	Mean square error	KWh	Kilowatt hour
MAE	Mean absolute error	°C	Degree Celsius
MAPE	Mean absolute percentage error	W/m^2	Watt per square meter
ARMA	Autoregressive moving average	MW	Megawatts
ARIMA	Autoregressive integrated moving average	CSV	Comma-separated values
SARIMA	Seasonal autoregressive integrated moving average	API	Application programming interface

2. Related Works

The worldwide growth in the use of photovoltaic energy has driven the development of various research initiatives aimed at obtaining high-precision models to forecast its generation. Due to this, the present research work begins with a bibliographical review of related works in this field in recent years to confirm which methodologies as well as techniques are at the forefront of research.

Yesilbudak et al. [3] provided a bibliographic review of a methodology for the data mining process for the forecast of electricity generation in solar plants. They presented a general data analysis process. As a result, they returned a table that lists different investigations that are referenced and points out the data that they use as input, as well as the model used for the prediction. Many of the works analyzed use ANN techniques.

The work of Maciel et al. [12], evaluates the forecast accuracy of the global horizontal irradiance, which is often used in short-term forecasts of solar radiation. The study uses ANN models with different construction structures and input weather variables to forecast photovoltaic energy production across three short-term forecast horizons using a single database. The analyses were conducted in a controlled experimental environment. The results indicate that ANNs using the global horizontal irradiance input variable provide higher accuracy (approximately 10%), while their absence increases error variability. No significant differences ($p > 0.05$) were identified in the forecast error models trained with different input data sets. Furthermore, forecast errors were similar for the same ANN model across different forecast horizons. The 30 and 60-neuron models with one hidden layer demonstrated similar or higher accuracy compared to those with two hidden layers.

In [13], a study is described that uses a time-frequency analysis based on short waveforms of data combined with an RNN to forecast sun irradiation in the next 10 min. This validation allows the amount of photovoltaic energy that is generated to be estimated. The validation results indicate that this forecast model has a deviation of less than 4% in 90.60% of the sample days analyzed. The MSE of the final model improved accuracy by 37.52% compared to the persistence reference model.

Carrera et al. [14] proposed the use of RNNs to forecast photovoltaic energy generation. They designed two types of RNNs: one using weather forecast data, and one using recent weather observations. Then, they combined both networks into PVHybNet, a hybrid network. The final model was successful in predicting photovoltaic energy generation at the Yeongam Solar Plant in South Korea, with an r^2 value of 92.7%. These results support the effectiveness of the combined network, which uses weather observations and forecasts. It also outperformed other machine learning models.

In the article of Rosato et al. [15], a new deep learning approach was proposed for the predictive analysis of energy-related time series trends, particularly those relevant to photovoltaic systems. The objective was to capture the trend of the time series; that is, if the series increases, decreases, or remains stable, instead of predicting the future numerical values. The modeling system is based on a RNN of a LSTM structure, which are capable of extracting information in samples located very far from the current one. This new approach has been tested in a real-world case study, showing good robustness and accuracy.

The work described in [16] uses an LSTM-based approach for short-term forecasts of global horizontal irradiance. Previous ANN and SVR results have demonstrated that they are inaccurate on cloudy days. To improve the accuracy on these days, the k-means clustering technique was used during data processing to classify the data into two categories: cloudy and mixed. RNN models were compared to assess different approaches, and an interregional study was conducted to assess their generalizability. The results showed that the r^2 coefficient of LSTM on cloudy and mixed days exceeded 0.9, while RNN only reached 0.70 and 0.79 in Atlanta and Hawaii, respectively. In the daily forecasts, all r^2 values on cloudy days were approximately 0.85. It was concluded that LSTM significantly improved accuracy compared to the other models.

The article by Hui et al. [17] proposed a hybrid learning method for weekly photovoltaic energy forecasting, utilizing weather forecast records and historical production data. The proposed algorithm combined bi-cubic interpolation and bi-directional LSTM (BiLSTM) to increase the temporal resolution of weather forecast data from three hours to one hour and improve forecast accuracy. Furthermore, a weekly photovoltaic energy classification strategy based on meteorological processes was established to capture the coupling relationships between weather elements, continuous climate changes, and weekly photovoltaic energy. The authors developed a scenario forecast method based on a closed recurrent unit GRU and a convolutional neural network (CNN) to generate weekly photovoltaic energy scenarios. The evaluation indices were presented to comprehensively assess the quality of the generated scenarios. Finally, the proposed method was validated using photovoltaic energy power records, observations, and meteorological forecasts collected from five solar plants in Northeast Asia to demonstrate its effectiveness and correctness.

In the study conducted by Xu et al. [18], the current state of research on renewable energy generation and predictive technology for wind and photovoltaic energy was described. The authors proposed a short-term forecast model for multivariable wind energy using the LSTM sequential structure with an optimized hidden layer topology. They evaluated physical models, statistical learning methods, and machine learning approaches based on historical data for wind and photovoltaic energy production forecasting. They examined the impact of cloud map identification on photovoltaic generation and focused on the impact of renewable energy generation systems on electrical grid operation and its causes. The article provided a summary of the classification of wind and photovoltaic power generation systems, as well as the advantages and disadvantages of photovoltaic systems and wind power forecasting methods based on various typologies and analysis methods.

In the article by Nkambule et al. [19], the authors introduced nine maximum power point tracking techniques for photovoltaic systems. These techniques were used to maintain the photovoltaic element array at its maximum power point and extract the maximum power available from the arrays. The authors evaluated and tested these techniques under different climatic conditions using the simulation software MATLAB SIMULINK. The tested machine learning algorithms included a decision tree, multivariate linear regression, Gaussian process regression, k-weighted nearest neighbors, linear discriminant analysis, packed tree, Naive Bayes classifier, support vector machine (SVM), and RNN. The experimental results showed that the k-weighted nearest neighbors technique performed significantly better compared to the other machine learning algorithms.

One interesting study related to the analyzed topic is presented in [20], which proposed an improved deep learning model based on the decomposition of small wavelet data for the prediction of solar irradiance the next day. The model uses CNN and LSTM and was established separately for four general types of climates (sunny, cloudy, rainy, and heavy rainy) due to the high dependence of sun radiation on weather conditions. For certain weather types, the raw solar irradiance sequence is decomposed into sub-sequences using discrete wavelet transformation. Each sub-sequence is then fed of a local CNN-based feature extractor to learn its abstract representation automatically. As the extracted features were also time-series data, they were individually input into LSTM to build the sub-sequence forecasting model. The final results of solar irradiance forecast for each weather type were obtained through the reconstruction of the small wavelet data of these forecast sub-sequences. The proposed method was compared with traditional deep learning models and demonstrated an improved predictive accuracy.

The article by Alkandari and Ahmand [21] describes the task of forecasting photovoltaic energy generation from weather variables such as solar radiation, temperature, precipitation, wind speed, and direction. The authors analyzed different techniques to determine the most suitable for photovoltaic energy forecasting. They proposed an approach that combined different techniques based on RNN models and statistical models based on their experimental results.

In [22], a data analysis process was developed to evaluate the performance of a predictive model generated using a database containing information on historical data of the energy produced. They highlighted the importance of performing good data preprocessing through various tasks in the initial stage of the work. They showed forecasts at different time horizons using ANN implementations, which have been used to solve similar problems in the past. First, they evaluated the interaction between anomaly detection techniques and predictive model accuracy. Second, after applying three performance metrics, they determined which one was the best for this particular application.

The research by Harrou et al. [23] proposed a model based on RNN with LSTM structure for the short-term prediction of photovoltaic energy production. The model was evaluated using records of power generation in 24-h segments, using data from a solar plant. The authors described the model used and highlighted its good performance during the training stage. In further development, they indicated their intention to incorporate weather variables into the model to further improve the model results.

The work of De et al. [24] proposed photovoltaic energy forecast models using RNNs with LSTM units. Limited datasets of one month were used with a frequency of 15 min. The goal was to achieve accurate forecasts with the LSTM framework. The results showed high precision, even with limited data, and in a reasonable amount of time. The hyperparameters were optimized, and variables such as temperature, panel temperature, stored energy, radiation, and output power were used.

In the work of Chen et al. [25], the authors analyzed the effects of various meteorological factors on the generation of photovoltaic energy and their impact during different periods. They proposed a simple radiation classification method based on the characteristics of the radiation records, which helps in selecting similar time periods. They employed the time series characteristic of photovoltaic energy production records to reconstruct the training dataset in a given period, which included output power and weather data. They presented the development of an RNN model with neurons in a LSTM structure, which was applied to data from two photovoltaic systems. The forecast results of this model stood out when they were compared to four other models.

The work of Sharadga et al. [26] evaluated various RNN models for forecasting photovoltaic energy output power using time series. Statistical techniques such as ARMA, ARIMA, and SARIMA were compared with RNN models and their variants, such as LSTM, BiLSTM, recurrent layer, direct RNN, MLP, and c-mean fuzzy clustering. The impact of the time horizon on the forecasts was analyzed, and hourly forecasts were made using data from a photovoltaic power station in China with a total of 3640 operating hours.

The study by Rajagukguk et al. [27] analyzed deep learning models for predicting solar radiation and photovoltaics in a time series. They compared four models: RNN, LSTM, GRU, and CNN–LSTM, considering accuracy, input data, forecast horizon, station type, weather, and training time. The results showed that each model had strengths and limitations under different conditions. LSTM stood out, with the best performance in terms of RMSE. The CNN–LSTM hybrid model outperformed the independent models, although it required more training time. Deep learning models are better suited to predict solar radiation and photovoltaics than conventional machine learning models. It is recommended to use the relative RMSE as a proxy metric to compare accuracy between models.

In the study provided by ref. [28], a methodology based on spectral irradiances and GA was presented to analyze the performance of photovoltaic modules. It was observed that the power conversion efficiency of these modules can vary, even under the same solar radiation. A case study was carried out in Malaysia, where twelve types of commercial photovoltaic modules were selected to simulate their conversion efficiencies and annual energy yields. This methodology provides detailed information on local spectral radiations and photovoltaic energy specifications, allowing for accurate analysis of module performance.

The work cited in [29] presents a methodology to calculate the energy conversion efficiency in organic photovoltaic cells by means of indoor measurements. A solar simulator and the measured local solar spectrum were used, considering optical and electrical factors. As a case study, random data of local solar spectra was collected throughout the year in Malaysia from 8:00 a.m. to 5:00 p.m. or 6:00 p.m. This analysis provides guidance for selecting the proper organic materials in solar cells and optimizing their performance at specific locations.

The study conducted by Jaber et al. [30] presented a forecast model based on a generalized regression ANN to compare the performance of six photovoltaic modules. Using variables such as cell temperature, irradiance, fill factor, peak power, short circuit current, open circuit voltage, and the product of the last two variables, 37,144 records from 247 module curves were collected under various climatic conditions in Malaysia. The results obtained showed a high precision in the prediction of the performance of the photovoltaic modules.

In the work of Diouf et al. [31], the impact of the operating temperature on the performance of photovoltaic modules was analyzed. A temperature forecast model was developed using ambient temperature and solar irradiance data obtained in a tropical region. The proposed approach captured the temperatures of the photovoltaic modules in different weather conditions, and they were compared with the experimentally measured values. The results showed that the proposed models outperformed those developed by other authors in terms of accuracy, which was evaluated using the MSE metric.

Bevilacqua et al. [32] investigated the effect of sun radiation on the temperature of photovoltaic panels. They proposed a one-dimensional finite-difference thermal model to calculate the temperature distribution within the panel and predict electricity production under various climatic conditions. The results revealed that, although the temperature could be predicted with high accuracy, the accuracy in predicting the power output varied. The model was validated using one year of experimental data at the University of Calabria, demonstrating excellent agreement between power predictions and actual measurements.

In the work of Zhang et al. [33], the influence of factors on photovoltaic energy forecasting was analyzed using ANN surface and small wave models. The effects of atmospheric temperature, relative humidity, and wind speed on polysilicon and amorphous silicon cells were examined. The experimental results revealed that atmospheric temperature had the highest correlation with output power in polysilicon cells, followed by wind speed and relative humidity. For amorphous silicon cells, relative humidity showed the highest correlation, followed by atmospheric temperature and wind speed.

He et al. [34] presented a forecast model for photovoltaic energy generation that uses a BiLSTM structure in an RNN. They selected the weather factors that affected energy generation using the Pearson correlation coefficient. Then, the design and implementation of the proposed model were detailed and evaluated using real data collected from a solar plant in China. The experimental results confirmed that the model had the low forecast error and highest accuracy of fit than the other tested models, such as SVR, decision tree, random forest, and LSTM.

Chen and Chang [35] proposed a method to forecast photovoltaic energy based on an RNN with a LSTM structure. They used Pearson's correlation coefficients to analyze the influence of external conditions on the variation of photovoltaic energy and eliminate irrelevant characteristics. The results of the case study showed that sun radiation, temperature, and humidity played a decisive role in this variation. Compared with conventional ANN algorithms, such as a radial basis ANN function and time series, the proposed method demonstrated superior performance in terms of accuracy.

In the work of Konstantinou et al. [36], an RNN model was evaluated to forecast photovoltaic energy generation 1.5 h in advance. Using the historical production records of a solar plant in Cyprus as input, the model was defined and trained. Performance evaluation was performed using graphical tools, calculating the RMSE metric, and applying cross-validation. The results showed that the proposed model made accurate predictions with a low RMSE value, and cross-validation confirmed its robustness by significantly reducing the average of the obtained RMSE values.

Nicolai et al. [37] presented three hybrid models that combine physical elements with ANNs to improve forecast accuracy. The first model uses a combination of ANNs and a five-parameter physical model. The second model uses a matching procedure with historical data and an evolutionary algorithm called social network optimization. The third model uses clear sky radiation as input. These models were compared with physical approaches and a simple forecast based on ANNs. The results demonstrated the effectiveness of these hybrid models in obtaining accurate forecasts.

In their classic article, Hochreiter and Schmidhuber [38] addressed the challenge of storing long-term information in RNNs and proposed a solution called LSTM. They noted that traditional recursive backpropagation presents difficulties due to the lack of adequate error flow. Therefore, LSTM was introduced, which utilizes special units and multiplicative gates to maintain a constant flow of error and control its access. They claimed that LSTM is computationally efficient and capable of learning to overcome significant time delays. Experiments using artificial data demonstrated that LSTM outperformed other RNN algorithms, exhibiting better performance and faster learning.

Schuster and Paliwal [39] presented the BiRNN, an extension of regular RNNs that overcomes limitations by training in both positive and negative time directions. They demonstrated its superior performance in regression and classification experiments using data and artificial phonemes from TIMIT. Furthermore, they proposed a modified two-way structure to estimate the conditional posterior probability of complete sequences without making any explicit assumptions. The results were supported by experiments using real data.

Learning with RNNs in long sequences presents significant challenges. Article [40] introduced the Dilated-RNN connection structure, which addresses the challenges of complex dependencies, vanishing or exploding gradients, and efficient parallelization. The Dilated-RNN utilizes dilated recurrent hop connections and can be combined with different RNN cells. Furthermore, it reduces the required parameters and improves training efficiency without compromising performance on tasks with long-term dependencies. A suitable memory capacity measure for RNNs with long hop connections was presented. The advantages of Dilated-RNNs were rigorously demonstrated, and the code is publicly available.

In [41], a quantum model was proposed that introduces a truly quantum version of classical neurons, enabling the formation of feed-forward quantum neural networks capable of universal quantum computing. The article described an efficient training method for these networks using fidelity as a cost function, providing both classical and quantum implementations. This method allows for fast optimization with minimal memory requirements, as the number of required qubits scales only with the network's width, facilitating the optimization of deep networks. Additionally, the study demonstrated the remarkable generalization behavior and impressive resilience to noisy training data exhibited by the proposed model when applied to the quantum task of learning an unknown unit.

Zhou et al. [42] highlighted that advantageous quantum computing and communication schemes have been proposed. However, the practical implementation of these schemes remains challenging due to the complexity of preparing quantum states. To address this, the authors introduced a quantum coupon collector protocol that utilizes coherent states and simple optical elements. Experimental demonstrations using realistic equipment showed a notable reduction in the number of samples required to learn a specific set, surpassing classical methods. Additionally, the study explored the potential of the protocol by constructing a quantum game that also exceeded classical limitations. These findings highlight the advantages of quantum mechanics in the realms of machine learning and communication complexity.

The work described in [43] introduced a novel approach for developing neural networks based on quantum computing devices. The proposed quantum neural network model leverages individual qubit operations and measurements in real-world quantum systems affected by decoherence. This approach effectively addresses the challenges associated with physical implementation by utilizing naturally occurring decoherence. Additionally, the model employs classically controlled operations to mitigate the exponential growth of the state space, resulting in reduced memory requirements and efficient optimization. Benchmark tests demonstrated the model's impressive nonlinear classification capabilities and robustness to noise. Moreover, the model extends the applicability of quantum computing and provides potential advancements in the field of quantum neural computers.

Finally, the objective of the study of Dairi et al. [44] was to develop accurate forecast models for photovoltaic energy production. The Variational AutoEncoder (VAE) model was used because of its performance in time series modeling and its flexibility in nonlinear approximations. Data from two photovoltaic plants were used to evaluate the performance of deep learning models. The results showed that the VAE outperformed other deep learning methods and benchmark machine learning models. Additionally, the performance of eight deep learning models, including RNN, LSTM, BiLSTM, GRU, CNN–LSTM, stacked autoencoders, VAE, and restricted Boltzmann machine, as well as two common machine learning models, logistic regression and support vector regression, were compared.

Based on the reviewed works, it is worth noting that RNNs are primarily used in the context of forecast models for photovoltaic energy production in solar plants. Within RNNs, the most used are those with a LSTM structure, followed by those based on a GRU structure. The works analyzed can be classified into three groups according to the techniques used:

- Machine learning: this order highlights the use of RNNs, ANNs, SVMs, and GAs.
- Statistical approach: this includes linear regressions, time series analysis, Bayesian networks, ARIMA, and ARMA.
- Hybrid approaches: these combine the two previous techniques with physical models.

Regarding the testing of these models, it is common for these works to focus on a single performance metric, such as RMSE. However, other metrics, such as MSE, MAE, MAPE, and the Pearson correlation coefficient, are often overlooked. The model assessment stage can be improved by employing a combination of metrics to measure performance.

Additionally, some works do not utilize large amounts of data for training and validation purposes. This highlights the need for more studies with larger datasets to ensure the accuracy and generalizability of the proposed models.

In this bibliographical review, another significant aspect stands out: the influence of various factors on the generation of photovoltaic energy [24,28–33,37]. These factors can be categorized into two groups:

- External factors are related to the weather, which include the intensity of solar radiation, ambient temperature, and relative humidity. These factors directly affect the generation of photovoltaic energy.
- Internal factors are components of photovoltaic modules, such as the material of the panels and their components, including silicon and organic cells, and the influence their performance. Sun radiation also has an impact on these factors and can cause a temperature increase in the layers of the panels. Therefore, it is important to consider the quality of the components when analyzing the production of photovoltaic energy.

Furthermore, recent works have focused on advancements in quantum machine learning and quantum computing. These developments have given rise to new approaches for learning using RNNs in long sequences, training quantum neural networks, and exploring quantum communication and computing. These advancements underscore the potential of quantum mechanics in surpassing the limitations of classical approaches in these fields [41–43].

The main innovation of this study compared to the analyzed works is its utilization of the RNN–ANN hybrid architecture designed and described in the previous work described in [11]. This architecture serves as the foundation for generating forecast models of photovoltaic energy production. It consists of two layers: the first layer utilizes LSTM or GRU recurrent units, while the second layer consists of surface neurons with an MLP structure. This approach is tested with consistent input and internal configurations for predicting PV power production.

In the previous work [11], the hybridization of this RNN–ANN architecture was introduced to improve the models' convergence. The results of the tests demonstrate that using solely layers with recurrent neurons does not yield superior performance when compared to incorporating an additional layer of shallow neurons. Although primary studies in the literature have reviewed explored hybrid models, they have not specifically combined RNN layers with ANN layers, as is done in this study [14,17,18,24,27,37].

Other important factors that differentiate this work from others are related to the large volume of data used, spanning a full year of EAE production records and weather variable measurements for the same period. Additionally, different models were generated by considering both the EAE and weather variables as inputs, as well as using only weather variables. The work examines several RNN–ANN hyperparameter configurations and assesses their performance using five performance metrics.

3. Materials and Methods

3.1. Data Origin

Based on the previous research described in [11], this study generated forecast models using records of EAE production combined with meteorological variables obtained from meteorological stations installed inside a solar plant. The meteorological variables included sun radiation (IRRAD), temperature (TEMP), wind speed (WS), wind angle (WANG), and a timeline (date and time).

The data used in this work were provided by Solar Brothers SPA, the owner of the Valle Solar Oeste photovoltaic plant. This dataset consists of more than one hundred thousand records of photovoltaic energy production, together with weather information corresponding to a period of one year.

The solar plant is located in the Atacama region of Chile and occupies an area of 30.2 hectares. It is part of a project that includes three other photovoltaic plants: Malaquita, Cachiyuyo, and Valle Solar Este. It has a generating capacity of 11.5 megawatts (MW). The photovoltaic modules used are composed of 325-watt polycrystalline silicon and equipped with horizontal single-axis solar trackers.

3.2. Work Methodology

The objective of this work was to develop models that can forecast the generation of photovoltaic energy with a high level of accuracy using historical production records and climatic measurements collected during one year. Figure 1 illustrates the general work method used to achieve this objective.

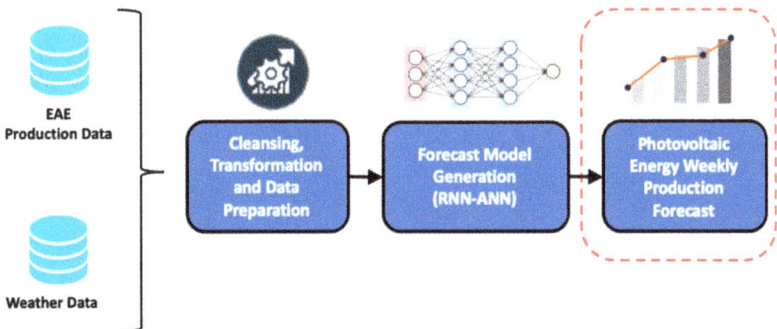

Figure 1. General working method.

As shown in Figure 1, the data for this study came from two sources: one providing EAE production records and the other providing weather variables collected from weather stations installed inside the solar plant. To achieve the study's objective, several operations were performed on the data, such as integration, exploration, cleansing, filling, and transformation. In addition, it was necessary to prepare an adequate data representation for handling time series with RNN techniques.

Subsequently, forecast models were generated using the RNN–ANN hybrid architecture designed and explained in [11]. These models were created using various hyperparameter configurations and trained, validated, and evaluated using five performance metrics. The models with the highest performance and accuracy were selected based on the evaluation metrics. A comparative analysis of the models was then carried out, and the results were interpreted.

3.3. Preliminary Analysis and Data Preparation

The dataset was stored in separate CSV files, with each file containing information for a single month of measurement. As a result, the frequency of the records varied. EAE measurements were taken hourly, while weather variables were measured every 5 min.

The daily production of EAE was recorded in kilowatt-hours (kWh). Weather variables such as compensated irradiation in watts per square meter (W/m^2), ambient temperature in degrees Celsius (°C), wind speed in kilometers per hour (km/h), and wind angle in degrees (°) were also available. These data are presented together with a timeline that includes date and time.

To integrate data from both sources, an exploratory analysis was first carried out. It was observed that the values of the weather variables did not vary substantially within one hour. Therefore, the average value of each weather variable for each hour was established by aligning it with the same hourly frequency of the data in the EAE variable.

The date and time information were combined into a single column. However, a challenge arose regarding the range of values for sun radiation due to the presence of negative readings in some pyranometers when there was no solar radiation. Instead of registering zero, the pyranometers registered a negative value. To address this issue, the negative readings of sun radiation were replaced by zeros. The dataset also contained missing data in various segments, particularly in weather variables. To address this, various data filling techniques were applied depending on the characteristics of the variables.

Figure 2 depicts a sample of weather variable records spanning one week. The temperature and sun radiation exhibited comparable behavior, showing a strong link. Wind speed and angle, on the other hand, followed a chaotic and unpredictable pattern. As a result, missing values for certain variables were handled differently. In particular, missing values for wind speed and angle were filled with the preceding value, because the curves of these variables indicated local patterns, and each value was strongly related to the previous one.

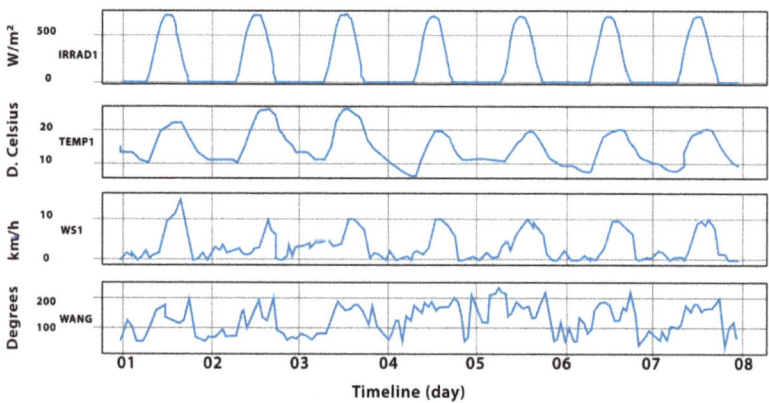

Figure 2. Exploratory sample of records in weather variables.

In the case of variable temperature and sun radiation, methods for filling in time series from different authors have been reviewed [45–48]. However, for this work, it was decided to use the technique described in [49] due to its simplicity of application and because it does not affect the performance of forecast models. This method involves completing the missing data based on the average. Each missing value was replaced by the average of the values of the seven days before or after, corresponding to the same time of day. For example, if the temperature value for 14 June at 10:25 a.m. was absent, the average of the temperature values at 10:25 a.m. of the seven days before was calculated, from 7 to 13 June. The value resulting from this calculation was used to replace the missing data. This method respects the local and daily trends of the variables. It was valid and could be carried out, as the missing data segments did not exceed 288 records. These methods were selected for their speed of execution and satisfactory results for relatively small missing segments.

On the other hand, the electrical variable EAE does not have missing values. However, it does present negative outliers in some records, which are not meaningful in this type of data. It is presumed that this anomaly can be attributed to the measuring instrument used. To solve this problem, the negative values are replaced with their absolute values, considering that the magnitude at the affected points aligns with the expected values.

Extreme values are identified in the EAE variable, and an analysis is carried out to establish a threshold limit within its range of values. Taking into account that the maximum power registered in the solar plant is approximately 9 MW, a threshold of 10 MW is defined. Because these cases are uncommon, values greater than 10 MW are replaced by the first value belonging to the 99th percentile of all records for this variable.

Additionally, as shown in Figure 3, the monthly generation of EAE by the solar plant during the observation period was examined. It can be seen that the months with the highest photovoltaic energy output, which run from October to March, must correlate to the spring and summer seasons in this location. In the autumn and winter seasons, the months of decreasing outputs were from April to September. This was primarily due to the sun radiation behavior at these sites, which is closely related to the EAE produced.

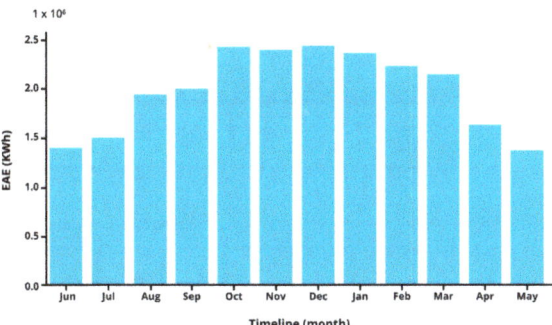

Figure 3. Monthly EAE production.

As mentioned above, the raw data was separated into different files per month. Therefore, a data integration task was initially performed by processing each file. Pre-processing tasks were performed for each variable. Once completed, the processed data were integrated into a single table containing all records for the work period, ordered chronologically.

3.4. Data Transformation

Once the previous data preparation has been completed, ad-hoc transformations must be carried out for appropriate use by the RNN technique. These transformations should be based on the characteristics of the technique and the model to be obtained. Both the inputs and the structure of the model must be prepared, and the dataset should be divided before moving on to the modeling process.

For this particular work, it was necessary to transform the data into a supervised structure, as RNN models require training that is defined by input and output labels. Furthermore, the research data was accompanied by a timestamp, and the research objectivewas to make time-based predictions.

Therefore, it was decided to define the inputs of the model as time series, which means that each input is composed of a sequence of n records. The models were trained, taking into account that for an output d_t, there is an input that covers several records from d_{t-1} to d_{t-n}. The data were transformed based on the size of the input and output streams. This process was performed iteratively. As a result, the data were restructured into input and output pairs, as shown in Figure 4.

It is common for such transformations to undergo multiple changes during the data analysis process, typically due to modifications to the model or during the evaluation stage. These changes often involve adjusting the sizes of the input and output sequences.

Finally, it is necessary to apply normalization to the data so that they can be rescaled and managed within the same range, which minimizes the effect of variation or noise. One of the most commonly used types of normalization is the minimum–maximum normalization, which involves transforming each data point according to the following equation:

$$x' = \frac{x - x_{min}}{x_{max} - x_{min}} \tag{1}$$

This process is carried out independently for each variable, as they each have their own range and scale. Once the model results are obtained, they must be inverted or denormalized to obtain the values in the original scale. For this work, standardization is used, since it yields better results.

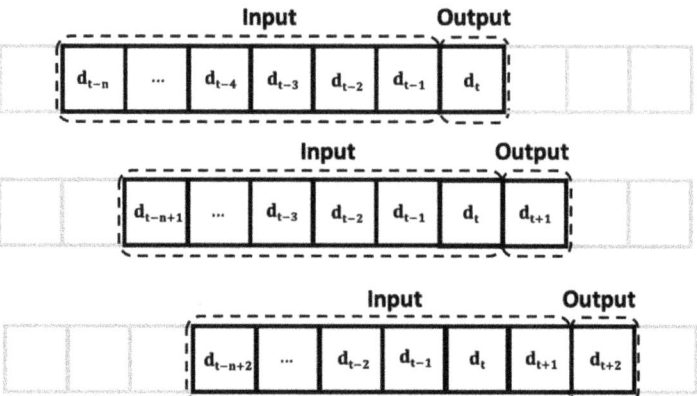

Figure 4. Sequence structure for time series.

3.5. Model Generation Tool

A computational tool was developed to automate the entire process, starting from data extraction and cleansing, to data preparation and transformation, as well as the generation of forecasting models with their corresponding graphs, model training and validation, and performance evaluation using various metrics. This tool provides a general framework for carrying out time series forecasting tasks and can be adapted to different scenarios and data sources.

For the development of this tool, the Python programming language was used in conjunction with the TensorFlow framework. The latter offers a comprehensive set of open-source libraries and resources to facilitate machine learning development. Additionally, the Keras API was used, which is one of the main components of TensorFlow and covers each step of the machine learning workflow.

As an input, the tool requires two files: one with the training and validation dataset and another with the configured hyperparameters. For each execution, the tool generates two output files. The first file contains the generated model and its graphs of loss, forecast, and dispersion function curves, comparing the forecast data with the actual data on the weekly production of EAE. The second file contains the results obtained for each of the metrics applied to the model.

This method of building the computational tool provides flexibility and generalization of the inputs. For example, it allows for the reconfiguration of hyperparameters to obtain a different model, changing the data set, or both inputs simultaneously.

4. RNN–ANN Models

This work is based on a hybrid RNN–ANN architecture that was designed in the previous section of this study and thoroughly described in [11]. The RNN–ANN architecture is made up of two hidden layers: the first uses recurrent neurons with LSTM or GRU units, and the second layer is composed of shallow neurons organized in an MLP structure. The significance of this architecture lies in its pre-existing and tested structure for generating forecast models of photovoltaic energy production using a single input variable. However, in this implementation, it has been configured to accommodate multiple variables as input for the models.

The contributions of this work build upon the previous part of this research by focusing on the validation of the RNN–ANN hybrid architecture through the generation of models that incorporate multiple input variables, as well as the exploration of various hyperparameter configurations. The variables used as inputs for the models included historical EAE records, as well as available weather variables such as sun radiation, temperature, and wind speed. These data corresponded to records collected throughout one year. In addition, the hyperparameters of the internal components of the model, such as the activation function and the loss function, were also fitted.

Different controlled experiments are conducted to obtain the models with the best performance, evaluated using a combination of appropriate metrics. Two types of models are generated for this purpose:

1. Models with EAE records and weather variable measurements as input variables, accompanied by a timeline;
2. Models that solely use weather variables as input variables, accompanied by a timeline.

To improve the performance of a model, it is important to configure several hyperparameters based on its features. For example, the number of neurons in the hidden layers can vary depending on whether the model has a single input variable or multiple input variables. Similarly, the number of batches and the activation function may need to be adjusted based on the number and type of input variables.

4.1. Models with EAE and Weather Variable Inputs

When configuring models, all necessary hyperparameters are considered, including the size of the input and output sequences, the division of the data set for training and validation, the type and number of recurring neurons in the hidden layers, and the batch size, activation functions, loss function, learning rate, optimizer, and performance metrics. Table 2 presents the hyperparameters used in the preliminary or test models. This aids in the identification and selection of optimal values for the final model configuration in this study. These adjustments were made through a series of experiments.

Table 2. Configuration of the models with all the variables.

Hyperparameters	Configuration
Number of recurrent neurons	100
Activation function	Relu
Loss function	Huber
Optimizer	Adam
Input sequence size	72
Dataset split	80% training, 20% testing

It is important to highlight that in the preliminary tests of the models using the entire provided dataset, undesired overtraining phenomena were observed when a training process of 100 epochs was defined. Therefore, after several tests, the number of epochs was set to 20, as the models were able to stabilize with this number.

Considering the exploratory analysis of the meteorological variables described in Section 3.3 and depicted in Figure 2, the decision was made to exclude the wind angle variable (WANG) from the models. This is attributed to its chaotic behavior and the absence of a direct relationship with the sun radiation and temperature variables. Thus, for model generation, only the following variables will be utilized: EAE, IRRAD, TEMP, WS, and Timestamp (date and time).

Starting from this base model, new experiments were carried out using different configurations for each hyperparameter until the results were within a good level of forecasting and acceptable ranges in the evaluation metrics were achieved. Based on the results obtained for each hyperparameter, models with the best performance were pre-selected, as shown in Table 3. Regarding the hyperparameter number of inputs, two types of models were selected: those with three input variables (EAE, IRRAD, and TEMP), and those with four input variables (EAE, IRRAD, TEMP, and WS), which were always accompanied by a timestamp. For all these models, 20 recurrent neurons and a dataset split of 90% for training and 10% for testing were used.

Table 3. Pre-selected models.

Models	Activation Function	Loss Function	Optimizer	Input Sequence Size	Number of Inputs
Model 1	Relu	MSE	RMSprop	72	3
Model 2	Relu	LogCosh	RMSprop	72	3
Model 3	LeakyReLU	MSE	RMSprop	72	3
Model 4	LeakyReLU	MSE	RMSprop	24	3
Model 5	LeakyReLU	MSE	RMSprop	24	4
Model 6	LeakyReLU	MSE	Adam	24	4

The results of the metrics for these models are presented in Table 4, where the best performance is compared to the other previously tested models.

Table 4. Metric results of preselected models.

Models	Correlation Coefficient	Determination Coefficient	MSE	MAE	RMSE
Model 1	0.962988	0.927196	0.045359	0.107983	0.212976
Model 2	0.963756	0.927210	0.043488	0.103623	0.208519
Model 3	0.962180	0.924341	0.040797	0.094496	0.201982
Model 4	0.965271	0.931373	0.039147	0.090114	0.197855
Model 5	0.964508	0.930250	0.040490	0.092352	0.201220
Model 6	0.960609	0.921630	0.043614	0.100860	0.208840

Figures 5 and 6 graphically present the results obtained from running the six preselected models with the indicated hyperparameter configurations. Models 1 and 4 stand out for their level of forecasting accuracy, closely resembling the actual curve of the EAE production data. However, Model 4 achieved the best results in all metrics. It exhibited the highest correlation coefficient (0.965271) and determination (0.931373), as well as the lowest errors (MSE = 0.039147, MAE = 0.090114, RMSE = 0.197855). This allowed us to deduce that the RNN–ANN hybrid architecture, with a smaller input sequence, achieves better performance in the models it generates.

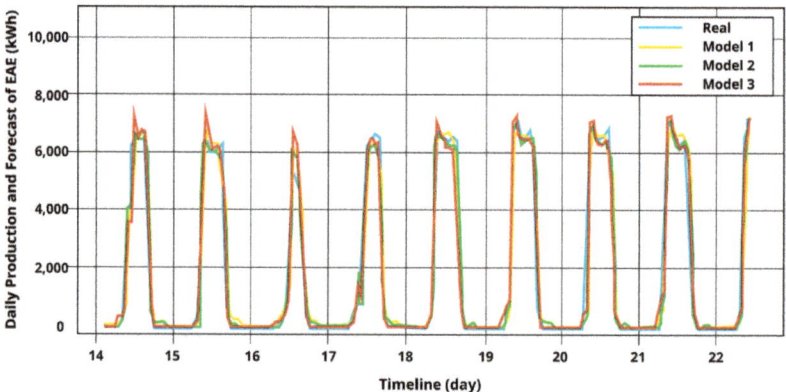

Figure 5. Daily forecast of pre-selected models with an input sequence size of 72.

In general, a reliable approximation to the actual production of EAE was noted, with the main failures occurring on very isolated days with irregular weather phenomena. Furthermore, it was observed that Model 6, despite not yielding the best metrics results, was the most stable and presented fewer disturbances during hours of absent sun due to the Adam optimizer used to implement this model.

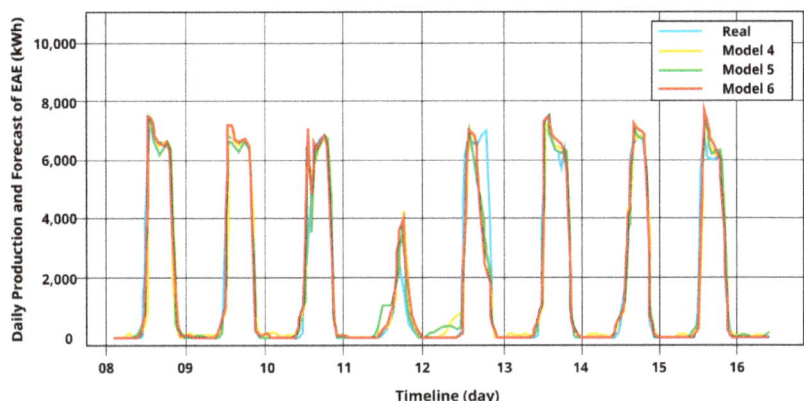

Figure 6. Daily forecast of pre-selected models with an input sequence size of 24.

The loss function of these models is shown in Figure 7, where an appropriate behavior can be observed for each model, as their training and testing curves converge in most cases, despite the small number of epochs used in training. Model 2 stands out due to its use of a different loss function, and the models that received an input sequence of 72 elements tended to undergo slight changes during the training process.

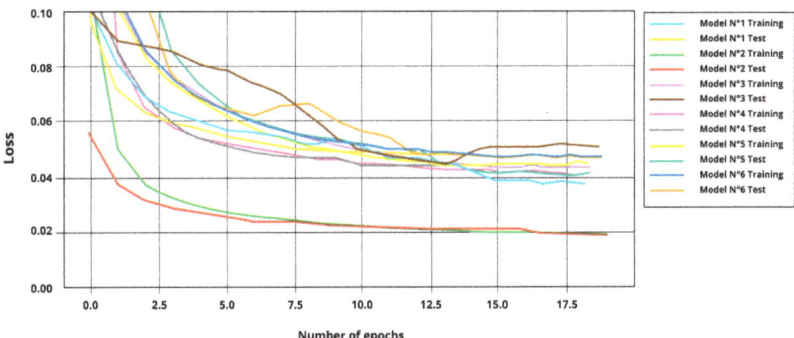

Figure 7. Loss curve graphs for pre-selected models.

4.2. Models with Only Weather Input Variables

For this type of model, experiments were also conducted to analyze which input variables were most appropriate. A base configuration was established to generate these models, with the main difference being the size of the input sequence. One set had a size of 72 elements, and the other had a size of 24 elements. A combination of input variables was also used. Table 5 presents the configuration of the hyperparameters for the base model.

Tables 6 and 7 show the results of the metrics achieved by the models with input sequence sizes of 72 and 24 elements, respectively, for different combinations of weather variables. In both cases, it was confirmed that the best combination of input variables was sun radiation and temperature, which achieved the best results in performance metrics such as the correlation coefficient and determination coefficient.

Table 5. Model setup with only weather variables.

Hyperparameters	Configuration
Number of recurrent neurons	20
Activation function	Relu
Loss function	LogCosh
Optimizer	RMSprop
Input sequence size	72/24
Data set split	90% training, 10% testing

Table 6. Results with a sequence size of 72 in the input.

Inputs	Correlation Coefficient	Determination Coefficient	MSE	MAE	RMSE
IRRAD, TEMP, WS	0.945908	0.888276	0.064001	0.114441	0.252984
IRRAD, TEMP	0.952505	0.906126	0.063654	0.121831	0.252297
IRRAD, WS	0.941199	0.868623	0.070948	0.127403	0.266360
TEMP, WS	0.893265	0.795375	0.129587	0.188416	0.359982

Table 7. Results with a sequence size of 24 in the input.

Inputs	Correlation Coefficient	Determination Coefficient	MSE	MAE	RMSE
IRRAD, TEMP, WS	0.950260	0.901154	0.061535	0.110532	0.248053
IRRAD, TEMP	0.951835	0.904166	0.060122	0.108557	0.245197
IRRAD, WS	0.940340	0.882897	0.065238	0.115602	0.255417
TEMP, WS	0.900719	0.806981	0.129571	0.186893	0.359959

Figures 8 and 9 display the daily forecasts obtained by these models for input sequence sizes of 72 and 24 elements, respectively. These graphs confirm that the combination of radiation and temperature variables provided a higher level of forecast accuracy.

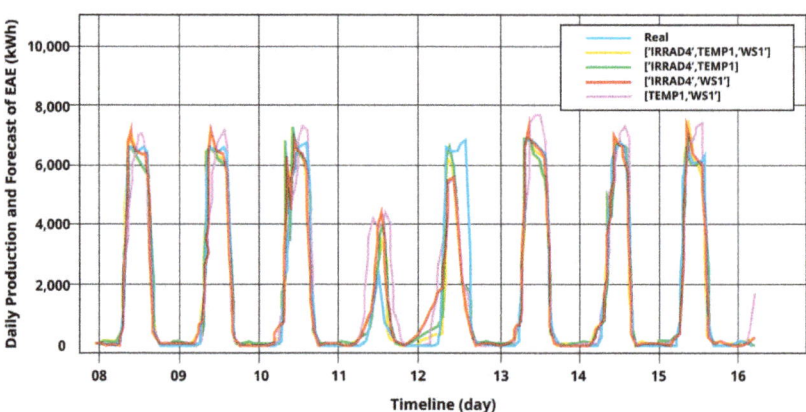

Figure 8. Daily forecast of models with input sequence sizes of 72.

Since these models only used weather variables, they did not achieve better metric results than the first type of model. However, they still provided a forecast that closely matched the real data.

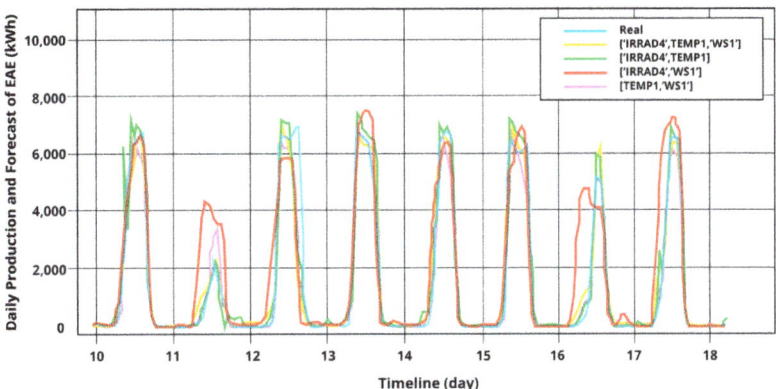

Figure 9. Daily forecast of models with input sequence sizes of 24.

5. Results and Discussion

It was possible to develop models to accurately forecast the weekly production of photovoltaic energy based on historical records of EAE and meteorological measurements, both accompanied by a timeline. The different related works analyzed in Section 2 were used as a reference. Specifically, the studies carried out in [25,26] were discussed due to their relevance to this research.

The main achievement of this work was to validate the RNN–ANN architecture for generating forecast models with multiple input variables. These models demonstrated high accuracy in forecasting photovoltaic energy generation using EAE production records and weather measurements collected over the course of a year.

There are hyperparameters that must be properly configured for the RNN–ANN forecast model. Many preliminary experiments were carried out from a base model with the goal of determining the appropriate hyperparameter configurations to generate the final forecast models. The experimental part of the work focused on generating two types of models based on the input variables.

The first type of model utilized the EAE variable, along with the IRRAD, TEMP, and WS weather variables. It used 20 recurrent neurons and divided the dataset into 90% for training and 10% for validation. The configurations are shown in Table 3. Six models of this type were obtained, which yielded good results in the evaluation metrics applied, as shown in Table 4.

For the second type of model, only weather variables were used, and eight models were obtained with different combinations of these variables, differentiated only by the input sequence size. The hyperparameters used for these models included 20 recurrent neurons and a 90% training and 10% validation data set split, which are shown in Tables 5–7.

The models of the second type yielded lower values in their metrics compared to the models of the first type, which can be observed by comparing Tables 4, 6 and 7. This result was expected, as the absence of the EAE variable as input made the model more prone to issuing output distortions. However, the obtained models could forecast photovoltaic energy generation in solar plants using conventional weather forecasts.

Table 8 shows the metrics results for the models with the best performance in each type. Model 4 excelled in all metrics for the first type, while the model that forecasted from the combination of solar radiation and temperature variables obtained the best results for the second type.

Table 8. Selected models for each type.

Selected Models	Correlation Coefficient	Determination Coefficient	MSE	MAE	RMSE
Model 4 (of Table 4)	0.965271	0.931373	0.039147	0.090114	0.197855
Model with IRRAD and TEMP (of Table 7)	0.951835	0.904166	0.060122	0.108557	0.245197

Although both models were able to forecast the weekly production of photovoltaic energy, they presented small errors and differences in some observed intervals. However, when comparing the results with those obtained in the works most closely related to this research (Che et al. [25] and Sharadga et al. [26]), it was found that Model 4 improved an average of 60% in the RMSE metric shared by both works, while the model of the second type improved in the RMSE metric by 45%. These results can still be improved upon by increasing the volume of data and extending the forecast period.

Figures 10 and 11 illustrate select results of the chosen models, as indicated in Table 8. In each figure, Graph (a) displays the weekly forecast for the months of May and June, while Graph (b) presents a scatterplot comparing the predicted values to the actual values of the solar plant's weekly EAE production. In the scatterplots, the red line represents the linear trend of EAE production in both the actual and forecasted data. The blue dots represent the spread of the forecasted data relative to their corresponding real EAE production data.

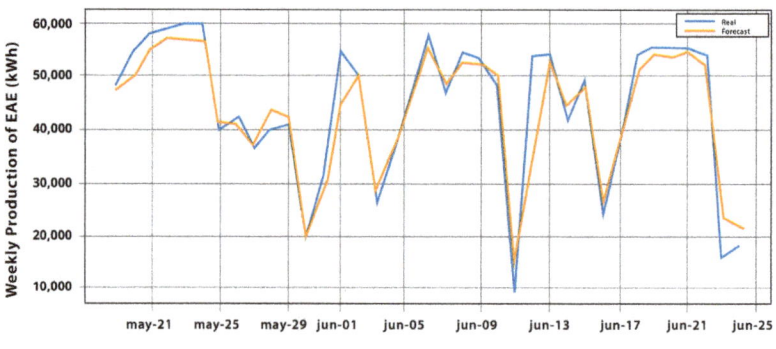

(a)

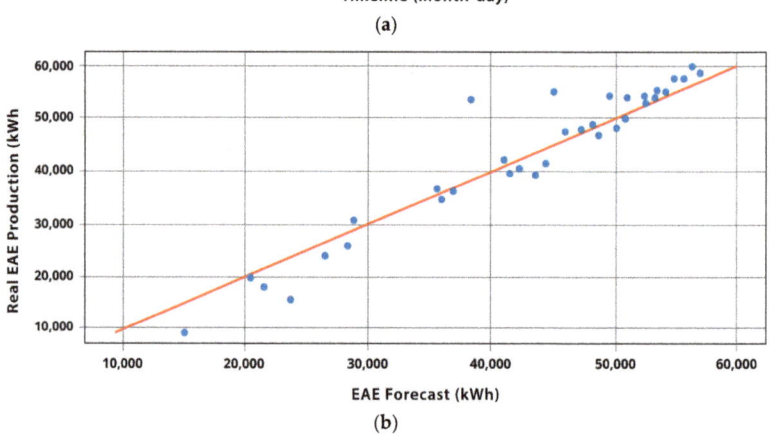

(b)

Figure 10. Model with EAE and weather variables. (**a**) Weekly forecast; (**b**) dispersion between forecast and real values.

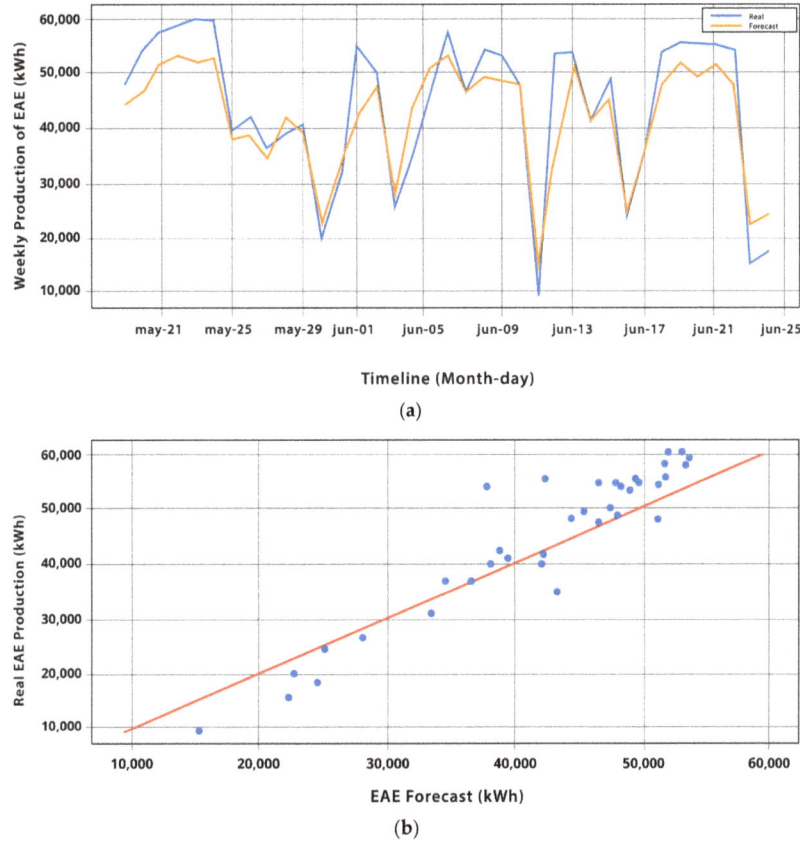

Figure 11. Model with only weather variables. (**a**) Weekly forecast; (**b**) dispersion between forecast and real values.

When Figures 10a and 11a are compared, it is clear that both models are capable of accurately estimating weekly photovoltaic energy production while maintaining a behavior similar to the real data curve. However, the model that combines the EAE and weather variables (model 4 in Table 4) showed higher precision and a better fit to the real data curve across the entire observed time.

Similar patterns can be observed in the scatter diagrams of Figures 10b and 11b. Although both models showed a clear correlation between the forecast and real data, Model 4 excelled with the EAE and meteorological variables as input, as it had less data dispersion points with regard to the real values. This was quantitatively confirmed by the correlation coefficients (0.965271) and determination (0.931373) shown in Table 8 compared to the same metrics obtained by the model that only used meteorological variables (correlation coefficient: 0.951835, determination: 0.904166). In addition, Model 4 surpassed the model of the second type in the other metrics by approximately 35% in the MSE, 10% in the MAE, and 20% in the RMSE.

To complement this analysis, Figure 12 presents a visual representation of the forecast errors of Model 4, which was selected as the best model in this study. The boxplot shows the distribution of errors for the training and test sets using the MSE metric. These errors are acceptable and support the reliability of the quantitative analysis performed. In this graph, the circles that appear represent outliers. The red line represents the third quartile, which means that 75% of the error values are less than or equal to the value at the top of the box.

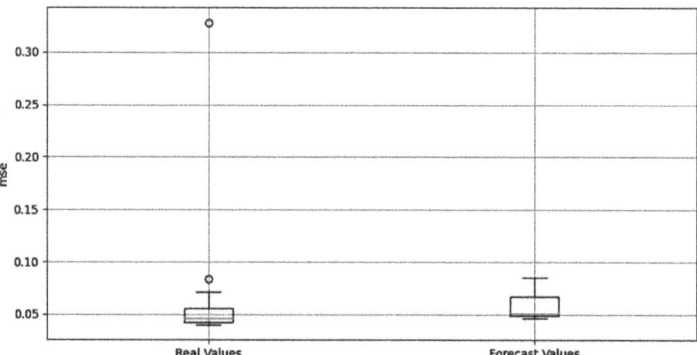

Figure 12. Distribution of Model 4 forecast errors observed using the MSE metric.

Overall, it can be concluded that for weekly analysis, the models that incorporated the EAE variable provided better forecast results compared to the models that only used meteorological variables as inputs. This suggests that the EAE variable is a relevant factor to consider when predicting the production of photovoltaic energy.

6. Conclusions

The forecast models are useful for solar plants and their operators, allowing efficient planning to balance the generation and consumption of photovoltaic energy. Improving the accuracy of these models is essential to obtain more reliable estimates of energy production, which can be integrated into existing electrical systems. In this study, it was possible to confirm and validate the previously described RNN–ANN hybrid architecture described in [11]. This approach generates forecast models of the weekly production of photovoltaic energy in a solar plant with a high degree of accuracy using multiple input variables. Two types of models were developed: one that uses EAE records and climate variables, and another that uses only climate variables. Both types of models achieved good accuracy in forecasting weekly energy production. Model 4 of the first type obtained the best results across all of the applied metrics (RMSE = 0.19, MSE = 0.03, MAE = 0.09, correlation coefficient = 0.96, and determination coefficient = 0.93). Although the selected model of the second type presented a lower precision in some metrics (RMSE = 0.24, MSE = 0.06, MAE = 0.10, correlation coefficient = 0.95, and determination coefficient = 0.90), it still showed a positive performance for making predictions. Compared with results of works directly related to this research ([25,26]), Model 4 showed improvements of 60% in the RMSE metric shared by both works, while the model of the second type exceeded an average of 45%. This work also stands out for the use of a large dataset (more than 100,000 records) for model training and validation, which contributed to its good level of precision. In addition, a computational tool was developed for the implementation of the models and experiments, which stands out for its simplicity and flexibility in the generation of different forecast models. Due to the generality of this tool, it can be applied to other contexts such as wind energy forecasting or others, adjusting the input data and hyperparameters according to the transformations described in Section 3.4.

As a future work, the architecture, performance, and accuracy of the models can be improved. This can be done by generating new models with different configurations and RNN structures using various combinations of hyperparameters. The data set for training and validation can also be increased by incorporating additional records. Another interesting line of research would be to integrate physical aspects, such as the internal composition of the photovoltaic modules or the temperature generated by sun radiation in these components. Finally, the application of this approach to other sources of renewable energy can be explored.

Author Contributions: W.C.-R., overall structure of work, introduction, related works, review of final results, and conclusions; C.H., development of experiments and testing of models; F.M.Q., analysis of results. All authors have read and agreed to the published version of the manuscript.

Funding: This research received no external funding.

Data Availability Statement: The data presented in this study are available from the corresponding author upon request. The data are not publicly available due to their containing confidential information from Solar Brothers SPA.

Acknowledgments: This work has been funded by the FIUDA2030 project of University of Atacama under Research CORFO/ANID 18ENI2-106198. The work was also supported by the Program "Nueva Ingeniería 2030" of the Faculty of Engineering and Architecture, Arturo Prat University.

Conflicts of Interest: The authors declare no conflict of interest.

References

1. International Energy Agency. *Trends in Photovoltaic Applications 2018*; Report publisher by IEA PVPS T1-34: Paris, France, 2018; Volume 23, ISBN 978-3-906042-79-4.
2. Arshian Sharif, A.; Saeed, M.; Ferdous, M.; Sohag, K. Role of solar energy in reducing ecological footprints: An empirical analysis. *J. Clean. Prod.* **2021**, *292*, 126028. [CrossRef]
3. Schloss, M.J. *Cambio climático y Energía: ¿Quo vadis?*, Encuentros multidisciplinares: Energía, Medio Ambiente y Avances Científicos; N° 62; Editorial Dialnet de la Universidad de la Rioja: La Rioja, España, 2019; Volume 21, ISSN 1139-9325.
4. Maleki, A.; Ahmadi, A.; Venkatesan, S. Optimal design and analysis of solar photovoltaic systems to reduce carbon footprint. *Renew. Energy* **2019**, *141*, 76–87. [CrossRef]
5. Boer, S.; Steinberger-Wilckens, R.; Buchholz, D.; Meissner, D.; Schebek, L. Environmental impact and economic analysis of an integrated photovoltaic-hydrogen system for residential applications. *Appl. Energy* **2020**, *276*, 115349.
6. Iheanetu, K.J. Solar Photovoltaic Power Forecasting: A Review. *Sustainability* **2022**, *14*, 17005. [CrossRef]
7. Yesilbudak, M.; Çolak, M.; Bayindir, R. A review of data mining and solar power prediction. In Proceedings of the 2016 IEEE International Conference on Renewable Energy Research and Applications (ICRERA), Birmingham, UK, 20–23 November 2016; pp. 1117–1121.
8. Berzal, F. *Redes Neuronales & Deep Learning*; Editorial Universidad de Granada: Granada, España, 2018; ISBN-10 1-7313-1433-7, ISBN-13 978-1-7313-1433-8.
9. Kukreja, H.; Bharath, N.; Siddesh, C.; Kuldeep, S. An Introduction to Artificial Neural Network. *Int. J. Adv. Res. Innov. Ideas Educ.* **2016**, *1*, 27–30.
10. Nwankpa, C.; Ijomah, W.; Gachagan, A.; Marshall, S. Activation Functions: Comparison of Trends in Practice and Research for Deep Learning. *arXiv* **2018**, arXiv:1811.03378.
11. Castillo-Rojas, W.; Bekios-Calfa, J.; Hernández, C. Daily Prediction Model of Photovoltaic Power Generation Using a Hybrid Architecture of Recurrent Neural Networks and Shallow Neural Networks. *Int. J. Photoenergy* **2023**, *2023*, 2592405. [CrossRef]
12. Maciel, J.N.; Wentz, V.H.; Ledesma, J.J.G.; Junior, O.H.A. Analysis of Artificial Neural Networks for Forecasting Photovoltaic Energy Generation with Solar Irradiance. *Braz. Arch. Biol. Technol.* **2021**, *64 no.spe*, e21210131. [CrossRef]
13. Rodríguez, F.; Azcárate, I.; Vadillo, J.; Galarza, A. Forecasting intra-hour solar photovoltaic energy by assembling wavelet-based time-frequency analysis with deep learning neural networks. *Int. J. Electr. Power Energy Syst.* **2021**, *137*, 107777. [CrossRef]
14. Carrera, B.; Sim, M.; Jung, J. PVHybNet: A hybrid framework for predicting photovoltaic power generation using both weather forecast and observation data. *IET Renew. Power Gener.* **2020**, *14*, 2192–2201. [CrossRef]
15. Rosato, A.; Araneo, R.; Andreotti, A.; Panella, M. Predictive Analysis of Photovoltaic Power Generation Using Deep Learning. In Proceedings of the IEEE International Conference on Environment and Electrical Engineering and IEEE Industrial and Commercial Power Systems Europe (EEEIC/I&CPS EUROPE), Genova, Italy, 10–14 June 2019.
16. Yu, Y.; Cao, J.; Zhu, J. An LSTM Short-Term Solar Irradiance Forecasting Under Complicated Weather Conditions. *IEEE Access* **2019**, *7*, 145651–145666. [CrossRef]
17. Hui, L.; Ren, Z.; Yan, X.; Li, W.; Hu, B. A Multi-Data Driven Hybrid Learning Method for Weekly Photovoltaic Power Scenario Forecast. *IEEE Trans. Sustain. Energy* **2022**, *13*, 91–100. [CrossRef]
18. Xu, D.; Shao, H.; Deng, X.; Wang, X. The Hidden-Layers Topology Analysis of Deep Learning Models in Survey for Forecasting and Generation of the Wind Power and Photovoltaic Energy. *Comput. Model. Eng. Sci.* **2022**, *131*, 567–597. [CrossRef]
19. Nkambule, M.S.; Hasan, A.N.; Ali, A.; Hong, J.; Geem, Z.W. Comprehensive Evaluation of Machine Learning MPPT Algorithms for a PV System Under Different Weather Conditions. *J. Electr. Eng. Technol.* **2020**, *16*, 411–427. [CrossRef]

20. Wang, F.; Yu, Y.; Zhang, Z.; Li, J.; Zhen, Z.; Li, K. Wavelet Decomposition and Convolutional LSTM Networks Based Improved Deep Learning Model for Solar Irradiance Forecasting. *Appl. Sci.* **2018**, *8*, 1286. [CrossRef]
21. AlKandari, M.; Ahmad, I. Solar power generation forecasting using ensemble approach based on deep learning and statistical methods. *Appl. Comput. Inform.* 2019. ahead-of-print. [CrossRef]
22. Sharma, E. Energy forecasting based on predictive data mining techniques in smart energy grids. *Energy Inform.* **2018**, *1*, 44. [CrossRef]
23. Harrou, F.; Kadri, F.; Sun, Y. Forecasting of Photovoltaic Solar Power Production Using LSTM Approach. In *Advanced Statistical Modeling, Forecasting, and Fault Detection in Renewable Energy Systems*; IntechOpen: London, UK, 2020. [CrossRef]
24. De, V.; Teo, T.; Woo, W.; Logenthiran, T. Photovoltaic power forecasting using LSTM on limited dataset. In Proceedings of the 2018 IEEE Innovative Smart Grid Technologies-Asia (ISGT Asia), Singapore, 22–25 May 2018; pp. 710–715.
25. Chen, B.; Lin, P.; Lai, Y.; Cheng, S.; Chen, Z.; Wu, L. Very-Short-Term Power Prediction for PV Power Plants Using a Simple and Effective RCC-LSTM Model Based on Short Term Multivariate Historical Datasets. *Electronics* **2020**, *9*, 289. [CrossRef]
26. Sharadga, H.; Hajimirza, S.; Balog, R.S. Time series forecasting of solar power generation for large-scale photovoltaic plants. *Renew. Energy* **2019**, *150*, 797–807. [CrossRef]
27. Rajagukguk, R.A.; Ramadhan, R.A.; Lee, H.-J. A Review on Deep Learning Models for Forecasting Time Series Data of Solar Irradiance and Photovoltaic Power. *Energies* **2020**, *13*, 6623. [CrossRef]
28. Seera, M.; Jun, C.; Chong, K.; Peng, C. Performance analyses of various commercial photovoltaic modules based on local spectral irradiances in Malaysia using genetic algorithm. *Energy J.* **2021**, *223*, 120009. [CrossRef]
29. Chong, K.-K.; Khlyabich, P.P.; Hong, K.-J.; Reyes-Martinez, M.; Rand, B.P.; Loo, Y.-L. Comprehensive method for analyzing the power conversion efficiency of organic solar cells under different spectral irradiances considering both photonic and electrical characteristics. *Appl. Energy* **2016**, *180*, 516–523. [CrossRef]
30. Jaber, M.; Hamid, A.S.A.; Sopian, K.; Fazlizan, A.; Ibrahim, A. Prediction Model for the Performance of Different PV Modules Using Artificial Neural Networks. *Appl. Sci.* **2022**, *12*, 3349. [CrossRef]
31. Diouf, M.C.; Faye, M.; Thiam, A.; Ndiaye, A.; Sambou, V. Modeling of the Photovoltaic Module Operating Temperature for Various Weather Conditions in the Tropical Region. *Fluid Dyn. Mater. Process.* **2022**, *18*, 1275–1284. [CrossRef]
32. Bevilacqua, P.; Perrella, S.; Bruno, R.; Arcuri, N. An accurate thermal model for the PV electric generation prediction: Long-term validation in different climatic conditions. *Renew. Energy* **2020**, *163*, 1092–1112. [CrossRef]
33. Zhang, S.; Wang, J.; Liu, H.; Tong, J.; Sun, Z. Prediction of energy photovoltaic power generation based on artificial intelligence algorithm. *Neural Comput. Appl.* **2020**, *33*, 821–835. [CrossRef]
34. He, B.; Ma, R.; Zhang, W.; Zhu, J.; Zhang, X. An Improved Generating Energy Prediction Method Based on Bi-LSTM and Attention Mechanism. *Electronics* **2022**, *11*, 1885. [CrossRef]
35. Chen, H.; Chang, X. Photovoltaic power prediction of LSTM model based on Pearson feature selection. *Energy Rep.* **2021**, *7*, 1047–1054. [CrossRef]
36. Konstantinou, M.; Peratikou, S.; Charalambides, A.G. Solar Photovoltaic Forecasting of Power Output Using LSTM Networks. *Atmosphere* **2021**, *12*, 124. [CrossRef]
37. Niccolai, A.; Dolara, A.; Ogliari, E. Hybrid PV Power Forecasting Methods: A Comparison of Different Approaches. *Energies* **2021**, *14*, 451. [CrossRef]
38. Hochreiter, S.; Schmidhuber, J. Long Short-Term Memory. *Neural Comput.* **1997**, *9*, 1735–1780. [CrossRef] [PubMed]
39. Schuster, M.; Paliwal, K.K. Bidirectional recurrent neural networks. *IEEE Trans. Signal Process.* **1997**, *45*, 2673–2681. [CrossRef]
40. Chang, S.; Zhang, Y.; Han, W.; Yu, M.; Guo, X.; Tan, W.; Cui, X.; Witbrock, M.J.; Hasegawa-Johnson, M.; Huang, T.S. Dilated Recurrent Neural Networks. In Proceedings of the Advances in Neural Information Processing Systems 30: Annual Conference on Neural Information Processing Systems 2017, Long Beach, CA, USA, 4–9 December 2017; pp. 76–86.
41. Beer, K.; Bondarenko, D.; Farrelly, T.; Osborne, T.J.; Salzmann, R.; Scheiermann, D.; Wolf, R. Training deep quantum neural networks. *Nat. Commun.* **2020**, *11*, 808. [CrossRef]
42. Zhou, M.-G.; Cao, X.-Y.; Lu, Y.-S.; Wang, Y.; Bao, Y.; Jia, Z.-Y.; Fu, Y.; Yin, H.-L.; Chen, Z.-B. Experimental Quantum Advantage with Quantum Coupon Collector. *Research* **2022**, *2022*, 9798679. [CrossRef]
43. Zhou, M.-G.; Liu, Z.-P.; Yin, H.-L.; Li, C.-L.; Xu, T.-K.; Chen, Z.-B. Quantum Neural Network for Quantum Neural Computing. *Research* **2023**, *6*, 0134. [CrossRef]
44. Dairi, A.; Harrou, F.; Sun, Y.; Khadraoui, S. Short-Term Forecasting of Photovoltaic Solar Power Production Using Variational Auto-Encoder Driven Deep Learning Approach. *Appl. Sci.* **2020**, *10*, 8400. [CrossRef]
45. Solanki, N.; Panchal, G. A Novel Machine Learning Based Approach for Rainfall Prediction. In *Information and Communication Technology for Intelligent Systems (ICTIS 2017)-Volume 1. ICTIS 2017. Smart Innovation, Systems and Technologies*; Satapathy, S., Joshi, A., Eds.; Springer: Cham, Switzerland, 2018; Volume 83, pp. 314–319. [CrossRef]
46. Choi, J.-E.; Lee, H.; Song, J. Forecasting daily PM10concentrations in Seoul using various data mining techniques. *Commun. Stat. Appl. Methods* **2018**, *25*, 199–215. [CrossRef]
47. Cambronero, C.G.; Moreno, I.G. Algoritmos de aprendizaje: KNN & KMeans. *Inteligencia en Redes de Comunicación*; Universidad Carlos III de Madrid: Madrid, Spain, 2006; p. 8. Available online: http://blogs.ujaen.es/barranco/wp-content/uploads/2012/02/Algoritmos-de-aprendizaje-knn-y-kmeans.pdf (accessed on 16 December 2022).

48. Orellana, M.; Cedillo, P. Detección de valores atípicos con técnicas de minería de datos y métodos estadísticos. *Rev. Enfoque UTE* **2020**, *11*, 56–67. [CrossRef]
49. Shabib, A.; Munir, A.; Noureen, H.; Muhammad, S.; Bashir, I.; Zahid, N. Rainfall Prediction in Lahore City using Data Mining Techniques. *Int. J. Adv. Comput. Sci. Appl. (IJACSA)* **2018**, *9*, 090439. [CrossRef]

Disclaimer/Publisher's Note: The statements, opinions and data contained in all publications are solely those of the individual author(s) and contributor(s) and not of MDPI and/or the editor(s). MDPI and/or the editor(s) disclaim responsibility for any injury to people or property resulting from any ideas, methods, instructions or products referred to in the content.

Communication

Exploring the PV Power Forecasting at Building Façades Using Gradient Boosting Methods

Jesús Polo *, Nuria Martín-Chivelet, Miguel Alonso-Abella, Carlos Sanz-Saiz, José Cuenca and Marina de la Cruz

Photovoltaic Solar Energy Unit, Renewable Energy Division, CIEMAT, Avda. Complutense 40, 28040 Madrid, Spain
* Correspondence: jesus.polo@ciemat.es

Abstract: Solar power forecasting is of high interest in managing any power system based on solar energy. In the case of photovoltaic (PV) systems, and building integrated PV (BIPV) in particular, it may help to better operate the power grid and to manage the power load and storage. Power forecasting directly based on PV time series has some advantages over solar irradiance forecasting first and PV power modeling afterwards. In this paper, the power forecasting for BIPV systems in a vertical façade is studied using machine learning algorithms based on decision trees. The forecasting scheme employs the skforecast library from the Python environment, which facilitates the implementation of different schemes for both deterministic and probabilistic forecasting applications. Firstly, deterministic forecasting of hourly BIPV power was performed with XGBoost and Random Forest algorithms for different cases, showing an improvement in forecasting accuracy when some exogenous variables were used. Secondly, probabilistic forecasting was performed with XGBoost combined with the Bootstrap method. The results of this paper show the capabilities of Random Forest and gradient boosting algorithms, such as XGBoost, to work as regressors in time series forecasting of BIPV power. Mean absolute error in the deterministic forecast, using the most influencing exogenous variables, were around 40% and close below 30% for the south and east array, respectively.

Keywords: BIPV; PV power forecasting; machine learning; gradient boosting algorithms

1. Introduction

The large expansion and growth of photovoltaic (PV) systems and the foreseen future increase are driving a strong impulse for distributed power generation. PV operation in urban environments and building integrated photovoltaics (BIPV) are good examples of topics that are significantly drawing the attention of the PV community and industry [1]. BIPV comprises those modules and systems that can serve as conventional building components and produce energy at the same time. Architectural, power and aesthetic aspects are all important in designing BIPV systems, and thus a wide variety of designs are emerging in the industry [2–4]. The specific features of BIPV systems have an impact on the thermal and electrical performance so adapted or new testing procedures, standards and modeling methodologies are being developed [5,6]. Modeling BIPV systems is challenging since the modules work under frequent partial shading conditions and also their thermal boundary conditions can be different from conventional PV plants [7–9]. Parametric 3D tools and models are being used to better approach the complex geometries and shading patterns produced by neighboring buildings [10]. In addition, the usual PV cell temperature models may be less accurate in the case of PV in façades affecting, consequently, the power prediction accuracy [11]. Challenges in modeling PV façades performance have been remarked on in several previous works of the authors at Ciemat using different approaches [12,13].

Solar forecasting is an important part of the management of solar power generation. In particular, PV solar power forecasting is helpful in electric grid management, load management and battery storage operation. A comprehensive overview of solar forecasting, including basic concepts, models and selected examples can be found in the reports delivered by IEA-PVPS Task 16 [14]. Most developments in solar forecasting have been made in the prediction of solar irradiance as a previous step to solar power forecasting, and many important contributions have been reported in recent years [15,16]. Thus, PV power forecast is performed by forecasting solar irradiance as a first step and deriving afterwards the PV power with a simulation model [17]. An alternative way consists of forecasting directly the AC PV power from historical time series, which requires no detailed knowledge of the PV system and the involved meteorological variables (module temperature and irradiance forecasts) and relying on the quality of the historical data [18,19].

Time series PV power forecasting is usually performed by autoregressive models or by machine learning methods. The latter are being recently used preferably due to the availability of advanced and powerful machine learning algorithms [20–23]. Artificial Neural Networks (ANNs) and Support Vector Machines (SVMs) are two of the most popular methods for forecasting time series of solar irradiance [24,25]. However, gradient boosting decision trees (GBDT) methods are gaining popularity in the most recent years due to their accuracy and computation speed proven in many Kaggle data science competitions. XGBoost (extreme gradient boosting) and CatBoost (categorical boosting) algorithms are two of the most successful GBDT methods for regression and classification [26,27].

Despite there being many works in the literature dealing with solar irradiance forecasting, PV power forecasting based on time series is much less studied and, in particular, BIPV power forecasting is practically not covered by the solar forecasting community. The present work is thus aimed at contributing to filling the gap of studies focused on BIPV power forecasting. BIPV power forecast applying the usual developments in solar irradiance forecasting involves deriving the Plane of Array (POA) irradiance from the forecasted global irradiance using a transposition model and then modeling the power with a PV model, which also requires the forecasting of the module temperature. Therefore, the forecasting uncertainty of the strategy based on solar irradiance forecasting has to include the combined uncertainty of the intermediate steps (transposition, power modeling, temperature and so on). In comparison, BIPV power forecasting using time series and machine learning only requires the measuring values of the power in the past, and it might be a more suitable approach. There are many works dealing with machine learning in solar forecasting, and most of them are based on solar irradiance forecasting. Support vector machines, neural networks and Long Short-Term Memory (LSTM) networks are very popular [28–30]. However, for large datasets, parameter tuning can be complicated [31]. Decision trees are versatile, fast and very efficient machine learning algorithms due to their simplicity. In this work, we are exploring the performance of the XGBoost and Random Forest models in forecasting hourly time series of BIPV power in a building at Ciemat headquarters using different exogenous variables. In addition to deterministic forecasting with machine learning, this work explores the capability of the XGBoost algorithm in probabilistic forecasting. Both Random Forest and XGBoost can be implemented in a straightforward way into forecasting schemes; in particular, they were implemented in the *skforecast* scheme (a very powerful library for addressing time series forecasting problems in python). In this work, the forecasting of BIPV power for two small arrays (south- and east-oriented) has been analyzed with these two algorithms. General good performance is observed in both methods for the case of deterministic forecasting, where the mean absolute error was placed at around 30% in the case of the east-oriented array and around 40% in the case of the south-oriented.

2. Materials and Methods

2.1. Test Facility and Experimental Data

In this work, we are using two years of monitored data corresponding to two PV arrays integrated into the south and east façades of Building 42 at Ciemat headquarters in Madrid (Spain). The geographic coordinates of the site are 40.45° N, −3.73° E, and the altitude is 695 m; the climatology according to the Koeppen climate classification is Csa (i.e., dry-summer subtropical, often referred to as Mediterranean climate). The PV modules are situated at the top of each façade (Figure 1). The arrays consist of monocrystalline silicon modules with seven series by two parallel (7sx2p) configurations for the east array and 7sx4p configuration for the south array. The south array, with a power of 8 kW, contains SunPower E18-325 modules (305 W each one) and a Fronius IG Plus 100 V-3 inverter. The east array, with a nominal power of 4 kW, consists of SunPower E20-327 modules (327 W each one) and a Fronius IG Plus 50 V-1 inverter.

Figure 1. View of the south and east arrays in the Ciemat building.

The experimental database contains hourly mean values of power, current and voltage at maximum power for each array, as well as hourly values of the module temperature and ambient temperature. Global horizontal irradiance and POA irradiance at south and east azimuths are measured with calibrated PV cells and are also available on an hourly basis.

2.2. Methodology

Gradient boosting decision trees (GBDT) are a machine learning technique that combines the prediction from multiple models (weak learners) to obtain a better predictive performance in an iterative and sequential way, where each predictor fixes its predecessor's error. XGBoost is a powerful and very popular open-source algorithm due to its speed and accuracy. XGBoost is a parallelized and optimized version of the gradient boosting algorithm [32]. It has been successfully used in many different disciplines involving big data science during the last recent years [26]. On the other hand, Random Forest is another popular effective ensemble machine learning algorithm, also based on decision trees, which has been used recently in solar irradiance forecasting [33,34]. Both algorithms can be implemented in a time series forecasting scheme. In this work, we have used the *skforecast* library in python, which contains the necessary classes and functions to adapt any Scikit-learn regression model, such as XGBoost and Random Forest, to forecasting problems [35].

The data used in this work consist of two years (2017–2018) of monitored PV power on an hourly basis of two BIPV arrays corresponding to the façade south and east of a building. The data are divided into three sets, namely the training, validation and test datasets. The model is first trained with the training set, and secondly, it is evaluated with the validation set using back-testing in order to select the combination of hyper-parameters and lags leading to the lowest error. Finally, the model is trained again with the best combination using both training and validation data. Figure 2 shows the different data sets selected for this work. Using the *skforecast* scheme, we have trained two different models to forecast hourly values of the power of each array using 72 lags. Explorative work, using back-testing, has been addressed by trying a different number of lags and has shown that 72 lags yield better results than larger or shorter ones. The hyper-parameters are certain values or weights that control the learning process. In this work, the hyper-parameters selected were: maximum depth per tree which took 3, 5 and 10 as possible values; the learning rate (0.01 and 0.1) for controlling the step size at each iteration; the number of trees in the ensemble, which was selected in 100 and 500.

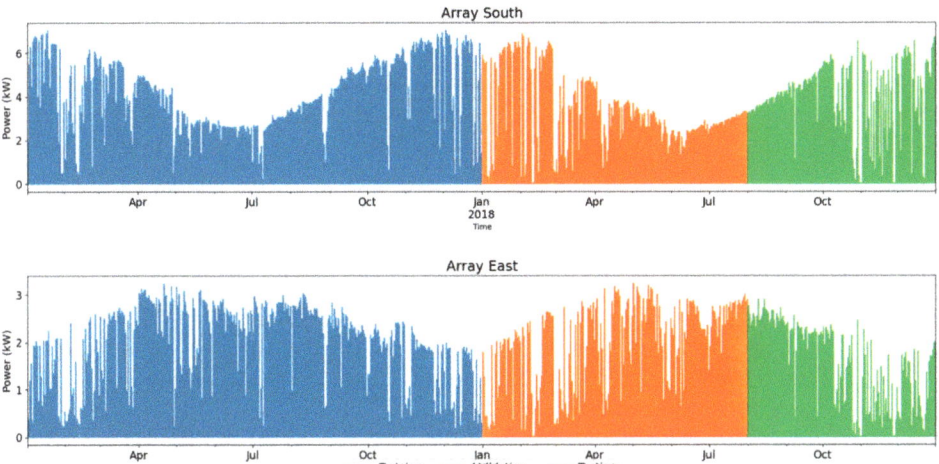

Figure 2. BIPV power datasets for south and east arrays.

In addition to the predictors (i.e., the array power), it is possible to add exogenous variables that may explain the regression model. Exogenous variables are those parameters that can be known or derived in the future. Clear sky irradiance, solar geometry-related variables and shadowing fraction are plausible examples of exogenous variables. In this work, we have explored the role of several exogenous variables: POA irradiance under clear sky (POA_cs), cosine of the incidence angle (cosAOI), shaded fraction of array surface (FS), sun azimuth (SunAz) and month number (m). The solar geometry and the POA irradiance under clear sky are calculated with the pvlib library [36], which contains the most updated information and models for solar resource computation. POA_cs is computed by calculating first the three solar irradiance components (global, direct and diffuse irradiance) for a horizontal surface using Ineichen's model [37]; then, Perez's model is used to transpose the horizontal components to the vertically tilted surfaces [38]. The shaded fraction of array surface was calculated in previous works where LIDAR data were used for computing a digital surface model (DSM) of the building and surroundings that allows shadow computation throughout the year [13]. In order to explore which exogenous variables work better in the forecasting scheme, the case matrix in Table 1 has been tested for each array and each algorithm.

Table 1. Case matrix for exploring the role of exogenous variables.

Case	Predictor	Exogenous Variables
Base Case	Power	None
Case 1	Power	POA_cs
Case 2	Power	POA_cs, cosAOI
Case 3	Power	POA_cs, cosAOI, FS
Case 4	Power	POA_cs, cosAOI, FS, SunAz
Case 5	Power	POA_cs, cosAOI, FS, SunAz, m

The correlation coefficients of each exogenous variable with the array power calculated with the Pearson linear correlation (R_{xy}) were, in descending order, 0.75, 0.63, 0.45, 0.09 and −0.08 for POA_cs, cosAOI, FS, m and SunAz, respectively.

$$R_{xy} = \frac{N \sum xy - \sum x \sum y}{\sqrt{N \sum x^2 - (\sum x)^2} \sqrt{N \sum y^2 - (\sum y)^2}} \quad (1)$$

where x represents the power and y refers to any exogenous variable.

Figure 3 shows the autocorrelation of the power time series for the two arrays under study.

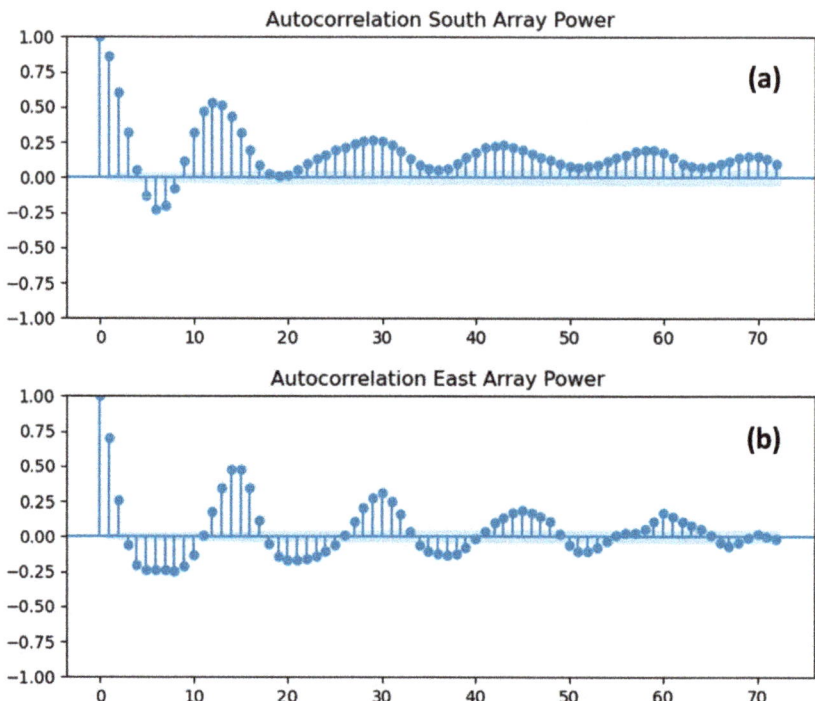

Figure 3. Autocorrelation plots for the array power: (**a**) South array. (**b**) East array.

3. Results

3.1. Deterministic Forecasting Using XGBoost and Random Forest

Deterministic forecasting refers to the prediction of single values (hourly values in the case of this work) in the future. Hence, hourly values of BIPV array power are forecasted for each array covering the different cases listed in Table 1 using XGBoost and Random Forest as regression algorithms in the skforecast scheme. The results are validated with the test dataset. Figures 4 and 5 show the scatter plot of the hourly power forecasted values for the south and east arrays, respectively.

Random Forest as a regressor in the forecasting model resulted in slightly more accurate forecasting than XGBoost. Furthermore, in both cases, the use of exogenous variables in the forecasting scheme improves the results.

The metrics used in the evaluation of forecasting the hourly power are mean bias error (MBE), normalized mean absolute error (nMAE) and root mean squared error (RMSE) [39].

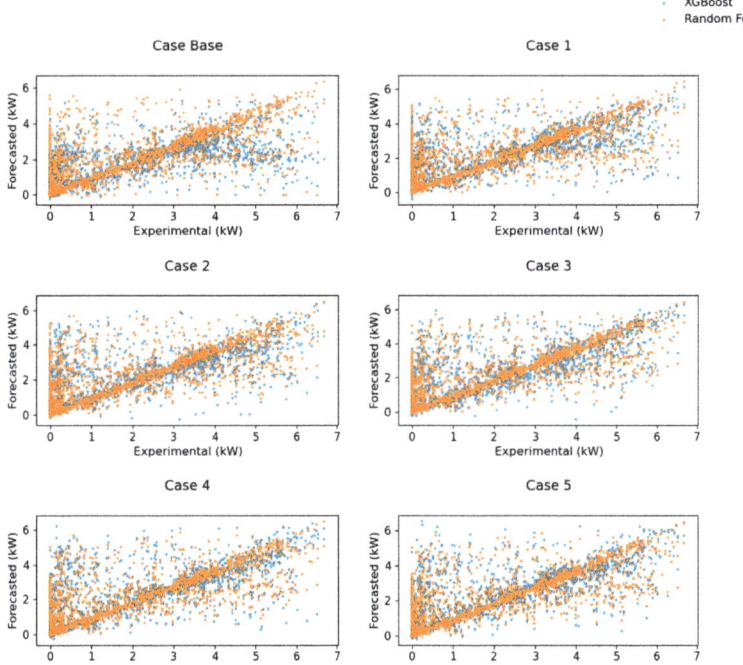

Figure 4. Scatter plot of forecasted power for south array.

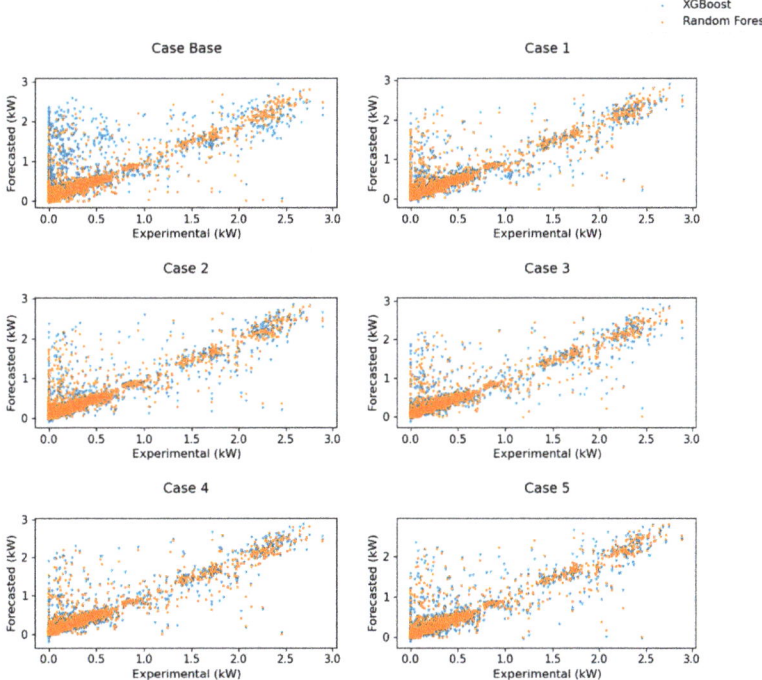

Figure 5. Scatter plot of forecasted power for east array.

$$MBE = \frac{1}{n}\sum\left(P_{measured} - P_{forecasted}\right) \qquad (2)$$

$$nMAE = \frac{1}{\langle P_{measured}\rangle}\frac{1}{n}\sum abs\left(P_{measured} - P_{forecasted}\right) \qquad (3)$$

$$RMSE = \sqrt{\frac{\sum\left(P_{measured} - P_{forecasted}\right)^2}{n}} \qquad (4)$$

where $P_{measured}$ is the experimental power of the array, $P_{forecasted}$ refers to the forecasted power values and $\langle P_{measured}\rangle$ is the arithmetic mean value of $P_{measured}$.

Figure 6 compares the MBE and RMSE metrics for XGBoost and Random Forest in both arrays. In the case of array south, the nMAE ranges from 54% to 42% with XGBoost, and from 43% to 40% with the Random Forest algorithm used in the *skforecast* scheme. On the other hand, in the case of array east, the nMAE is very high for the case base with XGBoost; the nMAE of all the studied cases varies from 72% to 28%. For Random Forest, the nMAE is in the range of 29–23%. The determination coefficient R^2 varies in the range of 0.60–0.69 in both methods (Random Forest and XGBoost) for the south array, and it reaches 0.80–0.85 in the case of the east array. Therefore, in all cases, the use of exogenous variables as additional explicative variables improves the performance of the forecasting. Moreover, the forecasting scheme performs better for the array east than for the south. For the south array, the use of clear sky in-plane irradiance (POA_cs) as an exogenous variable produces power forecasting with the minimum bias compared to the other cases. In the case of array east, the inclusion of shadowing information (FS) in addition to POA_cs as exogenous variables resulted in a more accurate forecast since this façade is much more influenced by shadows than the south-oriented one. Finally, Figure 7 illustrates the hourly power forecasted in several days for south and east arrays with the best performance cases, which are case 1 and case 3 (Table 1). The forecasting results improve significantly with the use of those exogenous variables with higher correlation coefficients, which correspond to case 3. Cases 4 and 5 do not add significant improvement to case 3. In terms of RMSE, the forecasting using Random Forest performs slightly better than XGBoost for most of the cases. However, it should be remarked that in the south array, case 3 (the best case of exogenous variables) resulted in much lower bias. Lowering the bias is important in forecasting when the dispersion of the forecasted data (RMSE) are very similar with both machine learning methods.

3.2. Probabilistic and Intervals Forecasting

The *skforecast* library allows the estimation of forecasting intervals based on bootstrapped residuals. Detailed information on the bootstrap method for interval prediction in solar power can be found in recent literature [40]. For forecasting intervals, case 3 of Table 1 has been selected since the inclusion of such exogenous variables improves the accuracy of the forecast. Moreover, preliminary simulations found that XGBoost was more suitable than Rain Forest for this type of forecast. Thus, the XGBoost regressor has been used with the bootstrap method to produce forecasting intervals. The results for forecasting 10–90% intervals with the bootstrap method for several days are illustrated for both arrays in Figure 8.

In order to evaluate the probabilistic prediction results, several metrics are frequently used. The Prediction Interval Coverage Probability (PICP) is defined as the proportion of the data covered by the forecasted interval [31].

$$\text{PICP} = \frac{1}{n}\sum c_i, \quad c_i = \begin{cases} 1, & lower_i \leq c_i \leq upper_i \\ 0, & otherwise \end{cases} \qquad (5)$$

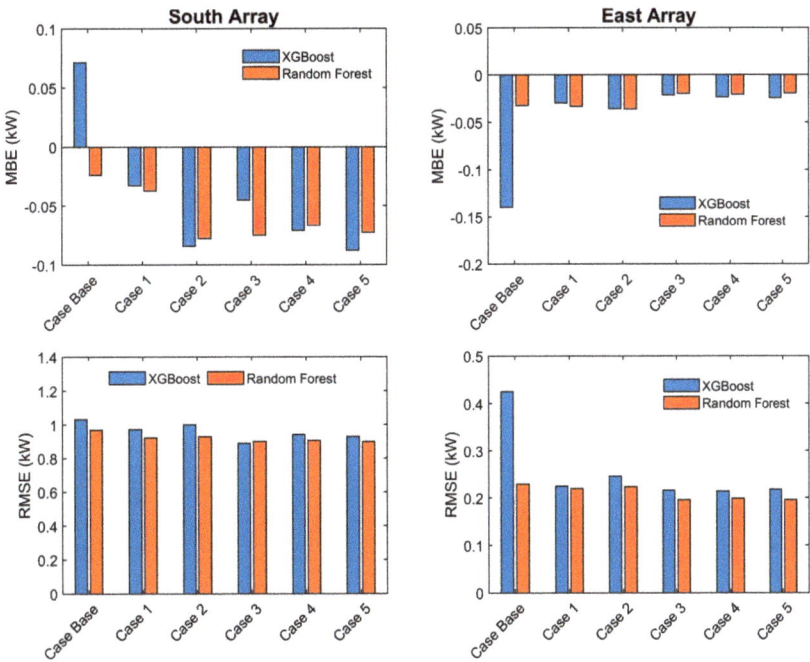

Figure 6. MBE and RMSE values for both arrays and all the cases.

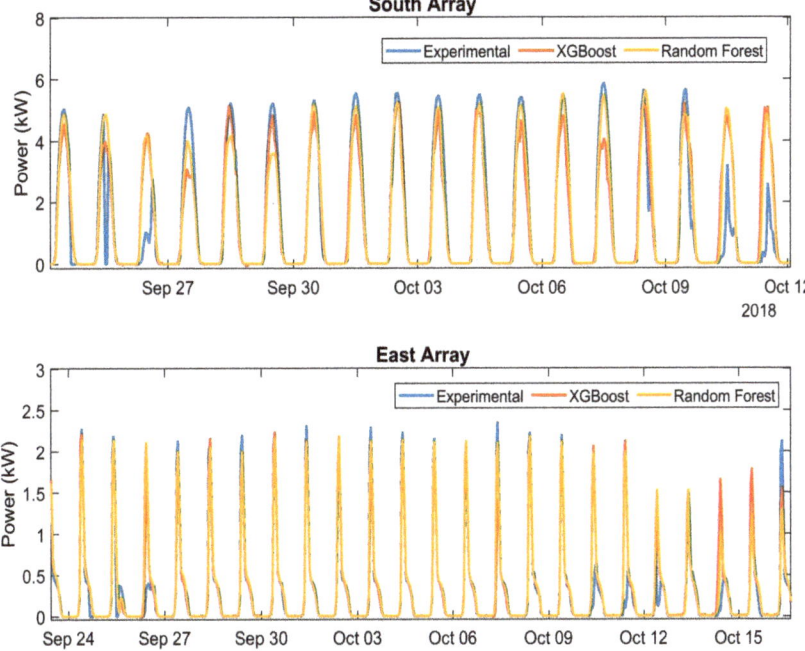

Figure 7. Hourly power forecasted for south and west arrays for the best performance cases.

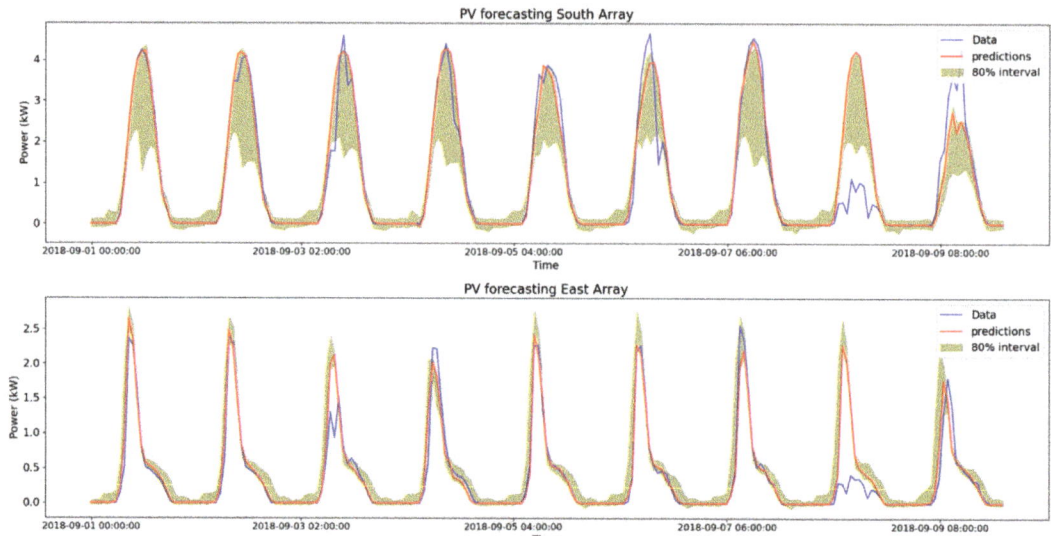

Figure 8. Probabilistic forecasting of the BIPV power for south and east arrays.

The Mean Prediction Interval Width (MPIW) is defined as,

$$\text{MPIW} = \frac{1}{R\,n} \sum (upper_i - lower_i) \qquad (6)$$

where R is the range of the target values (i.e., the difference between maximum and minimum power of the array). The higher the PICP value, the higher the reliability of the forecast, and the lower the MPIW value, the narrower the width of the forecasted interval. Table 2 shows the metrics for the south and east arrays. The coverage of both arrays is below 80% in both cases, but higher reliability is achieved in forecasting intervals for the east array. The intervals of probabilistic forecasting of the east array are narrower than in the case of the south array, and the coverage (PICP) is also greater (nearly 80%).

Table 2. Metrics for evaluating interval forecasting.

Array	PICP (%)	MPIW (%)
South	69.52	11.34
East	78.01	7.05

4. Discussion

Forecasting PV power directly offers some advantages over forecasting solar irradiance and modeling afterwards the PV power from the forecasted irradiance. In the case of BIPV, and particularly for PV modules in façade, the intermediate steps between solar irradiance forecasting and PV power forecasting include the use of transposition models, temperature forecasting and PV modeling. The alternative strategy is to directly forecast the PV power based on historical values (i.e., time series forecasting). Machine learning algorithms have evolved and grown considerably in the recent few years, and nowadays, there are available tools that integrate machine learning algorithms with forecasting schemes. The library *skforecast* is a good example of a tool that makes it easier to use scikit-learn machine learning regressors as forecasters.

Decision tree regressors such as XGBoost and Random Forest have been explored in this work as forecasters for BIPV power hourly forecasting. Both deterministic and probabilistic forecasting schemes have been applied to two BIPV arrays (south and east façades) monitored in a building in Madrid (Spain). Furthermore, XGBoost and Random Forest can be effectively integrated into a deterministic forecasting scheme. In both cases, the use of exogenous variables (i.e., those variables that can be securely known in the future), such as clear sky irradiance, solar geometry-related variables and shading patterns in the building, resulted in more accurate forecasted hourly values. The minimum mean absolute errors achieved were around 40% for the south array and close to 30% in the case of the East array. In addition, probabilistic forecasting has been explored using the XGBoost regressor with bootstrapped residuals. Better results were found for the East array, where the coverage of the forecasted interval was 78%. This work has shown the potential of these new forecasting tools for both deterministic and probabilistic forecasting of BIPV power on an hourly basis. The combination of different machine learning algorithms and different forecasting strategies (e.g., recursive multi-steps, hyper-parameter tuning, back-testing) could conduct more accurate results. Future work is expected in this regard to explore new forecasting schemes.

5. Conclusions

PV power forecasting is essential in managing the electrical grid and storage systems. In the particular case of BIPV, with the increasing growth of its deployment, it can be even more important. This paper has explored two machine learning algorithms based of decision trees in forecasting BIPV power from time series of power. Random Forest and XGBoost are able to forecast directly PV power with much better performance when highly correlated variables are used as exogenous variables. Random Forest achieved, in general, slightly better RMSE than XGBoost for most cases in deterministic forecasting. However, the best accuracy was observed in case 3, with XGBoost showing an RMSE of 0.89 kW and 0.21 kW for south and east arrays, respectively; moreover, very similar RMSE results of 0.9 kW and 0.20 kW for south and east arrays were found in the case of Random Forest. In probabilistic forecasting, XGBoost was used for south and east arrays with good results within the 10–90% interval.

XGBoost algorithm presents the advantage of a very easy and fast implementation method in forecasting schemes (as the *skforecast* library), having fast execution and making possible the use of both deterministic and probabilistic forecasting strategies based on time series forecasting. This versatility makes it a very interesting option in machine learning forecasting techniques for BIPV applications.

Author Contributions: Conceptualization, J.P. and N.M.-C.; methodology, J.P.; software, J.P.; validation, J.P., N.M.-C. and M.A.-A.; formal analysis, J.P., N.M.-C. and C.S.-S.; investigation, J.P., N.M.-C. and C.S.-S.; resources, M.A.-A., J.C. and M.d.l.C.; data curation, M.A.-A., J.C. and M.d.l.C.; writing—original draft preparation, J.P.; writing—review and editing, N.M.-C. and C.S.-S.; funding acquisition, J.P. and N.M.-C. All authors have read and agreed to the published version of the manuscript.

Funding: This research was funded by Spanish Ministry of Science and Innovation, grant number PID2021-124910OB-C31.

Institutional Review Board Statement: Not applicable.

Informed Consent Statement: Not applicable.

Data Availability Statement: Not applicable.

Acknowledgments: The authors would like to thank the RINGS-BIPV (Advanced Modeling and Prediction of BIPV) Project (PID2021-124910OB-C31), which is funded by the Ministerio de Ciencia e Innovación (Spain). The authors would also like to recognize the efforts, research and contributions of the experts groups of IEA PVPS Program, in particular those corresponding to Task 15 (BIPV) and Task 16 (Solar Resource), where the authors have an active collaboration.

Conflicts of Interest: The authors declare no conflict of interest.

References

1. Jakica, N.; Ynag, R.J.; Eisenlohr, J. *BIPV Design and Performance Modelling: Tools and Methods*; International Energy Agency: Paris, France, 2019; ISBN 9783906042862. Available online: https://www.iea.org/ (accessed on 21 December 2022).
2. Eder, G.; Peharz, G.G.; Trattni, R.; Bonomo, P.; Saretta, E.; Frontini, F.; Lopez, C.S.P.; Wilson, H.R.; Jakica, N.; Eisenlohr, J.; et al. *Report IEA-PVPS T15-07: 2019—Coloured BIPV Market, Research and Development*; International Energy Agency: Paris, France, 2019; Available online: https://www.iea.org/ (accessed on 21 December 2022).
3. Pelle, M.; Lucchi, E.; Maturi, L.; Astigarraga, A.; Causone, F. Coloured BIPV Technologies: Methodological and Experimental Assessment for Architecturally Sensitive Areas. *Energies* 2020, *13*, 4506. [CrossRef]
4. Kuhn, T.E.; Erban, C.; Heinrich, M.; Eisenlohr, J.; Ensslen, F.; Neuhaus, D.H. Review of technological design options for building integrated photovoltaics (BIPV). *Energy Build.* 2020, *231*, 110381. [CrossRef]
5. Martín-Chivelet, N.; Kapsis, K.; Wilson, H.R.; Delisle, V.; Yang, R.; Olivieri, L.; Polo, J.; Eisenlohr, J.; Roy, B.; Maturi, L.; et al. Building-Integrated Photovoltaic (BIPV) products and systems: A review of energy-related behavior. *Energy Build.* 2022, *262*, 111998. [CrossRef]
6. Berger, K.; Boddaert, S.; Del Buono, M.; Fedorova, A.; Frontini, F.; Inoue, S.; Ishii, H.; Kapsis, K.; Kim, J.-T.; Kovacs, P.; et al. Analysis of requirements, specifications and regulation of BIPV. In *Report IEA-PVPS T15-08: 2019*; Inoue, S., Wilson, H.R., Eds.; International Energy Agency—PVPS: Paris, France, 2019; Available online: https://www.iea.org/ (accessed on 21 December 2022).
7. Al-Janahi, S.A.; Ellabban, O.; Al-Ghamdi, S.G. A Novel BIPV Reconfiguration Algorithm for Maximum Power Generation under Partial Shading. *Energies* 2020, *13*, 4470. [CrossRef]
8. Zomer, C.; Custódio, I.; Antonolli, A.; Rüther, R. Performance assessment of partially shaded building-integrated photovoltaic (BIPV) systems in a positive-energy solar energy laboratory building: Architecture perspectives. *Sol. Energy* 2020, *211*, 879–896. [CrossRef]
9. Yadav, S.; Panda, S.; Hachem-Vermette, C. Optimum azimuth and inclination angle of BIPV panel owing to different factors influencing the shadow of adjacent building. *Renew. Energy* 2020, *162*, 381–396. [CrossRef]
10. Walker, L.; Hofer, J.; Schlueter, A. High-resolution, parametric BIPV and electrical systems modeling and design. *Appl. Energy* 2019, *238*, 164–179. [CrossRef]
11. Martín-Chivelet, N.; Polo, J.; Sanz-Saiz, C.; Tamara, L.; Benítez, N.; Alonso-Abella, M.; Cuenca, J. Assessment of PV Module Temperature Models for Building-Integrated Photovoltaics (BIPV). *Sustainability* 2022, *14*, 1500. [CrossRef]
12. Polo, J.; Martín-Chivelet, N.; Sanz-Saiz, C. BIPV Modeling with Artificial Neural Networks: Towards a BIPV Digital Twin. *Energies* 2022, *15*, 4173. [CrossRef]
13. Polo, J.; Martín-Chivelet, N.; Alonso-Abella, M.; Alonso-García, C. Photovoltaic generation on vertical façades in urban context from open satellite-derived solar resource data. *Sol. Energy* 2021, *224*, 1396–1405. [CrossRef]
14. Sengupta, M.; Habte, A.; Gueymard, C.; Wilbert, S.; Renne, D. *Best Practices Handbook for the Collection and Use of Solar Resource Data for Solar Energy Applications*, 2nd ed.; National Renewable Energy Lab. (NREL): Golden, CO, USA, 2017; Available online: https://www.iea.org/ (accessed on 21 December 2022). [CrossRef]
15. Yang, D.; Wang, W.; Gueymard, C.A.; Hong, T.; Kleissl, J.; Huang, J.; Perez, M.J.; Perez, R.; Bright, J.M.; Xia, X.; et al. A review of solar forecasting, its dependence on atmospheric sciences and implications for grid integration: Towards carbon neutrality. *Renew. Sustain. Energy Rev.* 2022, *161*, 112348. [CrossRef]
16. Yang, D.; Kleissl, J.; Gueymard, C.A.; Pedro, H.T.; Coimbra, C.F. History and trends in solar irradiance and PV power forecasting: A preliminary assessment and review using text mining. *Sol. Energy* 2018, *168*, 60–101. [CrossRef]
17. Lorenz, E.; Heinemann, D. 1.13—Prediction of Solar Irradiance and Photovoltaic Power. In *Comprehensive Renewable Energy*; Sayigh, A., Ed.; Elsevier: Oxford, UK, 2012; pp. 239–292. ISBN 978-0-08-087873-7.
18. Antonanzas, J.; Osorio, N.; Escobar, R.; Urraca, R.; Martinez-De-Pison, F.J.; Antonanzas-Torres, F. Review of photovoltaic power forecasting. *Sol. Energy* 2016, *136*, 78–111. [CrossRef]
19. Almeida, M.P.; Perpiñán, O.; Narvarte, L. PV power forecast using a nonparametric PV model. *Sol. Energy* 2015, *115*, 354–368. [CrossRef]
20. Sharadga, H.; Hajimirza, S.; Balog, R.S. Time series forecasting of solar power generation for large-scale photovoltaic plants. *Renew. Energy* 2020, *150*, 797–807. [CrossRef]
21. Theocharides, S.; Makrides, G.; Georghiou, G.E.; Kyprianou, A. Machine learning algorithms for photovoltaic system power output prediction. In Proceedings of the 2018 IEEE International Energy Conference (ENERGYCON), Limassol, Cyprus, 3–7 June 2018; pp. 1–6. [CrossRef]
22. Mittal, A.K.; Mathur, K.; Mittal, S. A Review on forecasting the photovoltaic power Using Machine Learning. *J. Physics Conf. Ser.* 2022, *2286*, 012010. [CrossRef]
23. Bae, D.J.; Kwon, B.S.; Song, K. Bin XGboost-based day-ahead load forecasting algorithm considering behind-the-meter solar PV generation. *Energies* 2022, *15*, 128. [CrossRef]
24. Das, U.K.; Tey, K.S.; Seyedmahmoudian, M.; Mekhilef, S.; Idris, M.Y.I.; Van Deventer, W.; Horan, B.; Stojcevski, A. Forecasting of photovoltaic power generation and model optimization: A review. *Renew. Sustain. Energy Rev.* 2018, *81*, 912–928. [CrossRef]
25. Narvaez, G.; Giraldo, L.F.; Bressan, M.; Pantoja, A. Machine learning for site-adaptation and solar radiation forecasting. *Renew. Energy* 2021, *167*, 333–342. [CrossRef]

26. Hancock, J.T.; Khoshgoftaar, T.M. CatBoost for big data: An interdisciplinary review. *J. Big Data* **2020**, *7*, 1–45. [CrossRef]
27. Divina, F.; Torres, M.G.; Vela, F.A.G.; Noguera, J.L.V. A Comparative Study of Time Series Forecasting Methods for Short Term Electric Energy Consumption Prediction in Smart Buildings. *Energies* **2019**, *12*, 1934. [CrossRef]
28. Qing, X.; Niu, Y. Hourly day-ahead solar irradiance prediction using weather forecasts by LSTM. *Energy* **2018**, *148*, 461–468. [CrossRef]
29. Kazem, H.A.; Yousif, J.H. Comparison of prediction methods of photovoltaic power system production using a measured dataset. *Energy Convers. Manag.* **2017**, *148*, 1070–1081. [CrossRef]
30. Zhang, J.; Verschae, R.; Nobuhara, S.; Lalonde, J.-F. Deep photovoltaic nowcasting. *Sol. Energy* **2018**, *176*, 267–276. [CrossRef]
31. Li, X.; Ma, L.; Chen, P.; Xu, H.; Xing, Q.; Yan, J.; Lu, S.; Fan, H.; Yang, L.; Cheng, Y. Probabilistic solar irradiance forecasting based on XGBoost. *Energy Rep.* **2022**, *8*, 1087–1095. [CrossRef]
32. Chen, T.; Guestrin, C. XGBoost: A scalable tree boosting system. In Proceedings of the 22nd ACM SIGKDD International Conference on Knowledge Discovery and Data Mining, San Francisco, CA, USA, 13–17 August 2016; ACM: San Francisco, CA, USA, 2016; pp. 785–794.
33. Ali, M.; Prasad, R.; Xiang, Y.; Khan, M.; Farooque, A.A.; Zong, T.; Yaseen, Z.M. Variational mode decomposition based random forest model for solar radiation forecasting: New emerging machine learning technology. *Energy Rep.* **2021**, *7*, 6700–6717. [CrossRef]
34. Liu, D.; Sun, K. Random forest solar power forecast based on classification optimization. *Energy* **2019**, *187*, 115940. [CrossRef]
35. Amat Rodrigo, J.; Escobar Ortiz, J. skforecast. Available online: https://www.cienciadedatos.net/py27-forecasting-series-temporales-python-scikitlearn.html (accessed on 26 September 2022).
36. Holmgren, W.F.; Hansen, C.W.; Mikofski, M.A. pvlib python: A python package for modeling solar energy systems. *J. Open Source Softw.* **2018**, *3*, 884. [CrossRef]
37. Ineichen, P.; Perez, R. A new airmass independent formulation for the Linke turbidity coefficient. *Sol. Energy* **2002**, *73*, 151–157. [CrossRef]
38. Perez, R.; Ineichen, P.; Seals, R.; Michalsky, J.; Stewart, R. Modeling daylight availability and irradiance components from direct and global irradiance. *Sol. Energy* **1990**, *44*, 271–289. [CrossRef]
39. Gueymard, C.A. A review of validation methodologies and statistical performance indicators for modeled solar radiation data: Towards a better bankability of solar projects. *Renew. Sustain. Energy Rev.* **2014**, *39*, 1024–1034. [CrossRef]
40. Li, K.; Wang, R.; Lei, H.; Zhang, T.; Liu, Y.; Zheng, X. Interval prediction of solar power using an Improved Bootstrap method. *Sol. Energy* **2018**, *159*, 97–112. [CrossRef]

Disclaimer/Publisher's Note: The statements, opinions and data contained in all publications are solely those of the individual author(s) and contributor(s) and not of MDPI and/or the editor(s). MDPI and/or the editor(s) disclaim responsibility for any injury to people or property resulting from any ideas, methods, instructions or products referred to in the content.

Article

Application of Temporal Fusion Transformer for Day-Ahead PV Power Forecasting

Miguel López Santos, Xela García-Santiago , Fernando Echevarría Camarero, Gonzalo Blázquez Gil and Pablo Carrasco Ortega *

Galicia Institute of Technology (ITG), 15003 A Coruña, Spain; mlopez@itg.es (M.L.S.); xgarcia@itg.es (X.G.-S.); fechevarria@itg.es (F.E.C.); gblazquez@itg.es (G.B.G.)
* Correspondence: pcarrasco@itg.es; Tel.: +34-981-173-206

Abstract: The energy generated by a solar photovoltaic (PV) system depends on uncontrollable factors, including weather conditions and solar irradiation, which leads to uncertainty in the power output. Forecast PV power generation is vital to improve grid stability and balance the energy supply and demand. This study aims to predict hourly day-ahead PV power generation by applying Temporal Fusion Transformer (TFT), a new attention-based architecture that incorporates an interpretable explanation of temporal dynamics and high-performance forecasting over multiple horizons. The proposed forecasting model has been trained and tested using data from six different facilities located in Germany and Australia. The results have been compared with other algorithms like Auto Regressive Integrated Moving Average (ARIMA), Long Short-Term Memory (LSTM), Multi-Layer Perceptron (MLP), and Extreme Gradient Boosting (XGBoost), using statistical error indicators. The use of TFT has been shown to be more accurate than the rest of the algorithms to forecast PV generation in the aforementioned facilities.

Keywords: photovoltaic power forecast; solar energy; Temporal Fusion Transformer; deep learning; artificial intelligence

Citation: López Santos, M.; García-Santiago, X.; Echevarría Camarero, F.; Blázquez Gil, G.; Carrasco Ortega, P. Application of Temporal Fusion Transformer for Day-Ahead PV Power Forecasting. *Energies* **2022**, *15*, 5232. https://doi.org/10.3390/en15145232

Academic Editors: Fouzi Harrou, Ying Sun, Bilal Taghezouit and Dairi Abdelkader

Received: 15 June 2022
Accepted: 16 July 2022
Published: 19 July 2022

Publisher's Note: MDPI stays neutral with regard to jurisdictional claims in published maps and institutional affiliations.

Copyright: © 2022 by the authors. Licensee MDPI, Basel, Switzerland. This article is an open access article distributed under the terms and conditions of the Creative Commons Attribution (CC BY) license (https://creativecommons.org/licenses/by/4.0/).

1. Introduction

Renewable energy is rapidly increasing worldwide since it became an economical alternative to conventional energy sources such as fossils fuels, which are responsible for greenhouse emissions (GHG), have a limited supply, and their prices are becoming increasingly unpredictable. Furthermore, the European Commission targets aim to reduce emissions by 50% to 55% by 2030 in comparison with 1990 and to become climate neutral in 2050 [1].

Electricity generated by solar photovoltaic (PV) systems has increased by 23% in 2020 to reach 821 TWh worldwide [2]. Projections indicate that the global installed capacity of this technology could rise by more than three times, reaching 2.840 GW in 2030, and 8.519 GW in 2050 [3]. The reason is solar energy presents many advantages: it is an environmentally friendly renewable source, is abundant, has a long service life [4], and as shown in Figure 1, it is becoming one of the most competitive power generation technologies after more than ten years of cost declines with a promising future ahead.

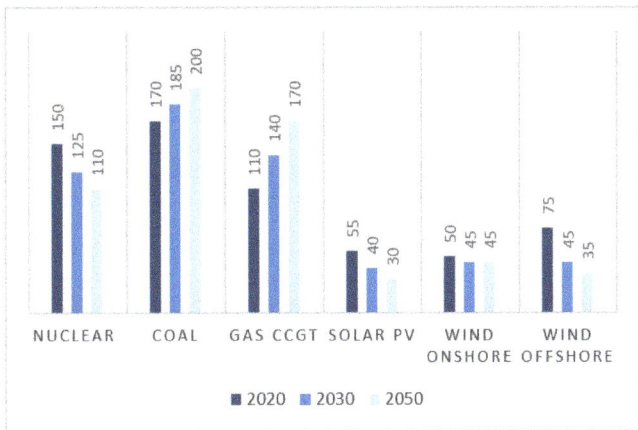

Figure 1. Levelized cost of electricity (USD/kWh) in European Union in the Stated Policies Scenario [5].

However, variations in solar irradiance and meteorological conditions cause fluctuation in solar power generation and lead to uncertainty in power output. This results in a power imbalance between the demand and the supply side of the grid [6]. Also, the unpredictable output significantly impacts the economic dispatch and the scheduling, stability, and reliability of the power system operation [7]. Precise forecasting of the energy produced is essential for grid operators, considering that deviations need to be compensated by the remaining generation technologies. Moreover, it is not only beneficial for system operators as PV plant managers can prevent potential penalties arising from differences between produced and predicted energy [8,9]. Therefore, PV power forecasting contributes to stabilize and optimize the operation and performance of the grid and renewable energy microgrids [10–13] by means of the comparative analysis between required and predicted energy. It also positively affects the customer by reducing the uncertainty and the generated energy cost [8,14].

Solar power forecasting ranges from ultra-short term to long-term forecasts. Long-term forecasts are especially relevant for planning the long duration power system. However, industry and researchers currently focus primarily on short-term or day-ahead predictions as these can account for cloud cover variability and provide more accurate results [15]. There are several approaches for solar power forecasting: physical models [16], persistence forecast [17], statistical models [18], artificial intelligence [19], including machine learning (ML) and deep learning (DL) [20,21], ensemble and hybrid-based models [14,22–26]. Common ML methods applied to PV power forecasting in literature are artificial neural networks (ANN) [20,27,28], support vector machine (SVM) [29,30] and extreme learning machine (ELM) [31,32]. Among all PV forecasting approaches, ANN have shown superior accuracy, being successfully applied in short-term forecast horizons [33–36]. In addition, machine learning methods, like ANN, can handle large amounts of data and produce accurate predictions for short-term periods, without the complexity of mathematical and physical relationships.

Some methods used for PV power forecasting present certain limitations. Persistence and statistical methods cannot handle nonlinear data. Physical methods depend on local meteorological data that can have limited access. Numerical weather prediction (NWP) models are widely used to provide forecasts of weather conditions, but they often lack sufficient spatial and temporal resolution. ANN are involved with problems of local minima, overfitting, and complex structure. DL methods have been developed to solve these limitations [37,38]. DL is an advanced branch of machine learning with the ability to process non-linear and complex relationships between various inputs and the forecasted output.

Examples of DL are Convolutional Neural Networks (CNN) [39–41], Recurrent Neural Networks (RNN) [42,43], Long Short-Term Memory (LSTM) [21,44] or Convolutional Self-Attention LSTM [45]. These methods have proven to achieve better prediction results when applied to solar power forecasting compared to other machine learning methods, especially those based on LSTM networks [46–49].

Time series can have seasonal patterns or increasing and decreasing trends. LSTM can learn to remember useful information from several time steps back that is relevant for producing the predicted output. Traditional recurrent networks do not have the ability to decide which information to remember. Nevertheless, LSTM has difficulty in determining long-term dependencies.

More complex deep learning architectures are constantly created that outperform previous ones. For example, Temporal Fusion Transformer (TFT) [50] is an Attention-Based Deep Neural Network for multi-horizon time series forecasting that integrates LSTM in its architecture. TFT also uses the attention mechanism to learn long-term dependencies in time series data, which means that it can directly learn patterns during training. This makes the TFT more advantageous than other time series methods in terms of interpretability. Moreover, TFT minimizes a quantile loss function, which enables it to generate a probabilistic forecast with a confidence interval.

This work aims to predict hourly day-ahead PV power generation by applying TFT as the forecasting method. TFT incorporates an interpretable explanation of temporal dynamics and high-performance forecasting over multiple horizons. It uses specialized components to choose important attributes and a series of gating layers to remove non-essential elements, resulting in high performance in a wide range of applications.

This paper contributes to extending the application of innovative DL methods to PV power forecasting. The novel aspect of this work is the use of TFT for PV power generation forecasting as there is no previous literature found that applies and compares this method for predicting PV output performance. TFT potentially enhances the accuracy of forecasts compared to other methods by learning short and long-term temporal relationships. This not only benefits the management of PV production systems but can also influence the stability and operation of the power system.

The predicting method is evaluated with common datasets used in literature. They include real data from six photovoltaic systems located in Germany and Australia. The results of the proposed DL method are compared with the following methods: Auto Regressive Integrated Moving Average (ARIMA), Multi-Layer Perceptron (MLP), LSTM, and Extreme Gradient Boosting (XGBoost).

2. Materials and Methods

The methodology applied in this study includes the following steps. (1) Data gathering, where data from different sources is collected to define the final dataset. The electrical energy produced by a photovoltaic system depends on variables such as horizontal irradiation, temperature, humidity, and solar zenith and azimuth, among others. (2) Data pre-processing, to transform raw data into a form more suitable for modeling, including data cleaning, feature selection, and data transformation (3) Model selection. (4) Training and tuning, where the selected model is trained for different combinations of hyperparameters, selecting the model with the best performance. (5) Results evaluation.

Figure 2 summarizes the process carried out.

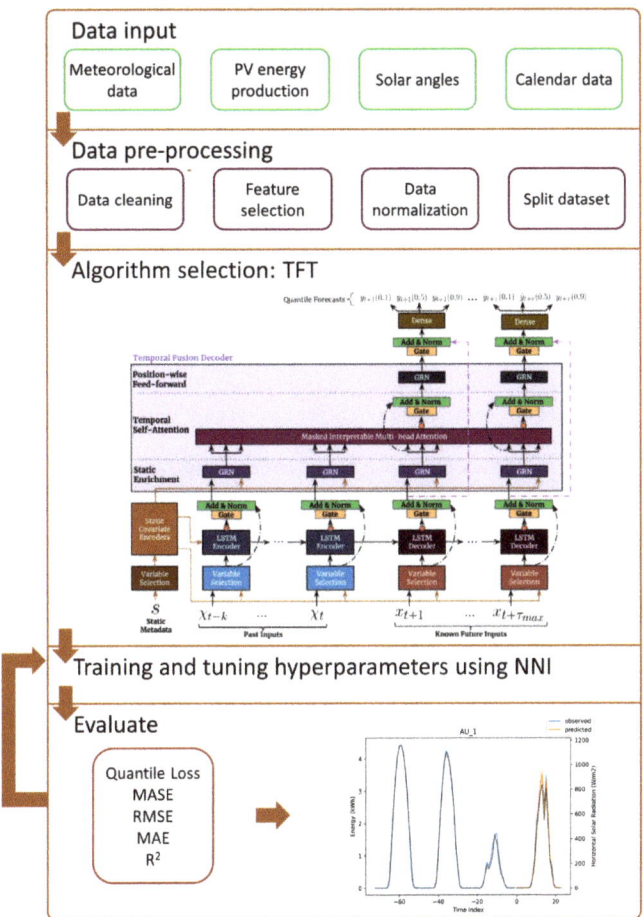

Figure 2. Structure of the proposed model. TFT architecture was adapted from [50].

2.1. Type of Data

The dataset used in this study includes historical power generation data from six different facilities as the dependent variables, and meteorological data, solar angles, and calendar data as independent variables.

The six facilities are located in Germany and Australia. Those located in Germany consist of three roof mounted systems situated on industrial and residential buildings in the city of Konstanz [51]. In this city, the average global horizontal irradiation is 1212 kWh/m^2 per year, the hottest month is July, with an average high of 25 °C and low of 15 °C, and the coldest month is January with an average low of -2 °C and high of 4 °C. The data is provided with a 5-min resolution.

The facilities in Australia are located at Desert Knowledge Australia Solar Centre (DKASC), in Alice Springs, which is a real-life demonstration of solar technologies in an area of high solar resources [52]. In this area, the average global horizontal irradiation is 2271 kWh/m^2 per year. The hottest month of the year in Alice Springs is January, with an average high of 35 °C and a low of 22 °C. The coldest month of the year in Alice Springs is July, with an average low of 5 °C and a high of 20 °C. The data is provided with 5-min resolution. Table 1 shows the specific information of each PV system and its data.

Table 1. Main characteristics of the PV facilities and datasets.

Facility	Array Rating (kW)	Characteristics	Start Day	Dataset Length
GE_1	17.0	Fixed, Roof mounted	25 October 2015	498 days
GE_2	5.0	Fixed, Roof mounted	29 February 2016	940 days
GE_3	10.0	Fixed, Roof mounted	11 October 2015	776 days
AU_1	4.9	Fixed, Roof mounted	13 October 2018	667 days
AU_2	6.0	Fixed, Ground mounted	13 October 2018	667 days
AU_3	5.8	Fixed, Ground mounted	13 October 2018	667 days

The meteorological variables used include global horizontal irradiance, wind speed, precipitation, temperature, and humidity. These factors affect to a greater or lesser extent the PV energy output of the system. The DKASC dataset used includes measurements of these variables, while for the systems of Konstanz this information is collected from a nearby weather station [53].

The solar angles, zenith and azimuth, were calculated based on the timestamp and the location of each PV system for each record of the dataset. The solar zenith angle is the angle between the sun's rays and the vertical direction, defining the sun's apparent altitude. The azimuth represents the sun's relative direction along the local horizon.

Figures 3 and 4 show the aforementioned variables during a five-day period in one of the facilities from Germany and one from Australia.

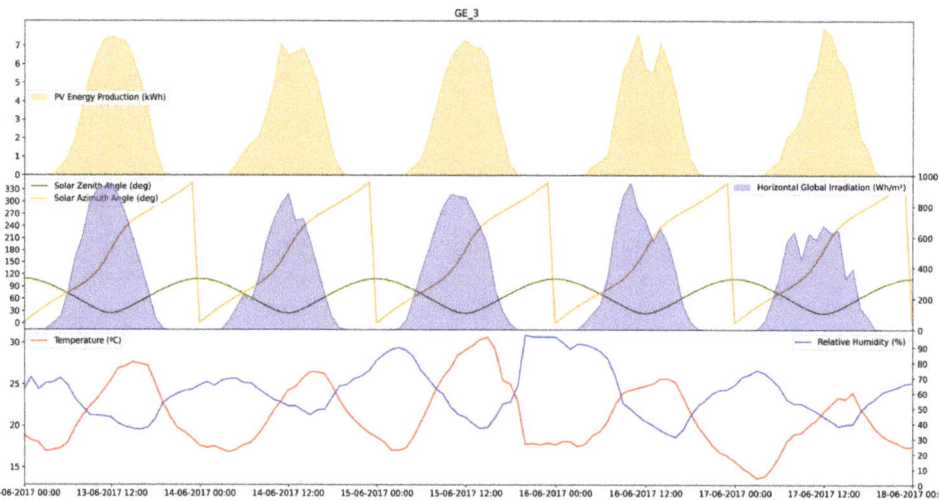

Figure 3. Photovoltaic (PV) energy production (kWh), horizontal global irradiation (Wh/m^2), solar zenith (°), solar azimuth (°), temperature (°C), and relative humidity (%) from one of the PV facilities in Germany (GE_3) during five days.

Regarding the calendar data, cyclical calendar variables need to be transformed to represent the data sequentially. For example, December and January are 1 month apart, although those months will appear to be separated by 11 months. To avoid this, 2 new features were created, deriving a sine and a cosine transform of the original feature.

Finally, the data was converted to hourly data and merged to create the final dataset, consisting of eleven independent variables, five meteorological variables, four calendar factors, and two variables to represent solar angles. Table 2 shows the variables initially considered.

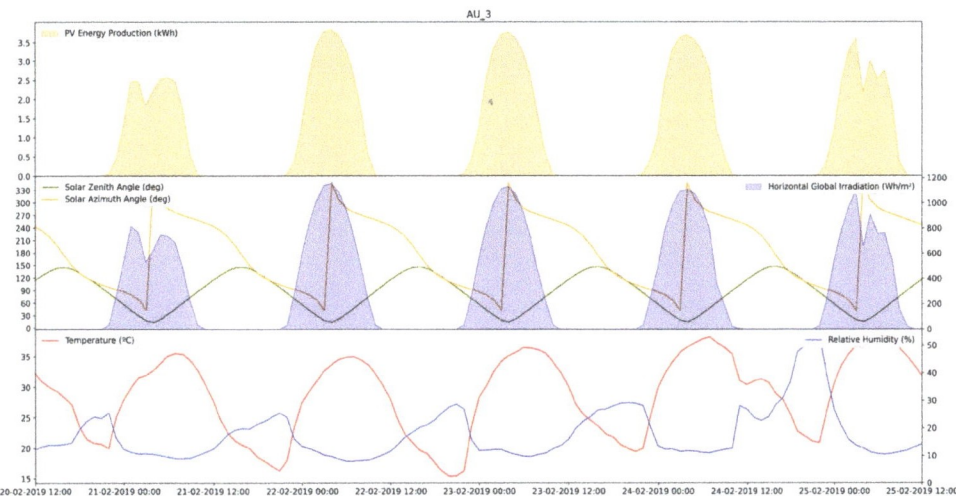

Figure 4. PV energy production (kWh), horizontal global irradiation (Wh/m^2), solar zenith (°), solar azimuth (°), temperature (°C), and relative humidity (%) from one of the PV facilities in Australia (AU_3) during five days.

Table 2. Dependent and independent variables initially considered.

Type of Variable	Variable Name	Source *
Dependent Variable	PV energy Production	PP
Independent Variable	Horizontal global irradiation	WS
	Solar zenith	DV
	Solar azimuth	DV
	Temperature	WS
	Relativity humidity	WS
	Wind speed	WS
	Precipitation	WS
	Hour sin	DV
	Hour cosine	DV
	Month sin	DV
	Month cosine	DV

* PP: Power Plant, WS: Weather Station, DV: Derived Variable.

2.2. Data Pre-Processing

Data pre-processing is defined as the transformation of raw data into a form more suitable for modeling. In this study, the following pre-processing tasks are included: data cleaning, feature selection, and data transformations.

Data cleaning:

The raw dataset has to be cleaned to identify and correct errors that may negatively impact the performance of the predictive model. For that, one important task is the detection of outliers taking into account the physical behavior of the system. DBSCAN (Density-Based Spatial Clustering of Application with Noise) was used to identify outliers in the dataset. This algorithm creates groups depending on a distance measurement between points, usually using Euclidean distance. A point is included in a cluster if the distance between this point and another point of the cluster is less than a parameter eps, taking into account a minimum number of points for each cluster. As a result, it identifies outliers as the points that do not belong to a cluster, which are those that are in low-density regions [54]. Considering that the PV energy production should fall within certain bounds for a given global horizontal irradiation, zenith angle and azimuth angle, these four features were considered to apply this algorithm.

Next, the missing values and the values of solar energy production identified as outliers were replaced taking into account the averaged coefficient between the PV generation and the horizontal global irradiation at the same hour on previous days. The new value for solar energy production is obtained by multiplying this coefficient by the horizontal global irradiation at the considered index.

Feature selection:

Feature selection is applied using wrapper methods. These methods train models using a subset of the input variables, where the objective is to find the subset that builds the model that yields the best results. As this process is computationally very expensive, we use TFT, a model that already has interpretable feature selection within its architecture to guide it.

The wrapper method used is Backward Elimination [55]. Initially, a TFT model is trained with all the variables, then, at each iteration, the least significant variable in the TFT model is removed, which should improve the performance of the model. Thus, this process is stopped when no improvement is observed after discarding another feature.

Data transforms:

Continuous input variables have different scales, which may result in a slow or unstable learning process. For that, they need to be normalized to make every datapoint have the same importance. In this study, standardization (of z-score normalization) was used to rescale the data. This is a technique where the final values have a zero mean and a unit standard deviation. The formula of the z-score normalization is:

$$x_{stand} = \frac{x_i - \mu}{\sigma} \qquad (1)$$

where x_i is the input data, μ is the average value of the feature, and σ is the standard deviation.

For the target variable, different transformations are applied. First the natural logarithm of the values, then the values are scaled by dividing each value by the median in its series.

2.3. Data Splitting

The dataset is divided into three sets for training purposes:

Training set: The sample of the data used to fit the model.

Validation set: The sample of data used to provide an unbiased evaluation of a fitted model while tuning its hyperparameters.

Test set: Part of the data used to fairly evaluate the final model fit on the training set.

This division is not done evenly; each photovoltaic installation in the dataset is divided so that 70% of its randomly selected samples go into the training set, 20% into the validation set, and 10% into the test set.

2.4. Forecasting Models

The solar energy production was predicted using TFT, although its performance was compared with other algorithms like ARIMA, MLP, LSTM, and XGBoost. MLP, LSTM, and TFT models were trained using the implementation in Pytorch Forecasting [56], while ARIMA and XGBoost used their own packages for Python.

2.4.1. TFT

TFT is an attention-based neural network architecture specially designed to combine multi-horizon forecasting with interpretable insights into temporal dynamics [50]. TFT utilizes specialized building blocks to select relevant features and leave out unused components, enabling high performance over a broad range of tasks. Their main components are:

- Gating mechanisms, named Gated Residual Network (GRN). They allow us to filter out any unnecessary elements of the architecture and avoid non-linear processing if it is not needed.
- Variable selection networks to choose important input features at each time step.
- Static covariate encoders that incorporate static variables into the network to condition temporal dynamics.
- Temporal processing to learn both long and short-term temporal patterns from both known and observed time-varying inputs. A temporal self-attention decoder, based on the Masked Multi-Head Attention layer, is employed to capture long-term dependencies, while a sequence-to-sequence layer is used to process local information.
- Allows us to calculate prediction intervals via quantile forecast to determine the likelihood of each target value.

TFT improves the interpretability of time series forecasting through the identification of the globally-important variables, the persistent temporal patterns, and the significant events for the prediction problem. It explains how and why the results are generated by the model, in contrast with the concept of a "black box" where it is difficult to explain how models arrive at their predictions. This makes the model's output more trustworthy and easier to work with, which is the objective of Explainable AI (XAI) [57].

2.4.2. ARIMA

ARIMA is a statistical model that predicts future values based on past time series data [58]. This algorithm consists of 3 components:

- Autoregression (AR), takes into account the dependence between an observation and certain past values.
- Integrated (I), uses the differencing of raw observations necessary to make the series stationary.
- Moving Average (MA), considers the dependent relationship between an observation and a residual error of a moving average model applied to certain past observations.

2.4.3. MLP

A MLP is a fully connected class of feedforward ANN [59]. It is made up of many interconnected computational units, called neurons. An artificial neuron receives inputs from other neurons, which are weighted and summed, establishing the impact of the information going through them. This weighted sum is then transformed by an activation function to generate the output of the neuron. These activation functions are needed to learn complex patterns and non-linear curves.

In a neural network, the neurons are arranged into multiple layers: an input layer, one or more hidden layers, and an output layer. The number of neurons of each layer and the number of hidden layers are the main parameters to optimize.

2.4.4. LSTM

LSTM networks are a special class of RNN, capable of learning long-term dependencies [60]. They can retain previous information and learn temporal correlations between consecutive data points. The memory block, its building structure, is composed of three interacting gates.

In LSTM, the core variable is the cell state, which allows for information to be carried from previous steps throughout the memory block. Its interacting gates control the addition or removal of information from the cell state. In particular, the first gate is called forget gate, and determines which information from previous steps to throw away from the cell state. The second one, the "input gate", controls the updating of the cell state. Finally, the last interacting gate, called the "output gate", provides the final output, based on a filtered version of the updated cell state.

2.4.5. XGBoost

XGBoost is a supervised predictive algorithm that uses the boosting principle [61]. The idea behind boosting is to generate multiple "weak" prediction models sequentially, each of these takes the results of the previous model to generate a "stronger" model. It uses different types of weak decision trees as its models. To get a stronger model from these weak models, an optimization algorithm is used, in this case, Gradient Descent.

2.5. Hyperparameter Tuning

The different hyperparameters of the model are predefined with default values, although better performance is achieved if they are optimized for the problem under study. Neural Network Intelligence (NNI) is used to tune these hyperparameters [62]. This tool allows us to define a search space, generating different configurations of the parameters. Next, NNI performs training for each combination, in order to find the best outcome. NNI trains the model by generating its own random training, validation, and test sets from the dataset, and training it with a combination of the defined hyperparameters.

2.6. Evaluation Metrics

To evaluate and compare the forecasting performances, several statistical error metrics were employed: root mean square error ($RMSE$), mean absolute error (MAE), mean absolute scaled error ($MASE$), coefficient of determination (R^2), and quantile loss. These evaluation metrics are defined as:

$$RMSE = \sqrt{\frac{1}{N} \sum_{i=1}^{N} |y_i - \hat{y}_i|^2} \tag{2}$$

$$MAE = \frac{1}{N} \sum_{i=1}^{N} |y_i - \hat{y}_i| \tag{3}$$

$$MASE = \frac{MAE}{MAE_{naive}} \tag{4}$$

$$R^2 = 1 - \frac{\sum_{i=1}^{N}(y_i - \hat{y}_i)^2}{\sum_{i=1}^{N}(y_i - y_{avg})^2} \tag{5}$$

$$QuantileLoss = \sum_{q \in Q} \max((q(y_i - \hat{y}_i), (q-1)(y_i - \hat{y}_i)) \tag{6}$$

where y_i and $\hat{y}_i$ represent the real and forecasted values, respectively, y_{avg} shows the mean of real values, MAE_{naive} is the MAE of a naïve model that predicts the values by shifting actual values into the future, and Q is the set of quantile values to be fitted in our study $Q = \{0.02, 0.1, 0.25, 0.5, 0.75, 0.9, 0.98\}$.

3. Results and Discussion

3.1. Outliers Detection

The percentage of missing values and outliers detected in each dataset are shown in Table 3. The number of outliers identified is greater in the facilities from Germany than in those from Australia. The reason for this behavior could be the distance between the PV facilities and the weather station in Konstanz. Although the tower is located in the same city not far from the facilities, the irradiance recorded at the same moment can vary significantly on partially cloudy days. The analysis of outliers is, therefore, of great importance for those facilities that do not have their own weather station.

Table 3. Missing values and outliers detected in each dataset.

Facility	Missing Values (%)	Outliers (%)	Facility	Missing Values (%)	Outliers (%)
GE_1	0.60	0.49	AU_1	1.83	0.00
GE_2	1.13	1.85	AU_2	1.83	0.00
GE_3	0.68	1.05	AU_3	1.83	0.00

3.2. Data Analysis

The dataset was analyzed once it was cleaned. First, Figure 5 shows the probability density function (PDF) of the PV energy production data, taking only into account values between sunrise and sunset. These datasets present a bimodal distribution for the Australian facilities, with a peak close to cero and another at high PV energy production. On the other hand, the distributions are left-skewed for the installations located in Germany, with its highest point at low PV energy production. In both cases, the first peak is derived from the hours near sunset and sunrise, where the global horizontal radiation is low.

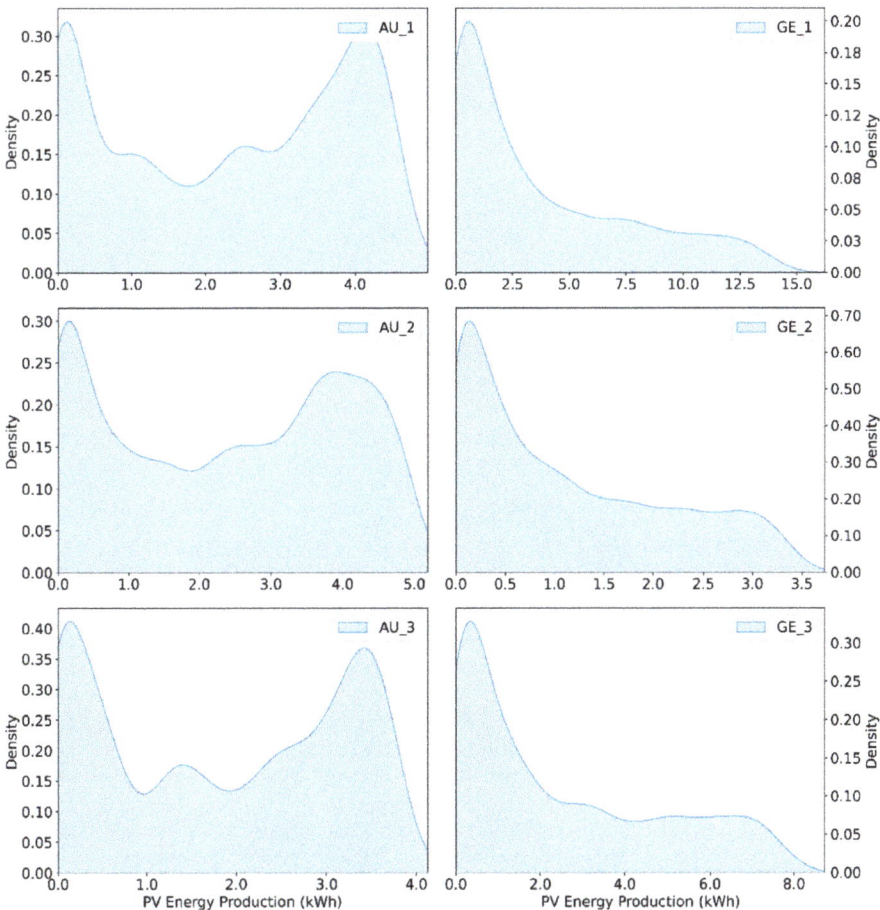

Figure 5. Probability density function (PDF) of the PV energy production for the different facilities.

Figure 6 shows the autocorrelation function (ACF) of PV energy production for two of the time series considered, one for each location. This ACF represents the similarity between two observations depending on the lag time among them. In this case, the results indicate that the PV energy production presents a clear periodic pattern with an interval of 24h. These results are equivalent for the rest of the facilities.

The Pearson correlation coefficient was also calculated to measure the correlation between the PV energy production and both the meteorological variables and the solar angles (Table 4).

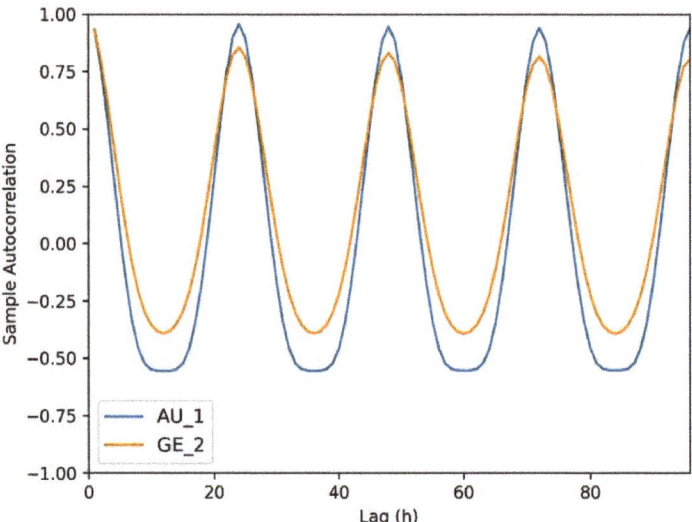

Figure 6. Autocorrelation function (ACF) of PV energy production time series data.

Table 4. Pearson correlation coefficient (PCC) between target value (PV energy production) and the meteorological variables and solar angles.

PCC	GE_1	GE_2	GE_3	AU_1	AU_2	AU_3
Horizontal global irradiation	0.91	0.97	0.89	0.98	0.99	0.98
Temperature	0.56	0.57	0.54	0.40	0.44	0.40
Relative humidity	−0.74	−0.69	−0.74	−0.37	−0.39	−0.36
Wind speed	0.08	0.07	0.10	0.09	0.10	0.09
Precipitation	−0.13	−0.11	−0.12	−0.03	−0.03	−0.03
Solar zenith	−0.77	−0.83	−0.77	−0.84	−0.85	−0.83
Solar azimuth	0.21	0.11	0.25	0.03	0.04	0.05

The correlation between PV energy production and the different meteorological variables varies between the location, showing a different influence of these features depending on the climatic conditions. With respect to the correlation with the horizontal global irradiation, it is stronger in the case of the facilities from Australia. Among the facilities in Germany, the highest correlation was found in the GE_2 facility. The differences in the correlations obtained may be due to several factors. First, the sky conditions in Konstanz are much more diverse than the sky conditions in Alice Springs, which has an impact in the relation between horizontal irradiation and plane-of-array (POA) irradiation [63], and therefore, in energy production. Secondly, the GE_1 and GE_3 installations are not oriented towards the south, but slightly towards the southwest, which produces a certain gap between the maximum generation and the maximum irradiation points, as shown in Figure 7. Thirdly, the tilt of the different systems is not the same: the lower the tilt, the greater the correlation. Finally, the facilities in Germany are located on roofs of urbanized areas, which results in a more obstructed horizon that also decreases the correlation.

Finally, Figure 8 represents the relation between the PV energy production and the horizontal global irradiation for the different facilities, highlighting the differences between the months of the year.

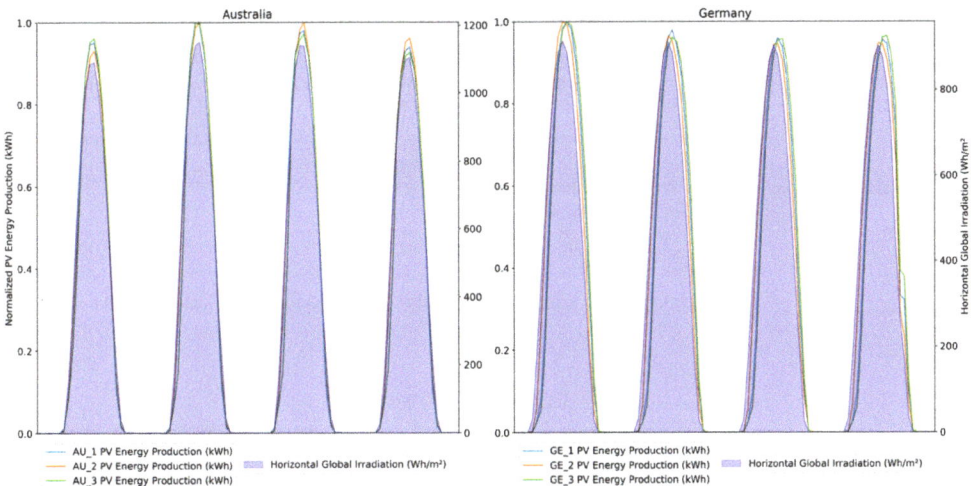

Figure 7. Normalized PV energy production and horizontal solar irradiation for the facilities from Germany and Australia during a four-day period.

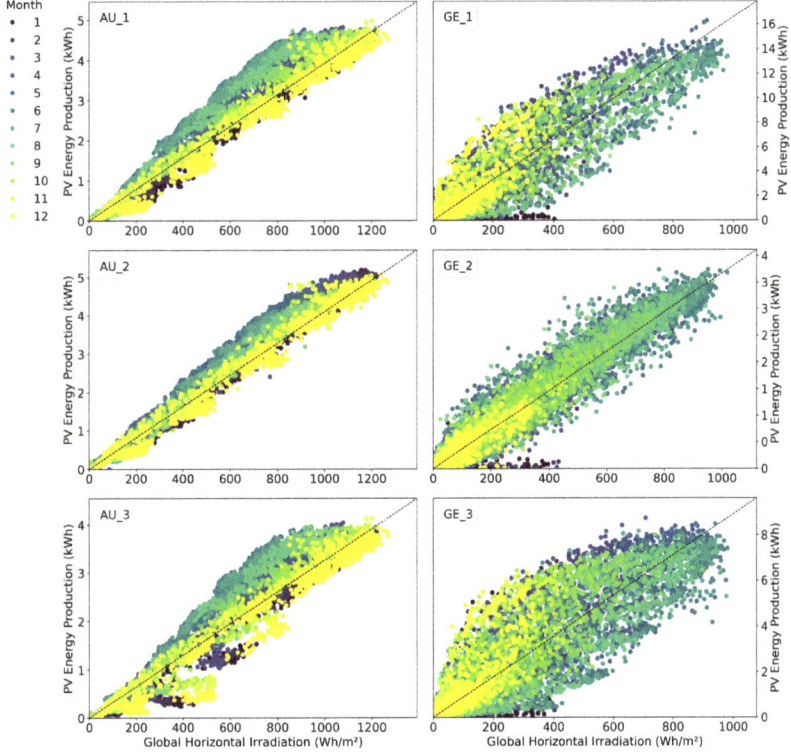

Figure 8. Relation between PV energy production (kWh) and global horizontal irradiation (Wh/m^2) for the different locations.

3.3. Feature Selection

From the dataset, solar horizontal irradiation, temperature, humidity, zenith angle, azimuth angle, and the sine and cosine transformation of the month were found to be valuable parameters for the model, whereas the rest of the variables considered were discarded. Although different feature sets were used, temperature and solar angles were also selected variables in [64], while precipitation was also discarded.

3.4. Forecasting Results

Using the variables selected, the hourly day-ahead PV power generation was predicted using different models for the two locations. The hyperparameters of MLP, LSTM, and XGBoost were established based on the best models in [28,48,65]. For TFT, the hyperparameters were tuned with NNI and the best performance was obtained for the values in Table 5.

Table 5. Selected hyperparameters for TFT model.

Hyperparameter	Value
LSTM layers	2
Hidden size	60
Hidden continuous size	30
Attention head size	2
Learning rate	0.001
Encoder length	72
Dropout	0.7
Batch size	1024

Figure 9 shows the results for different combinations of hyperparameters.

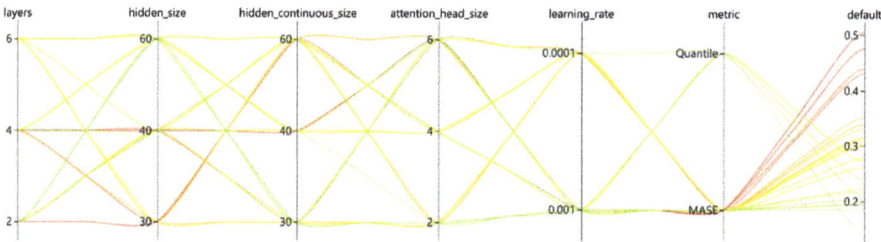

Figure 9. Results during the tuning of the hyperparameters for TFT with NNI.

The variables related to the complexity of the neural network based models are shown in Table 6. TFT is the most complex model considering the three variables: number of parameters, model size, and training time per epoch showing an 82.6% and 86.6% increase in size and in time complexity, respectively, compared to LSTM.

Table 6. Variables related to neural networks complexity.

	Total Parameters (K)	Estimated Parameter Size (MB)	Training Time per Epoch (s)
MLP	8.7	0.035	15
LSTM	48.1	0.192	16
TFT	361	1.44	92

The forecasting errors using these different models are shown in Table 7. As can be seen, TFT outperforms the other models with lowest values for all the indicators in both locations. Comparing TFT with LSTM, the second-best model, the indicators of RMSE, MAE, and MASE, for Australia are 46%, 48%, 48% lower, respectively. The same behavior can be observed for Germany, with a reduction of 20%, 26%, and 54% in RMSE, MAE, and MASE from TFT with respect to LSTM. These results may be explained by the different components integrated in TFT. This algorithm incorporates temporal self-attention decoder to capture long-term dependencies, allowing to learn relationships at different scales. It also supports to efficiently address features for each input type: static or time-invariant features, past-observed time varying input and future-known time varying input. It was also found to exceed other predictions models in other areas like the forecasting of wind speed or freeway traffic speed [66,67].

Table 7. Forecasting errors for the different models in both locations: Germany and Australia.

	RMSE		MAE		MASE		R^2	
	GE	AU	GE	AU	GE	AU	GE	AU
ARIMA	1.441	0.219	1.106	0.187	-	-	0.640	0.978
MLP	0.786	0.593	0.370	0.331	1.458	0.961	0.816	0.853
LSTM	0.343	0.118	0.162	0.064	0.846	0.191	0.975	0.994
XGBoost	1.124	0.336	0.497	0.137	1.105	1.242	0.577	0.945
TFT	0.276	0.064	0.120	0.033	0.390	0.100	0.983	0.998

LSTM showed good accuracy and better performance than XGBoost, MLP, and ARIMA. This behavior was also found in [47,48]. Unlike XGBoost and MLP, both LSTM and TFT can retain previous information and learn temporal correlations between consecutive data points, giving these models a better performance. Besides, while the ARIMA model was only developed taking into account a linear relationship between the exogenous variables and the target variable, both LSTM and TFT can include non-linear approximations. Therefore, these results indicate that both mechanisms are important for the forecasting of day-ahead solar production.

The performance of TFT on each facility was compared using MASE and R^2, the two metrics that are scale invariant. The results for Germany are always worse than those for Australia, with a significant reduction in accuracy for both metrics. The forecasting errors with TFT for the different indicators and the different series considered are shown in Table 8.

Table 8. TFT performance for the 6 locations.

	RMSE	MAE	MASE	R^2	Quantile Loss
GE_1	0.432	0.187	0.346	0.983	0.053
GE_2	0.105	0.050	0.513	0.987	0.014
GE_3	0.291	0.123	0.312	0.980	0.035
AU_1	0.062	0.032	0.091	0.999	0.009
AU_2	0.070	0.035	0.097	0.998	0.010
AU_3	0.061	0.032	0.112	0.998	0.009

The highest accuracy in forecasting the day-ahead PV power generation is always achieved in AU_1, although the performance of the TFT is very similar for the three Australian PV plants. In this case, the coefficient of variation, which establish the extent of the variability in relation to the mean, is 3.73% and 0.05% for MASE and R^2, respectively. In the case of Germany, the coefficients of variation are 27.62% and 0.29% for MASE and R^2, showing a great variability between the performance of the model in German facilities.

The forecast accuracy in the German facilities is still not as favorable as the one in the facilities in Australia, this may be due to the greater variability in the weather conditions experienced by the solar facilities in Konstanz.

However, the forecast in the facilities in Germany has improved drastically, especially in GE_1 and GE_3. As mentioned, the other factors which could be damaging the Pearson correlation between horizontal irradiation and energy production (the different orientation and tilt of the panels and the more blocked horizon) could have been corrected with the implementation in the model of the solar angles (zenith and azimuth), the meteorological variables (temperature and humidity) and the calendar data. The solar angles help to predict the relationship between the horizontal irradiation and the irradiation in the plane of the panels [68], which is reinforced with the meteorological variables [63] that also influence other factors, such as the efficiency of the panels [69].

Figures 10 and 11 show the results of PV power generation forecasting based on TFT and the real solar energy production for representative rainy and sunny days in both locations. These graphs represent the global horizontal irradiation and the observed values from the past 72 h to the prediction length. The predicted value is represented with the prediction intervals, showing the uncertainty of the forecasted values. This information is important when managing the operation of the facilities.

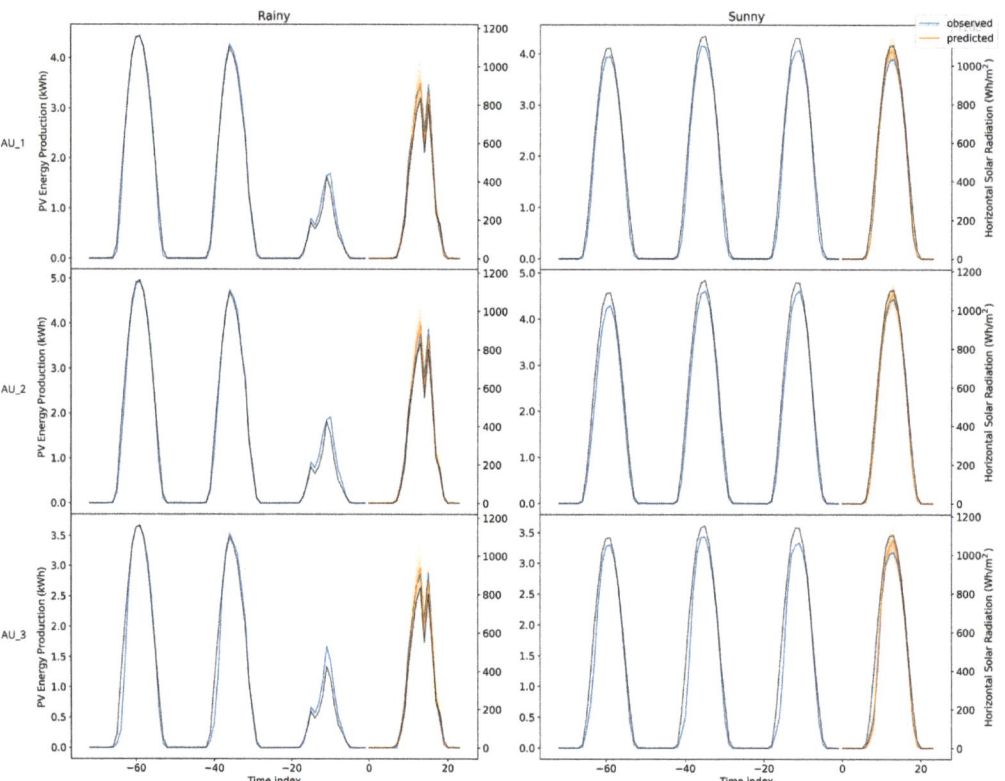

Figure 10. Observed and predicted PV energy production forecasting for a sunny and a rainy day in the facilities from Australia. Global horizontal radiation is represented in grey.

For AU_1 on a rainy day, the maximum solar energy production predicted is 3.50 kWh, where 3.22 kWh and 3.76 kWh are the 0.1 and 0.9 percentiles, respectively. The interval between the tenth and the ninetieth percentile is 0.54 kWh. Considering the hours with energy production, the mean and standard deviation for half of this interval are 0.19 kWh and 0.07 kWh, respectively, with a maximum value of 0.27 kWh and a minimum of 0.07 kWh. For the example of a sunny day, the value predicted for the hour with maximum solar output is 4.05 kWh. In this case, the mean and standard deviation of the mid-range between the considered percentiles during the day is 0.12 kWh and 0.03 kWh, respectively, indicating lower variation in these values. Analyzing these results for this case, it seems that the uncertainty is higher and more varied for rainy days.

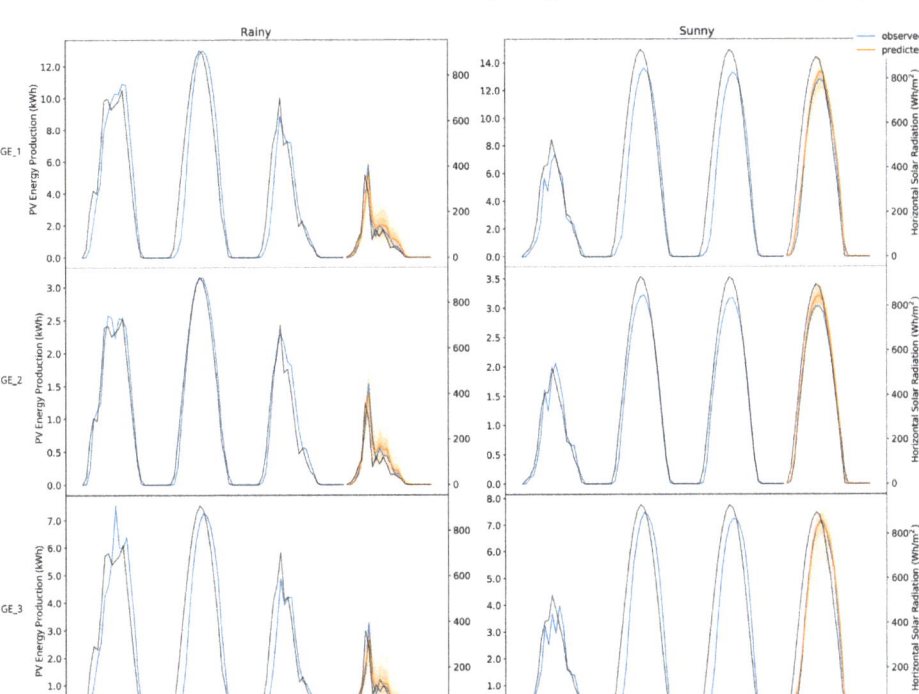

Figure 11. Observed and predicted PV energy production forecasting for a sunny and a rainy day in the facilities from Germany. Global horizontal irradiation is represented in grey.

For the case of GE_2, the maximum production on the example for a rainy day is 1.39 kWh, and the mean and standard deviation of the half of the interval between 0.1 and 0.9 percentiles along the day is 0.20 kWh and 0.07 kWh, respectively. The maximum is 0.35 kWh and the minimum is 0.08 kWh. In the case of a sunny day, the values are 0.17 kWh and 0.02 kWh for the mean and the standard deviation, respectively, with a solar energy production of 3.2 kWh. In this case, the uncertainty is higher than in the case of Australia, although it is constant throughout the day. Comparing the examples of a rainy and a sunny day, the mean values are similar, although the rainy day is over a peak of solar energy production of 1.39 kWh, whereas on a sunny day, the maximum output is 3.2 kWh. This indicates that the uncertainty is also higher on rainy days as in the case of Germany.

One possible explanation for the lower accuracy during cloudy or rainy days could be the higher variability of the irradiance levels recorded during such days. This implies that the training of the network, and therefore, the prediction of PV energy production, becomes less reliable under these circumstances.

3.5. TFT Interpretability

TFT improves the interpretability of time series forecasting through the calculation of the variable importance scores for the different types of features, and also through the representation of the attention weight patterns. These results can be seen in Figure 12, which shows the importance of the past-observed time varying inputs, Figure 13, representing the importance of the future-known time varying features, and Figure 14 showing the attention weight patterns for one-step-ahead forecasts.

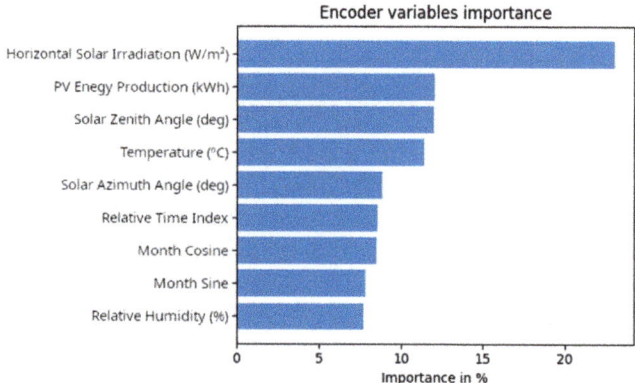

Figure 12. Importance of encoder variables.

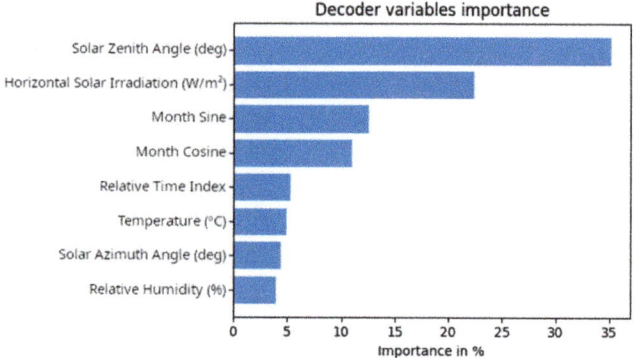

Figure 13. Importance of decoder variables.

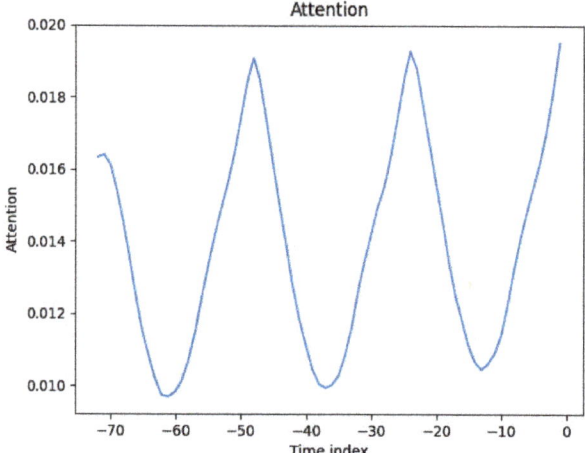

Figure 14. Attention weight patterns.

These datasets also have three static inputs: target center, target scale, and the identification of the facility, aiming at providing additional information and context to the model. This last variable is needed to identify each series, since TFT allows to train all of them together, learning also from general patterns amongst series. The first two are related to the standardization of the target variable, and included as static variables in the model. For these series, target center has a value of 0 and target scale is the median of the time series. The importance of these variables is as follows: target center> series id> target scale.

The encoder variables contain the features for which past values are known at prediction time, and consist of the features selected previously in addition to the index indicating the relative time. In this case, the relative time takes values between -72 (input length) and 0. The importance of each of these variables can be seen in Figure 12. The horizontal solar irradiation received most of the attention (almost 25%), followed by the target variable and the solar zenith (around 12.5% each). Relative humidity and the sine and cosine transformation of the month are variables with a limited weight on the encoder side.

Decoder variables are those features for which future values are known at prediction time. For the decoder, the relative time index takes values between -72 and 24 (prediction length). The importance of each of these variables for the prediction model can be observed in Figure 13. Solar zenith and horizontal solar irradiation play a significant role, summing almost 60% of the weighted importance.

The results from both the encoder and decoder weighted importance highlight the necessity of having a good representation of solar zenith and horizontal solar irradiation to achieve high prediction performance.

Finally, Figure 14 represents the attention weight patterns for one-step-ahead forecasts, which can be used to understand the most important past time steps that the TFT model focused on. It shows that the attention displays a cyclic pattern, with clear attention peaks at daily intervals. Thus, the attention is focused on the closest values, and in values at the same hour of previous days. This behavior is understandable since the PV energy production follows the same periodic pattern, as can be seen in Figure 6.

4. Conclusions

PV energy production varies significantly due to many factors, including weather conditions, time of day, season, solar irradiance, panel degradation, shading, and other uncontrollable factors. These variations create challenges for power systems because they cause grid instability and imbalances in the supply and demand of electricity amongst other complications. An accurate forecast of the PV power generation helps to guarantee the operation of the power system.

In this study, the TFT, a novel deep learning algorithm, is tested to address the hourly day-ahead PV energy production on datasets from different facilities. This algorithm is able to learn long-term and short-term temporal relationships respectively, and also helps to efficiently build feature representations of static variables, observed and known time-varying inputs. These different components allow the model to be successful in producing accurate forecasts, outperforming other advanced methods like LSTM.

TFT outperformed the other models for predicting PV energy production in the six facilities analyzed, providing better values for all the accuracy indicators. Comparing TFT with LSTM, the second-best model, the indicators of RMSE, MAE, and MASE, for the facilities in Australia are 46%, 48%, 48% lower, and 20%, 26%, and 54% lower for the facilities in Germany.

The TFT model has also performed well in facilities which did not have an on-site weather station where the meteorological variables had to be collected from the nearest meteorological station. This is of great importance since a large number of small and medium solar PV facilities do not have a pyranometer on site. The study shows the importance of detection and replacement of outliers in these types of facilities.

The importance of the decoder and encoder variables has been also calculated, revealing that solar horizontal irradiation and the zenith angle are the key variables for the model.

This model can also calculate the prediction intervals, estimating the uncertainty of the forecast which facilitates the operation and management of the facilities and for economic dispatch optimization.

In relation to the limitations and complexity of the model used, it should be noted that TFT needs a larger amount of data to achieve good prediction results. Besides, it is also a complex model, requiring higher maintenance due to higher computational and storage resources. When this is not an issue, the outcomes show that this research can be of great benefit to grid operators, plant managers and customers. The use of more complex models, such as TFT, provides more accurate PV production predictions, which contributes to improve the management of the power system.

Author Contributions: Conceptualization, M.L.S., X.G.-S., F.E.C., P.C.O. and G.B.G.; methodology, M.L.S.; software, M.L.S.; validation, M.L.S., X.G.-S.; formal analysis, M.L.S.; investigation, M.L.S., X.G.-S. and F.E.C.; data curation, M.L.S.; writing—original draft preparation, M.L.S., X.G.-S. and F.E.C.; writing—review and editing, M.L.S., X.G.-S., G.B.G. and F.E.C.; visualization, M.L.S., X.G.-S., G.B.G.; supervision, G.B.G., F.E.C. and P.C.O.; project administration, F.E.C. and P.C.O.; funding acquisition, F.E.C. and P.C.O. All authors have read and agreed to the published version of the manuscript.

Funding: This research was funded by CERVERA Research Program of CDTI, the Industrial and Technological Development Centre of Spain, through the Research Projects HySGrid+, grant number CER-20191019, and CEL.IA, grant number CER-20211022. The APC was funded by CERVERA Research Program of CDTI, through the Research Project HySGrid+, grant number CER-20191019.

Institutional Review Board Statement: Not applicable.

Informed Consent Statement: Not applicable.

Data Availability Statement: Not applicable.

Conflicts of Interest: The authors declare no conflict of interest. The funders had no role in the design of the study; in the collection, analyses, or interpretation of data; in the writing of the manuscript, or in the decision to publish the results.

References

1. European Commission. *The European Green Deal*; European Commission: Brussels, Belgium, 2019.
2. IEA. *Solar PV*; International Energy Agency: Paris, France, 2021.
3. International Renewable Energy Agency. *Future of Solar Photovoltaic Deployment, Investment, Technology, Grid Integration and Socio-Economic Aspects A Global Energy Transformation Paper About IRENA*; International Renewable Energy Agency: Masdar City, Abu Dhabi, 2019; ISBN 978-92-9260-156-0.
4. Raza, M.Q.; Nadarajah, M.; Ekanayake, C. On Recent Advances in PV Output Power Forecast. *Sol. Energy* **2016**, *136*, 125–144. [CrossRef]
5. International Energy Agency. *World Energy Outlook 2021*; International Energy Agency: Paris, France, 2021.
6. Akhter, M.N.; Mekhilef, S.; Mokhlis, H.; Ali, R.; Usama, M.; Muhammad, M.A.; Khairuddin, A.S.M. A Hybrid Deep Learning Method for an Hour Ahead Power Output Forecasting of Three Different Photovoltaic Systems. *Appl. Energy* **2022**, *307*, 118185. [CrossRef]
7. Shivashankar, S.; Mekhilef, S.; Mokhlis, H.; Karimi, M. Mitigating Methods of Power Fluctuation of Photovoltaic (PV) Sources—A Review. *Renew. Sustain. Energy Rev.* **2016**, *59*, 1170–1184. [CrossRef]
8. Antonanzas, J.; Osorio, N.; Escobar, R.; Urraca, R.; Martinez-de-Pison, F.J.; Antonanzas-Torres, F. Review of Photovoltaic Power Forecasting. *Sol. Energy* **2016**, *136*, 78–111. [CrossRef]
9. Pierro, M.; Moser, D.; Perez, R.; Cornaro, C. The Value of PV Power Forecast and the Paradox of the "Single Pricing" Scheme: The Italian Case Study. *Energies* **2020**, *13*, 3945. [CrossRef]
10. Zahraoui, Y.; Alhamrouni, I.; Mekhilef, S.; Basir Khan, M.R. Chapter One-Machine Learning Algorithms Used for Short-Term PV Solar Irradiation and Temperature Forecasting at Microgrid. In *Applications of AI and IOT in Renewable Energy*; Academic Press: Cambridge, MA, USA, 2022; pp. 1–17. ISBN 978-0-323-91699-8.

11. López, E.; Monteiro, J.; Carrasco, P.; Sáenz, J.; Pinto, N.; Blázquez, G. Development, Implementation and Evaluation of a Wireless Sensor Network and a Web-Based Platform for the Monitoring and Management of a Microgrid with Renewable Energy Sources. In Proceedings of the 2019 International Conference on Smart Energy Systems and Technologies (SEST), Porto, Portugal, 9–11 September 2019; pp. 1–6.
12. Hao, Y.; Dong, L.; Liang, J.; Liao, X.; Wang, L.; Shi, L. Power Forecasting-Based Coordination Dispatch of PV Power Generation and Electric Vehicles Charging in Microgrid. *Renew. Energy* **2020**, *155*, 1191–1210. [CrossRef]
13. Aslam, M.; Lee, J.M.; Kim, H.S.; Lee, S.J.; Hong, S. Deep Learning Models for Long-Term Solar Radiation Forecasting Considering Microgrid Installation: A Comparative Study. *Energies* **2019**, *13*, 147. [CrossRef]
14. Ramsami, P.; Oree, V. A Hybrid Method for Forecasting the Energy Output of Photovoltaic Systems. *Energy Convers. Manag.* **2015**, *95*, 406–413. [CrossRef]
15. Ahmed, R.; Sreeram, V.; Mishra, Y.; Arif, M.D. A Review and Evaluation of the State-of-the-Art in PV Solar Power Forecasting: Techniques and Optimization. *Renew. Sustain. Energy Rev.* **2020**, *124*, 109792. [CrossRef]
16. Dolara, A.; Leva, S.; Manzolini, G. Comparison of Different Physical Models for PV Power Output Prediction. *Sol. Energy* **2015**, *119*, 83–99. [CrossRef]
17. Dutta, S.; Li, Y.; Venkataraman, A.; Costa, L.M.; Jiang, T.; Plana, R.; Tordjman, P.; Choo, F.H.; Foo, C.F.; Puttgen, H.B. Load and Renewable Energy Forecasting for a Microgrid Using Persistence Technique. *Energy Procedia* **2017**, *143*, 617–622. [CrossRef]
18. Shireen, T.; Shao, C.; Wang, H.; Li, J.; Zhang, X.; Li, M. Iterative Multi-Task Learning for Time-Series Modeling of Solar Panel PV Outputs. *Appl. Energy* **2018**, *212*, 654–662. [CrossRef]
19. Ardila, S.; Maciel, V.M.; Ledesma, J.N.; Gaspar, D.; Dinho Da Silva, P.; Pires, L.C.; María, V.; Nunes Maciel, J.; Javier, J.; Ledesma, G.; et al. Fuzzy Time Series Methods Applied to (In)Direct Short-Term Photovoltaic Power Forecasting. *Energies* **2022**, *15*, 845. [CrossRef]
20. Almonacid, F.; Pérez-Higueras, P.J.; Fernández, E.F.; Hontoria, L. A Methodology Based on Dynamic Artificial Neural Network for Short-Term Forecasting of the Power Output of a PV Generator. *Energy Convers. Manag.* **2014**, *85*, 389–398. [CrossRef]
21. Wang, F.; Xuan, Z.; Zhen, Z.; Li, K.; Wang, T.; Shi, M. A Day-Ahead PV Power Forecasting Method Based on LSTM-RNN Model and Time Correlation Modification under Partial Daily Pattern Prediction Framework. *Energy Convers. Manag.* **2020**, *212*, 112766. [CrossRef]
22. Massucco, S.; Mosaico, G.; Saviozzi, M.; Silvestro, F. A Hybrid Technique for Day-Ahead PV Generation Forecasting Using Clear-Sky Models or Ensemble of Artificial Neural Networks According to a Decision Tree Approach. *Energies* **2019**, *12*, 1298. [CrossRef]
23. Li, P.; Zhou, K.; Lu, X.; Yang, S. A Hybrid Deep Learning Model for Short-Term PV Power Forecasting. *Appl. Energy* **2020**, *259*, 114216. [CrossRef]
24. Raza, M.Q.; Mithulananthan, N.; Summerfield, A. Solar Output Power Forecast Using an Ensemble Framework with Neural Predictors and Bayesian Adaptive Combination. *Sol. Energy* **2018**, *166*, 226–241. [CrossRef]
25. Dolara, A.; Grimaccia, F.; Leva, S.; Mussetta, M.; Ogliari, E. A Physical Hybrid Artificial Neural Network for Short Term Forecasting of PV Plant Power Output. *Energies* **2015**, *8*, 1138–1153. [CrossRef]
26. Lotfi, M.; Javadi, M.; Osório, G.J.; Monteiro, C.; Catalão, J.P.S. A Novel Ensemble Algorithm for Solar Power Forecasting Based on Kernel Density Estimation. *Energies* **2020**, *13*, 216. [CrossRef]
27. Radicioni, M.; Lucaferri, V.; de Lia, F.; Laudani, A.; Presti, R.L.; Lozito, G.M.; Fulginei, F.R.; Schioppo, R.; Tucci, M. Power Forecasting of a Photovoltaic Plant Located in ENEA Casaccia Research Center. *Energies* **2021**, *14*, 707. [CrossRef]
28. Cervone, G.; Clemente-Harding, L.; Alessandrini, S.; Delle Monache, L. Short-Term Photovoltaic Power Forecasting Using Artificial Neural Networks and an Analog Ensemble. *Renew. Energy* **2017**, *108*, 274–286. [CrossRef]
29. Pan, M.; Li, C.; Gao, R.; Huang, Y.; You, H.; Gu, T.; Qin, F. Photovoltaic Power Forecasting Based on a Support Vector Machine with Improved Ant Colony Optimization. *J. Clean. Prod.* **2020**, *277*, 123948. [CrossRef]
30. Zendehboudi, A.; Baseer, M.A.; Saidur, R. Application of Support Vector Machine Models for Forecasting Solar and Wind Energy Resources: A Review. *J. Clean. Prod.* **2018**, *199*, 272–285. [CrossRef]
31. Tang, P.; Chen, D.; Hou, Y. Entropy Method Combined with Extreme Learning Machine Method for the Short-Term Photovoltaic Power Generation Forecasting. *Chaos Solitons Fractals* **2016**, *89*, 243–248. [CrossRef]
32. Hossain, M.; Mekhilef, S.; Danesh, M.; Olatomiwa, L.; Shamshirband, S. Application of Extreme Learning Machine for Short Term Output Power Forecasting of Three Grid-Connected PV Systems. *J. Clean. Prod.* **2017**, *167*, 395–405. [CrossRef]
33. Almonacid, F.; Rus, C.; Hontoria, L.; Muñoz, F.J. Characterisation of PV CIS Module by Artificial Neural Networks. A Comparative Study with Other Methods. *Renew. Energy* **2010**, *35*, 973–980. [CrossRef]
34. Oudjana, S.H.; Hellal, A.; Mahammed, I.H. Power Forecasting of Photovoltaic Generation. *Int. J. Electr. Comput. Eng.* **2013**, *7*, 627–631.
35. Monteiro, R.V.A.; Guimarães, G.C.; Moura, F.A.M.; Albertini, M.R.M.C.; Albertini, M.K. Estimating Photovoltaic Power Generation: Performance Analysis of Artificial Neural Networks, Support Vector Machine and Kalman Filter. *Electr. Power Syst. Res.* **2017**, *143*, 643–656. [CrossRef]
36. Matteri, A.; Ogliari, E.; Nespoli, A.; Rojas, F.; Herrera, L.J.; Pomare, H. Enhanced Day-Ahead PV Power Forecast: Dataset Clustering for an Effective Artificial Neural Network Training. *Eng. Proc.* **2021**, *5*, 16. [CrossRef]

37. Mellit, A.; Pavan, A.M.; Lughi, V. Deep Learning Neural Networks for Short-Term Photovoltaic Power Forecasting. *Renew. Energy* **2021**, *172*, 276–288. [CrossRef]
38. Mishra, M.; Byomakesha Dash, P.; Nayak, J.; Naik, B.; Kumar Swain, S. Deep Learning and Wavelet Transform Integrated Approach for Short-Term Solar PV Power Prediction. *Measurement* **2020**, *166*, 108250. [CrossRef]
39. Zang, H.; Cheng, L.; Ding, T.; Cheung, K.; Liang, Z.; Wei, Z.; Sun, G. A Hybrid Method for Short-Term Photovoltaic Power Forecasting Based on Deep Convolutional Neural Network. *IET Gener. Transm. Distrib.* **2018**, *12*, 4557–4567. [CrossRef]
40. Suresh, V.; Janik, P.; Rezmer, J.; Leonowicz, Z. Forecasting Solar PV Output Using Convolutional Neural Networks with a Sliding Window Algorithm. *Energies* **2020**, *13*, 723. [CrossRef]
41. Yu, D.; Lee, S.; Lee, S.; Choi, W.; Liu, L. Forecasting Photovoltaic Power Generation Using Satellite Images. *Energies* **2020**, *13*, 6603. [CrossRef]
42. Yona, A.; Senjyu, T.; Funabashi, T.; Kim, C. Determination Method of Insolation Prediction with Fuzzy and Applying Neural Network for Long-Term Ahead PV Power Output Correction. *IEEE Trans. Sustain. Energy* **2013**, *4*, 527–533. [CrossRef]
43. Li, G.; Wang, H.; Zhang, S.; Xin, J.; Liu, H. Recurrent Neural Networks Based Photovoltaic Power Forecasting Approach. *Energies* **2019**, *12*, 2538. [CrossRef]
44. Maitanova, N.; Telle, J.S.; Hanke, B.; Grottke, M.; Schmidt, T.; von Maydell, K.; Agert, C. A Machine Learning Approach to Low-Cost Photovoltaic Power Prediction Based on Publicly Available Weather Reports. *Energies* **2020**, *13*, 735. [CrossRef]
45. Yu, D.; Choi, W.; Kim, M.; Liu, L. Forecasting Day-Ahead Hourly Photovoltaic Power Generation Using Convolutional Self-Attention Based Long Short-Term Memory. *Energies* **2020**, *13*, 4017. [CrossRef]
46. Abdel-Nasser, M.; Mahmoud, K. Accurate Photovoltaic Power Forecasting Models Using Deep LSTM-RNN. *Neural Comput. Appl* **2019**, *31*, 2727–2740. [CrossRef]
47. Zheng, J.; Zhang, H.; Dai, Y.; Wang, B.; Zheng, T.; Liao, Q.; Liang, Y.; Zhang, F.; Song, X. Time Series Prediction for Output of Multi-Region Solar Power Plants. *Appl. Energy* **2020**, *257*, 114001. [CrossRef]
48. Luo, X.; Zhang, D.; Zhu, X. Deep Learning Based Forecasting of Photovoltaic Power Generation by Incorporating Domain Knowledge. *Energy* **2021**, *225*, 120240. [CrossRef]
49. Kim, B.; Suh, D.; Otto, M.O.; Huh, J.S. A Novel Hybrid Spatio-Temporal Forecasting of Multisite Solar Photovoltaic Generation. *Remote Sens.* **2021**, *13*, 2605. [CrossRef]
50. Lim, B.; Arık, S.; Loeff, N.; Pfister, T. Temporal Fusion Transformers for Interpretable Multi-Horizon Time Series Forecasting. *Int. J. Forecast.* **2021**, *37*, 1748–1764. [CrossRef]
51. Data Platform–Open Power System Data. Available online: https://data.open-power-system-data.org/household_data/ (accessed on 24 March 2022).
52. DKASC, Alice Springs DKA Solar Centre. Available online: http://dkasolarcentre.com.au/locations/alice-springs (accessed on 24 March 2022).
53. Wetter Und Klima-Deutscher Wetterdienst-Our Services-Open Data Server. Available online: https://www.dwd.de/EN/ourservices/opendata/opendata.html (accessed on 24 March 2022).
54. Ram, A.; Kumar, M. A Density Based Algorithm for Discovering Density Varied Clusters in Large Spatial Databases Sunita Jalal. *Int. J. Comput. Appl.* **2010**, *3*, 975–8887.
55. Witten, I.H.; Frank, E.; Hall, M.A. Data Transformations. In *Data Mining: Practical Machine Learning Tools and Techniques*; Elsevier: Amsterdam, The Netherlands, 2011; pp. 305–349. [CrossRef]
56. PyTorch Forecasting Documentation—Pytorch-Forecasting Documentation. Available online: https://pytorch-forecasting.readthedocs.io/en/stable/# (accessed on 2 June 2022).
57. Gunning, D.; Stefik, M.; Choi, J.; Miller, T.; Stumpf, S.; Yang, G.Z. XAI—Explainable Artificial Intelligence. *Sci. Robot.* **2019**, *4*, eaay7120. [CrossRef]
58. Asteriou, D.; Hall, S.G. ARIMA Models and the Box-Jenkins Methodology. *Appl. Econom.* **2016**, *2*, 275–296. [CrossRef]
59. Haykin, S.S. *Neural Networks: A Comprehensive Foundation*; Prentice Hall PTR: Hoboken, NJ, USA, 1994.
60. Hochreiter, S.; Schmidhuber, J. Long Short-Term Memory. *Neural Comput.* **1997**, *9*, 1735–1780. [CrossRef]
61. Chen, T.; Guestrin, C. XGBoost: A Scalable Tree Boosting System. In Proceedings of the 22nd ACM SIGKDD International Conference on Knowledge Discovery and Data Mining, San Francisco, CA, USA, 13–17 August 2016. [CrossRef]
62. NNI Documentation—Neural Network Intelligence. Available online: https://nni.readthedocs.io/en/stable/index.html (accessed on 2 June 2022).
63. Cheng, H.Y.; Yu, C.C.; Hsu, K.C.; Chan, C.C.; Tseng, M.H.; Lin, C.L. Estimating Solar Irradiance on Tilted Surface with Arbitrary Orientations and Tilt Angles. *Energy* **2019**, *12*, 1427. [CrossRef]
64. Kraemer, F.A.; Palma, D.; Braten, A.E.; Ammar, D. Operationalizing Solar Energy Predictions for Sustainable, Autonomous IoT Device Management. *IEEE Internet Things J.* **2020**, *7*, 11803–11814. [CrossRef]
65. Wang, J.; Li, P.; Ran, R.; Che, Y.; Zhou, Y. A Short-Term Photovoltaic Power Prediction Model Based on the Gradient Boost Decision Tree. *Appl. Sci.* **2018**, *8*, 689. [CrossRef]
66. Wu, B.; Wang, L.; Zeng, Y.-R. Interpretable Wind Speed Prediction with Multivariate Time Series and Temporal Fusion Transformers. *Energy* **2022**, *252*, 123990. [CrossRef]
67. Zhang, H.; Zou, Y.; Yang, X.; Yang, H. A Temporal Fusion Transformer for Short-Term Freeway Traffic Speed Multistep Prediction. *Neurocomputing* **2022**, *500*, 329–340. [CrossRef]

68. Olmo, F.J.; Vida, J.; Foyo, I.; Castro-Diez, Y.; Alados-Arboledas, L. Prediction of Global Irradiance on Inclined Surfaces from Horizontal Global Irradiance. *Energy* **1999**, *24*, 689–704. [CrossRef]
69. Said, S.A.M.; Hassan, G.; Walwil, H.M.; Al-Aqeeli, N. The Effect of Environmental Factors and Dust Accumulation on Photovoltaic Modules and Dust-Accumulation Mitigation Strategies. *Renew. Sustain. Energy Rev.* **2018**, *82*, 743–760. [CrossRef]

Article

Revolutionizing Photovoltaic Systems: An Innovative Approach to Maximum Power Point Tracking Using Enhanced Dandelion Optimizer in Partial Shading Conditions

Elmamoune Halassa [1], Lakhdar Mazouz [1], Abdellatif Seghiour [2,3], Aissa Chouder [3] and Santiago Silvestre [4,*]

1. Applied Automation and Industrial Diagnostic Laboratory (LAADI), Ziane Achour University of Djelfa, Djelfa 17000, Algeria
2. Ecole Supérieure en Génie Electrique et Énergétique d'Oran, Laboratory of Electrical and Materials Engineering (LGEM), Oran 31000, Algeria
3. Electrical Engineering Laboratory (LGE), University Mohamed Boudiaf of M'sila, BP 166, M'sila 28000, Algeria
4. MNT Group, Electronic Engineering Department, Universitat Politécnica de Catalunya (UPC) BarcelonaTech, C/Jordi Girona 1-3, Campus Nord UPC, 08034 Barcelona, Spain
* Correspondence: santiago.silvestre@upc.edu

Abstract: Partial shading (PS) is a prevalent phenomenon that often affects photovoltaic (PV) installations, leads to the appearance of numerous peaks in the power-voltage characteristics of PV cells, caused by the uneven distribution of solar irradiance on the PV module surface, known as global and local maximum power point (GMPP and LMPP). In this paper, a new technique for achieving GMPP based on the dandelion optimizer (DO) algorithm is proposed, inspired by the movement of dandelion seeds in the wind. The proposed technique aimed to enhance the efficiency of power generation in PV systems, particularly under PS conditions. However, the DO-based MPPT is compared with other advanced maximum power point tracker (MPPT) algorithms, such as Particle Swarm Optimization (PSO), Grey Wolf Optimization (GWO), Artificial Bee Colony (ABC), Cuckoo Search Algorithm (CSA), and Bat Algorithm (BA). Simulation results establish the superiority and effectiveness of the used MPPT in terms of tracking efficiency, speed, robustness, and simplicity of implementation. Additionally, these results reveal that the DO algorithm exhibits higher performance, with a root mean square error (RMSE) of 1.09 watts, a convergence time of 2.3 milliseconds, and mean absolute error (MAE) of 0.13 watts.

Keywords: maximum power point tracker (MPPT); photovoltaic; partial shading conditions (PSCs); dandelion optimizer; optimization

Citation: Halassa, E.; Mazouz, L.; Seghiour, A.; Chouder, A.; Silvestre, S. Revolutionizing Photovoltaic Systems: An Innovative Approach to Maximum Power Point Tracking Using Enhanced Dandelion Optimizer in Partial Shading Conditions. *Energies* 2023, *16*, 3617. https://doi.org/10.3390/en16093617

Academic Editor: Enrique Romero-Cadaval

Received: 24 March 2023
Revised: 11 April 2023
Accepted: 20 April 2023
Published: 22 April 2023

Copyright: © 2023 by the authors. Licensee MDPI, Basel, Switzerland. This article is an open access article distributed under the terms and conditions of the Creative Commons Attribution (CC BY) license (https://creativecommons.org/licenses/by/4.0/).

1. Introduction

The growing population has led to a higher demand for electricity, as it has become a crucial aspect of modern life, and a blackout could cause serious disruptions and losses. With the world's economy and social life recovering, especially post-pandemic, increasing electricity generation capacity is imperative to meet these demands. However, traditional electricity generation methods such as using coal, gas, and fossil fuels have a harmful effect on the environment. As per the International Energy Agency (IEA), the global power sector's CO_2 emissions rose to nearly 700 million tons in 2021, surpassing the previous record by over 14 Gt. The United Nations (UN) views electricity generation as a major contributor to global climate change, with fossil fuels still accounting for over 80% of global energy production [1].

The degradation of PV modules can negatively impact MPP tracking, particularly in regions with low humidity. Over time, the performance parameters of PV modules, such as efficiency, current, and series resistance, may change due to degradation, which could necessitate adjustments to MPP tracking algorithms. When a PV module experiences a decline in efficiency, the MPP tracking algorithm might need to be modified to optimize power generation in light of the reduced output power. Similarly, if the series resistance of the PV module increases as a result of degradation, the MPP tracking algorithm might need to account for this change in impedance and be adjusted accordingly to ensure accurate MPP tracking. In general, the degradation of PV modules can affect the precision and efficacy of MPP tracking algorithms. As such, PV system designers and operators should keep this in mind when implementing MPP tracking algorithms in regions with low humidity. Appropriate updates or adjustments may be necessary to ensure optimal power generation from the PV system [2,3].

Solar power is the most widely popular renewable source because it is clean, accessible, and freely available. However, solar PV systems have limitations, with their output dependent on climate conditions and affected by non-linear characteristics of current–voltage and power–voltage [4]. To overcome these limitations, an effective MPPT is required to retrieve the utmost power from PV systems and ensure they operate at optimal levels under different conditions. The MPPT must operate with speed and efficiency to maintain stability in the PV system, particularly through rapidly changing shading situations. In order to maintain a steady output voltage for the photovoltaic (PV) system, a DC–DC converter is necessary to control the maximum power point (MPP) through adjusting its duty cycle [5]. Figure 1 demonstrates the positioning of a boost converter between the PV array and the load within the MPPT, and various algorithms can be utilized to adjust its duty cycle, which form the basis of the MPPT controller and are often implemented using a microcontroller.

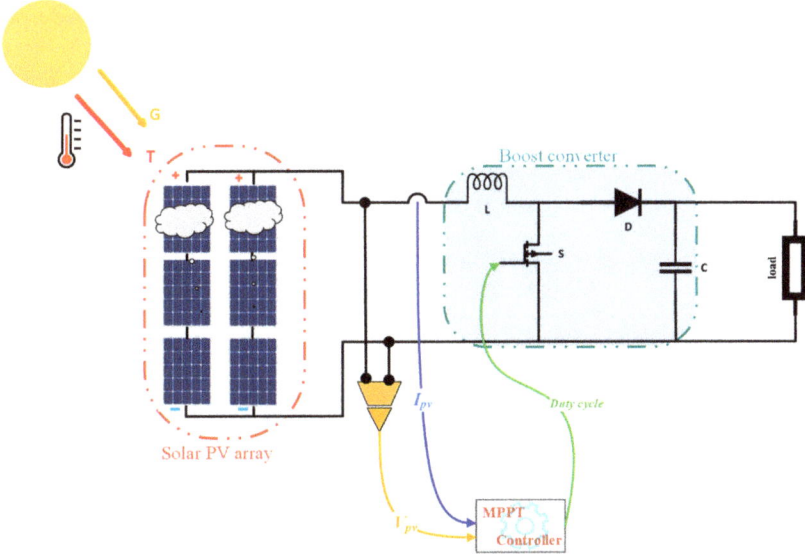

Figure 1. Illustration of PV System with Boost Converter for MPPT.

However, traditional MPPT techniques, such as Perturb and Observe (P&O) and Incremental Conductance (IC), fail to track the GMPP, as they are unable to distinguish between the LMPP and GMPP. This can lead to being stuck at one of the LMPPs and greatly reducing the energy generated by the system. To overcome this problem effectively, various computational intelligence techniques have been suggested by many authors to address these limitations and track the MPP regardless of weather conditions. The optimization algorithms possess several valuable features, including the capability to efficiently solve non-linear optimization problems with low failure rates, fast convergence times, and minimal oscillations, covering a broad range of research [6]. These attributes are highly desirable for researchers who intend to monitor the GMPP across diverse weather conditions. The first feature is crucial in avoiding the algorithm becoming fixed at a local peak, thus minimizing the loss of production power from the PV system. The second attribute ensures stability in the PV system, particularly during online optimization with substantial dynamic changes in PSCs. The last feature ensures the attainment of the GMPP. Metaheuristic techniques constitute a set of algorithms used to address optimization problems. These algorithms are influenced by natural phenomena such as evolution, migration, and swarm behavior and are employed when traditional optimization methods are either infeasible or too slow. With several beneficial characteristics, including the ability to effectively solve non-linear optimization problems with low failure rates, quick convergence times, and minimal oscillation, they have gained popularity among researchers seeking to track the GMPP under any weather conditions. The first advantage of these techniques prevents the algorithm from becoming stuck at a local peak, thereby avoiding significant losses in the output power of the PV system. The second characteristic helps maintain the stability of the PV system during online optimization with changing PSCs.

In the field of MPPT, numerous optimization algorithms have been developed, including HOA [1], PSO [7], GWO [8], ABC [9], Cuckoo Search Optimization (CSO) [10], Group Teaching Optimization (GTO) [11], Harris Hawk Optimization (HHO) [12], Grasshopper Optimization (GHO) [13], Bat Algorithm (BA) [14], Improved Team Game Optimization (TGO) [10], Ant Colony Optimization (ACO) [11], Modified Butterfly Optimization (MBO) [15], Henry Gas Solubility Optimization (HGSO) [16], and Pattern Search (PS) [17]. Most of these algorithms are based on updating the position of the agent based on its location, making them less susceptible to high oscillation and weak convergence [1,18]. However, the main difference between these algorithms lies in the use of various strategies in the initial and final steps of optimization to enhance exploration and exploitation, respectively [6]. The PSO algorithm is based on the social behavior of bird flocks and fish schools. It utilizes a group of particles that navigate the search space to find the optimal solution. Each particle's movement, consisting of its position and speed, is impacted by its personal best solution, and the best solution found by the entire swarm [19]. The PSO algorithm targets the solution space, where each location signifies a particular level of problem-solving potential [20]. To determine the best solution, it guides particles throughout the solution space, with each particle relying on its understanding of nearby particles [21]. The particle position is defined by the duty cycle value of the DC–DC converter, with the generated power serving as the fitness value evaluation function.

The ABC algorithm is a metaheuristic optimization method inspired by the foraging behavior of honeybee swarms [22]. This algorithm integrates local search techniques performed by employed bees with global search techniques carried out by onlookers and scouts to strike a balance between exploration and exploitation. The GWO algorithm is based on the hunting behavior of a grey wolf pack. The pack consists of Alpha, Beta, Delta, and Omega wolves with a strict hierarchical structure. Alpha wolves are the leaders, Beta wolves provide support, Delta wolves follow instructions, and Omega wolves occupy the lowest rank and may be used as scapegoats [23]. The MPPT-based GWO approach optimizes the power output of photovoltaic systems by combining the strengths of the GWO algorithm and the MPPT technique. MPPT-based PSO is a popular optimization method in photovoltaic systems. Despite its widespread use, it is not without limitations. One of its major drawbacks is the slow convergence time, which can occur when particles move at a low speed, leading to longer optimization times and reduced efficiency of the system. Another issue is the tendency for the algorithm to diverge when particles move too quickly, resulting in suboptimal solutions [15]. A significant issue with the ABC algorithm is its failure to distinguish between uniform and partial shading conditions, as the same termination criteria are used for both. Consequently, uniform shading conditions may lead to a slower convergence time, as the controller must undergo repeated iterations to establish the steady-state duty cycle, just as in complex partial shading conditions [15]. In one study, a proposed enhanced CS algorithm is recommended as the MPPT approach for PV systems under dynamic partial shading. The research found that the improved CS strategy outperforms other swarm optimization techniques, addressing the problem of local peaks and improving the performance of the CS algorithm. Otherwise, the paper [10] mentions that optimization techniques, in general, can suffer from long convergence times. The authors of [14] propose using bat-based optimization techniques for MPPTs in PV systems and compare the performance of these techniques, including Bat-P&O, Bat-Beta, and Bat-IC, to traditional algorithms. The paper also suggests combining bat-based algorithms with traditional algorithms to reduce power oscillations and improve system performance.

The latter metaheuristic optimization algorithms have been widely used due to their ability to handle complex and non-linear systems. The dandelion algorithm is an innovative optimization method inspired by the sowing behavior of dandelions. Specifically, it incorporates self-learning capability and dynamic radius adjustment to efficiently explore the solution space and optimize extreme learning machines (ELM). Notably, the algorithm has exhibited superior performance compared to other optimization algorithms in terms of convergence speed and accuracy [24]. Further, in one study, the DA is applied to optimize extreme learning machines (ELM) for biomedical classification problems, resulting in significant enhancements in classification accuracy. Moreover, the study delves into exploring different fusion methods to generate fusion classifiers with superior accuracy and stability [25]. The authors in [26] postulate using DO to identify the Proton Exchange Membrane Fuel Cells (PEMFC) model parameters with precision, overcoming the pitfalls of metaheuristic algorithms. The study appraises the DO approach under steady-state and dynamic conditions and gauges its efficacy against other techniques, evincing a promising yield and superior performance. To improve the DO algorithm's exploration ability and prevent it from falling into local optima, ref. [27] proposes a novel competition mechanism that incorporates historical information feedback. The fitness value of each dandelion in the next generation is compared with the current best dandelion, and the weaker dandelion is replaced by a new offspring. This approach improves the offspring generation process by utilizing an estimation-of-distribution algorithm to exploit historical information. Three historical information models are designed: the best, worst, and hybrid historical information feedback models. The authors in [28] have presented a novel approach, the dandelion code, as an alternative to the widely used Pruumlfer code for finding optimal spanning trees. While the Pruumlfer code has been criticized for its low locality, the dandelion code exhibits higher efficiency and greater locality. Although direct encoding and NetKeys currently outperform the dandelion code in test problems, the proposed method is still a strong alternative, particularly for larger networks.

Reference [29] introduces a new swarm intelligence bioinspired optimization algorithm named DO to tackle continuous optimization problems. The DO algorithm is inspired by the flight patterns of dandelion seeds carried by the wind, which are modeled into three stages: rising, descending, and landing. The DO algorithm employs Brownian motion and a Levy random walk to simulate the flying trajectory of a seed during the descending stage and landing stage. The DO algorithm can be used as an MPPT method in photovoltaic systems. It is capable of effectively balancing the trade-offs between tracking speed, accuracy, and convergence. By simulating the process of dandelion seed long-distance flight relying on wind, the DO algorithm can optimize the efficiency and performance of solar PV systems. In the rising stage, the seeds rise in a spiral manner due to the eddies from above or drift locally in communities according to different weather conditions. In the descending stage, flying seeds steadily descend by constantly adjusting their direction in global space. In the landing stage, seeds land in randomly selected positions so that they grow. The moving trajectory of a seed in the descending stage and landing stage is described by Brownian motion and a Levy random walk.

Although widely used, some optimization algorithms have limitations in tracking MPP for PV systems, as previously mentioned. DO is a promising solution, inspired by the dispersal mechanism of dandelion plants. Its unique features make it a strong candidate for MPPT algorithms in photovoltaic systems. A comprehensive evaluation of

DO's performance is provided in Table 1, in comparison to existing optimization algorithms. This article aims to thoroughly investigate the potential of DO for MPPTs in photovoltaic systems. This paper focuses on the following key contributions:

- This work introduces a novel optimization algorithm referred to as DO, which is designed to determine the GMPP of the Algerian PV system. The DO algorithm employs advanced mathematical techniques to search for and locate the optimal operating point of the system, thereby ensuring the system operates at its highest possible efficiency.
- The paper presents a comprehensive comparison between the newly proposed DO optimization algorithm and five established benchmark optimization algorithms, namely, PSO, ABC, GWO, CSA, and BA, utilizing a simulation model for a photovoltaic (PV) system with maximum power point tracking (MPPT). The comparative analysis evaluates the algorithms' performance based on various performance metrics, including convergence speed, accuracy, and robustness. The results of the analysis demonstrate the superior performance of the DO algorithm over the benchmark algorithms, indicating its potential for effective optimization of PV systems with MPPT.
- A dataset is utilized consisting of records collected over a two-day period of uniform irradiance and complex PS. These databases are employed in a co-simulation paradigm, leveraging MATLAB-PSIM software, to undertake dynamic validation of the proposed approach. Such an approach enables the investigation of the system's behavior over time, considering the impact of changing environmental conditions, and facilitates the assessment of model robustness and accuracy. By integrating the databases with the simulation software, the approach provides a comprehensive platform for testing and validating the proposed methodology, thereby enabling its effective implementation in real-world applications.

Table 1. Comparison study between metaheuristic algorithms' MPPT techniques.

Methods	Reference	Year	Convergence Speed	Tracking Efficiency	Implementation Complexity	Oscillation
GWO	[8]	2016	Low	High	High	Medium
ACO	[30]	2017	Medium	Medium	Medium	Low
PSO	[7]	2018	High	High	High	Low
BA	[31]	2020	Medium	High	High	Medium
GHO	[13]	2020	High	High	High	Low
CS	[10]	2021	Low	Low	Medium	Low
ABC	[9]	2021	High	High	High	Low
DO	Proposed		Very High	Very High	Medium	Very Low

The structure of the rest of this paper is as follows: The modeling of the photovoltaic cell is outlined in Section 2. Section 3 delves into the topic of partial shading's effects and its characteristics. Section 4 provides a thorough explanation of the novel DO algorithm as well as the simulation results. The paper concludes in Section 5.

2. PV System Modelling

2.1. Overview of the PV System

This study examines a 9.54 kW PV system placed at the "Centre de Développement des Energies Renouvelables" (CDER) in Algiers, Algeria. The system comprises 30 photovoltaic modules (Isofoton 106W) arranged in 2 strings of 15 modules each. Both horizontal and plane irradiances are measured using a thermoelectric pyranometer, while the temperature of the PV modules is monitored with a thermocouple (refer to Figure 2). The data acquisition system is used to measure weather conditions such as solar irradiance and temperature, as well as electrical parameters such as voltage, current, and power. The main electrical specifications of the PV modules under Standard Test Conditions (STC) are listed in Table 2. The weather and MPP current and voltage measurements were taken at 1-min intervals.

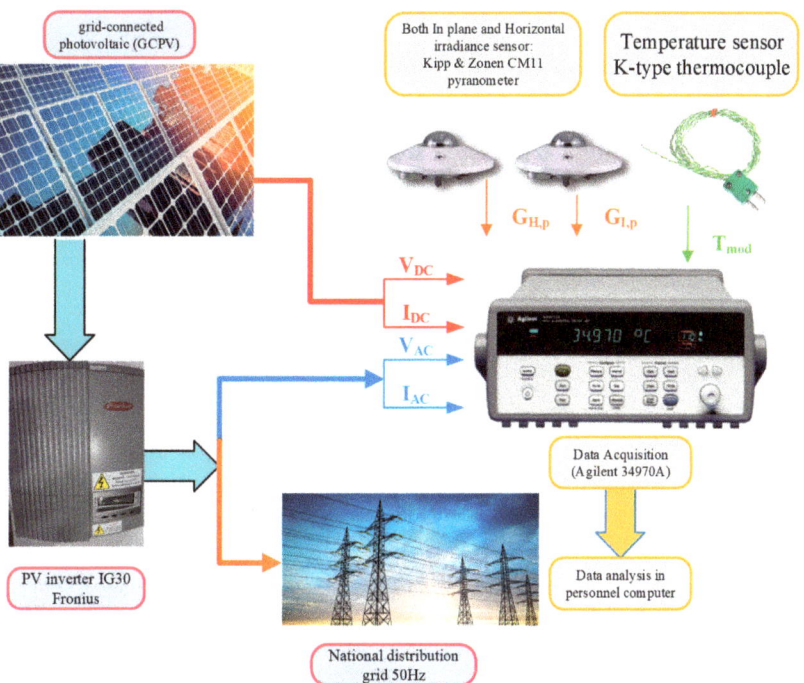

Figure 2. PV study plant and the monitored system.

Table 2. Standard Test Conditions "Isofoton 106-12" parameters.

Parameters	I_{sc} [A]	I_{mpp} [A]	V_{oc} [V]	V_{mpp} [V]	P_{mpp} [W]
Values	6.54	6.4	21.6	17.4	106

2.2. The Modeling of the Photovoltaic Cell

The modeling process requires collecting data to experimentally determine the relationships between the inputs and outputs. The data are then used to develop a mathematical model that describes the cell's behavior. The model's accuracy depends heavily on the quality of the data. Generally, the One-Diode Model (ODM) represents the actual behavior of a PV module (refer to Figure 3). It is presented in an analytical form that establishes a relationship between the PV current (I_{PV}) and PV voltage (V_{PV}) through the following equation [32,33]:

$$I_{PV} = I_{ph} - I_0 \overbrace{\left(exp\left(\frac{q(V_{PV} + R_s I_{PV})}{nk_B T_p} \right) - 1 \right)}^{I_d} - \overbrace{\frac{V_{PV} + R_s I_{PV}}{R_{sh}}}^{I_{sh}} \quad (1)$$

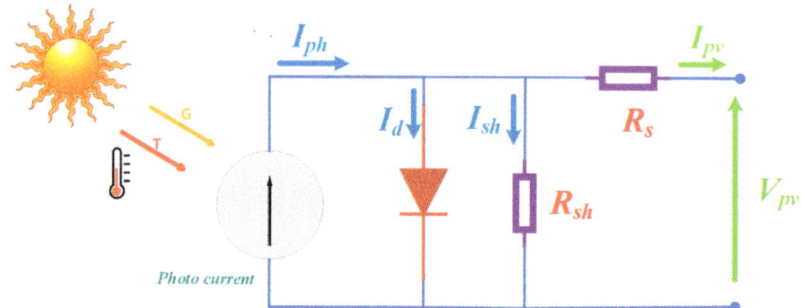

Figure 3. ODM of PV cell.

The optimization algorithm is a powerful tool for extracting the parameters of solar cells. The optimization algorithm works by finding the values of the parameters that minimize the difference between the modeled and experimental data. This is done by adjusting the parameters until the model provides the best fit to the data. There are several optimization algorithms that can be used for parameter extraction in solar cells, which are presented in [26,27]. In this research, the effective parameters of a PV cell are considered to be of great importance. To this end, the effective parameters that were reported in References [25,28] have been selected for use in this study. The reason for this choice is that these parameters have been experimentally validated and found to be highly accurate. The effective parameters of a PV cell play a crucial role in determining its performance, including its power output and conversion efficiency. These parameters describe the internal characteristics of the cell and the way it behaves under different operating conditions. By using accurate and experimentally validated effective parameters, this study aims to ensure that the results obtained are reliable and representative of the actual behavior of the PV cell. The Coyote Optimization Algorithm (COA) identified the best selected parameters, including R_{sh}, R_s, I_{ph}, I_0, and n, which are presented in Table 3 in [32].

Table 3. Isofoton 106W-12V PV module extracted parameters.

Parameter	Estimated Values
I_{ph} [A]	6.44
I_0 [A]	2.5×10^{-5}
N	1.63
R_s [Ω]	0.1403
R_{sh} [Ω]	202.46
RMSE [A]	0.011

3. Partial Shading and Its Effects

The effect of partial shading on the PV module's power–voltage (P–V) curve can be significant. The P–V curve is a graphical representation of the relationship between the module's output power and voltage at different levels of solar irradiance. When the module is not shaded, the P–V curve has a characteristic shape with a single maximum power point (MPP), which represents the optimal operating point of the module.

However, when the module is partially shaded, the P–V curve undergoes changes. The shading can cause multiple MPPs to occur, which can lead to significant power losses. The MPP is no longer a single point but rather a range of points, which makes it challenging to determine the optimal operating point. Additionally, shading can cause some of the shaded cells to become reverse-biased, leading to their degradation and potential hotspots, which can cause permanent damage to the module.

Partial shading in PV systems (see Figure 4) refers to a situation where some portions of a solar panel are obstructed from receiving direct sunlight. This can be caused by a variety of factors, including trees, buildings, or other objects that cast a shadow on the panels. The effects of partial shading can be significant, as it can impact the performance of an entire PV system. When a portion of a panel is shaded, it can diminish the overall power output, as well as the performance of the other panels connected to the same string. The MATLAB-PSIM software was employed in this study to execute multiple shading scenarios, utilizing a reliable model.

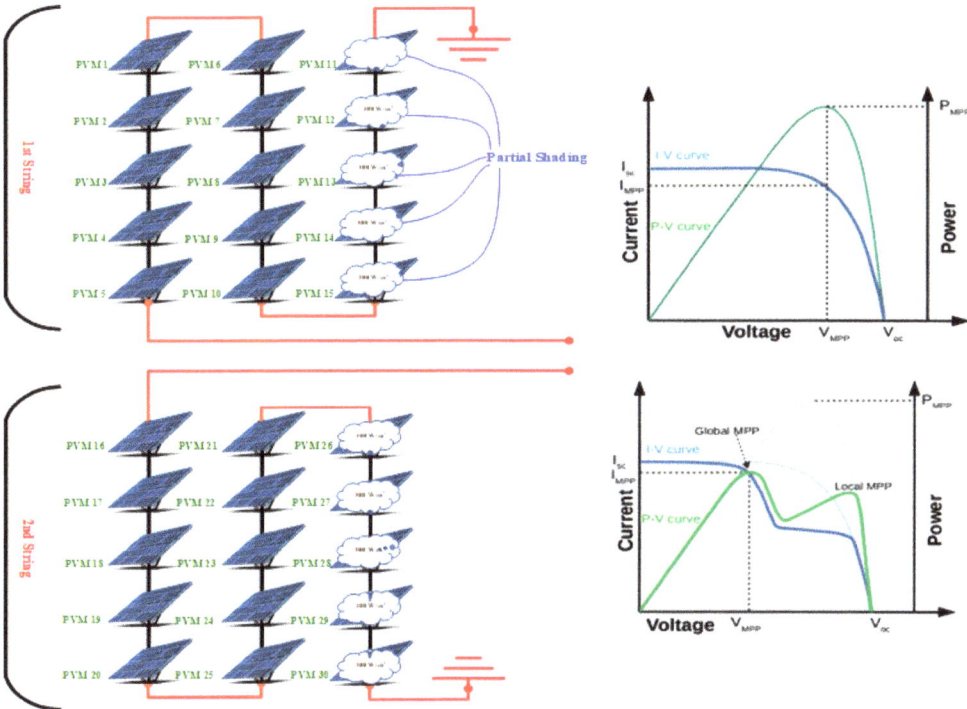

Figure 4. PV study plant under partial shading and its effects on P–V curve.

4. Implementing Dandelion Optimizer Algorithm as MPPT

In 2022, Shijie Zhao introduced a highly effective global optimization algorithm that leverages the mechanism by which dandelion seeds are dispersed over long distances by the wind, as shown in Figure 5, to achieve faster convergence rates on globally smooth problems, surpassing previous methods that only utilized local smoothness of the function. This algorithm demonstrates exceptional results and has been mathematically proven to outperform a pure random search algorithm [29].

The optimization process in dandelion optimization is based on how dandelion seeds spread in the wind, allowing them to colonize new environments and adapt to changing conditions. Similarly, the DO algorithm generates multiple solutions and explores different areas of the solution space using randomness and variability to find the best solution [29].

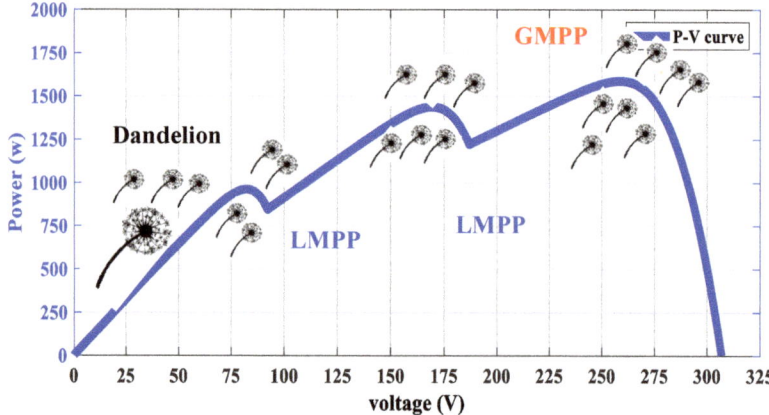

Figure 5. Wind-borne dandelion flowers searching for GMPP.

4.1. Mathematical Model

The DO algorithm repeats the wind and reproduction operators until an ending criterion is met, such as a desired level of fitness or a maximum number of iterations. The algorithm selects the top solution found during the optimization process as the final solution. This subsection specifically discusses the mathematical formulas for DO.

4.1.1. Initialization

Like other nature-inspired metaheuristic algorithms, DO implements population evolution and iterative optimization based on population initialization, i.e., seed generation. In the proposed MPPT-based DO, the algorithm generates multiple solutions that are duty cycles of boost converter (D), which represent potential solutions to our optimization problem, and the population is represented as

$$\text{population} = \begin{bmatrix} D_1 \\ \vdots \\ \vdots \\ D_{pop} \end{bmatrix} \qquad (2)$$

where pop represents the population size.

Every potential solution is generated at random between the upper bound (UB) and lower bound (LB), and the expression of the *i*th individual D_i is

$$D_i = \text{rand} \times (UB - LB) + L \qquad (3)$$

where rand stands for a random number between 0 and 1, and i is an integer between 1 and pop.

During the initialization stage, DO identifies the participant with the best fitness value as the initial elite, which is considered the most suitable starting point for the dandelion seed to grow and flourish. The mathematical expression of the initial elite (D_{elite}) is then defined as where the function find() refers to two equal-valued indexes.

$$\begin{aligned} f_{best} &= \min(fD_i) \\ D_{elite} &= D(\text{find}(f_{best} = f(D_i))) \end{aligned} \qquad (4)$$

4.1.2. Rising Stage

Dandelion seeds must reach a certain height during the rising stage before they can float away from their parent. Dandelion seeds rise to different heights depending on wind speed, air humidity, and other factors. The weather is divided into two categories in this case.

Case 1: On a clear day, wind speeds can be assumed to have a lognormal distribution. The Y-axis is where random numbers are more distributed in this distribution, increasing the likelihood that dandelion seeds will travel to distant regions, with the goal of exploring new regions of the search space and discovering new potential solutions that are better than the current best solution. The higher the wind, the higher the dandelion flies and the farther the seeds spread. The vortexes above the dandelion seeds are constantly adjusted by the wind speed to cause them to rise in a spiral form. In this case, the corresponding mathematical expression is

$$D_{t+1} = D_t + \alpha \times v_x \times v_y \times \ln Y \times (D_s - D_t) \quad (5)$$

where

$$v_x = r \times \cos \theta$$
$$v_y = r \times \sin \theta \quad (6)$$

θ is a random number between $[-\pi, \pi]$ and $r = \frac{1}{e^\theta}$.

The position of the dandelion seed during iteration t is represented by D_t; however, D_s is the randomly chosen position in the search space during iteration t. The expression for the randomly generated position is given by Equation (7).

$$D_s = \text{rand}(1,1) \times (\text{UB} - \text{LB}) + \text{LB} \quad (7)$$

ln Y signifies a lognormal distribution subject to $\mu = 0$ and $\delta^2 = 1$, and its mathematical formula is

$$\ln Y = \begin{cases} \frac{1}{y\sqrt{2\pi}} \exp\left[-\frac{1}{2\delta^2}(\ln y)^2\right] & y \geq 0 \\ 0 & y < 0 \end{cases} \quad (8)$$

y symbolizes the standard normal distribution $N(0, 1)$ in Equation (8). α is an adaptive parameter used to adjust the search step length, and the mathematical expression is

$$\alpha = \text{rand}() \times (\frac{1}{T^2}t^2 - \frac{2}{T}t + 1) \quad (9)$$

Case 2: When it is raining, dandelion seeds are unable to be carried away by the wind due to factors such as air resistance and humidity. This leads to the seeds staying in their local area, which can be represented mathematically by the equation

$$D_{t+1} = D_t \times k \quad (10)$$

where k is used to organize a dandelion's local search domain, which is determined using Equation (11).

$$qd = \frac{1}{T^2 - 2T + 1}t^2 - \frac{2}{T^2 - 2T + 1}t + 1 + \frac{1}{T^2 - 2T + 1} \quad (11)$$

$$k = 1 - \text{rand}() \times qd$$

At the conclusion of each iteration, the value of the parameter k gradually moves closer to 1, ensuring that the population ultimately reaches the optimal search agent. To sum up, the mathematical representation of dandelion seeds in the rising stage is given by the expression

$$D_{t+1} = \begin{cases} D_t + \alpha \times v_x \times v_y \times \ln Y \times (D_s - D_t) & \text{randn} < 1.5 \\ D_t \times k & \text{else} \end{cases} \quad (12)$$

where the random number generated by the function randn() follows the normal distribution.

4.1.3. Descending Stage

During this phase, the DO algorithm places a strong emphasis on exploration. The motion of dandelion seeds is modeled in DO using Brownian motion, which simulates their descent after rising to a certain height. This motion allows individuals to easily explore a wider range of search communities during the iteration process, as Brownian motion follows a normal distribution at each step. To reflect the stability of dandelion descent, the DO algorithm utilizes the average position information after the rising stage, which helps guide the overall population towards more promising communities. The mathematical representation for this process is

$$D_{t+1} = D_t - \alpha \times \beta_t \times (D_{mean\_t} - \alpha \times \beta_t \times D_t) \quad (13)$$

where β_t is a random number drawn from the normal distribution and denotes Brownian motion.

The mathematical expression of D_{mean_t}, which stands for the population's average position in the ith iteration, is

$$D_{mean\_t} = \frac{1}{pop} \sum_{i=1}^{pop} D_i \quad (14)$$

4.1.4. Landing Stage

During the exploitation phase of the DO algorithm, the dandelion seed selects its landing spot based on the results of the first two stages. As the iteration process continues, the algorithm aims to reach the global optimal solution. This process is represented by Equation (12).

$$D_{t+1} = D_{elite} + levy(\lambda) \times \alpha \times (D_{elite} - D_t \times \delta) \quad (15)$$

where D_{elite} denotes the dandelion seed's optimal position in the ith iteration. $levy(\lambda)$ denotes the Levy flight function and is calculated using Equation (16), and σ is a linear increasing function between [0, 2] and is calculated by Equation (17).

$$levy(\lambda) = s \times \frac{\omega \times \sigma}{|t|^{\frac{1}{\beta}}} \quad (16)$$

$$\delta = \frac{2t}{T} \quad (17)$$

A random number between [0, 2] called β is used in Equation (16). In this study, $\beta = 1.5$, ω, and t are random numbers between [0, 1], while s is a fixed constant of 0.01. The mathematical expression of σ is

$$\sigma = \left(\frac{\Gamma(1+\beta) \times \sin\left(\frac{\pi\beta}{2}\right)}{\Gamma(\frac{1+\beta}{2}) \times \beta \times 2^{\left(\frac{\beta-1}{2}\right)}} \right) \quad (18)$$

A detailed description of the MPPT-based DO is shown in the flowchart Figure 6.

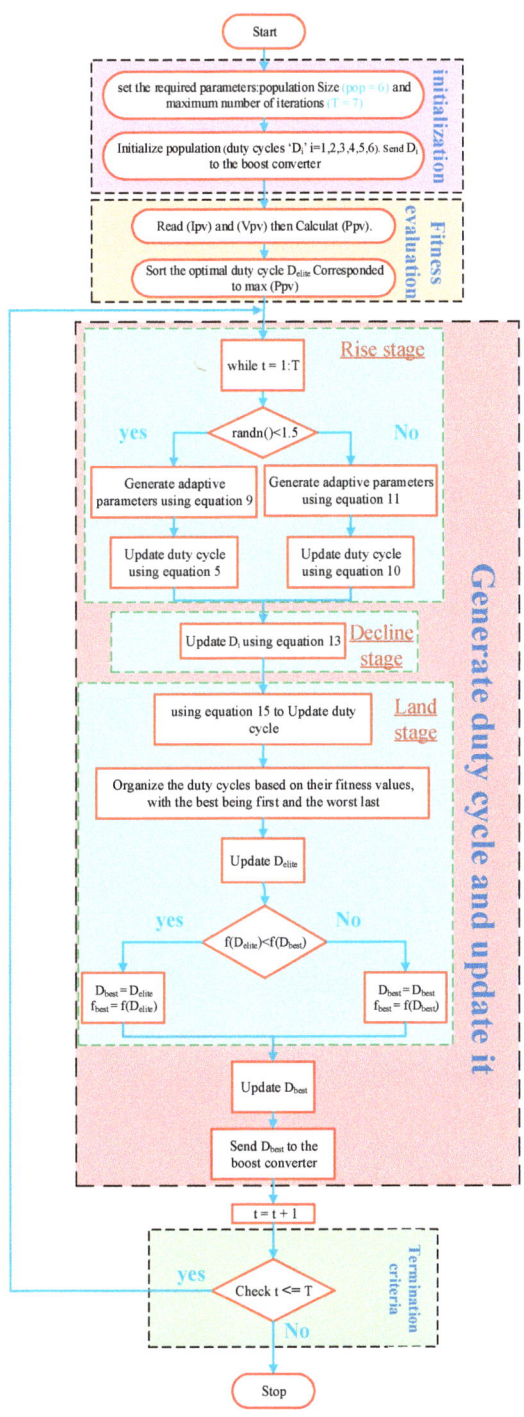

Figure 6. Flowchart of the MPPT-based DO.

4.2. Simulation Results

4.2.1. Ability to Track GMPP

Extensive simulation studies have been conducted to evaluate the performance of the proposed MPPT algorithm. The PV system in Figure 4 has been specifically designed for this purpose, consisting of two series-connected PV modules, a DC–DC boost converter, a DC load, and an MPPT controller. The evaluation has been performed using a co-simulation methodology that combines the Matlab/Simulink and PSIM platforms. The co-simulation enables the assessment of the proposed DO-based MPPT algorithm's feasibility and effectiveness, as well as the comparison of its performance against the PSO, GWO, ABC, BA, and CS algorithms, under stable and dynamic climatic conditions. Table 4 presents the parameters for the optimization algorithms utilized in this study.

The MPPT algorithms have been implemented in a Matlab/Simulink environment, as shown in Figure 7, while the PSIM platform has been utilized to implement the DC–DC boost converter and the PV array as illustrated in Figure 8.

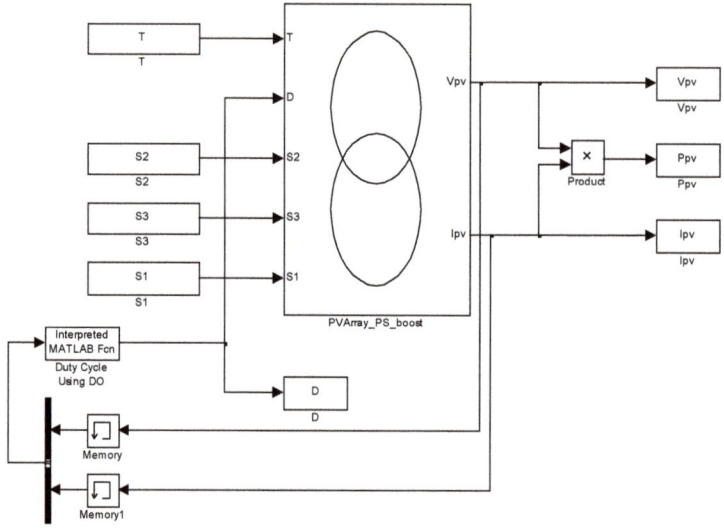

Figure 7. Implemented Matlab/Simulink model for MPPT algorithms.

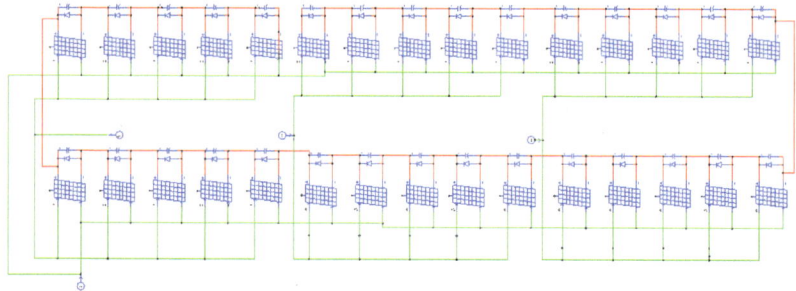

Figure 8. PV array and DC–DC boost converter circuits employed in Psim environment.

Assessing all non-uniform climatic conditions can be challenging, which is why three preselected shading patterns (SPs) have been used to evaluate the performance of the proposed DO-based MPPT algorithm. These shading patterns, designated as SP1, SP2, and SP3 and shown in Figure 9, are used to evaluate the algorithm's ability to track the variant GMPP under static solar insolation. By using these preselected shading patterns, it is possible to evaluate the performance of the algorithm under a range of different conditions, without the need to assess all possible non-uniform climatic conditions, which can be time-consuming and resource-intensive. The following are the three different shade patterns with different irradiance levels, as shown in Figure 9: SP1 involves no shading; SP2 includes partial shading; and SP3 introduces partial shading.

Table 4. Optimization techniques and their control parameters investigated in the study.

Technique	Parameters	Number of the Population	Maximum Number of Iterations
PSO	W = 0.4, c1 = 1.2, c2 = 1.6 and r1, r2 = random [0, 1]	10	17
GWO	r1, r2 = random [0, 1], A = 2 × 0.1 × r1 − 0.1 and C = 2 × r2	6	10
ABC	50% employed bees and 50% onlooker bees	6	10
BA	Fmin = 0, Fmax = 2, A = 0.5, r = 0.5, alpha = 0.9, gamma = 0.9	7	10
CS	k = 0.8 Beta = 1.5	4	10
DO	α and β_t are random numbers $a = \dfrac{-1}{Max\ iteration^2 - 2 \times Max\ iteration + 1}$ $b = -2 \times a$ $c = 1 - a - b$	4	7

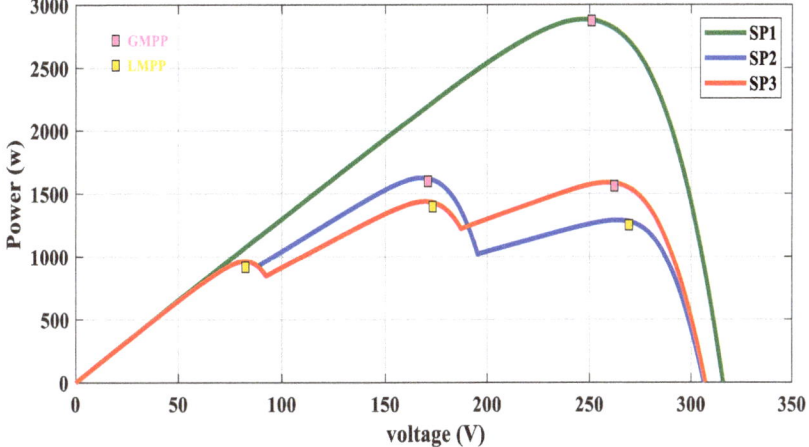

Figure 9. Shading patterns.

The simulation results present in Figure 10 show that the proposed MPPT algorithm is capable of accurately tracking the GMPP of the PV array under various environmental conditions, and it achieves a fast convergence to the GMPP.

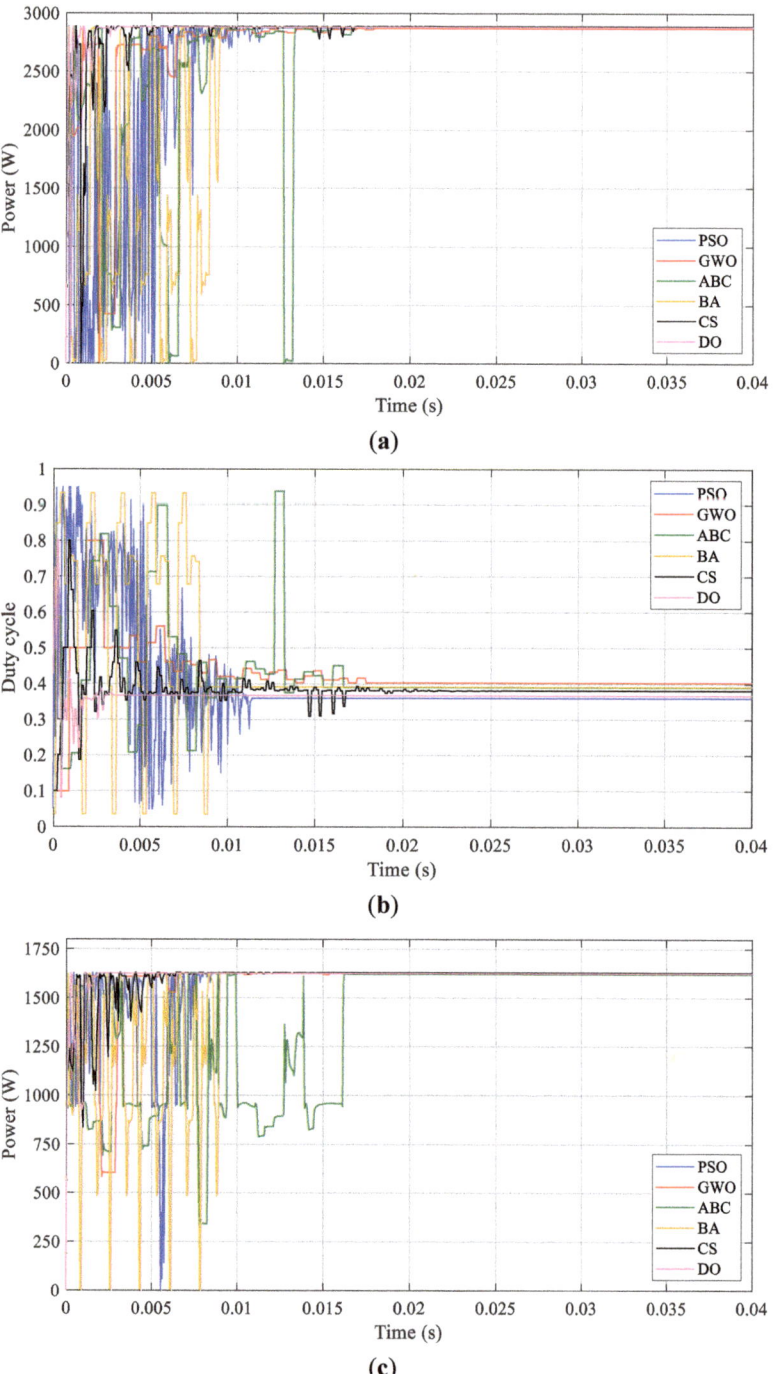

Figure 10. *Cont.*

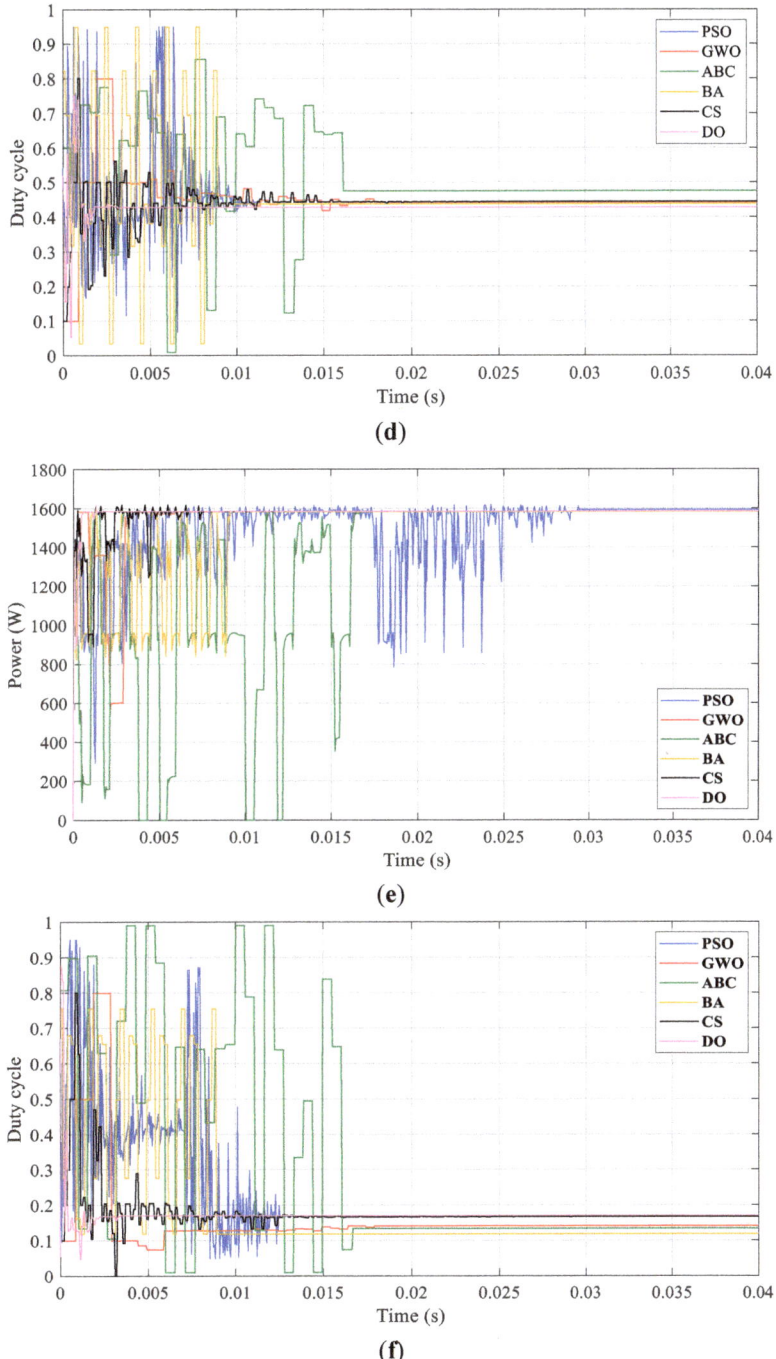

Figure 10. Simulated mean power and duty cycle of PSO, GWO, ABC, BA, CS, and DO for PV string ((**a**,**b**) for SP1, (**c**,**d**) for SP2, (**e**,**f**) for SP3).

4.2.2. Tracking and Comparing Performance

To demonstrate the tracking capability of the proposed DO-based MPPT algorithm under dynamic solar insolation conditions, a transient shading pattern (SP1 to SP3) is generated at t = 0.02 s, where the total simulation time is 0.4 s. The tracking curves obtained by the algorithm are shown in Figure 11. The DO-based MPPT algorithm is able to catch the GMPP of pattern SP1 in less than a 0.005 s, demonstrating its quick response time. When the solar insolation changes to SP3 at 0.02 s, the algorithm restarts the search process based on Equation (12) and is able to successfully track the new GMPP of SP3 in 0.024 s, clearly proving the robustness of the proposed algorithm in handling dynamic partial shading. These results demonstrate the effectiveness of the DO-based MPPT algorithm in tracking the maximum power point under changing solar insolation conditions, which is a critical requirement for achieving high efficiency and performance in PV systems.

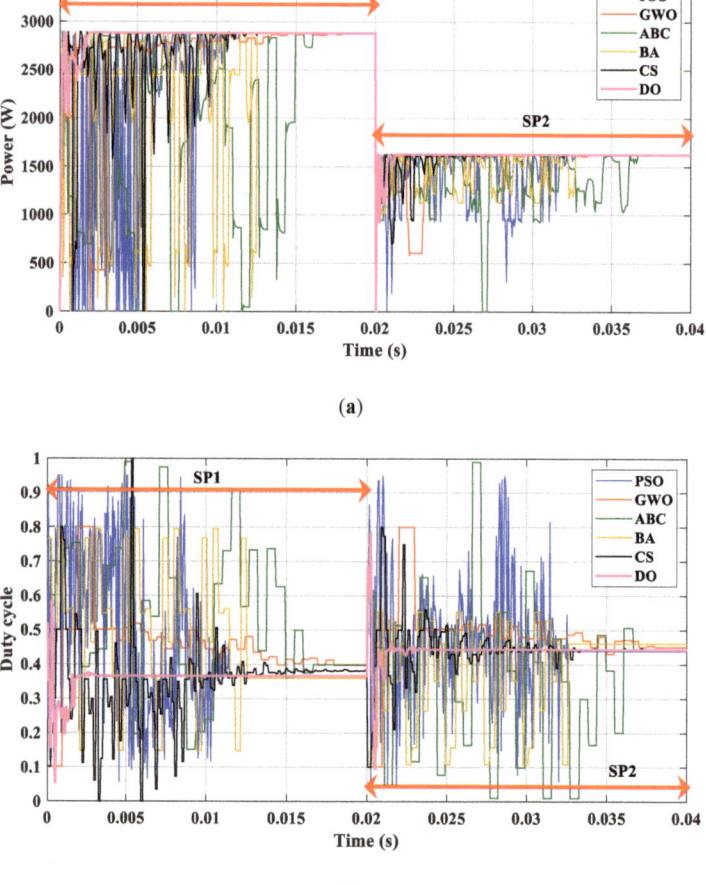

Figure 11. *Cont.*

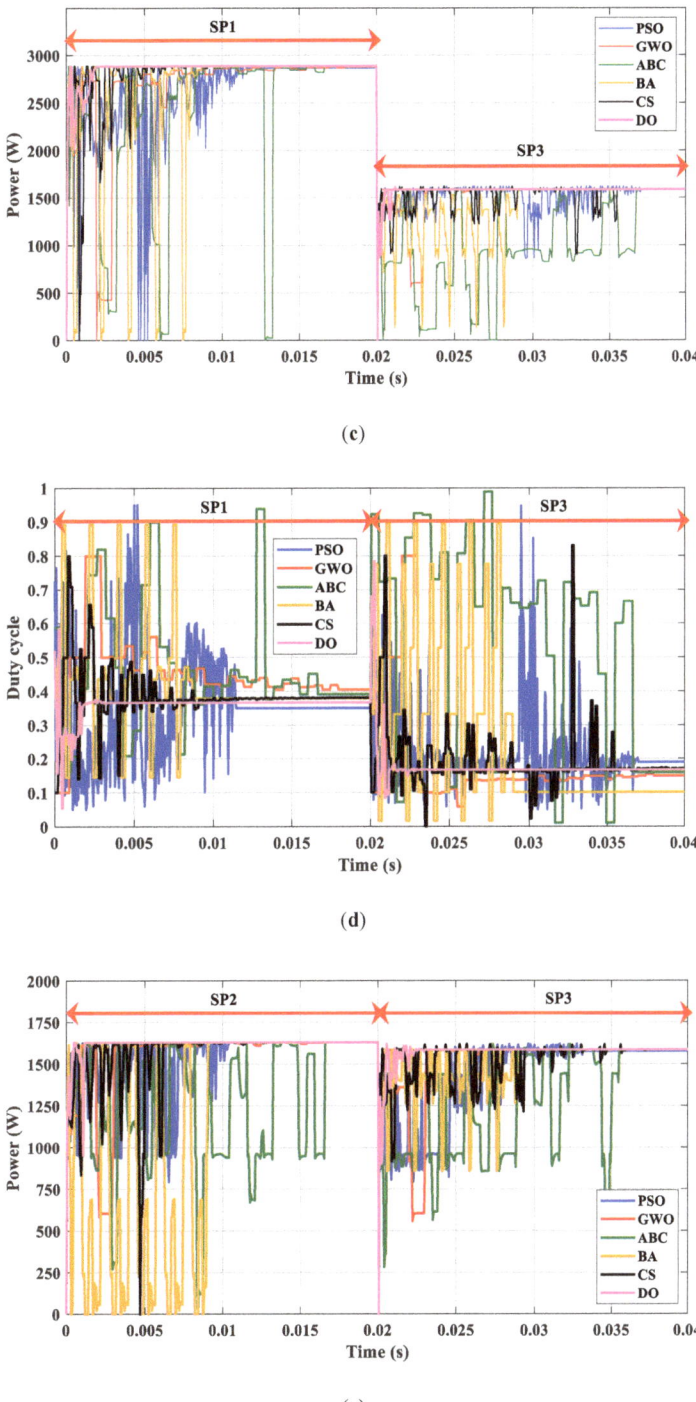

Figure 11. Cont.

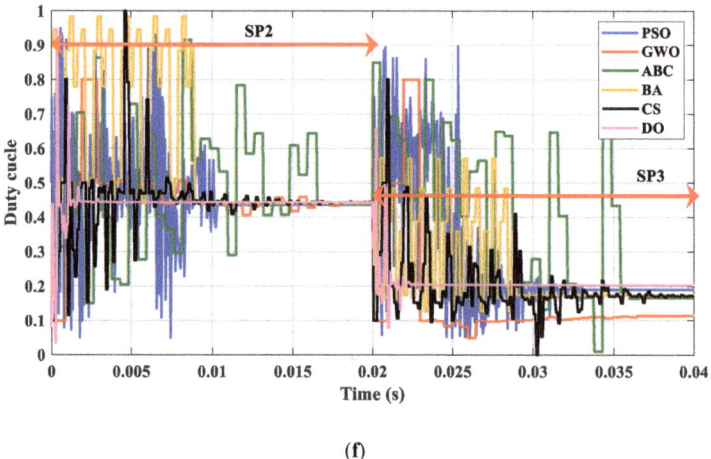

(**f**)

Figure 11. Tracking curves under shading pattern variation from SP1 to SP2 ((**a**,**b**)), SP1 to SP3 ((**c**,**d**)), and SP2 to SP3 ((**e**,**f**)).

4.2.3. Statistical Analysis

The MPPT techniques presented in Figure 12 were analyzed using three metrics: convergence time, the mean absolute error (MAE) calculated using Equation (19), and the root mean square error (RMSE) calculated using Equation (20).

$$\text{Error}_{\text{MAE}} = \frac{\sum_{i=1}^{n}(P_{pve} - P_{pv})}{n} \tag{19}$$

$$\text{Error}_{\text{RMSE}} = \sqrt{\frac{\sum_{i=1}^{n}(P_{pve} - P_{pv})^2}{n}}$$

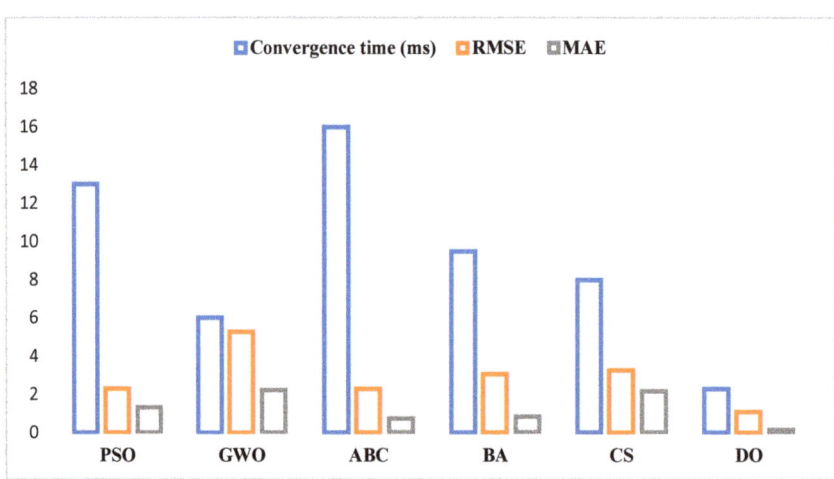

Figure 12. Comparison of RMSE and MAE.

In these equations, P_{pve} represents the expected power, P_{pv} is the power tracked, and n is the number of samples. The study found that MPPTs based on DO have the lowest convergence time compared to the other techniques (the convergence time of shading pattern 3 was used as a reference or sample). On the other hand, the results also show that the DO technique had the lowest RMSE among all the compared techniques, indicating that it tracks the GMPP with higher efficiency and generates negligible oscillations. Additionally, the MAE had a lower magnitude, demonstrating effective GM detection under all operating conditions.

4.2.4. Dynamic Validation

This subsection aims to validate a proposed DO-based MPPT technique using real-world data under varying environmental conditions. To validate its effectiveness, the algorithm was tested on multiple samples during full-day intervals using experimental measurements. In addition, to assess the MPPT algorithm's capability to track the GMPP, actual daily solar irradiation profiles and their corresponding temperatures were utilized to evaluate the algorithm's performance on clear and cloudy days, as presented in Figures 13 and 14.

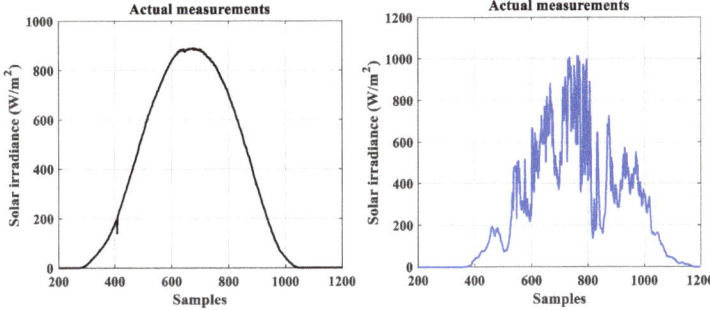

Figure 13. Distinct solar irradiance patterns on clear and shady days based on actual measurements.

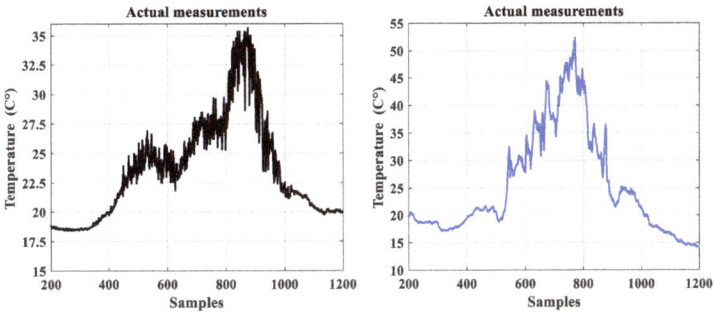

Figure 14. Distinct temperature patterns on clear and shady days based on actual measurements.

The obtained results show that the DO-based MPPT outperformed the other algorithms in terms of convergence speed and achieving maximum power point under varying solar irradiance and temperature conditions. Figures 15 and 16, presenting the results for powers, are provided to support these findings.

According to the findings, among the tested methods, the DO-based MPPT algorithm has demonstrated the most favorable performance with the lowest RMSE and MAE values. This suggests that the DO-based algorithm is capable of achieving more precise and accurate MPP tracking compared to the other methods assessed. Although the other methods performed reasonably well, the results imply that they may not attain the same level of precision as the DO-based algorithm. Consequently, the results indicate that the DO-based MPPT algorithm is the most promising option for accurate MPP tracking in PV.

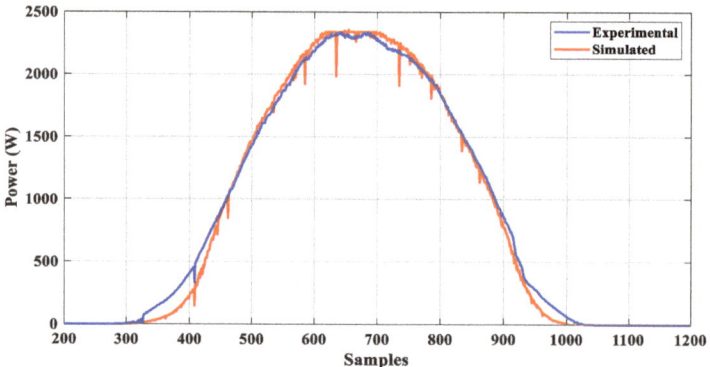

Figure 15. Comparison of experimental and simulated powers at MPP under clear conditions using DO-based MPPT.

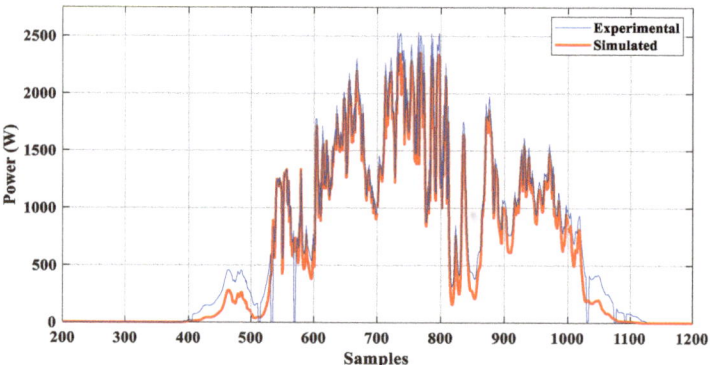

Figure 16. Comparison of experimental and simulated powers at MPP under shading conditions using DO-based MPPT.

5. Conclusions

The utilization of the DO algorithm in MPPT controllers presents a promising approach towards improving the efficiency and performance of solar PV systems. The DO algorithm offers an effective means of balancing the trade-offs between tracking speed, accuracy, and convergence. Through the experiments detailed in this scientific paper, it has been demonstrated that the MPPT-based DO algorithm outperforms other widely used MPPT-based metaheuristic algorithms, including PSO, GWO, ABC, CS, and BA, thereby establishing its superiority. The results show that the proposed MPPT was able to achieve faster tracking speed, higher tracking accuracy, and better stability under changing weather conditions. One of the key advantages of the dandelion optimizer algorithm is its ability to dynamically adjust the search space based on the current operating conditions, which can result in significant improvements in the overall performance of the system. Moreover, the DO algorithm is relatively easy to implement and does not require complex mathematical models or extensive training datasets. Furthermore, the proposed MPPT can provide a cost-effective solution for renewable energy production, which can lead to increased adoption of solar energy systems in both developed and developing countries. The performance of the DO algorithm is sensitive to the initial parameter settings, and different initial parameter values could lead to different results. Careful parameter tuning and optimization would be required to achieve optimal performance. While the DO algorithm is relatively simple compared to other optimization algorithms, it still requires significant computational resources, especially for larger-scale systems. This could limit the practical application of the algorithm in real-world PV systems. Further research and development are needed to optimize the algorithm's performance and address these limitations. This article has presented a newly proposed MPPT algorithm based on DO. Through simulation and experimentation, it has been shown that the DO-based MPPT algorithm outperforms other commonly used MPPT algorithms such as PSO, GWO, ABC, BA, and CS. Additionally, a real-world validation has been conducted to demonstrate the practical applications of the proposed algorithm. In future work, a comparison of the computational complexity and required computational power of the hardware of various MPPT algorithms could be conducted. Overall, the DO-based MPPT algorithm has demonstrated promising results and has the potential to be applied in PVs.

Author Contributions: Methodology, L.M. and A.C.; Validation, L.M.; Formal analysis, A.S.; Investigation, A.S.; Writing—original draft, E.H.; Writing—review & editing, A.C. and S.S. All authors have read and agreed to the published version of the manuscript.

Funding: This research received no external funding.

Data Availability Statement: The data presented in this study are available on request from the corresponding author. The data are not publicly available due to privacy restrictions.

Conflicts of Interest: The authors declare no conflict of interest.

References

1. Sarwar, S.; Hafeez, M.A.; Javed, M.Y.; Asghar, A.B.; Ejsmont, K. A Horse Herd Optimization Algorithm (HOA)-Based MPPT Technique under Partial and Complex Partial Shading Conditions. *Energies* **2022**, *15*, 1880. [CrossRef]
2. Khan, F.; Kim, J.H. Performance Degradation Analysis of C-Si PV Modules Mounted on a Concrete Slab under Hot-Humid Conditions Using Electroluminescence Scanning Technique for Potential Utilization in Future Solar Roadways. *Materials* **2019**, *12*, 4047. [CrossRef]
3. Khan, F.; Alshahrani, T.; Fareed, I.; Kim, J.H. A Comprehensive Degradation Assessment of Silicon Photovoltaic Modules Installed on a Concrete Base under Hot and Low-Humidity Environments: Building Applications. *Sustain. Energy Technol. Assess.* **2022**, *52*, 102314. [CrossRef]
4. Kichou, S.; Wolf, P.; Silvestre, S.; Chouder, A. Analysis of the Behaviour of Cadmium Telluride and Crystalline Silicon Photovoltaic Modules Deployed Outdoor under Humid Continental Climate Conditions. *Solar Energy* **2018**, *171*, 681–691. [CrossRef]
5. Taghezouit, B.; Harrou, F.; Larbes, C.; Sun, Y.; Semaoui, S.; Arab, A.H.; Bouchakour, S. Intelligent Monitoring of Photovoltaic Systems via Simplicial Empirical Models and Performance Loss Rate Evaluation under LabVIEW: A Case Study. *Energies* **2022**, *15*, 7955. [CrossRef]
6. Eltamaly, A.M. A Novel Musical Chairs Algorithm Applied for MPPT of PV Systems. *Renew. Sustain. Energy Rev.* **2021**, *146*, 111135. [CrossRef]
7. Li, H.; Yang, D.; Su, W.; Lu, J.; Yu, X. An Overall Distribution Particle Swarm Optimization MPPT Algorithm for Photovoltaic System under Partial Shading. *IEEE Trans. Ind. Electron.* **2019**, *66*, 265–275. [CrossRef]
8. Mohanty, S.; Subudhi, B.; Ray, P.K. A New MPPT Design Using Grey Wolf Optimization Technique for Photovoltaic System under Partial Shading Conditions. *IEEE Trans. Sustain. Energy* **2016**, *7*, 181–188. [CrossRef]
9. Gonzalez-Castano, C.; Restrepo, C.; Kouro, S.; Rodriguez, J. MPPT Algorithm Based on Artificial Bee Colony for PV System. *IEEE Access* **2021**, *9*, 43121–43133. [CrossRef]
10. Eltamaly, A.M. An Improved Cuckoo Search Algorithm for Maximum Power Point Tracking of Photovoltaic Systems under Partial Shading Conditions. *Energies* **2021**, *14*, 953. [CrossRef]
11. Zafar, M.H.; Al-Shahrani, T.; Khan, N.M.; Mirza, A.F.; Mansoor, M.; Qadir, M.U.; Khan, M.I.; Naqvi, R.A. Group Teaching Optimization Algorithm Based MPPT Control of PV Systems under Partial Shading and Complex Partial Shading. *Electronics* **2020**, *9*, 1962. [CrossRef]
12. Mansoor, M.; Mirza, A.F.; Ling, Q. Harris Hawk Optimization-Based MPPT Control for PV Systems under Partial Shading Conditions. *J. Clean. Prod.* **2020**, *274*, 122857. [CrossRef]
13. Mansoor, M.; Mirza, A.F.; Ling, Q.; Javed, M.Y. Novel Grass Hopper Optimization Based MPPT of PV Systems for Complex Partial Shading Conditions. *Solar Energy* **2020**, *198*, 499–518. [CrossRef]
14. da Rocha, M.V.; Sampaio, L.P.; da Silva, S.A.O. Comparative Analysis of MPPT Algorithms Based on Bat Algorithm for PV Systems under Partial Shading Condition. *Sustain. Energy Technol. Assess.* **2020**, *40*, 100761. [CrossRef]
15. Shams, I.; Mekhilef, S.; Tey, K.S. Maximum Power Point Tracking Using Modified Butterfly Optimization Algorithm for Partial Shading, Uniform Shading, and Fast Varying Load Conditions. *IEEE Trans. Power Electron.* **2021**, *36*, 5569–5581. [CrossRef]

16. Mirza, A.F.; Mansoor, M.; Ling, Q. A Novel MPPT Technique Based on Henry Gas Solubility Optimization. *Energy Convers. Manag.* **2020**, *225*, 113409. [CrossRef]
17. Javed, M.Y.; Murtaza, A.F.; Ling, Q.; Qamar, S.; Gulzar, M.M. A Novel MPPT Design Using Generalized Pattern Search for Partial Shading. *Energy Build.* **2016**, *133*, 59–69. [CrossRef]
18. Yousri, D.; Babu, T.S.; Allam, D.; Ramachandaramurthy, V.K.; Etiba, M.B. A Novel Chaotic Flower Pollination Algorithm for Global Maximum Power Point Tracking for Photovoltaic System under Partial Shading Conditions. *IEEE Access* **2019**, *7*, 121432–121445. [CrossRef]
19. Eberhart, R.; Kennedy, J. New Optimizer Using Particle Swarm Theory. In Proceedings of the International Symposium on Micro Machine and Human Science, Nagoya, Japan, 4–6 October 1995.
20. Loukriz, A.; Haddadi, M.; Messalti, S. Simulation and Experimental Design of a New Advanced Variable Step Size Incremental Conductance MPPT Algorithm for PV Systems. *ISA Trans.* **2016**, *62*, 30–38. [CrossRef]
21. Wasim, M.S.; Amjad, M.; Habib, S.; Abbasi, M.A.; Bhatti, A.R.; Muyeen, S.M. A Critical Review and Performance Comparisons of Swarm-Based Optimization Algorithms in Maximum Power Point Tracking of Photovoltaic Systems under Partial Shading Conditions. *Energy Rep.* **2022**, *8*, 4871–4898. [CrossRef]
22. Alorf, A. A Survey of Recently Developed Metaheuristics and Their Comparative Analysis. *Eng. Appl. Artif. Intell.* **2023**, *117*, 105622. [CrossRef]
23. Mirjalili, S.; Mirjalili, S.M.; Lewis, A. Grey Wolf Optimizer. *Adv. Eng. Softw.* **2014**, *69*, 46–61. [CrossRef]
24. Gong, C.; Han, S.; Li, X.; Zhao, L.; Liu, X. A New Dandelion Algorithm and Optimization for Extreme Learning Machine. *J. Exp. Theor. Artif. Intell.* **2017**, *30*, 39–52. [CrossRef]
25. Li, X.; Han, S.; Zhao, L.; Gong, C.; Liu, X. New Dandelion Algorithm Optimizes Extreme Learning Machine for Biomedical Classification Problems. *Comput. Intell. Neurosci.* **2017**, *2017*. [CrossRef]
26. Li, B.; Abbassi, R.; Saidi, S.; Abbassi, A.; Jerbi, H.; Kchaou, M.; Alhasnawi, B.N. Accurate Key Parameters Estimation of PEMFCs’ Models Based on Dandelion Optimization Algorithm. *Mathematics* **2023**, *11*, 1298. [CrossRef]
27. Han, S.; Zhu, K.; Zhou, M.C. Competition-Driven Dandelion Algorithms With Historical Information Feedback. *IEEE Trans. Syst. Man. Cybern. Syst.* **2022**, *52*, 966–979. [CrossRef]
28. Thompson, E.; Paulden, T.; Smith, D.K. The Dandelion Code: A New Coding of Spanning Trees for Genetic Algorithms. *IEEE Trans. Evol. Comput.* **2007**, *11*, 91–100. [CrossRef]
29. Zhao, S.; Zhang, T.; Ma, S.; Chen, M. Dandelion Optimizer: A Nature-Inspired Metaheuristic Algorithm for Engineering Applications. *Eng. Appl. Artif. Intell.* **2022**, *114*, 105075. [CrossRef]
30. Titri, S.; Larbes, C.; Toumi, K.Y.; Benatchba, K. A New MPPT Controller Based on the Ant Colony Optimization Algorithm for Photovoltaic Systems under Partial Shading Conditions. *Appl. Soft Comput.* **2017**, *58*, 465–479. [CrossRef]
31. Eltamaly, A.M.; Al-Saud, M.S.; Abokhalil, A.G. A Novel Scanning Bat Algorithm Strategy for Maximum Power Point Tracker of Partially Shaded Photovoltaic Energy Systems. *Ain Shams Eng. J.* **2020**, *11*, 1093–1103. [CrossRef]
32. Seghiour, A.; Abbas, H.A.; Chouder, A.; Rabhi, A. Deep Learning Method Based on Autoencoder Neural Network Applied to Faults Detection and Diagnosis of Photovoltaic System. *Simul. Model. Pract. Theory* **2023**, *123*, 102704. [CrossRef]
33. Bhukya, L.; Kedika, N.R.; Salkuti, S.R. Enhanced Maximum Power Point Techniques for Solar Photovoltaic System under Uniform Insolation and Partial Shading Conditions: A Review. *Algorithms* **2022**, *15*, 365. [CrossRef]

Disclaimer/Publisher's Note: The statements, opinions and data contained in all publications are solely those of the individual author(s) and contributor(s) and not of MDPI and/or the editor(s). MDPI and/or the editor(s) disclaim responsibility for any injury to people or property resulting from any ideas, methods, instructions or products referred to in the content.

Article

A Sensorless Intelligent System to Detect Dust on PV Panels for Optimized Cleaning Units

Faris E. Alfaris

Department of Electrical Engineering, College of Engineering, King Saud University, Riyadh 11421, Saudi Arabia; falfaris@ksu.edu.sa

Abstract: Deployment of photovoltaic (PV) systems has recently been encouraged for large-scale and small-scale businesses in order to meet the global green energy targets. However, one of the most significant hurdles that limits the spread of PV applications is the dust accumulated on the PV panels' surfaces, especially in desert regions. Numerous studies sought the use of cameras, sensors, power datasets, and other detection elements to detect the dust on PV panels; however, these methods pose more maintenance, accuracy, and economic challenges. Therefore, this paper proposes an intelligent system to detect the dust level on the PV panels to optimally operate the attached dust cleaning units (DCUs). Unlike previous strategies, this study utilizes the expanded knowledge and collected data for solar irradiation and PV-generated power, along with the forecasted ambient temperature. An expert artificial intelligence (AI) computational system, adopted with the MATLAB platform, is utilized for a high level of data prediction and processing. The AI was used in this study in order to estimate the unprovided information, emulate the provided measurements, and accommodate more input/output data. The feasibility of the proposed system is investigated using actual field data during all possible weather conditions.

Keywords: artificial intelligence (AI); photovoltaic (PV) systems; dust cleaning; renewable energy; optimization; cost minimization

---

Citation: Alfaris, F.E. A Sensorless Intelligent System to Detect Dust on PV Panels for Optimized Cleaning Units. *Energies* **2023**, *16*, 1287. https://doi.org/10.3390/en16031287

Academic Editors: Fouzi Harrou, Ying Sun, Bilal Taghezouit and Dairi Abdelkader

Received: 28 November 2022
Revised: 8 January 2023
Accepted: 16 January 2023
Published: 25 January 2023

Copyright: © 2023 by the author. Licensee MDPI, Basel, Switzerland. This article is an open access article distributed under the terms and conditions of the Creative Commons Attribution (CC BY) license (https:// creativecommons.org/licenses/by/ 4.0/).

1. Introduction

Driven by ambitious national green energy targets and agreements, conventional power systems are currently witnessing an accelerated modernization, where renewable energy power resources are being implemented in power plants as an alternative to fossil fuel electrical generators [1]. In addition, other local constraints imposed by governments, such as the Saudi Vision 2030, to reduce greenhouse gas emission have made renewable energy sources (RESs) attractive power sources in the electricity production sector.

RESs are characterized by their low operation costs and carbon dioxide "CO_2" emissions, making the energy they produce more environmentally friendly; however, these resources face massive technical and economic challenges, such as frequency instability, voltage deviation, and output power uncertainty. These issues contribute to reducing RESs' feasibility and reliability, especially when utilized for stand-alone applications [2–4]. Consequently, governments and energy lanners and developers should reconsider the technical challenges and different cost aspects of the widespread deployment of RESs. For example, one of the most important key influences on PV power sources is the existence of dust on the surface of PV panels. Dust and any other accumulated objects have a major impact on a PV system's performance and cost effectiveness. Accumulated soiling over PV panels could reduce the PV system efficiency by between 8 and 12% per month, as concluded in [5]. Moreover, daily or unoptimized processes for cleaning PV panels reduce the electrical feasibility of the PV system in addition to increasing the operational and maintenance costs [6–8].

The studies conducted in [9,10] used actual annual collected PV data to compare with present PV output power in order to detect the presence of dust. Kelebaone T. et al.

examined the use of light sensors to operate PV cleaning units when the light passing through the PV panels was less than 20% of the atmospheric sunlight [11]. Studies in [12–15] relied on collected PV power data to estimate the impact of dust on PV panels and then model the effect of dust on PV performance. Russell K. Jones et al. in [16] used a long-term observation on average soiling rates to propose an optimal schedule for PV panel cleaning in central Saudi Arabia. Another methodology of detecting dust was introduced in [17], where the PV output voltage and current are monitored to operate the washing unit when the output power is less than 50% of the rated power during the daytime. Researchers in [18,19] investigated the feasibility of imaging process technology to detect dust on PV panels. An approach based on optical imaging and the routine measurement of aerosols was also explored in [20] to obtain PV panels' dust. Moreover, the study utilized mathematical models in order to normalize the calculated panel efficiency, whereas other influencing factors, such as solar radiation, ambient temperature, and inverter efficiency, were not initially accounted for.

The relation between the PV output voltage and the particle size of soiling was investigated in [21]. The study showed that as the size of the soiling particles covering the panel gets smaller, the output voltage of the panel decreases linearly, thus negatively affecting the PV panel's efficiency. Hence, the use of detecting cameras or photodiode sensors, as used in the study, might be not sufficient where the size of the contaminated particles could not be measured precisely.

Based on the aforementioned dust detection techniques, it is noticeable that the use of cameras, sensors, or other detection elements to measure the dust on PV panels inevitably poses more issues and costs, as the additional devices are considerably expensive and need to be cleaned and calibrated in addition to requiring access to electricity on the top of the PV panels. Figure 1 summarizes a comparative study on PV cleaning units after an intensive review of the above literature. The cost and size in the comparison were estimated, relying on some commercially available detection elements, whereas the reliability and simplicity were estimated based on the required controller circuits and lifetime of the basic utilized components. All results were normalized to be a percentage of each individual comparative aspect. It should be noted that the comparison in Figure 1 is not applicable for any detecting and cleaning approach; however, it is valid for the strategies in the literature, i.e., [9–11,16–19], as they compared detection systems with no additional imaging or sensing devices.

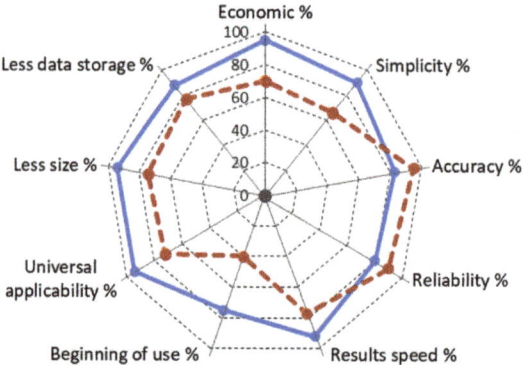

Figure 1. Comparison of different aspects of PV cleaning units (blue) without using an additional device and (dotted red) with using additional devices.

Therefore, this present study proposes an intelligent computational system to detect the dust level on PV panel surfaces without integrating any external imaging, measuring, or monitoring devices. The innovative aspect of this work is its contribution in reducing the cost and complexity of PV cleaning units at any location and under any PV system specifications. The importance and feasibility of the proposed system comes from the ability of operation from the first day after installing the PV system and providing results in real-time manner. The analysis of this work mainly relies on an estimation model of solar radiation along with an expert artificial-intelligence (AI)-based system [22]. The detailed analysis procedures are as follows:

1. Estimating the solar radiation energy;
2. Obtaining the output power for a specific PV system;
3. Injecting an estimated air temperature to the process;
4. Scaling and calibrating the estimated PV power;
5. AI computational process to analyze the PV performance.

The output decision of the proposed methodology is fed to the attached cleaning system to choose the optimal time and level of cleaning. Different cleaning devices, such as robotic systems and automated water pumps, were discussed and analyzed in previous studies [23–25]. Furthermore, modern techniques of PV panel cleaning were recently proposed, such as utilizing drones for getting rid of dust over the panels' surfaces, as in [26]. Due to the fact that this study focuses only on detecting the dust on PV panels and optimizing the time and level of the cleaning process, the physical cleaning tools will not be discussed further in this paper.

The rest of the paper is organized as follows: Section 2 introduces the mathematical solar irradiation model and the methodology of estimating the PV output power for different PV system size and orientation. Section 3 discusses the strategy of detecting the dust over the surfaces of the PV panels, while the utilization of the AI system for the computational and logical processes is explained in Section 4. Acquisition and illustration of actual PV data is discussed in Section 5, and an evaluation of the derived solar irradiation model is shown in Section 6. Section 7 investigates the feasibility of the proposed AI system using actual PV data. Significant deliverables and conclusions for this study are discussed in Section 8.

2. Prediction of PV Output Power

2.1. Modeling Solar Radiation Energy

The solar irradiation model relies on the knowledge of the sun's location (azimuth and altitude angles), date and time (within the year), and area and location of interest. In order to predict the output power for a PV generation unit, other parameters should be considered, such as the specifications of the real PV system and the ground coverage ratio (GCR). These additional parameters will be discussed and included in the model in the last section. Figure 2 shows the necessary atmosphere angles to assign the sun's location with respect to a certain point on the earth.

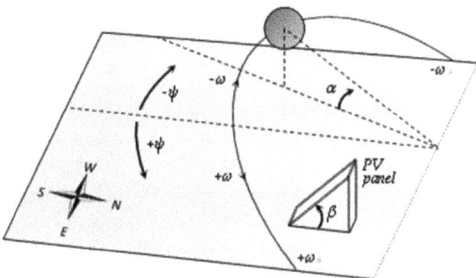

Figure 2. Sun angles (altitude angle α, azimuth angle ψ, and hour angle ω) with respect to a static object on the earth.

To obtain the solar radiation energy received by a flat surface on the earth (in watt/m^2), the Meinel and Meinel model is used due to its accuracy and fewer number of needed parameters [27,28]. Moreover, this model assigns the sunrise and sunset times without further calculations, unlike other commonly used models.

The Meinel and Meinel model can estimate the solar radiation energy relying on the air-mass coefficient (AM). The air-mass is a function of the sun altitude angle α. In order to account for tilted surface angles (with tilt angle β and azimuth angle ψ), a correlation factor (C_F) is introduced to the sun energy expression as in Equation 1 [28]. Eventually, the sun radiation energy received by a tilted angle is defined as follows:

$$\begin{cases} I_T = I_0 \, C_F = 1376 \times (0.7)^{AM^{0.678}} \, C_F(\beta, \psi) \\ AM = 1/\sin(\alpha) \end{cases} \quad (1)$$

The correlation factor in Equation 1 is added to the initial solar radiation energy (I_0) when the PV panels are not laid horizontally on the earth. In other words, the correlation factor appears only when the PV panels have a tilt angle and/or azimuth angle and can be expressed as:

$$\begin{cases} C_F = \frac{\cos(\theta)}{\sin(\alpha)} \\ \cos(\theta) = \sin(\delta)\sin(\phi)\cos(\beta) + \cos(\delta)\cos(\omega)\cos(\phi)\cos(\beta) \\ + \sin(\delta)\sin(\psi)\cos(\phi)\cos(\beta) - \cos(\delta)\cos(\omega)\sin(\psi)\sin(\phi)\cos(\beta) \\ + \cos(\delta)\sin(\beta)\sin(\psi)\sin(\omega) \end{cases} \quad (2)$$

The altitude angle α is dependent on the declination angle δ, hour angle ω, and the earth latitude of the location of interest ϕ. The altitude angle is a time-variant variable, where the hour angle varies with the location of the sun throughout the day with respect to a fixed point on the earth. From Figure 2, and after an intensive mathematical analysis, the altitude angle α could be obtained using the inverse of the triangular sine function as follows:

$$\alpha = \sin^{-1}\{\cos(\omega)\cos(\delta)\cos(\phi) + \sin(\phi)\sin(\delta)\} \quad (3)$$

2.2. Prediction of PV Output Power

The transmission from the inherited estimated sun radiation energy to the output power for a certain PV system requires knowledge of the actual system specifications. Therefore, this section aims to utilize the solar radiation model to predict the extracted power from a specific PV system. This can be achieved by considering other parameters, like PV system capacity and efficiency, I-V module characteristics versus temperature, panel azimuth and tilt angles, entire PV system power loss (from cables, regulators, and inverters), and the ground coverage ratio (GCR). The GCR factor determines the shaded (untapped) area after installing the PV panels. For the sake of ensuring the validity of the model, a comparison process could be applied between the model output data and an actual PV measurement to enhance and validate the prediction tool performance. The flowchart shown in Figure 3 illustrates the estimation processing stages.

The output of the above assessment model is considered as the main building block of the intelligent processing system proposed in this work. The ambient temperature is an essential parameter that has a significant impact on the PV panels' performance; therefore, it is necessary to integrate it to the prediction model. In order to ensure that the control stage has no costly physical elements, an estimation of the ambient temperature is included in the model instead of a physical heat sensor.

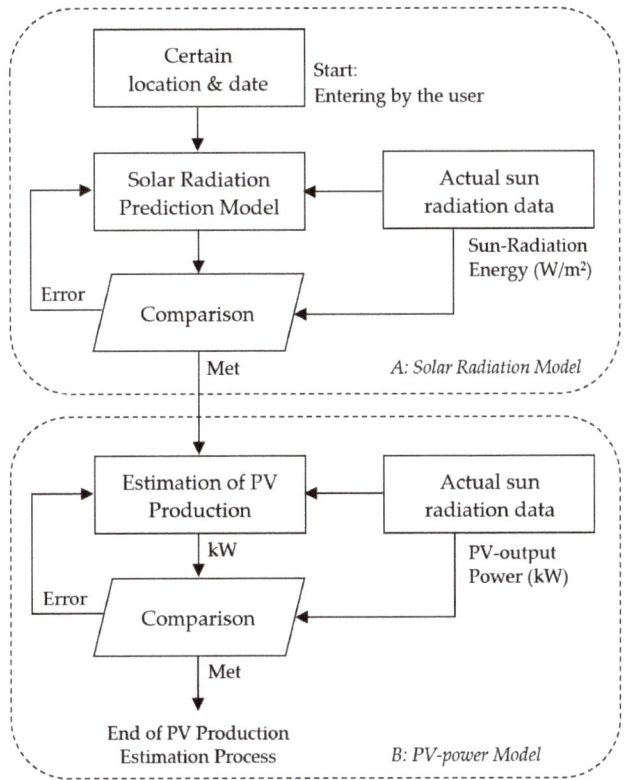

Figure 3. Flowchart of the solar radiation and PV power estimation process.

2.3. Ambient Temperature Estimation Model

The ambient temperature is normally periodical throughout the Gregorian year, especially for desert areas. In other words, the ambient temperature for a certain location could be estimated based on the temperature data collected over a year. For example, the average weekly temperature based on data collected from 2015 to 2022 in Riyadh, Saudi Arabia, where this study was conducted, is illustrated in Figure 4. Moreover, Table 1 summarizes the average monthly temperature for the interval from 1973 to 2017 for the same region.

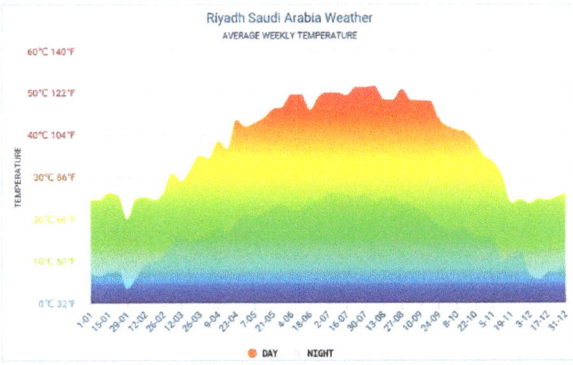

Figure 4. Average weekly temperature for Riyadh, Saudi Arabia from 2015–2022 [29].

Table 1. Average monthly temperature for Riyadh, Saudi Arabia from 2015–2022 [29].

Month	Daytime (°C)	Nighttime (°C)
January	25	7
February	25	8
March	31	15
April	38	18
May	45	22
June	49	23
July	51	26
August	50	25
September	48	22
October	41	17
November	29	13
December	25	8

The above temperature data are processed along with the temperature-variant I-V module characteristics to include the heat impact on the PV panels, considering that the intelligent system must be able to sort out the unreliable or unusual temperature data and that the prediction model must have the capability to recognize the impact of high temperature, due to any external causes, via analyzing the behavior of the PV output power. The I-V module characteristics for the used panel is mentioned in the Appendix A.

3. Correlation of Dust to the PV Output Power

It is well-known that the produced power by PV panels is affected negatively by the accumulation of dust on the surface; however, there are no determined formulas to describe this relationship specifically. Due to the fact that this relationship is necessary to complete the construction of the intelligent detection tool in this work, the PV output power versus the accumulated dust was formulated through an intensive survey study on the performance of PV panels in the presence of accumulated dust [19,20]. Figure 5 shows two PV panels with different cleaning conditions.

Figure 5. PV panels to study the impact of soiling on the output power: (**left**) cleaned PV panel and (**right**) dirty PV panel [19].

From the previous conducted studies [10,13], the average generated power (in W) for a normalized size of PV system under different levels of dust concentration (in g/m^2) was collected and listed in Table 2.

In order to extract the dust versus PV power relationship, the data in Table 2 were plotted, as shown in Figure 6, and the formula was generated. It is worth mentioning that the PV output power was converted to its percentage values (considering the maximum power in Table 2 as the rated power) to generalize the extracted formula so it could be applied for any size and any combination of PV panels and arrays.

Table 2. Normalized PV output power versus dust weight.

PV Power (W)	PV Power (%)	Dust Weight (g/m^2)
309.28	100	0
285.43	92.28	0.1
236.40	76.43	0.28
182.28	58.93	0.4
137.32	44.39	0.46
112.04	36.22	0.6
87.371	28.24	0.8

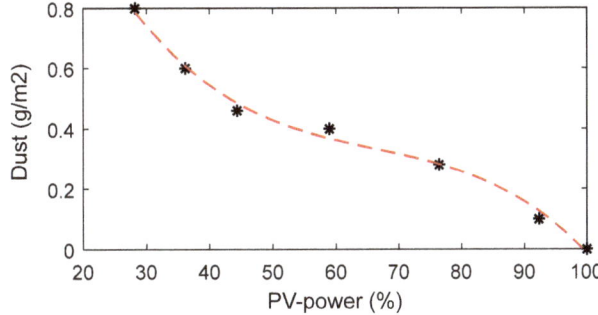

Figure 6. Percentage of normalized PV output power versus dust weight: (starred black) collected data, (dotted red) fitting curve.

From the dotted black curve shown in Figure 6, we could generate the relationship between accumulated dust and reduction in PV panels' output power. This step was accomplished with the help of the curve fitting tool in MATLAB software. Furthermore, in the interest of obtaining a very precise fitting formula, the third-degree polynomial type of curve fitting was carefully chosen, and the final fitting expression was established, as expressed in the following equation.

$$W_{DUST} = \{-0.0514\, P_{PV\%}^3 + 10.2\, P_{PV\%}^2 - 723\, P_{PV\%} + 21300\} \times 10^{-4} \quad (g/m^2) \quad (4)$$

It can be concluded from Equation (4) that the negative impact of the contaminated dust on the PV output power is more severe at the dust weight of 0.25 g/m^2 to 0.5 g/m^2 (where the PV output power reduced by 20% to 60% of its rated power). This verifies the importance of this study, as the need for the panel to be washed arises only after a specific amount of dust. The next section discusses the intelligent system methodology.

4. Artificial-Intelligence-Based Prediction Model

The main objective of this paper is to give optimized decisions on the cleaning of PV panels, using a fewer number of external measuring elements, with the help of an intelligent computational engine. Hence, this section demonstrates the methodology of gathering the entire discussed knowledge to generate a reliable and feasible processing unit. An expert artificial intelligence system was utilized for this aim. The flowchart in Figure 7 shows the mechanism of the expert system, where the computational algorithm, along with the prediction and analyzing knowledge, interacts with the information entered by the end user to generate suitable decisions.

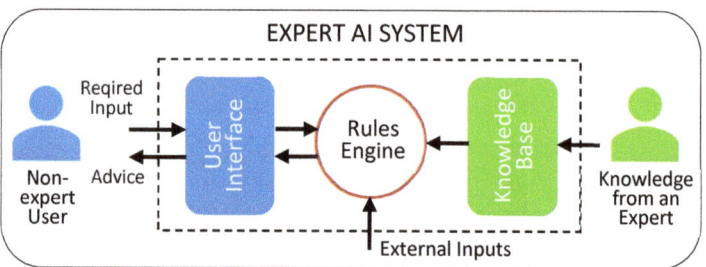

Figure 7. The flowchart of the expert artificial intelligence system.

Recently, expert system (ES) and expert control system (ECS) techniques are utilized for renewable energy systems in order to enhance the operating and control decisions of non-expert users [30–32]. For example, the expert artificial intelligence system can be used in the pitch control of wind turbines for improved system performance [31]. The proposed expert system in the aforementioned study was applied to recognize the pattern of the generated power of the wind system in order to apply the predictive model. Second, the AI system must collect all required data from the interfaced user to analyze the wind system output power to determine suitable control decisions and deliver them to the end user via the user interface. Figure 8 illustrates the control schematic diagram of that study.

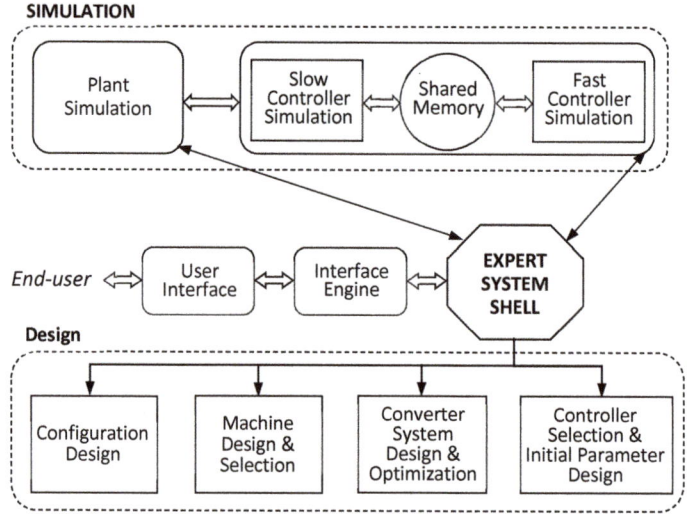

Figure 8. Expert system based automated design for the wind system proposed in [31].

Figure 9 virtually shows the processing flow of the proposed expert artificial intelligence system. First, the user must enter the time, location of interest, and the private PV system specifications. Second, the processing unit estimates the output power of the PV system after including the ambient temperature parameter. Third, the resultant information is calibrated and up/down-scaled to the actual PV output production. This step is necessary to take into account the unprovided input information, such as the type of PV panels, performance of the DC-DC regulator, and the panel highest from the sea level.

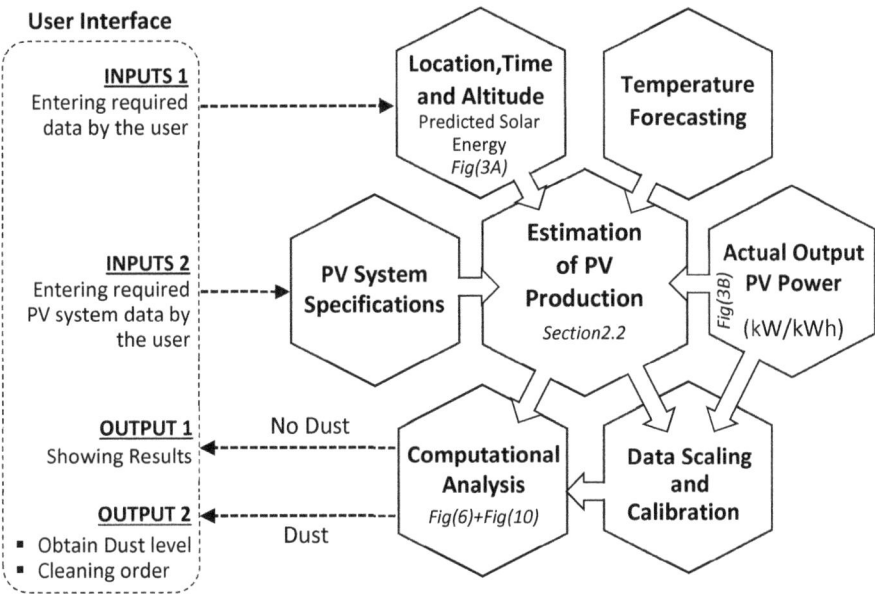

Figure 9. Methodology of the proposed intelligent dust detection unit (expert system).

The calibration process is designed to use the actual data collected from the first day of installation to identify the exact PV performance. Eventually, the production of the PV system (in kW) is analyzed with the help of the calibrated predicted results in order to detect the existence of accumulated dust.

The computational analysis shown in Figure 9 is responsible for intelligently analyzing the behavior of the PV output power in order to discover the indicators hiding behind each performance change. For instance, the fluctuation and intermittence in the PV power could indicate cloudy weather, shading, a temperature rise, or dust. In addition, the degradation in PV performance might be due to manufacturing causes, hardware issues, the PV life span, contaminated dirt, or any other possible causes. Consequently, the analysis should differentiate among the aforementioned causes and recognize the indication of accumulated dust.

Of course, determining the exact problem is difficult, since the number of inputs to the processing unit are kept few, and the impacts on the PV performance are considerably high. However, since the scope of this study focuses on detecting the existence of dust, the objective is possible and can be achieved.

The key factor in recognizing the accumulated dust is the fact that the PV power has a special pattern when it operates under several levels of dust conditions. The PV performance with dust has a cumulative dwindling pattern, and it is repetitive every day. In addition, the percentage of power reduction is related to the amount of dust in a way that can be logically differentiated from other impacts by analyzing the trending behavior and the moving average of the PV output power performance. It is well-known that the degradation in PV output power is caused by several influential factors, such as shading, clouds, raised temperature, and dust. However, the nature of the impact of each factor has its own distinguishable characteristics.

For example, if the PV power, during a normal ambient temperature, is fluctuating up and down wildly, and its moving average follows the same estimated trend of the output power, as in Figure 10a, then the impact in this case is considered as cloudy weather. On the other hand, in the event that the moving average of the PV output power is dropping with a rate of change similar to the change of the altitude angle, as in Figure 10b, then the shade effect is considered in this case. The rate of change of the altitude angle is considered here due to the fact that the increase/decrease in the shaded area over the PV panel is directly related to the sun trajectory. The failure of the PV system can be distinguished by the sharp degradation in the power, as in Figure 10c, whereas the effect of dust can be detected by the downward trending of the output power with a low-rate descent of the moving average, as in Figure 10d. After detecting the effect of dust, the amount (weight) of the contaminated soiling is determined using Equation (4). If more than one factor is detected, such as dust with cloud or dust with shade, the order of cleaning will not operate in this case due to the unfeasibility of the cleaning process.

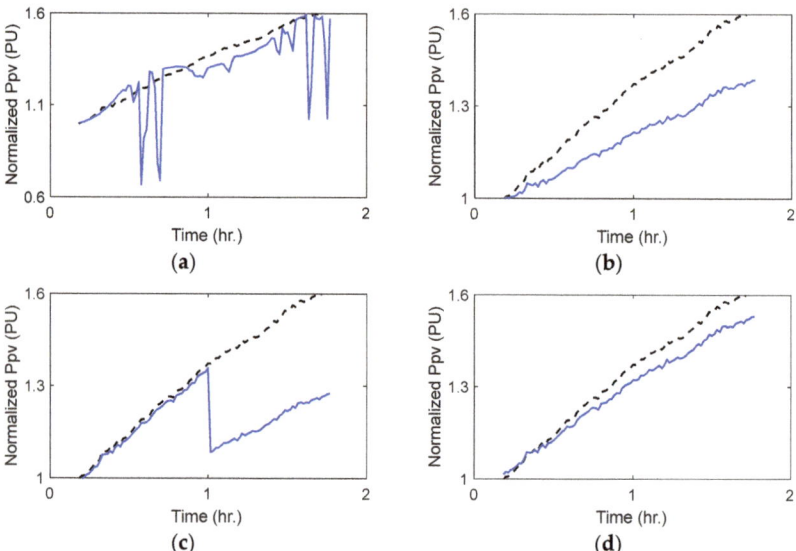

Figure 10. Different case scenarios of the PV output power pattern where (dotted-black line) for estimated power, while (solid-blue line) for actual PV power: (**a**) during cloudy weather; (**b**) with shading impact; (**c**) with a failure in PV panels; (**d**) with an accumulating dust.

The time window of the process is designed to be 24 h, starting from 12:00 PM, based on an intensive analysis. The ultimate outcome of the processing operation can be classified into two possible decisions: either "No dust" and showing results or "existence of dust" and commanding for panel cleaning.

5. Acquisition and Illustration of Actual PV Data

In order to validate the study feasibility, actual field PV data were used for this purpose. The realistic PV measurements of clean and dusty PV panels were collected from the Sustainable Energy Technologies Center (SET), King Saud University, Riyadh, Saudi Arabia [33]. The SET center has a completed test set to investigate the impact of dust on PV panels. The dust impact was evaluated by measuring and analyzing the performance of the PV panels under different dust level conditions. A set of four PV panels, with disparate cleaning time intervals, was used in that study. Based on the cleaning strategies, the collected data can be broken down into four main categories:

1. PV data with daily cleaned panels;
2. PV data with panels cleaned every week;
3. PV data with panels cleaned every month;
4. PV data with panels not cleaned for a year.

All data were collected in 2020 for 12 months. The tilt angle is 24 degrees toward the south. The SCADA system collects open voltage, short circuit current and temperature every single minute (1 min sampling rate). The validity of the proposed system was investigated by processing the four sets of panel data in order to evaluate the ability of the AI system to take the right course of action. The AI system here is responsible for detecting the cause of the PV power degradation as well as determining whether the cleaning command is feasible or not.

Figures 11–13 show the number of selected PV measurements during certain days. In Figure 11, the data for every panel are shown during a sunny day. As observed, the panel output power for the daily cleaned panel is more than the output power for the other panels, where the accumulated dust is inversely related with the panel output efficiency. In this case, the dust detection process is obvious, and the outcome from the AI system must be the cleaning order when the amount of dust exceeds the allowable limit (0.15 g/m^2). Figure 12 shows the collected data during a partly cloudy day. In this case, the PV panel produced a fluctuated output power during the morning due to the presence of clouds. Since the timeframe of the computational process is 24 h, the AI system must be able to differentiate the amount of dust despite the presence of clouds for part of the day and then give the order to the cleaning unit when it is feasible. Figure 13 illustrates the PV data during cloudy weather for the entire day, and it is obvious that the AI system must not operate the cleaning unit since the panels will not be able to capture the sun light for that day.

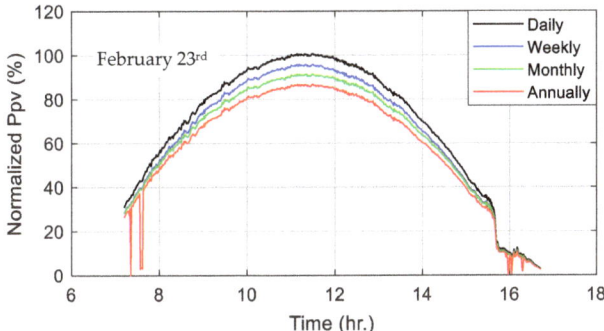

Figure 11. Actual PV data under different cleaning periods (sunny day).

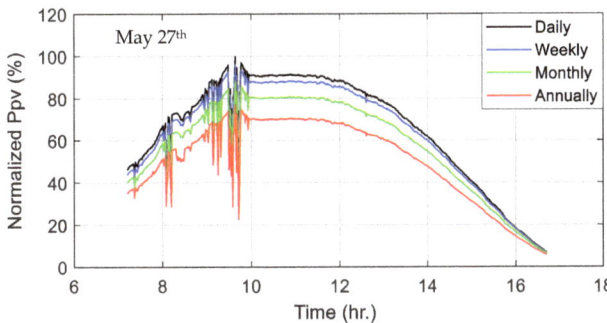

Figure 12. Actual PV data under different cleaning periods (partly cloudy day).

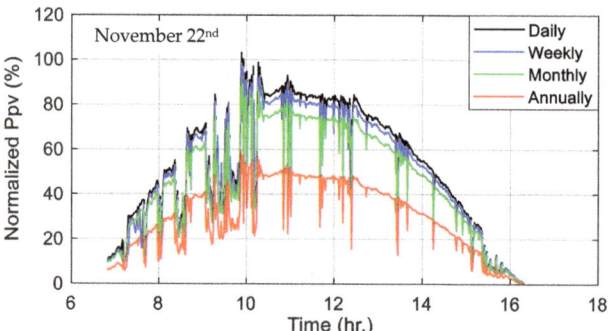

Figure 13. Actual PV data under different cleaning periods (cloudy day).

6. Evaluation of the Estimating Model

In the interest of validating the proposed assessment tool, an evaluation analysis was conducted to test the outcomes of the sun energy predictor. Three days were selected carefully (beginning, middle, and end of the year) to cover all possible sun angle conditions. Figures 14 and 15 show the sun energy estimation for the Riyadh region on 23 February, 27 May and 22 November 22. Figure 14 shows the estimated sun energy on a flat surface, while the results in Figure 15 are for a surface with a 24-degree tilt angle and 10-degree azimuth angle toward the south. These predicted curves and those for all remaining days will be utilized to estimate the PV output power and then detect the dust level with the help of the AI system.

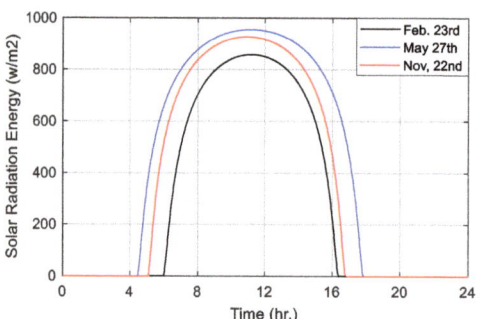

Figure 14. Estimated sun energy on a flat surface.

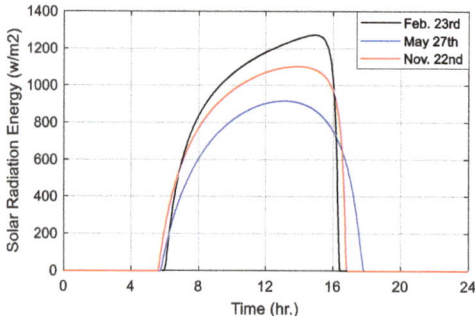

Figure 15. Estimated sun energy on a tilted surface (10-degree tilt angle).

It is worth mentioning that the power scale of the estimated sun energy is in W/m^2; hence, it is necessary to normalize it (in scale of 100%) to be compatible with any size of PV system. In addition, the sun energy data must be clipped to the same time interval of the actual data, as some unwanted real PV data were rejected due to technical errors during data collection.

7. Evaluation of the Proposed AI System

The feasibility of the proposed AI system, shown in Figure 9, is investigated by combining all required inputs and observing the ultimate system outputs. The detection unit is responsible for assigning the level of the accumulated dust on PV panels as well as sending a command signal to the cleaning system at the correct time. Table 3 lists the parameters of the studied PV system.

Table 3. Specifications of the studied PV system.

PV System Parameters	
Rated power	1000 W
Total panel area	9.35 m × 4.82 m (45 m^2)
Panel efficiency	21%
Tilt and azimuth angles	(24°), (0° S)
Input data by the user	
Day numbers	53, 147, 322
Longitude and latitude of the PV System location	46.6753° E–24.7136° N Riyadh, Saudi Arabia
Time zone	GMT+3
Calculated parameters	
Ground Coverage Ratio	0.78
Noontime	12:06PM, 11.50AM, 11.38AM Obtained by longitude, sun location, and local time zone

Different weather conditions on different days were considered to test the detection unit under all possible consequences. The output results from the AI unit are shown in Figures 16 and 17. The analysis outcomes of the AI unit are delivered to the end user via the interactive user interface, as illustrated in Figure 9.

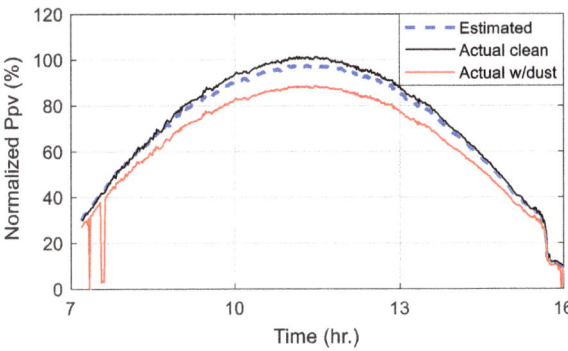

Figure 16. Estimated and actual PV output power during a sunny day.

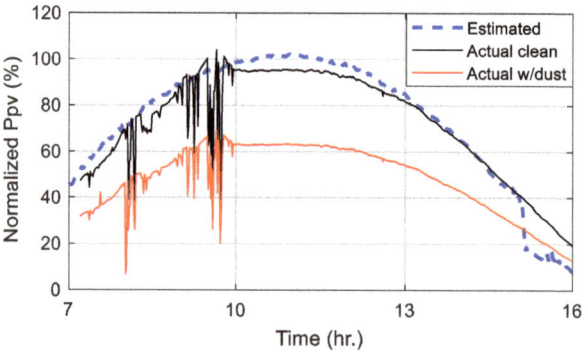

Figure 17. Estimated and actual PV output power during a partly cloudy day.

The outcome figures, Figures 16 and 17, show only three plots for the PV system: the estimated delivered power, actual delivered power with cleaned panels, and actual delivered power with uncleaned panels, while the proposed system can virtually accommodate any type of PV power data. The reason for not showing all collected data is to not repeat the previously shown figures as well as to explain the basic process with obvious graphs. However, the completed analysis for all available data, including weekly and monthly cleaned panel data, are illustrated in Table 4.

Table 4. Outcome results of the proposed AI system under different days, weather conditions, and dust levels.

Day	Weather Condition	Cleaning Period	Dust Level (g/m^2)	Cleaning Order	Reasons
23 February 2020	Sunny	Daily	0.041	NO	Low dust level
		Weekly	0.066	NO	Low dust level
		Monthly	0.152	YES	High dust level
		Annually	0.217	YES	High dust level
27 May 2020	Partly cloudy	Daily	0.094	NO	Low dust level
		Weekly	0.161	NO	Low dust level
		Monthly	0.242	YES	High dust level (detected pre-clouds)
		Annually	0.314	YES	High dust level (detected pre-clouds)
22 November 2020	Mostly cloudy	Daily	0.164	NO	Cloudy weather
		Weekly	0.234	NO	Cloudy weather
		Monthly	0.264	NO	Cloudy weather
		Annually	0.423	NO	Cloudy weather

The final decision of the AI system not only relies on the comparison between the estimated and actual PV output power, but also depends on a deep intelligent computational analysis where the dust versus PV power, as in Equation (4), is one of the main key detection factors. For instance, on 27 May (and for the monthly cleaned panel), the order was not given for cleaning due to the existence of clouds; however, on the same day (and for the annually cleaned panel), the decision for cleaning the panel was suggested, where the AI system detected a high level of dust despite the presence of clouds. Moreover, despite the fact that the dust level on 22 November exceeded 0.15 g/m^2, the dust detection unit did not order cleaning due to the presence of heavy clouds throughout the day. In other words, the proposed system is responsible for giving the order for cleaning when it is logically feasible.

The validity process is not limited to the days shown in Table 4; however, it has been conducted for more than 300 days throughout the year of 2020. The days in Table 4 were carefully selected to clearly demonstrate the outcomes of the proposed technique during different seasons and weather conditions in order to ensure the feasibility of the proposed PV cleaning technique.

8. Conclusions

This paper proposes an artificial-intelligence-based prediction model (AIPM) in order to detect the amount of dust accumulated on PV panels; consequently, it operates the attached cleaning units using an optimal strategy. Unlike the use of cameras, sensors, power datasets, and other detection elements, this paper attempted to determine the dust level by utilizing the expanded knowledge on solar irradiation models and logical/intelligent computational analysis. The expert artificial intelligence (AI) computational system is used in this study for a high level of data processing and to accommodate more input/output data. The feasibility of the proposed dust detection strategy was investigated using actual field data during all possible weather conditions. The results proved the ability of the detection unit for commanding the cleaning system at the optimal time as well as the capability of determining the dust level.

The proposed strategy contributes by simplifying the attached dust detection unit in terms of lower cost and higher usage flexibility. In addition, the beginning of use time for the proposed system is considerably faster than other actual-data-based methodologies. On the other hand, the proposed system must be investigated with different PV case scenarios in future work in order to fulfill the accuracy and reliability requirements. The allowable dust level in this study is 0.15 g/m^2 (corresponds to 12% PV power reduction) during a sunny day, while it is dependent on the intelligent computational analysis during cloudy and high-temperature weather conditions.

Funding: This work was supported by the Researchers Supporting Project number (RSPD2023R578), King Saud University, Riyadh, Saudi Arabia.

Data Availability Statement: Not applicable.

Conflicts of Interest: The author declares no conflict of interest.

Abbreviations

The following abbreviations are used in this manuscript:

DCUs	Dust Cleaning Units
AI	Artificial Intelligence
RESs	Renewable Energy Sources
CO2	Carbon Dioxide
GCR	Ground coverage ratio
AM	Air-mass coefficient
CF	Correlation Factor
WDUST	Weight of Dust
SET	Sustainable Energy Technologies Center
GMT	Greenwich Mean Time
AIPM	Artificial-Intelligence-based Prediction Model

Appendix A

The Figure A1 shows the current–voltage curve of the panel heat versus output power characteristic. This curve was used in the dust detection process to estimate the heat impact on the PV power.

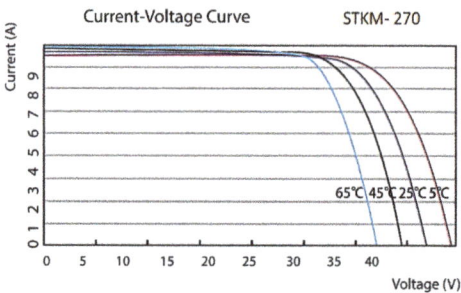

Figure A1. Current–voltage heat characteristic used in this study [34].

References

1. Ismael, S.M.; Aleem, S.H.E.A.; Abdelaziz, A.Y.; Zobaa, A.F. State-of-the-art of hosting capacity in modern power systems with distributed generation. *Renew. Energy* **2019**, *130*, 1002–1020. [CrossRef]
2. Ayadi, F.; Colak, I.; Garip, I.; Bulbul, H.I. Impacts of Renewable Energy Resources in Smart Grid. In Proceedings of the 8th International Conference on Smart Grid (icSmartGrid), Paris, France, 17–19 June 2020. [CrossRef]
3. Varma, R.K. Impact of High Penetration of Solar PV System and Smart Inverter Developments. In *Smart Solar PV Inverters with Advanced Grid Support Functionalities*, 1st ed.; Wiley-IEEE Press: New York, NY, USA, 2022; pp. 1–34. [CrossRef]
4. Ndirangu, K.; Tafti, H.D.; Fletcher, J.E.; Konstantinou, G. Impact of Grid Voltage and Grid-Supporting Functions on Efficiency of Single-Phase Photovoltaic Inverters. *IEEE J. Photovolt.* **2022**, *12*, 421–428. [CrossRef]
5. Salimi, H.; Lavasani, A.M.; Ahmadi-Danesh-Ashtiani, H.; Fazaeli, R. Effect of dust concentration, wind speed, and relative humidity on the performance of photovoltaic panels in Tehran. *Energy Sources Part A Recovery Util. Environ. Eff.* **2019**, *72*, 1–11. [CrossRef]
6. Paul, D.I. Dust Deposition on Photovoltaic Modules: Its Effects on Performance. In *The Effects of Dust and Heat on Photovoltaic Modules: Impacts and Solutions*, 1st ed.; Springer Press: Cham, Switzerland, 2022; pp. 3–46.
7. Tarigan, E. The Effect of Dust on Solar PV System Energy Output Under Urban Climate of Surabaya, Indonesia. *J. Phys.* **2019**, *1373*, 012025. [CrossRef]
8. Darwish, Z. Effect of Dust on Photovoltaic Performance Review and Research Status. In Proceedings of the Latest Trends in Renewable Energy and Environmental Informatics, Kuala Lumpur, Malaysia, 2–4 April 2013. [CrossRef]
9. Abuqaaud, K.A.; Ferrah, A. A Novel Technique for Detecting and Monitoring Dust and Soil on Solar Photovoltaic Panel. In Proceedings of the Advances in Science and Engineering Technology International Conferences (ASET), Dubai, United Arab Emirates, 4–9 February 2020. [CrossRef]
10. Shaaban, M.F.; Alarif, A.; Mokhtar, M.; Tariq, U.; Osman, A.H.; Al-Ali, A.R. A New Data-Based Dust Estimation Unit for PV Panels. *Energies* **2020**, *14*, 3601. [CrossRef]
11. Tsamaase, K.; Ramasesane, T.; Zibani, I.; Matlotse, E.; Motshidisi, K. Automated dust detection and cleaning system of PV module. *J. Electr. Electron. Eng. (IOSR-JEEE)* **2017**, *12*, 2320–3331. [CrossRef]
12. Zorrilla-Casanova, J.; Philiougine, M.; Carretero, J.; Bernaola, P.; Carpena, P.; Mora-Lopez, L.; Sidrach-De-Cardona, M. Analysis of Dust Losses in Photovoltaic Modules. In Proceedings of the World Renewable Energy Congress, Linköping, Sweden, 8–13 May 2011. [CrossRef]
13. Sulaiman, S.A.; Mat, M.N.H.; Guangul, F.M.; Bou-Rabee, M.A. Real-time study on the effect of dust accumulation on performance of solar PV panels in Malaysia. In Proceedings of the International Conference on Electrical and Information Technologies (ICEIT), Marrakech, Morocco, 25–27 March 2015. [CrossRef]
14. Ketjoy, K.; Konyu, M. Study of Dust Effect on Photovoltaic Module for Photovoltaic Power Plant. *Energy Procedia* **2014**, *52*, 431–437. [CrossRef]
15. Wu, Z.; Zhou, Z.; Alkahtani, M. Time-Effective Dust Deposition Analysis of PV Modules Based on Finite Element Simulation for Candidate Site Determination. *IEEE Access* **2020**, *8*, 65137–65147. [CrossRef]
16. Jones, R.K.; Baras, A.; Al Saeeri, A.; Al Qahtani, A.; Al Amoudi, A.O.; Al Shaya, Y.; Alodan, M.; Al-Hsaien, S.A. Optimized Cleaning Cost and Schedule Based on Observed Soiling Conditions for Photovoltaic Plants in Central Saudi Arabia. *IEEE J. Photovolt.* **2016**, *6*, 730–738. [CrossRef]
17. Mohammed, H.A.; Al Hilli, B.A.M.; Al-Mejibli, I.S. Smart system for dust detecting and removing from solar cells. *J. Phys. Conf. Ser.* **2018**, *1032*, 012055. [CrossRef]
18. Dantas, G.M.; Mendes, O.L.C.; Maia, S.M.; De Alexandria, A.R. Dust detection in solar panel using image processing techniques: A review. *Research. Res. Soc. Dev.* **2020**, *9*, e321985107. [CrossRef]
19. Yfantis, E.; Fayed, A. A Camera System for Detecting Dust And Other Deposits On Solar Panels. *Adv. Image Video Process.* **2014**, *2*, 1–10. [CrossRef]

20. Roumpakias, E.; Stamatelos, T. Surface Dust and Aerosol Effects on the Performance of Grid-Connected Photovoltaic Systems. *Sustainability* **2020**, *12*, 569. [CrossRef]
21. Coşgun, A.E.; Demir, H. The Experimental Study of Dust Effect on Solar Panel Efficiency. *J. Polytech.* **2021**, *25*, 1429–1434. [CrossRef]
22. Puri, V.; Jha, S.; Kumar, R.; Priyadarshini, I.; Son, L.H.; Abdel-Basset, M.; Elhoseny, M.; Long, H.V. A Hybrid Artificial Intelligence and Internet of Things Model for Generation of Renewable Resource of Energy. *IEEE Access* **2019**, *7*, 111181–111191. [CrossRef]
23. Parrott, B.; Zanini, P.C.; Shehri, A.; Kotsovos, K.; Gereige, I. Automated, robotic dry-cleaning of solar panels in Thuwal, Saudi Arabia using a silicone rubber brush. *Sol. Energy* **2018**, *171*, 526–533. [CrossRef]
24. Cai, S.; Bao, G.; Ma, X.; Wu, W.; Bian, G.-B.; Rodrigues, J.J.; de Albuquerque, V.H.C. Parameters optimization of the dust absorbing structure for photovoltaic panel cleaning robot based on orthogonal experiment method. *J. Clean. Prod.* **2019**, *217*, 724–731. [CrossRef]
25. Alghamdi, A.S.; Bahaj, A.S.; Blunden, L.S.; Wu, Y. Dust Removal from Solar PV Modules by Automated Cleaning Systems. *Energies* **2019**, *12*, 2923. [CrossRef]
26. Rehman, S.; Mohandes, M.A.; Hussein, A.E.; Alhems, L.M.; Al-Shaikhi, A. Cleaning of Photovoltaic Panels Utilizing the Downward Thrust of a Drone. *Energies* **2022**, *15*, 8159. [CrossRef]
27. Roger, A.; Amir, A. *Photovoltaic Systems Engineering*, 4th ed.; CRC Press: New York, NY, USA, 2020; pp. 133–356.
28. Alfaris, F.; Alzahrani, A.; Kimball, J.W. Stochastic model for PV sensor array data. In Proceedings of the International Conference on Renewable Energy Research and Application (ICRERA), Milwaukee, WI, USA, 19–22 October 2014. [CrossRef]
29. Riyadh Saudi Arabia Weather 2022 Climate and Weather in Riyadh. Available online: http://hikersbay.com/climate/saudiarabia/riyadh?lang=en (accessed on 19 December 2022).
30. Expert Systems in Artificial Intelligence—Javatpoint. Available online: https://www.javatpoint.com/expert-systems-in-artificial-intelligence (accessed on 21 December 2022).
31. Bose, B.K. Artificial Intelligence Techniques in Smart Grid and Renewable Energy Systems—Some Example Applications. *Proc. IEEE* **2017**, *105*, 2262–2273. [CrossRef]
32. Navarrete, E.C.; Perea, M.T.; Correa, J.J.; Serrano, R.C.; Ríos-Moreno, G. Expert Control Systems Implemented in a Pitch Control of Wind Turbine: A Review. *IEEE Access* **2019**, *7*, 13241–13259. [CrossRef]
33. Sustainable Energy Technologies Center (SET) 2022. Available online: https://set.ksu.edu.sa/en (accessed on 6 November 2022).
34. Solar Electric, UK Office. Available online: http://www.solarelectricuk.com/high-power-pv-solar-panels/data-sheets.html (accessed on 15 November 2022).

Disclaimer/Publisher's Note: The statements, opinions and data contained in all publications are solely those of the individual author(s) and contributor(s) and not of MDPI and/or the editor(s). MDPI and/or the editor(s) disclaim responsibility for any injury to people or property resulting from any ideas, methods, instructions or products referred to in the content.

Article

Approximating Shading Ratio Using the Total-Sky Imaging System: An Application for Photovoltaic Systems

Mahmoud Dhimish [1,*] and Pavlos I. Lazaridis [2]

[1] Laboratory of Photovoltaics, School of Physics, Engineering and Technology, University of York, York YO10 5DD, UK
[2] Department of Engineering and Technology, University of Huddersfield, Huddersfield HD1 3DH, UK
* Correspondence: mahmoud.dhimish@york.ac.uk

Abstract: In recent years, a determined shading ratio of photovoltaic (PV) systems has been broadly reviewed and explained. Observing the shading ratio of PV systems allows us to navigate for PV faults and helps to recognize possible degradation mechanisms. Therefore, this work introduces a novel approximation shading ratio technique using an all-sky imaging system. The proposed solution has the following structure: (i) we determined four all-sky imagers for a region of 25 km^2, (ii) computed the cloud images using our new proposed model, called color-adjusted (CA), (iii) computed the shading ratio, and (iv) estimated the global horizontal irradiance (GHI) and consequently, obtained the predicted output power of the PV system. The estimation of the GHI was empirically compared with captured data from two different weather stations; we found that the average accuracy of the proposed technique was within a maximum ±12.7% error rate. In addition, the PV output power approximation accuracy was as high as 97.5% when the shading was zero and reduced to the lowest value of 83% when overcasting conditions affected the examined PV system.

Keywords: shading ratio estimation; photovoltaics; total-sky imaging; cloud estimation

Citation: Dhimish, M.; Lazaridis, P.I. Approximating Shading Ratio Using the Total-Sky Imaging System: An Application for Photovoltaic Systems. *Energies* **2022**, *15*, 8201. https://doi.org/10.3390/en15218201

Academic Editors: Fouzi Harrou, Ying Sun, Bilal Taghezouit and Dairi Abdelkader

Received: 6 October 2022
Accepted: 1 November 2022
Published: 3 November 2022

Publisher's Note: MDPI stays neutral with regard to jurisdictional claims in published maps and institutional affiliations.

Copyright: © 2022 by the authors. Licensee MDPI, Basel, Switzerland. This article is an open access article distributed under the terms and conditions of the Creative Commons Attribution (CC BY) license (https://creativecommons.org/licenses/by/4.0/).

1. Introduction

The appearance of solar power is faced with challenges unique to the solar resource. Namely, variability in ground irradiance makes regulating and maintaining power both challenging and costly, as the uncertainty of solar generation compared to conventional fossil power sources requires considerable regulation and reserve capacities to meet ancillary service requirements. Of particular interest to the energy industry are sudden and sweeping changes in irradiance, termed "ramp events", typically caused by large clouds or widespread changes in cloud cover.

Solar forecasting models have been widely presented in literature, although they mainly focus on two main approaches: (i) physical numerical-based weather predictions [1–3] and (ii) solar forecasting that is more directly based on real-time long-term data measurements from the ground [4,5] or from satellites [6] with the support of machine learning algorithms [7]. In the field, the accuracy of the second approach customarily attains higher prediction and forecasting accuracy.

The ground-based forecasting models use total-sky imagers (TSI). For example, Yang et al. [8] developed a solar irradiance forecasting model using all-sky imager images applied in UC San Diego. Their proposed model can accurately forecast the global horizontal irradiance for 3–15 min at a 90% accuracy rate. A similar approach was also presented by Nouri et al. [9], where the all-sky imager cloud transmittance was determined. Figure 1 shows the actual TSI images of the sky where the transmittance is known/unknown. Their proposed techniques relied on three input parameters: (i) height of the cloud, (ii) probability analysis of the historical data for the cloud vs transmittance rate, and (iii) recent transmittance measurements and their corresponding cloud heights.

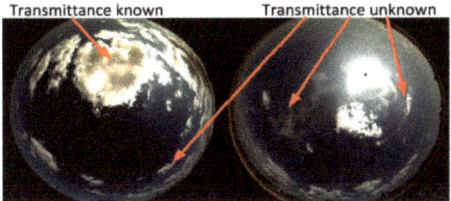

Figure 1. Sky images of a TSI [9].

Other recent studies [10–12] showed that TSI could potentially be used to determine the shading factors for PV applications; nevertheless, this has not been developed yet. For example, ref. [13] proposed a cloud motion estimation using an artificial neural network (ANN). Their model has a relatively low estimation error rate ($\pm 5\%$) and can be used within a broader range of applications.

The approximation of shading in a PV system can also be obtained using the determination of the current-voltage (I-V) curves, applied with maximum power point tracking (MPPT) units [14–16]. The problem with these models is that they can predict the amount of loss in the PV output power; however, they cannot indicate the shading factor resulting from the clouds in the sky. In contrast, the output power losses in PV systems can also result from cumulative dust [17], snow [18], hotspots [19–21], or cracks [22–25]. Therefore, assuming that all PV output power losses are caused by shading is substantially incorrect.

Artificial intelligence-based techniques have also recently been applied to approximate the sky's shading ratio or cloud coverage [26,27]. For example, a recent study [28] demonstrated a cloud cover estimation from images taken by sky-facing cameras using a multi-level machine learning technique. Another recent study [29] explored the applicability of the impact factors to estimate solar irradiance using multiple machine learning algorithms such as support vector machines, a long short-term memory (LSTM) neural network, linear regression, and a multi-layer neural network. They found that the LSTM model provided the best prediction accuracy using weather data without installing and maintaining on-site solar irradiance sensors. In contrast, numerous algorithms have been developed to predict the output power of a typical PV system using weather station data, all of which can be used within a moderately small-scale geographical area of less than 2 km^2. When, for example, a location is 20 km apart from the weather station, these algorithms fail to predict the output power accurately; in some cases, even with a closer location (<5 km), it is hard to achieve good prediction results.

2. Aim of This Work

In previous publications, we presented and validated forecasting and predicting shading ratios in a PV system or GHI forecasting from a more comprehensive point of view. However, previous publications did not address the TSI adoption in PV output power forecasting and prediction shading factors expressly within a large-scale area (>20 km^2). Therefore, in this article, we aimed to present our work on developing a multi-stage process to accurately approximate the shading ratio of clouds in the sky and apply the method to predict the output power of PV systems. The actual implementation of the algorithm developed was to allocate four TISs within a 25 km^2 area and then apply a cloud cover fraction approximation model, named the CA algorithm. Consequently, we predicted the output power of different PV systems within this area. In this article, we also used weather station data to measure the actual GHI and compare it with the obtained GHI from the proposed algorithm; this step was necessary to demonstrate the accuracy of our algorithm.

3. Experimental Setup

Four identical field-mounted TSI 440A total-sky imagers were located in Huddersfield, UK (Figure 2a). TSI-A and TSI-B were 5 km apart; there was also an equivalent distance from TSI-B to TSI-C. It was decided to set up the TSIs in the range of 5 km, as this would give more accurate predictions, since, for example, the Met Office and many researchers propose fixing the TSIs in the field at a distance of 1 to 5 km maximum. The instrument consisted of a spherical mirror and a downward-pointing camera (Figure 2b). For the best image resolution, images had to be taken every 1 min. The camera provided images that were 420 × 420 pixels, which were un-adjustable. Therefore, a cloud identification (filtering) algorithm had to be applied.

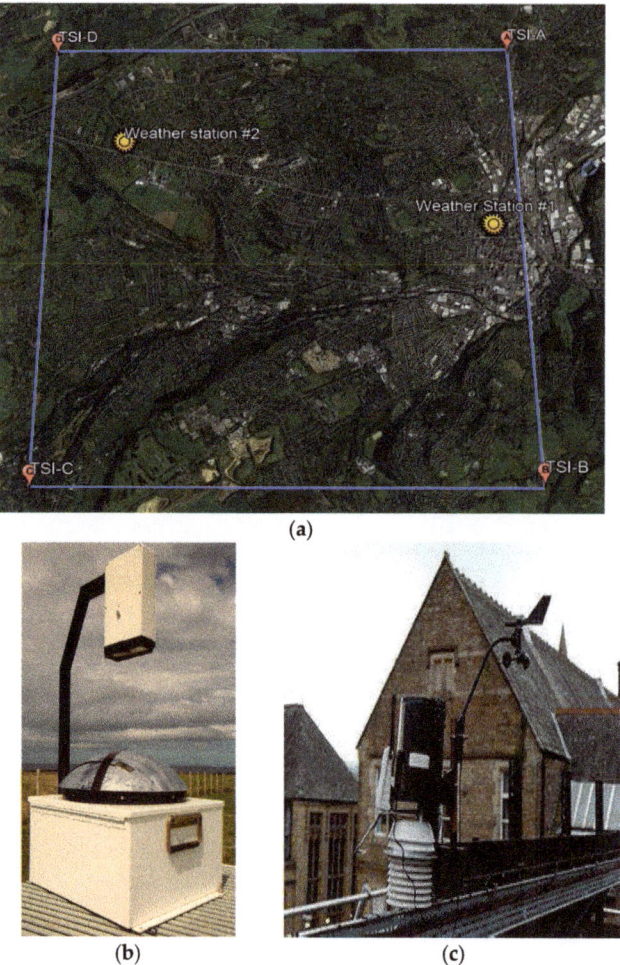

Figure 2. Experimental setup: (**a**) Map showing the sky imager locations and the weather stations. The actual distance from TSI-A to TSI-B was 5 km. The region displayed in this figure was approximately 5 km^2, taken from @Google Maps, 2022, (**b**) TSI 440A total-sky imager, (**c**) Davis weather station.

Two identical Davis weather stations (Figure 2c) were used to validate the accuracy of the shading ratio algorithm. (They will be discussed later in this section). The weather station can measure the solar irradiance in a range of 0–1000 W/m^2, with a high accuracy of ± 0.5 W/m^2. We mounted the weather stations without any slope, as we did for the TSIs.

The data of both the TSIs and the weather stations were taken wirelessly (via cloud-based software) and logged for the duration of the experiments. In addition, the summary of the coordinates of the sites (TSIs and weather stations) are summarized in Table 1.

Table 1. Site coordinates.

TSI/Weather Stations	Latitude	Longitude
TSI-A	53°40′1.87″ N	1°46′51.78″ W
TSI-B	53°37′20.80″ N	1°46′39.65″ W
TSI-C	53°37′22.57″ N	1°51′14.75″ W
TSI-D	53°40′3.13″ N	1°51′18.08″ W
Weather Station #1	53°38′49.31″ N	1°47′3.30″ W
Weather Station #2	53°39′22.65″ N	1°50′34.38″ W

4. Methods

4.1. Cloud Decision Algorithm

To date, the most adaptable cloud estimation algorithms are the blue/red-plus-blue/green-ratio algorithm (BRBG) and the cloud detection and opacity classification algorithm (CDOC). The first algorithm, BRBG, uses the difference in light scattering by clouds compared to a clear-sky day [30]; the result will indicate a factor between 0 and 1, which ultimately describes the cloudiness of an image. On the other hand, the CDOC algorithm is constructed upon the BRBG [31]. This algorithm identifies the cloudiness in the TSI image using the classification of the thickness and the red–blue ratio of the sky image.

The cloud cover fraction (CCF), defined as the fraction of sky covered by clouds, of both algorithms were calculated (Figure 3) for two conditions. In Figure 3a, the CCF equaled 0.58 and 0.76 for BRBG and CDOC, respectively. In this example, the sky was partially covered by thick clouds, covering the sun. In contrast, in Figure 3b, both algorithms had extremely high CCF for the overcasting condition. In this paper, we proposed an adjusted cloud-decision algorithm, and we called it color-adjusted (CA). We can not only determine an accurate measurement for the CCF, but the actual distribution can also be further exaggerated, compared with the BRBG and the CDOC.

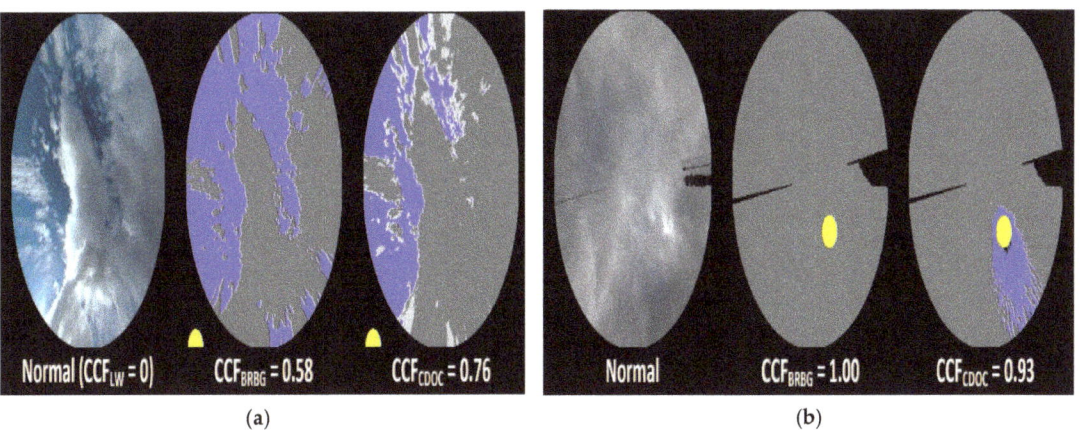

Figure 3. Evaluation of the CCF ratio for the BRBG and CDOC algorithms under two different shading conditions (note, the yellow cycle represents the actual position of the sun in the sky, and the "normal" is the actual image captured using the full-sky imager): (a) partial shading, (b) overcasting.

The normal image captured using the sky imager was an RGB color image (Figure 4a). The quaternion (red, green, yellow, and blue) pixel values were deposited and combined into a single image, as shown in Figure 4b. Here, the vector of each color was filtered using the hypercomplex convolution,

$$\overline{g}(n,m) = \sum_{s=-S}^{S} \sum_{k=-K}^{K} h_L(s,k)\, g(n-s \bmod N,\, m-k \bmod M) h_R(s,k) \quad (1)$$

where $\bar{g}(n, m)$ is the filtered image in a quaternion array $((N + 2) \times (M + 2))$, $g(n - s \bmod N, m - k \bmod M)$ is the actual image in quaternion array $(N \times M)$, $h_L(s, k)$ is the quaternion left mask $((2S + 1) \times (2K + 1))$, and $h_R(s, k)$ is the quaternion right mask $((2S + 1) \times (2K + 1))$.

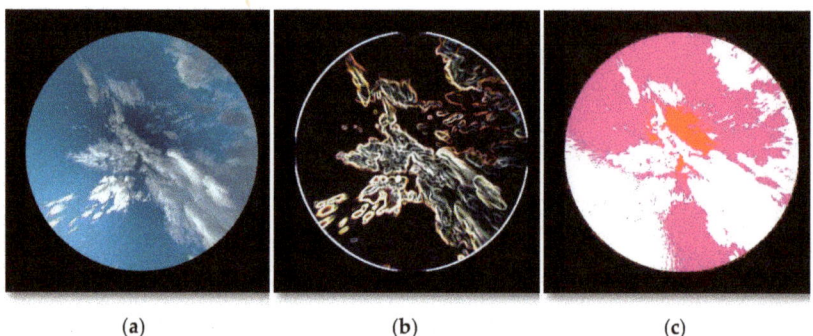

(a) (b) (c)

Figure 4. Evaluation of the proposed cloud decision algorithm: (**a**) Normal image captured using the full-sky imager, (**b**) the quaternion values of the image, (**c**) output image of the CA algorithm (blue–green color ratio); the back area represents CCF ratio = 1.0, blue area represents sky-free, and green is partial clouds.

The cloudiness was observed by selecting the most appropriate color ratio. We found that red–white, Figure 4c, was the most precise color ratio that could instantly discover the clouds, and, therefore, it was used to calculate the CCF.

To verify the differences between our model and the pre-existing models (BRBG and CDOC), the image in Figure 3a was used. The results of our cloud decision algorithm are shown in Figure 4. Initially, the image taken from the TSI was populated into the quaternion values, as shown in Figure 4a, and next, the image color was adjusted to a red–white ratio. Here, the red area represented full shade, the CCF = 1.0, and white or pink (0 being white and 1 being red) represented the free sky (i.e., no, or partial clouds), whereas green was the partial shading area. The CCF value was then calculated by subtracting the ratio of the colors, and we found that in Figure 4c, CCFCA = 0.63, compared with CCFBRBG = 0.58 and CCFCDOC = 0.76. The results of the cloud decision algorithm were in the ranges of the BRBG and CDOC algorithms. However, it is worth noting that the cloud decision algorithm did not take the average values of both algorithms.

4.2. Cloud Cover Fraction Approximation

After completing the CA algorithm, the shading ratio approximation for the selected area was formulated. This approximation aimed to find the shading in the area; that way, the approximation of the cloud coverage can be further improved. First, to identify any position/location on the map, the coordinates of the TSIs must be known, as we have already seen in Figure 2a. If the location of the PV system or the weather station is closer to a particular TSI, the CCF of the TSI will contribute more to the approximation of the shade. This approach is usually referred to as the "adjusted weighted average". For example, if the weather station was located precisely on the TSI-A location, only the CCF value of the TSI-A would be considered. The distance between the location at (x, y) and the four TSI locations was calculated using (2), and the sum was calculated using (3), where $(x1, y2)$, $(x2, y3)$, $(x3, y3)$, and $(x4, y4)$ are the coordinates of the TSIs.

Note that the actual distances were measured in km, where TSI-A was located at (5,5), TSI-B at (5,0), TS-C at (0,0), which in this case, represented the origin of the map, and finally, TSI-D at (0,5).

$$D1 = \sqrt{(x - x1)^2 + (y - y1)^2};$$

$$D2 = \sqrt{(x - x2)^2 + (y - y2)^2};$$

$$D3 = \sqrt{(x-x3)^2 + (y-y3)^2};$$
$$D4 = \sqrt{(x-x4)^2 + (y-y4)^2} \qquad (2)$$
$$Sum = D1 + D2 + D3 + D4 \qquad (3)$$

The contribution of the *CCF* from each *TSI* at a particular location were, therefore, calculated based on the ratios of the sum of the distances subtracted by the actual distance from the site, using (4). Then, each *CCF* contribution was multiplied by the actual *CCF*, determined using the *CA* algorithm; consequently, the weighted average *CCF* was calculated. This was accomplished by calculating the highest two values of the determined *CCF* contributions.

$$CCF\ contribution\ TSI-A = \frac{Sum - D1}{Sum};$$
$$CCF\ contribution\ TSI-B = \frac{Sum - D2}{Sum};$$
$$CCF\ contribution\ TSI-C = \frac{Sum - D3}{Sum};$$
$$CCF\ contribution\ TSI-D = \frac{Sum - D4}{Sum} \qquad (4)$$

Let us now consider the weather stations #1 and #2, located at (4.7,3) and (0.8,4), respectively, where the origin was at *TSI-C* (0,0). The calculations of all the parameters are compiled in Table 2. The optimum distances (shortest) between the weather stations and the actual *TSIs* are highlighted in the table. The output *CCFs* at both weather stations were calculated using (5) and (6). The *CCF* values for the TSIs were taken from Figure 5 (on 15 June 2022 at 11:30).

$$CCF\ weather\ station\ \#1 = \frac{(0.87 \times 0.66) + (0.81 \times 0.52)}{2} = 0.50 \qquad (5)$$

$$CCF\ weather\ station\ \#2 = \frac{(0.74 \times 0.63) + (0.92 \times 0.77)}{2} = 0.59 \qquad (6)$$

Table 2. Results of the parameters with respect to both weather stations.

Weather Station	D1 (km)	D2 (km)	D3 (km)	D4 (km)	Sum (km)	CCF Contribution TSI-A	CCF Contribution TSI-B	CCF Contribution TSI-C	CCF Contribution TSI-D	Output CCF
#1	2	3	5.6	5.1	15.7	0.87	0.81	0.64	0.68	0.50
#2	4.3	5.8	4.1	1.3	15.5	0.72	0.63	0.74	0.92	0.59

4.3. Shading Ratio Approximation Flowcode

In summary, the flowcode of the developed shading ratio approximation is presented in Figure 6. Initially, the TSI locations were identified, and then a reference TSI was selected. This corresponded to the actual origin of the map ($x = 0, y = 0$); this step was critical in measuring the distances of D1, D2, D3, D4, and their sum. Our previous calculation assumed that TSI-C was the origin (Figure 2a).

$$GHI\ Approximation\ Error\ (\%) = 100 - \left(\frac{GHI_{weather\ station}}{GHI_{proposed\ technique}} \times 100 \right) \qquad (7)$$

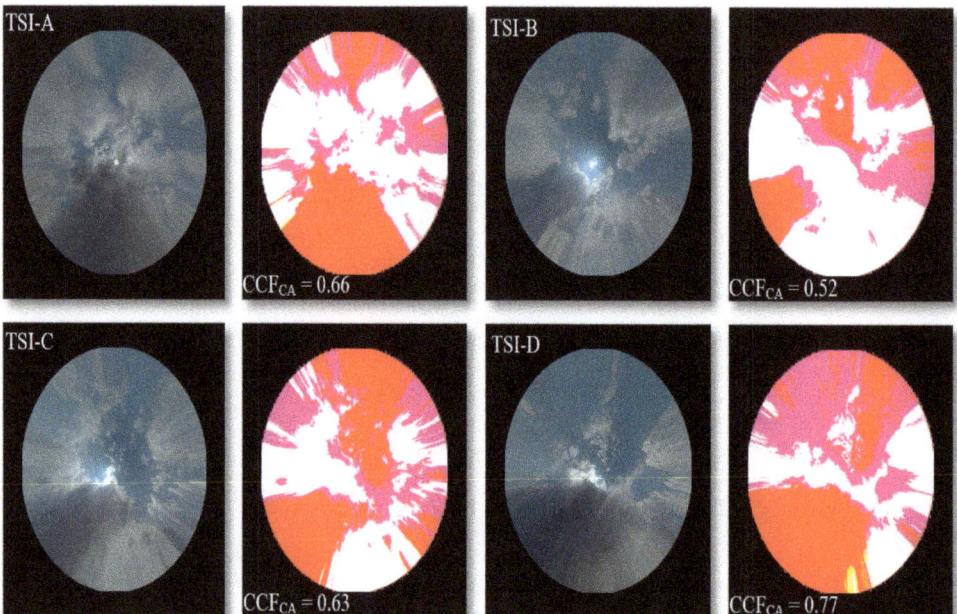

Figure 5. Normal TSI and the calibrated images using the developed CA algorithm (15 June 2022 11:30).

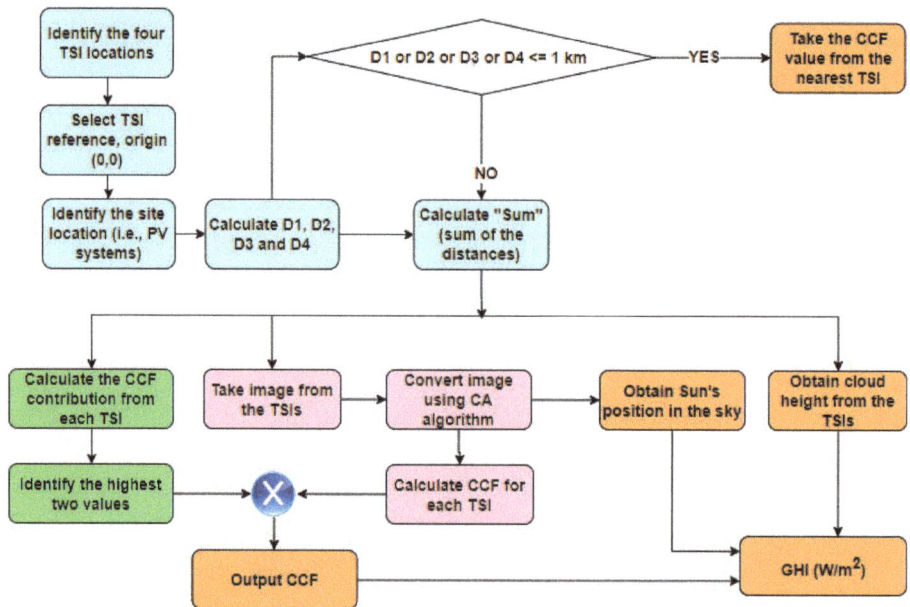

Figure 6. Flowcode of the developed shading ratio approximation algorithm.

If any of the measured distances were less than or equal to 1 km, the CCF would be taken directly to the adjacent/nearest TSI. This arrangement would give a 97% accuracy of the shade ratio in the location, as empirically evidenced by previous research [32–34]. On the other hand, if the location was more than 1 km away from any available TSIs, as with both weather stations in our experiment, the calculations of the CCF contribution and the CCF from the CA algorithm were obtained. Subsequently, the output CCF was determined, corresponding to the actual estimation of the cloud coverage at the site. Therefore, the correlation between the CCF and global horizontal irradiance (GHI) can be obtained using the GHI prediction interval computation models that have been widely presented in literature [35–39]. This depends on three variables: output CCF, sun position in the sky, and the cloud height measured using the TSIs. This step is practically useful when predicting the output power of a PV system (discussed in the next section).

We used the error function as a metric to analyze the performance of the approximation for the GHI; this was calculated using (7).

5. Results

5.1. Accuracy of the Proposed Shading Ratio Approximation Technique

To test the accuracy of the developed technique, we compared the estimated GHI to the actual GHI determined by weather stations #1 and #2 (Figure 7). According to Figure 7a, taken from weather station #1, two conditions were observed on the first day: partial clouds from 6:00–14:00 and clear skies from then onward. We noticed that the error (difference between the actual vs the estimated GHI) was equal to ±7.1% during partial cloud conditions. In contrast, there was a limited error (±2.3%) in the estimated GHI during clear sky conditions.

During the second day (Figure 7b), the sky was masked by heavy clouds or what is known as overcasting. This data was taken from weather station #1. In this case, the error in estimating the GHI was ±12.7%. This is likely the case in many cloud estimation techniques [38,39] because, in this specific condition, the sky imager usually fails to measure the height of the clouds precisely, and the output CCF is likely to have a more elevated distribution. In addition, on the third day, and according to Figure 7c, the sky was masked by partial clouds; this measurement was taken from weather station #2. The observed error in the estimation of the GHI was equal to 6.3%.

The above results confirm and validate the idea that the developed algorithm has high accuracy (low error) in estimating the GHI, compared with the actual weather station data.

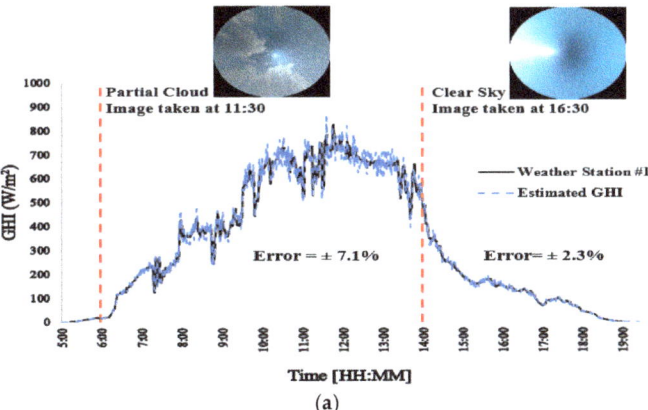

Figure 7. Cont.

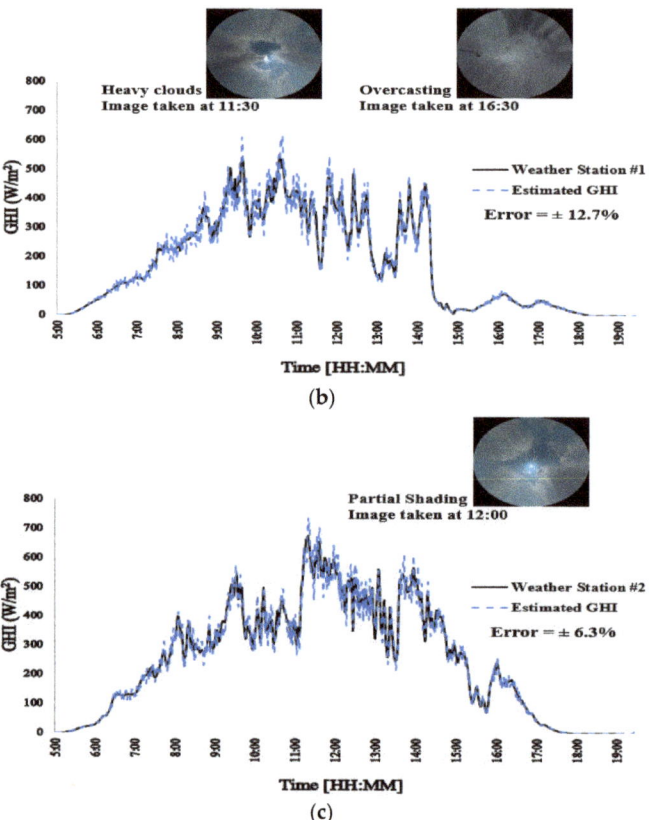

Figure 7. Output results of the estimated vs actual weather station GHIs under different shading conditions: (**a**) partial shading and clear sky, taken from weather station #1 (21 July 2022), (**b**) overcasting (heavy clouds), taken from weather station #1 (22 July 2022), and (**c**) partial shading, taken from weather station #2 (23 July 2022). (The sky images were taken from the nearest TSI, TSI-A for weather station #1 and TSI-D for weather station #2).

5.2. Estimating the Output Power of PV Systems

The ultimate aim of the proposed technique is to estimate the shading within an area and hence, predict the output power of PV systems. The advantages here are:

1. Weather stations are no longer needed.
2. It can predict the shade in relatively large areas (in our case, 25 km^2).
3. If a high variance is found between the estimated PV power vs the actual measured power in the PV system, a fault identification can be reported.

The temperature of any selected site/location can be taken from the online database available in the Met Office (or simply, using BBC weather as an example in the UK). In this section, to obtain the temperature in the examined PV systems, we used the data available in the Met Office; an update on the temperature can be found in the 5-min resolution, including one-day high-precision measured temperature.

We examined the accuracy of the PV output power estimation using two PV systems located within the studied area (Figure 8a), and the physical images of both PV systems are shown in Figure 8b. PV system #1 was comprised of eight series-connected PV modules and two strings, with a total capacity of 4320 W. PV system #2 also had the same configuration as PV system #1 but with a slightly lower rating power of 3520 W. Neither of the PV systems had a maximum power point tracking unit and were directly connected to the grid via Victron Energy 5 kW inverters that were installed back in May–June 2018. Both systems were maintained, and their data were managed via Solar UK Ltd.; we were given permission to access the data of both PV systems. A loss of 8% in the output power was expected, due to the non-ideal tilt and azimuth arrangements, so we included this ratio in our estimation for the output power.

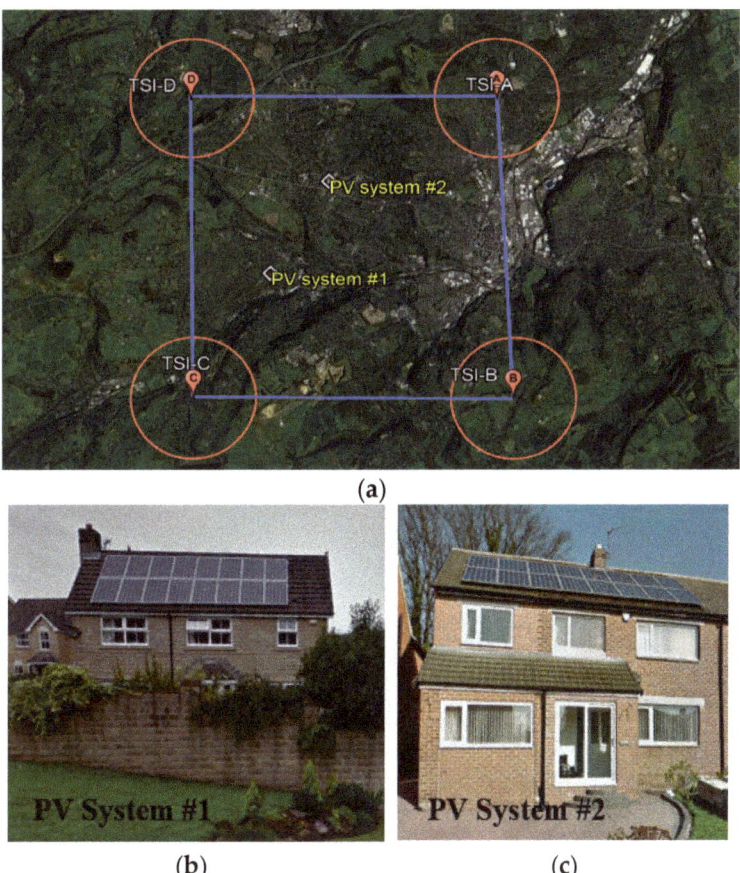

Figure 8. PV setups: (**a**) map representing the locations of the examined PV systems and (**b**,**c**) physical images of the PV systems.

We followed the same procedure to estimate the GHI in the PV system locations (as detailed in Figure 6). Next, we used (8) and (9) to estimate the output power of the PV systems, where N is the number of solar cells in a PV module (N = 60), and 16 is the total number of PV modules in the system. The parameters 0.00422 and 0.00343 are the equivalent output power of each solar cell, and $T^{0.021}$ is the weighted temperature.

$$Estimated\ Power\ (PV\ system\ \#1) = (N \times 16 \times 0.00422)\ GHI^{0.9998} \times T^{0.021} \qquad (8)$$

$$Estimated\ Power\ (PV\ system\ \#2) = (N \times 16 \times 0.00343)\ GHI^{0.9998} \times T^{0.021} \qquad (9)$$

To summarize the overall performance of the proposed model, we considered plotting the PV output power approximation accuracy against the CCF, presented in Figure 9. We observed that while the CCF was in the range of 0–0.6, the prediction accuracy of the PV output power was above 90%. In contrast, the prediction accuracy decreased when heavy clouds (i.e., overcasting) were present in the sky, and the CCF ratio was above 0.6. In this case, the PV output power prediction accuracy might decrease to as low as 83%.

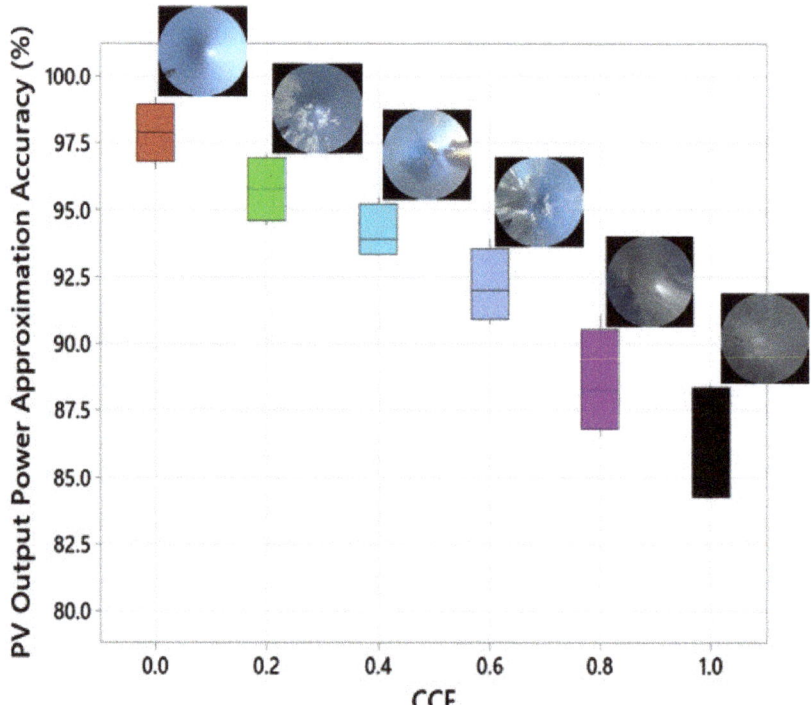

Figure 9. CCF versus the accuracy of the PV output power prediction.

The actual measured power from the PV systems versus the estimated power using the proposed technique is shown in Figure 10a. The experiment was conducted during a cloudy day, evidenced by the fluctuation in the output power and the actual TSI images taken at 12:00 (Figure 10b). The average temperature of the PV systems is also presented in Figure 10a, taken from the Met Office online database. For PV system #1, the error in estimating the output power was equal to ±3.1%. However, a more significant error was observed when estimating the power of PV system #2, which was ±7.3%. Nevertheless, the developed technique achieved a high accuracy rate in predicting the output power.

We further analyzed the data captured during this experiment using a cumulative density function (CDF) distribution, presented in Figure 10c. As a result, we proved a considerable similarity between the actual and the estimated power of both PV systems over the entire spectrum. For example, there was no noticeable difference in predicting the power in low irradiance compared with high irradiance levels. In addition, the standard deviation (StDev) and the mean of the experimental datasets were relatively identical.

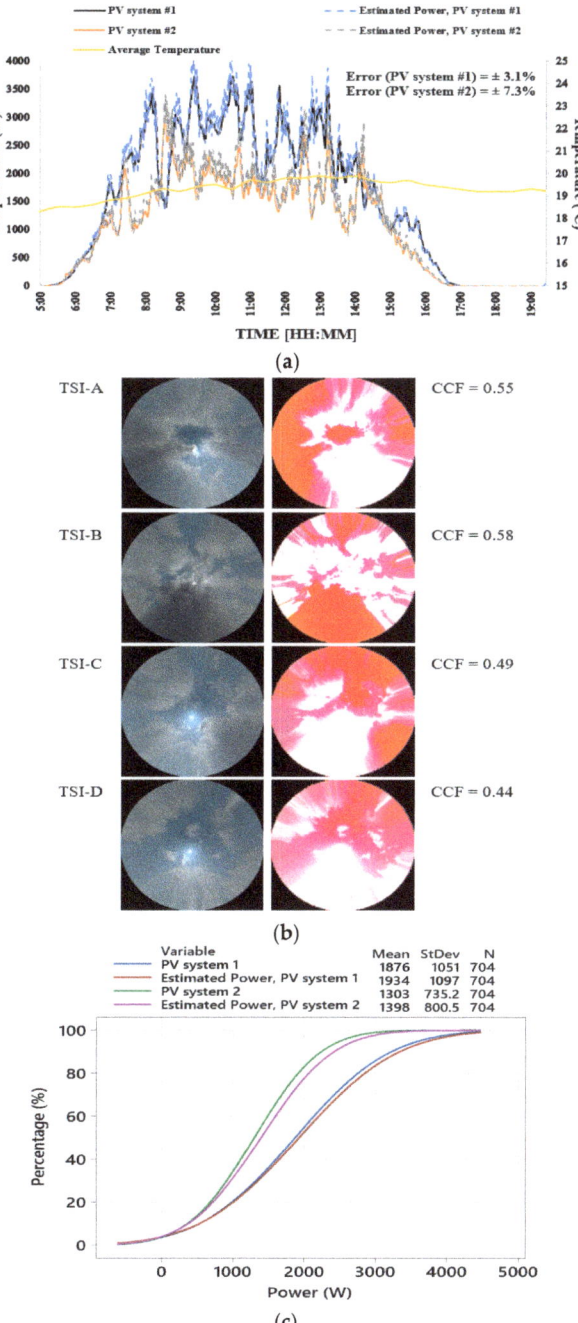

Figure 10. Output results when using the algorithm with PV systems: (**a**) output estimated power vs actual measured power in the examined PV systems (03 August 2022), (**b**) TSI image taken at 12:00, and (**c**) CDF distribution plot of the data taken from (**a**).

6. Comparative Study

This section compares the work presented in this paper against several recently published articles [40–43]. A summary of the comparisons is presented in Table 3. In [40,41], the authors have presented some interesting results on approximating the GUI and cloud cover, mainly using artificial intelligence-based algorithms. Specifically, in [40], a prediction of the GUI using an LM-BP model was proposed. However, the algorithm appeared more accurate when the solar irradiance was lower than 80–100 W/m^2. In addition, ref. [41] proposed a total cloud cover approximation algorithm using a CNN model, yet the proposed solution was unautomated and required intensive human input in the loop. Furthermore, on May 2021, a new paper was published demonstrating how to forecast solar irradiance using an LSTM model. The proposed solution was attractive; however, it needs more clarity on whether the LSTM will work when solar irradiance is under low levels and how far the algorithm can predict solar irradiance from the single-use sky imager. In addition, most recently, in March 2022, authors of [43] demonstrated a new prediction of the solar irradiance algorithm using minute-by-minute images taken with a TSI sky camera. The sky images were taken from the TSI and optimized. However, the algorithm lacked the ability to detect atmospheric attenuation, which resulted in high prediction errors in some instances.

Table 3. Comparison of this work and previously published papers [40–43].

Item	[40]	[41]	[42]	[43]	This Work
Month/Year of Study	October 2018	January 2021	May 2021	March 2022	Novemebr 2022
Desctiption of the proposed approximation shading ratio technique	Predicting GHI using feed-forward neural network with Levenberg–Marquardt backpropagation (LM-BP)	Total cloud cover optimization using convolutional neural networks (CNN)	Estimation of 10 min ahead of solar irradiance using long short-term memory (LSTM) algorithm	Predicting the irradiance at the solar-field level using minute-by-minute images taken with a TSI	Using the images of four TSIs and converting the images using the proposed cloud approximation model
GHI Estimation	Included	Excluded	Included	Included	Included
Method disadvantages	The algorithm does not accurately predict one hour ahead for low irradiation levels under 80–100 W/m^2	No estimation of the cloud base height, and the algorithm is unautomated for cloud cover identification	There are no details on the total GHI prediction area covered. n addition, it is unclear how low irradiance levels affect the accuracy of the algorithm	The algorithm lack the ability to detect atmospheric attenuation, which resulted in high prediction errors in some instances	If the area is increased, a reduction of the shading approximation accuracy is expected

In comparison, our algorithm in this paper relied on acquiring four sky images taken from a network of four TSIs. The images were then converted into better quality to identify the clouds/shading in the sky. Our work resulted in a high prediction accuracy of GHI or cloud coverage within 25 km^2. More errors are expected from prediction accuracy when the area coverage is increased.

7. Conclusions

This paper presents the development of an approximation for shading using TSI system pictures. The algorithm can estimate the shading ratio in the sky using a color-adjusted processing technique, and subsequently, it can aid in calculating the GHI in the sky. The method was applied to two different PV systems within four TSIs distributed in an area of 25 km^2. It was found that, in this case, the GHI can be estimated with a maximum ±12.7% error rate. In addition, the PV output power approximation accuracy was as high as 97.5% when the shading approximation was zero and reduced to the lowest value of 83% when shading was at its maximum. This work can be extended to deploy the developed algorithm in a more comprehensive TSI network, say in an area bigger than 50 km^2. This more comprehensive TSI network could further justify the proposed algorithm's accuracy and support the shading estimation of more PV systems.

Author Contributions: Conceptualization, M.D.; methodology, M.D. and P.I.L.; validation, P.I.L.; formal analysis, M.D.; data curation, M.D. and P.I.L.; writing—original draft preparation, M.D.; writing—review and editing, M.D. and P.I.L. All authors have read and agreed to the published version of the manuscript.

Funding: This research received no external funding.

Conflicts of Interest: The authors declare no conflict of interest.

Abbreviations

The following abbreviations are used in this manuscript:

PV	photovoltaic
CA	color-adjusted
GHI	global horizontal irradiance
TSI	total-sky imagers
ANN	artificial neural network
I-V	current-voltage
MPPT	maximum power point tracking
LSTM	long short-term memory
BRBG	blue/red-plus-blue/green-ratio algorithm
CDOC	cloud-detection and opacity classification algorithm
CCF	cloud cover fraction
CDF	cumulative density function
StDev	standard deviation
CNN	convolutional neural network
LM-BP	Levenberg–Marquardt backpropagation

References

1. Su, H.Y.; Liu, T.Y.; Hong, H.H. Adaptive residual compensation ensemble models for improving solar energy generation forecasting. *IEEE Trans. Sustain. Energy* **2019**, *11*, 1103–1105. [CrossRef]
2. Bochenek, B.; Ustrnul, Z. Machine learning in weather prediction and climate analyses—Applications and perspectives. *Atmosphere* **2022**, *13*, 180. [CrossRef]
3. Yang, D.; Wang, W.; Hong, T. A historical weather forecast dataset from the European Centre for Medium-Range Weather Forecasts (ECMWF) for energy forecasting. *Sol. Energy* **2022**, *232*, 263–274. [CrossRef]
4. Zhen, Z.; Zhang, X.; Mei, S.; Chang, X.; Chai, H.; Yin, R.; Wang, F. Ultra-short-term irradiance forecasting model based on ground-based cloud image and deep learning algorithm. *IET Renew. Power Gener.* **2022**, *16*, 2604–2616. [CrossRef]
5. Lee, S.; Kim, G.; Lee, M.I.; Choi, Y.; Song, C.K.; Kim, H.K. Seasonal Dependence of Aerosol Data Assimilation and Forecasting Using Satellite and Ground-Based Observations. *Remote Sens.* **2022**, *14*, 2123. [CrossRef]
6. Yang, D.; Perez, R. Can we gauge forecasts using satellite-derived solar irradiance? *J. Renew. Sustain. Energy* **2019**, *11*, 023704. [CrossRef]
7. Deif, M.A.; Solyman, A.A.; Alsharif, M.H.; Jung, S.; Hwang, E. A hybrid multi-objective optimizer-based SVM model for enhancing numerical weather prediction: A study for the Seoul metropolitan area. *Sustainability* **2021**, *14*, 296. [CrossRef]
8. Yang, H.; Kurtz, B.; Nguyen, D.; Urquhart, B.; Chow, C.W.; Ghonima, M.; Kleissl, J. Solar irradiance forecasting using a ground-based sky imager developed at UC San Diego. *Sol. Energy* **2014**, *103*, 502–524. [CrossRef]
9. Nouri, B.; Wilbert, S.; Segura, L.; Kuhn, P.; Hanrieder, N.; Kazantzidis, A.; Schmidt, T.; Zarzalejo, L.; Blanc, F.; Pitz-Paal, R. Determination of cloud transmittance for all sky imager based solar nowcasting. *Sol. Energy* **2019**, *181*, 251–263. [CrossRef]
10. Kong, W.; Jia, Y.; Dong, Z.Y.; Meng, K.; Chai, S. Hybrid approaches based on deep whole-sky-image learning to photovoltaic generation forecasting. *Appl. Energy* **2020**, *280*, 115875. [CrossRef]
11. Zhen, Z.; Liu, J.; Zhang, Z.; Wang, F.; Chai, H.; Yu, Y.; Lu, X.; Wang, T.; Lin, Y. Deep learning based surface irradiance mapping model for solar PV power forecasting using sky image. *IEEE Trans. Ind. Appl.* **2020**, *56*, 3385–3396. [CrossRef]
12. Nouri, B.; Blum, N.; Wilbert, S.; Zarzalejo, L.F. A hybrid solar irradiance nowcasting approach: Combining all sky imager systems and persistence irradiance models for increased accuracy. *Sol. RRL* **2022**, *6*, 2100442. [CrossRef]

13. Eşlik, A.H.; Akarslan, E.; Hocaoğlu, F.O. Cloud Motion Estimation with ANN for Solar Radiation Forecasting. In Proceedings of the 2021 International Congress of Advanced Technology and Engineering (ICOTEN), Taiz, Yemen, 4–5 July 2021; pp. 1–5.
14. Dhimish, M. 70% decrease of hot-spotted photovoltaic modules output power loss using novel MPPT algorithm. *IEEE Trans. Circuits Syst. II Express Briefs* **2019**, *66*, 2027–2031.
15. Guerra, M.I.; Ugulino de Araújo, F.M.; Dhimish, M.; Vieira, R.G. Assessing maximum power point tracking intelligent techniques on a pv system with a buck–boost converter. *Energies* **2021**, *14*, 7453. [CrossRef]
16. Dhimish, M. Assessing MPPT techniques on hot-spotted and partially shaded photovoltaic modules: Comprehensive review based on experimental data. *IEEE Trans. Electron Devices* **2019**, *66*, 1132–1144. [CrossRef]
17. Aslam, A.; Ahmed, N.; Qureshi, S.A.; Assadi, M.; Ahmed, N. Advances in Solar PV Systems; A Comprehensive Review of PV Performance, Influencing Factors, and Mitigation Techniques. *Energies* **2022**, *15*, 7595. [CrossRef]
18. Van Noord, M.; Landelius, T.; Andersson, S. Snow-Induced PV Loss Modeling Using Production-Data Inferred PV System Models. *Energies* **2021**, *14*, 1574. [CrossRef]
19. Vieira, R.G.; de Araújo, F.M.U.; Dhimish, M.; Guerra, M.I.S. A Comprehensive Review on Bypass Diode Application on Photovoltaic Modules. *Energies* **2020**, *13*, 2472. [CrossRef]
20. Muteri, V.; Cellura, M.; Curto, D.; Franzitta, V.; Longo, S.; Mistretta, M.; Parisi, M.L. Review on Life Cycle Assessment of Solar Photovoltaic Panels. *Energies* **2020**, *13*, 252. [CrossRef]
21. Olalla, C.; Hasan, M.N.; Deline, C.; Maksimović, D. Mitigation of Hot-Spots in Photovoltaic Systems Using Distributed Power Electronics. *Energies* **2018**, *11*, 726. [CrossRef]
22. Kim, J.; Rabelo, M.; Padi, S.P.; Yousuf, H.; Cho, E.-C.; Yi, J. A Review of the Degradation of Photovoltaic Modules for Life Expectancy. *Energies* **2021**, *14*, 4278. [CrossRef]
23. Dhimish, M.; Mather, P. Ultrafast high-resolution solar cell cracks detection process. *IEEE Trans. Ind. Inform.* **2019**, *16*, 4769–4777. [CrossRef]
24. Libra, M.; Daněček, M.; Lešetický, J.; Poulek, V.; Sedláček, J.; Beránek, V. Monitoring of Defects of a Photovoltaic Power Plant Using a Drone. *Energies* **2019**, *12*, 795. [CrossRef]
25. Goudelis, G.; Lazaridis, P.I.; Dhimish, M. A Review of Models for Photovoltaic Crack and Hotspot Prediction. *Energies* **2022**, *15*, 4303. [CrossRef]
26. Li, Z.; Rahman, S.M.; Vega, R.; Dong, B. A Hierarchical Approach Using Machine Learning Methods in Solar Photovoltaic Energy Production Forecasting. *Energies* **2016**, *9*, 55. [CrossRef]
27. Khandakar, A.; Chowdhury, M.E.H.; Kazi, M.-K.; Benhmed, K.; Touati, F.; Al-Hitmi, M.; Gonzales, A.J.S.P. Machine Learning Based Photovoltaics (PV) Power Prediction Using Different Environmental Parameters of Qatar. *Energies* **2019**, *12*, 2782. [CrossRef]
28. Park, S.; Kim, Y.; Ferrier, N.J.; Collis, S.M.; Sankaran, R.; Beckman, P.H. Prediction of Solar Irradiance and Photovoltaic Solar Energy Product Based on Cloud Coverage Estimation Using Machine Learning Methods. *Atmosphere* **2021**, *12*, 395. [CrossRef]
29. Cha, J.; Kim, M.K.; Lee, S.; Kim, K.S. Investigation of Applicability of Impact Factors to Estimate Solar Irradiance: Comparative Analysis Using Machine Learning Algorithms. *Appl. Sci.* **2021**, *11*, 8533. [CrossRef]
30. Esteves, J.; Cao, Y.; da Silva, N.P.; Pestana, R.; Wang, Z. Identification of clouds using an all-sky imager. In Proceedings of the 2021 IEEE Madrid PowerTech, Madrid, Spain, 28 June–2 July 2021; pp. 1–5.
31. Pu, R.; Landry, S.; Zhang, J. Evaluation of atmospheric correction methods in identifying urban tree species with WorldView-2 imagery. *IEEE J. Sel. Top. Appl. Earth Obs. Remote Sens.* **2014**, *8*, 1886–1897. [CrossRef]
32. Logothetis, S.-A.; Salamalikis, V.; Nouri, B.; Remund, J.; Zarzalejo, L.F.; Xie, Y.; Wilbert, S.; Ntavelis, E.; Nou, J.; Hendrikx, N.; et al. Solar Irradiance Ramp Forecasting Based on All-Sky Imagers. *Energies* **2022**, *15*, 6191. [CrossRef]
33. Zuo, H.M.; Qiu, J.; Jia, Y.H.; Wang, Q.; Li, F.F. Ten-minute prediction of solar irradiance based on cloud detection and a long short-term memory (LSTM) model. *Energy Rep.* **2022**, *8*, 5146–5157. [CrossRef]
34. Du, J.; Min, Q.; Zhang, P.; Guo, J.; Yang, J.; Yin, B. Short-term solar irradiance forecasts using sky images and radiative transfer model. *Energies* **2018**, *11*, 1107. [CrossRef]
35. Zhang, X.; Fang, F.; Wang, J. Probabilistic solar irradiation forecasting based on variational Bayesian inference with secure federated learning. *IEEE Trans. Ind. Inform.* **2020**, *17*, 7849–7859. [CrossRef]
36. Zhang, R.; Ma, H.; Hua, W.; Saha, T.K.; Zhou, X. Data-driven photovoltaic generation forecasting based on a Bayesian network with spatial–temporal correlation analysis. *IEEE Trans. Ind. Inform.* **2019**, *16*, 1635–1644. [CrossRef]
37. Andrade, J.R.; Bessa, R.J. Improving renewable energy forecasting with a grid of numerical weather predictions. *IEEE Trans. Sustain. Energy* **2017**, *8*, 1571–1580. [CrossRef]
38. Jiang, H.; Gu, Y.; Xie, Y.; Yang, R.; Zhang, Y. Solar irradiance capturing in cloudy sky days–a convolutional neural network based image regression approach. *IEEE Access* **2020**, *8*, 22235–22248. [CrossRef]
39. Kumar, U.; Sahoo, B.; Chatterjee, C.; Raghuwanshi, N.S. Evaluation of simplified surface energy balance index (S-SEBI) method for estimating actual evapotranspiration in Kangsabati reservoir command using landsat 8 imagery. *J. Indian Soc. Remote Sens.* **2020**, *48*, 1421–1432. [CrossRef]
40. Crisosto, C.; Hofmann, M.; Mubarak, R.; Seckmeyer, G. One-Hour Prediction of the Global Solar Irradiance from All-Sky Images Using Artificial Neural Networks. *Energies* **2018**, *11*, 2906. [CrossRef]
41. Krinitskiy, M.; Aleksandrova, M.; Verezemskaya, P.; Gulev, S.; Sinitsyn, A.; Kovaleva, N.; Gavrikov, A. On the Generalization Ability of Data-Driven Models in the Problem of Total Cloud Cover Retrieval. *Remote Sens.* **2021**, *13*, 326. [CrossRef]

42. Rajagukguk, R.A.; Kamil, R.; Lee, H.-J. A Deep Learning Model to Forecast Solar Irradiance Using a Sky Camera. *Appl. Sci.* **2021**, *11*, 5049. [CrossRef]
43. Alonso-Montesinos, J.; Monterreal, R.; Fernandez-Reche, J.; Ballestrín, J.; López, G.; Polo, J.; Barbero, F.J.; Marzo, A.; Portillo, C.; Batlles, F.J. Nowcasting System Based on Sky Camera Images to Predict the Solar Flux on the Receiver of a Concentrated Solar Plant. *Remote Sens.* **2022**, *14*, 1602. [CrossRef]

Article

Modeling of Photovoltaic Array Based on Multi-Agent Deep Reinforcement Learning Using Residuals of I–V Characteristics

Jingwei Zhang [1], Zenan Yang [1], Kun Ding [1,*], Li Feng [2], Frank Hamelmann [2], Xihui Chen [1], Yongjie Liu [3] and Ling Chen [4]

[1] College of Mechanical and Electrical Engineering, Hohai University, Changzhou 213022, China
[2] Solar Computing Laboratory, University of Applied Sciences Bielefeld, Artilleriestraße 9, 32427 Minden, Germany
[3] Engineering Research Center of Dredging Technology of Ministry of Education, Changzhou 213022, China
[4] School of Physics and Electronic Electrical Engineering, Huaiyin Normal University, Huai'an 223300, China
* Correspondence: dingk@hhu.edu.cn

Abstract: Currently, the accuracy of modeling a photovoltaic (PV) array for fault diagnosis is still unsatisfactory due to the fact that the modeling accuracy is limited by the accuracy of extracted model parameters. In this paper, the modeling of a PV array based on multi-agent deep reinforcement learning (RL) using the residuals of I–V characteristics is proposed. The environment state based on the high dimensional residuals of I–V characteristics and the corresponding cooperative reward is presented for the RL agents. The actions of each agent considering the damping amplitude are designed. Then, the entire framework of modeling a PV array based on multi-agent deep RL is presented. The feasibility and accuracy of the proposed method are verified by the one-year measured data of a PV array. The experimental results show that the higher modeling accuracy of the next time step is obtained by the extracted model parameters using the proposed method, compared with that using the conventional meta-heuristic algorithms and the analytical method. The daily root mean square error (RMSE) is approximately 0.5015 A on the first day, and converges to 0.1448 A on the last day of training. The proposed multi-agent deep RL framework simplifies the design of states and rewards for extracting model parameters.

Keywords: deep reinforcement learning; double deep Q network; parameter estimation; photovoltaic mathematical model

Citation: Zhang, J.; Yang, Z.; Ding, K.; Feng, L.; Hamelmann, F.; Chen, X.; Liu, Y.; Chen, L. Modeling of Photovoltaic Array Based on Multi-Agent Deep Reinforcement Learning Using Residuals of I–V Characteristics. *Energies* 2022, 15, 6567. https://doi.org/10.3390/en15186567

Academic Editors: Fouzi Harrou, Ying Sun, Bilal Taghezouit and Dairi Abdelkader

Received: 25 July 2022
Accepted: 4 September 2022
Published: 8 September 2022

Publisher's Note: MDPI stays neutral with regard to jurisdictional claims in published maps and institutional affiliations.

Copyright: © 2022 by the authors. Licensee MDPI, Basel, Switzerland. This article is an open access article distributed under the terms and conditions of the Creative Commons Attribution (CC BY) license (https://creativecommons.org/licenses/by/4.0/).

1. Introduction

As an important form of renewable energy, solar photovoltaic (PV) systems have developed rapidly in the last decade. In the recent report of International Energy Agency (IEA), China is likely to account for almost half of the global increase in renewable electricity generation, with over 900 TWh from solar PV and wind in 2021 [1]. The huge renewable energy market attracts more attention on the intelligent operation and maintenance and fault diagnosis technology of the PV systems, which can directly enhance the efficiency and reduce the labor cost of maintenance. As the first-level energy conversion devices in the PV systems, the PV array directly converts solar energy into electrical energy and suffers long-term outdoor uncertain meteorological factors, e.g., thermal cycles, ultraviolet radiation, dust, and hail. Therefore, in recent years, many researchers have carried out the study of the fault detection and diagnosis (FDD) of the PV array [2,3]. The model-based FDD methods are proposed to diagnose most faults or abnormalities, e.g., open-circuit, line-line or line-ground short-circuit fault of the PV array [4–6], cable aging or series impedance abnormality [7,8], partial shading [8–11], etc. For the FDD of the PV arrays, the modeling of the PV array is required [8–10]. The greater modeling error may also lead to the misdiagnosis of the PV array. Additionally, the online FDD of the PV array has a higher requirement for the real-time performance of modeling. Thus, it challenges the accuracy and adaptivity of the mathematical model under various ambient conditions. Unfortunately, the conventional modeling methods cannot satisfy the accuracy and real-time demands for FDD.

Commonly, the mathematical models of PV array are derived from the equivalent single-diode model (SDM), double-diode model (DDM), or multi-dimension diode model of solar cells. Then, the I–V curves of the PV array can be estimated based on the measured irradiance on the plane of the PV array and module temperature after extracting the model parameters [7,12–16]. At present, the model parameter extracting methods can be divided into two main categories. One is to analytically or numerically solve the model parameters based on the measured or rated electrical parameters of PV modules, commonly provided by manufacturers [7,12]. In [12], the equation to estimate the temperature coefficient of voltage is proposed to build the equation systems and to solve the model parameters. In [7], the explicit methods to solve the model parameters are analyzed to detect the degradation of the PV module. However, few methods exhibit acceptable accuracy and reliability to estimate the model parameters. Nevertheless, the model parameters may vary with the change of the ambient irradiance or temperature conditions. The model parameter, e.g., series resistance and ideal factor, are considered as constants which may deteriorate the accuracy of the model.

Another category of parameter extraction attempts to minimize an objective function, which represents the error between the measured I–V curve and the modeled one. Then, the model parameters are extracted by the meta-heuristic optimizers [13–19], e.g., particle swarm optimizer (PSO) [8], culture algorithm (CA) [17], and artificial bee colony (ABC) [18]. This category of methods uses the data points on the entire measured I–V curve. The accuracy of modeling is much higher than that of the analytical method. At present, some PV inverter products have the capability to measure the I–V curves of PV arrays, which makes the above methods suitable for applications, e.g., the FDD. However, the referenced I–V curve at each time step of diagnosis should be modeled based on the optimized model parameters. Thus, the meta-heuristic optimizers cannot estimate the variation in model parameters. In addition, some researchers have directly used the supervised learning algorithms to model the PV array, e.g., by training a one-dimensional deep residual network [20]. To ensure the good generalization of the network, the training samples under different irradiation and temperature levels are required [20]. Once the above model is applied to the fault diagnosis of PV arrays, the samples should be periodically updated, and the model needs be retrained to ensure the long-term stability of the model accuracy. In recent years, reinforcement learning (RL) has been applied in the electrical power engineering area. The RL is a machine learning process that leads the RL agents to interact with the designed environment by constructing a Markov decision process (MDP). The optimal action strategies are gradually learned based on the feedback of the environment state and the rewards of corresponding actions. Thus, the RL can be used as a self-learning approach, which is quite different from the conventional supervised or unsupervised learning models. The multi-agent RL is commonly used for solving cooperative or adversarial scenarios. The cooperative tasks are realized by evaluating the action of each agent according to the unified and observable environment state and collaborative rewards. Then, the overall optimal action strategy can be obtained after multi-agent collaboration.

In this paper, the modeling of a PV array based on the multi-agent deep RL is proposed. The novelty of this paper is that the RL agents can dynamically adjust the model parameters considering the variation of the ambient conditions for the PV array. The contribution of this paper includes:

- The design of the states and rewards of the RL agents in the modeling process are simplified for the researchers in PV engineering. The conventional methods for designing the states and rewards of the RL agents are commonly relied in the design of a virtual training environment to interact with RL agents and train them. The design of the states and rewards are according to the virtual training environment [21]. In this paper,

- the designed states of the RL agents are in terms of the variation of I–V characteristics in the training process, and the reward is designed according to the modeling error of I–V characteristics. For the researchers in PV engineering, the understanding of the modeling process in this paper is easier.
- The continuous state space is designed for training the RL agents by considering the continuous variation of I–V curves, which can enhance the generalization of the RL agents for estimating variation of model parameters.

At first, the state of the art for the model parameter extraction is briefly reviewed. The mathematical model of the PV array is introduced. Then, the double deep Q network (DDQN) is designed as the value network of the RL model. The multi-agent deep RL framework for the modeling of the PV array is proposed, including the RL states based on the high dimensional residuals of I–V characteristics, multi-agent cooperative rewards, and the agent actions with the damping amplitude. The measured annual I–V curves of a PV array are used to verify the modeling accuracy of the proposed method. Due to the fact that most model parameters extraction methods are currently based on meta-heuristic algorithms, the model estimation results using the model parameters extracted by different meta-heuristic and analytical methods are compared. Finally, the time cost of different model parameter extraction methods are investigated.

This paper is organized as follows: Section 1 briefly reviews the state of the art of model parameter extraction. Section 2 explains the mathematical model of the PV array used in this paper. The proposed modeling method of the PV array based on multi-agent deep RL is presented in Section 3. Section 4 elaborates the experimental verification of the proposed method using the measured data of an actual PV array. Section 5 summarizes the conclusions of this paper.

2. Mathematical Model of PV Array

PV arrays are usually composed of PV modules connected in series and parallel, and each PV module is composed of solar cells connected in series. The bypass diodes are connected in anti-parallel to alleviate the hot spot effect when the cells are mismatched [7]. The physical model of the PV module is commonly described by the SDM, and the corresponding I–V equation is [8]:

$$I_{PV} = I_{ph} - I_s\left[\exp\left(\frac{q(V_{PV} + R_s I_{PV})}{akT}\right) - 1\right] - \frac{V_{PV} + R_s I_{PV}}{R_{sh}} \quad (1)$$

where I_{PV} and V_{PV} are the output current and voltage of the PV module, respectively; q, k, T are the electronic charge (1.60217662 $\times 10^{-19}$ C), the Boltzmann constant (1.38064852 $\times 10^{-23}$ JK^{-1}) and the temperature of the solar cell (in K), respectively. $I_{ph}, I_s, a, R_s, R_{sh}$ are the five parameters of the mathematical model, which represents the photocurrent, the saturation current of the diode, the ideal factor of diode, the equivalent series, and shunt resistance, respectively. Among them, the photocurrent I_{ph} can be estimated by the irradiation G on the plane of the PV array [8]:

$$I_{ph} = I_{SC,stc}[1 + K_i(T - T_{stc})]\frac{G}{G_{stc}} \quad (2)$$

$I_{SC,stc}$ is the short-circuit current of the PV module under the standard test conditions (STC), K_i is the temperature coefficient of the current, which can be obtained from the specification of the PV module. G_{stc} and T_{stc} are the irradiance (1000 W/m^2) and temperature (25 °C) under STC, respectively. The saturation current of diode I_s can be estimated by the ideal factor of diode a and the temperature T [8]:

$$I_s = I_{s,stc}\left(\frac{T}{T_{stc}}\right)^{\frac{3}{a}}\exp\left(\frac{qE_g}{akT_{stc}} - \frac{qE_g}{akT}\right) \quad (3)$$

E_g is the band gap energy, $I_{s,stc}$ is the saturation current of diode under the STC, which can be expressed as [8]:

$$I_{s,stc} = \frac{I_{SC,stc}}{\exp\left(\frac{qV_{OC,stc}}{N_{cs}akT_{stc}}\right) - 1} \quad (4)$$

where $V_{OC,stc}$ is the open-circuit voltage of the PV module under STC, and N_{cs} is the number of cells connected in series of the PV module.

Therefore, only the three model parameters, i.e., the ideal factor of diode a, the equivalent series resistance R_s and the equivalent parallel resistance R_{sh} should be determined. Then, substituting the model parameters into (1), the I–V equation of the PV module can be established. The model of the PV array can be obtained by multiplying the current and voltage of the PV module with the corresponding number of modules connected in series and parallel. Additionally, considering the measurement error of the pyranometer, a compensation value of irradiance ΔG is introduced as an additional model parameter to correct the measured co-plane irradiance G_{meas}:

$$G = G_{meas} + \Delta G \quad (5)$$

The above equations show that the accuracy of the model estimated I–V curve is directly influenced by the extracted model parameters, i.e., the ideal factor of diode a, the equivalent series resistance R_s and the equivalent parallel resistance R_{sh}. The output current can be estimated by the corresponding voltage once the irradiance and temperature are known.

3. Modeling of PV Array Based on Multi-Agent Deep Reinforcement Learning

3.1. Design of State and Reward Based on Residuals of I–V Characteristics

In this paper, a multi-agent deep RL framework is proposed for modeling the PV array considering the continuous variation of RL states. In the MDP, the environment state represents the environment change after the act of all agents in the previous time step, i.e., episode. During the extraction of the model parameters, the I–V curves of the PV array can be modeled based on the model parameters estimated by the agents, then the residuals of the modeled I–V curve relative to the measured one are used as the environment state. In this paper, the RL environment state is proposed based on the time-series images of the residual curves of I–V characteristics. Figure 1 represents the flowchart for constructing the environment state of multi-agent deep RL.

At first, the model parameters output by the multi-agent are used to estimate the I–V curve of the PV array according to (1)–(4). The I–V curve measured by the inverter is pre-processed and normalized. Then, the residual value of the current at the same voltage point on the I–V curve is calculated to obtain the residual I–V curve image, and the auxiliary information in the image is removed to form a 160×120 pixel image. Considering the time-varying trend of the residual curves during the RL process of the multi-agent, the residual curve images of the latest $t-4$ to t time step are combined into the $4 \times 160 \times 120$ high-dimensional residuals of I–V characteristics in the time step t, which represents the environment state for training the multi-agent. Obviously, if the value of the current on the residual curve tends towards 0, this indicates that the modeled I–V curve using the parameters estimated by the action of the multi-agent are consistent with the measured I–V curve at time step t, i.e., the modeling accuracy is high sufficient. Due to the residuals of the I–V characteristic being represented by a curve in the image, the lesser resolution is selected. To accurately represent the residuals of the I–V characteristic, the 160×120 resolution is enough. The time steps from the latest $t-4$ to t is chosen according to the fact that the convergence of the DDQN model is more stable if using the latest four time steps [22]. Furthermore, the root mean square error (RMSE) of the current between the estimated and measured I–V curves is used as the criterion for evaluating the effectiveness of the multi-agent actions:

$$\text{RMSE} = \sqrt{\frac{1}{N_{points}} \sum_{i=1}^{N_{points}} \left(\frac{I_{model,i} - I_{meas,i}}{I_{meas,i}}\right)^2} \qquad (6)$$

where N_{points} is the number of points on the I–V curve, and $I_{model,i}$ and $I_{meas,i}$ are the estimated and measured value at the i-th point in the I–V curve, respectively. Additionally, the mean absolute error (MAE) and mean absolute percentage error (MAPE) are used to assess the model accuracy during verification:

$$\text{MAE} = \frac{1}{N_{points}} \sum_{i=1}^{N_{points}} \left|I_{model,i} - I_{meas,i}\right| \qquad (7)$$

$$\text{MAPE} = \frac{1}{N_{points}} \sum_{i=1}^{N_{points}} \frac{\left|I_{model,i} - I_{meas,i}\right|}{\left|I_{meas,i}\right|} \qquad (8)$$

In order to ensure the convergence of the model parameters estimated by the multi-agent, the multi-agent collaborative rewards are designed according to the gradient descent to guarantee the RMSE converging. Therefore, the multi-agent collaborative reward is designed as:

$$\Re = \begin{cases} +1, \text{RMSE}_t \leq \text{RMSE}_{t-1} \\ -1, \text{RMSE}_t > \text{RMSE}_{t-1} \end{cases} \qquad (9)$$

when the RMSE at time step t decreases or keeps the same value as that at the previous time step $t-1$, the reward $\Re$ is set as 1, otherwise the reward is -1.

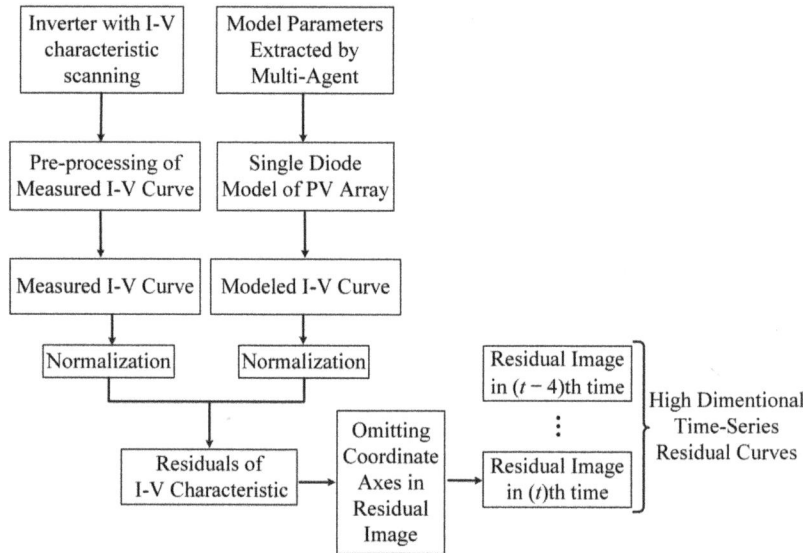

Figure 1. Design of states based on the time-series images of residual curves of I-V characteristics.

3.2. Design of Actions Considering Amplitude Attenuation

For the accurate parameter extraction and modeling, the designed action should be able to directly estimate the model parameter of the next time step. In this paper, multiple independent agents are used to estimate the corresponding model parameters. The three actions of each agent for the model parameters are designed as follows [23]:

$$\begin{cases} M_{t+1} = M_t + rM_{stc} \\ M_{t+1} = M_t \\ M_{t+1} = M_t - rM_{stc} \\ M \in \{a, R_s, R_{sh}, \Delta G\} \\ M_{stc} \in \{a_{stc}, R_{s,stc}, R_{sh,stc}, \Delta G_{stc}\} \end{cases} \quad (10)$$

where $a_{stc}, R_{s,stc}$ and $R_{sh,stc}$ are the corresponding initial model parameters of a, R_s, R_{sh} under the STC, respectively, solved by the module of the PV array in MATLAB/Simulink based on the specification of the PV module [24]. ΔG_{stc} is changing in the range of 1–2% of irradiance under the STC. r is the ratio to turn the amplitude during the RL. At the beginning of the RL, the model parameters should be explored in a greater range. Furthermore, the model parameters should be kept as stable as possible after the RMSE converges. Considering that, the total RL time step is at least 10,000 steps, r is designed to decay with the RL time step t as the trend of sigmoid function:

$$r = \begin{cases} 0.02 - \dfrac{0.01}{1 + \exp\left(-\left(\frac{t}{500} - 10\right)\right)}, t \leq 10{,}000 \\ 0.01, t > 10{,}000 \end{cases} \quad (11)$$

As shown in Figure 2, at the beginning of the training, the r is greater and the adjustment step for each model parameter is approximately 2% of the model parameters under STC, i.e., $a_{stc}, R_{s,stc}, R_{sh,stc}$ and G_{stc}. This mechanism can promote the RL agents to explore the action space and enhance the diversity of the replay memory. After approximately 4000 time steps, the adjustment step of each model parameter is gradually reduced towards 1%, and a more stable action selection strategy is used after the Q network is converged.

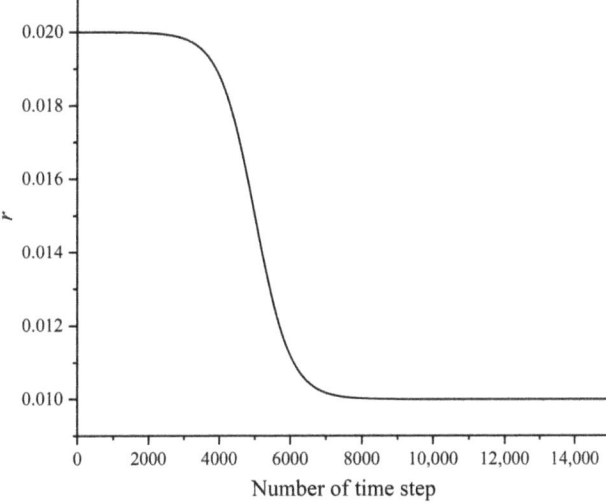

Figure 2. Trend of the coefficient r with the training time step.

3.3. Agents Based on Double Deep Q Network

The DDQN originates from the double Q-learning algorithm [21]. Similarly to the deep Q network, the DDQN improves the description of the value function of action policy using a deep Q-value network, instead of the Q-table. The advantage of DDQN is that the continuous changes in the environment state are considered, and high-dimensional continuous state input can be realized [22]. In the DDQN, the evaluation Q-network with the network weight set θ is used to determine the value function of the action a_t under the environment state s_t at the current time step t, which is denoted as $Q(s_t, a_t; \theta)$. Then, the target Q-network is used to estimate the target Q-value $Q(s_{t+1}, a_{t+1}; \theta')$ of the next state s_{t+1} at the next time step. The network weight set θ of the evaluation Q-network is trained by the adaptive moment estimation (ADAM) algorithm and the network loss function $L(\theta)$ is minimized, which is defined as [21,22]:

$$L(\theta) = E\left[\left(\Re + \gamma Q(s_{t+1}, \arg\max_{a_{t+1}} Q(s_{t+1}, a_{t+1}; \theta), \theta') - Q(s_t, a_t; \theta)\right)^2\right] \quad (12)$$

where γ is the discount factor taking values between (0,1), and E represents the mathematical expectation of the error. θ' is the network parameter set for the target Q network. A batch of samples are randomly selected from the experience replay memory to train the current network [21,22]. After the evaluation, Q-network is trained, and the target Q-network can be periodically updated by the evaluation Q-network. Then, the target Q-value is estimated by the target Q-network to realize the further training of the evaluation Q-network.

The deep convolutional networks are the type of networks most commonly used to identify patterns in images. Considering the designed environment state based on the residuals of I–V characteristics, the deep convolutional network is used as the Q-network of each agent, due to its fast training and ability to capture the local features of images [25–27]. The network structure is shown in Figure 3. At first, the 4 × 160 × 120 high-dimensional residuals of I–V characteristics are fed into the convolutional network with three 20 × 20 filters, and the rectified linear unit (ReLU) is used as the activation function to form a 3 × 15 × 11 matrix. Then, the 4 × 4 averaging pooling is connected to form a 3 × 3 × 2 matrix, which is further flattened into an 18 × 1 vector. Finally, the vector is fed to the fully connected layer with the sigmoid activation function to obtain the estimated value of the actions for each agent. The action with the estimated maximum value is selected as the final action.

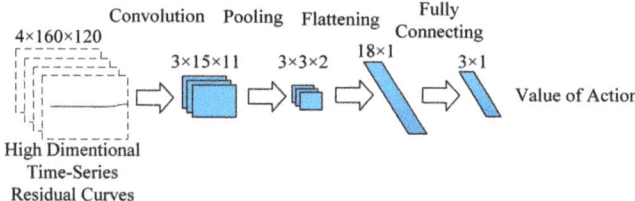

Figure 3. Structure of Q network in the DDQN of each agent, where blue blocks represent convolutional or fully connecting networks.

3.4. Modeling Framework of PV Array Based on Multi-Agent Deep RL

The proposed modeling framework of the PV array based on the multi-agent deep RL is shown in Figure 4. At first, the I–V curves of the PV array measured by the inverter and the I–V curve estimated by the model are compared to construct the residuals of I–V characteristics, which is used as the environment state to train each agent of the model parameter. Then, the RMSE of the I–V curve is calculated via (6), and the multi-agent cooperative reward is obtained via (9). Additionally, the loss function of the Q network is optimized by the ADAM algorithm, and the residuals of I–V characteristics are fed to the DDQN of each agent to estimate the result of value function. After determining the optimal action strategy, the model parameters can be estimated via (10). Then, the model parameters are obtained and input to the mathematical model of the PV array to estimate the I–V curve at the next time step, based on the measured in-plane irradiance and module temperature. Finally, the model parameter extraction and modeling of the PV array is realized.

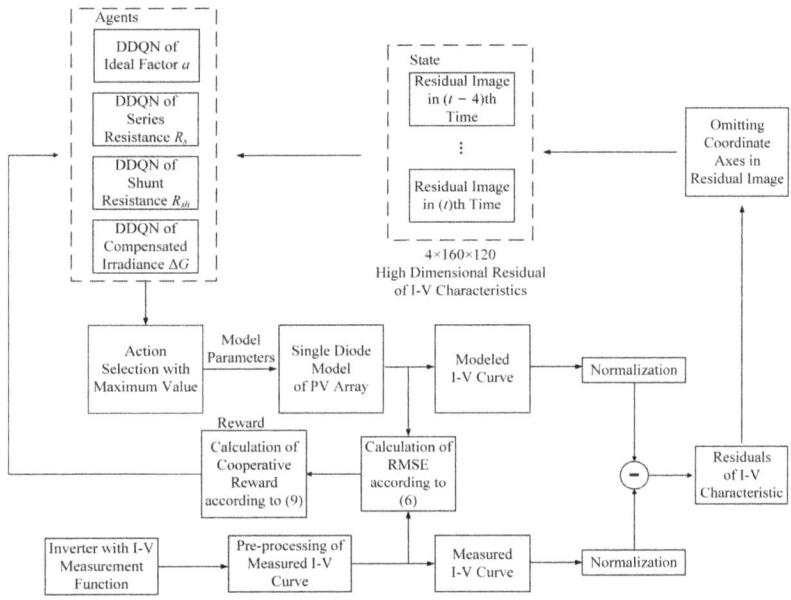

Figure 4. Framework of proposed multi-agent deep RL-based model parameter extraction of PV array.

4. Experimental Verification of Proposed Method Based on Multi-Agent Deep Reinforcement Learning

In order to verify the accuracy of the proposed method based on multi-agent deep RL, a 5.28 kWp PV array, formed by 22 multi-crystalline PV modules TSM-240, is used for experimental verification. The specification of the PV module TSM-240 under STC provided by the manufacturer is shown in Table 1. The PV system is equipped with the three-phase grid-connected inverter GW20KN-DT, which can measure the I–V curves of the PV array. At least 256 points on the I–V curve can be measured in 2 s. The pyranometer TBQ-2 is used to measure the in-plane irradiance of the PV array. The platinum resistors Pt100 are pasted on the back sheet of the PV modules to measure the temperature of PV module. I–V curves of the PV array, in-plane irradiance, and temperature of the PV module are transmitted via the RS485 bus to an indoor monitor computer with proposed modeling method. Data measured from 27 June 2018 to 31 July 2019 are used for verification. Considering that the measured I–V characteristic of the PV array may lead to the power loss of the PV plant, the measurement and modeling cannot be too frequent. However, the total number of training samples should be guaranteed, as a greater time interval leads to longer training duration. Therefore, the time interval should be determined in a trade-off. In the experiments, the measurement interval is 2 min. The measured I–V curves are pre-processed. The data measured with the irradiation less than 200 W/m^2 are neglected to reduce the influence of measurement errors. Additionally, the distorted I–V curves or data measured under the mismatch conditions of the PV array, e.g., the partial shading or other abnormalities, are filtered to ensure that the RL multi-agent are trained with normal samples. The number of local maximum and minimum on the second order derivative curve d^2I/dV^2 is used as an indicator to identify these abnormal I–V curves [8]. Then, the proposed multi-agent deep RL-based method is used to estimate the model parameters of the next time step. The modeling accuracy of the proposed method is statistically analyzed and compared with the conventional or recently presented model extraction methods, including the particle swarm optimizer (PSO) [8], culture algorithm (CA) [17], and analytical method [12]. The modeling accuracy of the next time step, using the above different parameter extraction methods, are focused upon herein.

Table 1. Specification of PV module TSM-240.

Parameters	Value
Maximum power $(P_{mpp,stc})$	240 W
Voltage at maximum power point $(V_{mpp,stc})$	29.7 V
Current at maximum power point $(I_{mpp,stc})$	8.1 A
Open circuit voltage $(V_{OC,stc})$	37.3 V
Short circuit current $(I_{SC,stc})$	8.62 A
Temperature coefficient of current (K_i)	0.047%/°C
Temperature coefficient of voltage (K_v)	−0.32%/°C

Figure 5 shows the histogram of the annual accuracy comparison of modeling the I–V curve at the next time step based on the model parameters extracted by the proposed method and other algorithms. The annual RMSEs of the proposed method converge to approximately 0.1 A. The proposed multi-agent deep RL-based method shows better performance for modeling the I–V curves at the next time step, compared with the PSO, CA, or the analytical method. The reason for which the meta-heuristic algorithms or the analytical method fail is that, the meta-heuristic optimizers only use the measured I–V curve at the current time step to extract the model parameters, and can only guarantee the accuracy of modeling at the current time step. This may cause difficulty in accurately modeling for the (t + 1)-th time step. The dynamic change of model parameters cannot be considered. However, once the loss function of DDQN is converged, the proposed multi-agents can select the correct action to regulate the model parameters according to the residuals of I–V characteristics by training the DDQN. Thus, more accurate model parameters can be estimated for the next time step, which enhances the adaptability of the modeling. Figure 6 shows the moving average of 20 adjacent values of the RMSE and corresponding fitted trend line. Due to the fact that the initial date is approximately in early July 2018, the trend of the RMSE shows that the RL agents basically converge in the beginning of December 2018, which is approximately 5 months. The RMSE is disconnected due to the data missing or filtering of the abnormal measured I–V curves. The convergence can be accelerated if more I–V curves are measured to train the RL agents, or increasing the sample frequency of the I–V characteristics.

The average RMSEs of different methods in typical dates of the entire RL period are listed in Table 2. On the first day, i.e., 27 June 2018, the daily average RMSE of modeling using the multi-agent deep RL-based method is approximately 0.5015 A. The RMSE is even higher than that of the other meta-heuristic methods. The reason is that the training of DDQN is not completed. The RMSE of the proposed method converges to 0.1448 A in the last day of verification, i.e., 31 July 2019. However, for the PSO-based and CA-based methods, the daily RMSEs show no obvious convergence trend. Similar results can also be observed from Figure 5.

Table 3 shows the annual MAE, RMSE, and MAPE for different methods. The annual MAE of the proposed method is 0.24 A and is approximately 2.44% of the short-circuit current of the PV array under the STC. The annual MAPE of the proposed method is approximately 12.20%, which is acceptable for modeling a PV array, considering the fact that the error is relatively greater when the training process of DDQN is uncompleted.

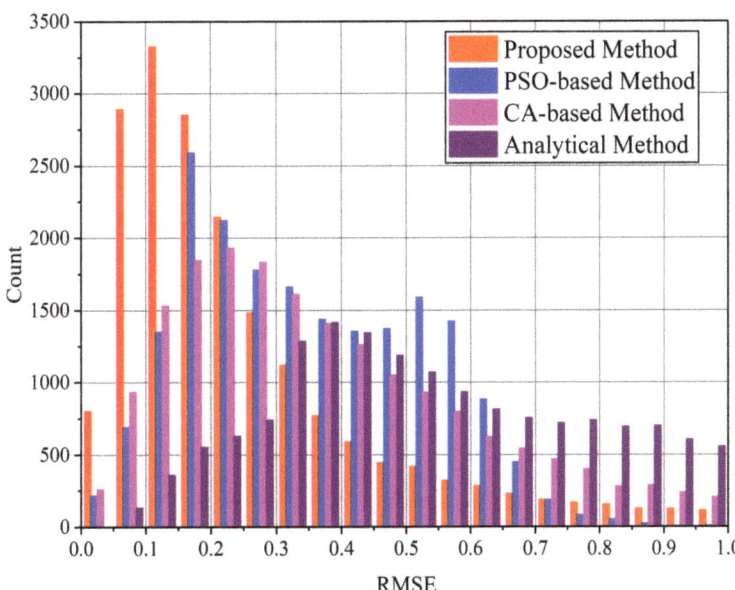

Figure 5. Distribution of annual accuracy of modeling based on different model parameter extraction methods.

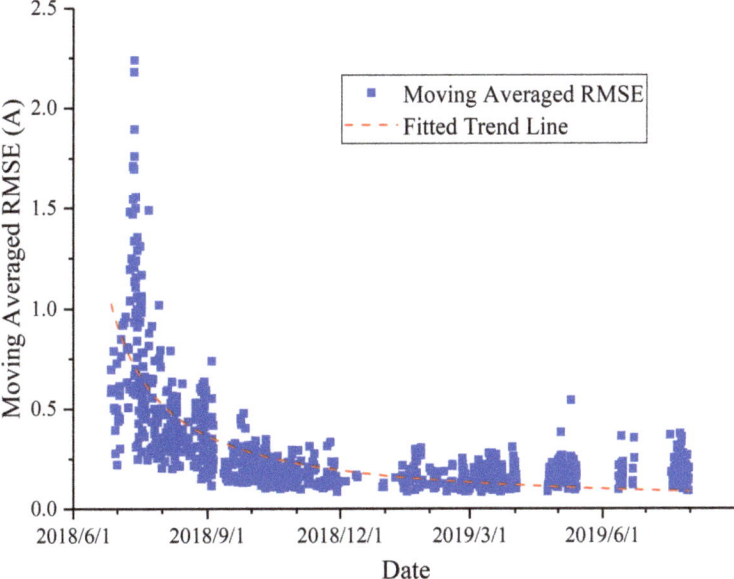

Figure 6. Convergence trend of RMSE.

Table 2. Daily average RMSE (A) in typical days for different extraction methods.

Extraction Methods	27 June 2018	30 September 2018	31 December 2018	31 March 2019	31 July 2019
Proposed multi-agent deep RL-based method	0.5015	0.1970	0.0932	0.2026	0.1448
PSO-based method	0.1662	0.3572	0.2135	0.5504	0.3551
CA-based method	0.3986	0.3392	0.2274	0.6905	0.2188
Analytical method	0.4755	0.7190	0.6486	0.7860	0.8170

Table 3. Statistical results of annual errors.

Metrics	Proposed Multi-Agent Deep RL-Based Method	PSO-Based Method	CA-Based Method	Analytical Method
MAE (A)	0.24	0.28	0.31	0.42
RMSE (A)	0.29	0.35	0.41	0.69
MAPE (%)	12.20	22.11	19.52	48.17

Figure 7 presents the comparison results between the measured and the modeled I–V curves based on the above parameter extraction methods in the typical days of four seasons. The estimation results of the multi-agent deep RL-based method obtains greater errors compared with the measured I–V curves in Figure 7a due to the insufficient training samples and un-converged DDQN for the proposed method. However, Figure 7b–d show that the modeling results of the proposed method are more consistent with the measured curves. Compared with the conventional meta-heuristic methods for estimating the model parameters of the next time step, the proposed method obtains a better modeling accuracy under lower irradiation levels, e.g., approximately 200 W/m^2. Tables 4 and 5 list the calculated MAE and MAPE for each I–V curve in Figure 7, using different modeling methods. The same results can be observed that the proposed multi-agent deep RL-based method does not perform well in 28 September 2018. It results in more uncertain model parameters and reduces the modeling accuracy. With the training of RL agents, the MAE and MAPE both show that the performance of the proposed method is significantly enhanced.

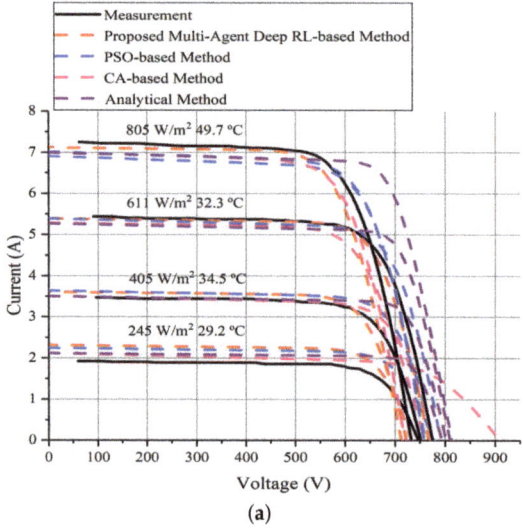

Figure 7. Cont.

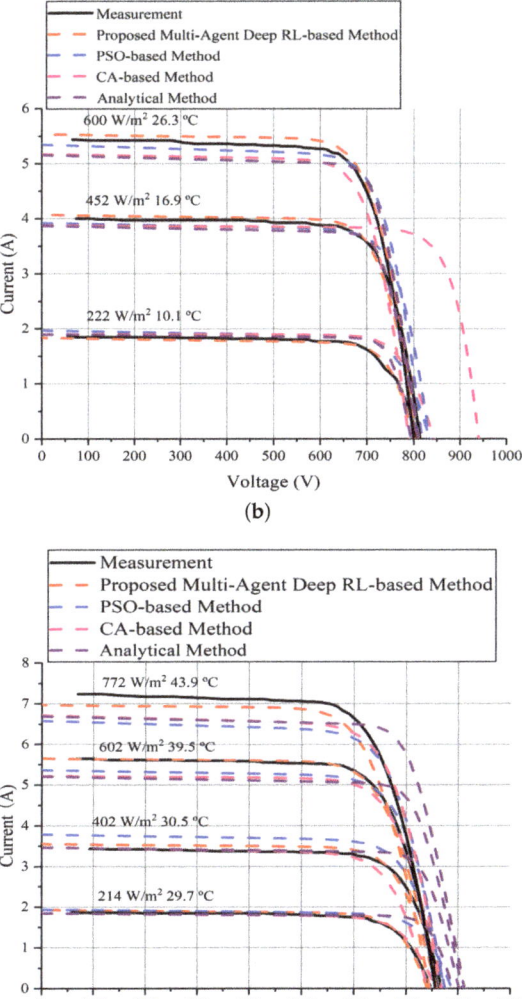

Figure 7. Cont.

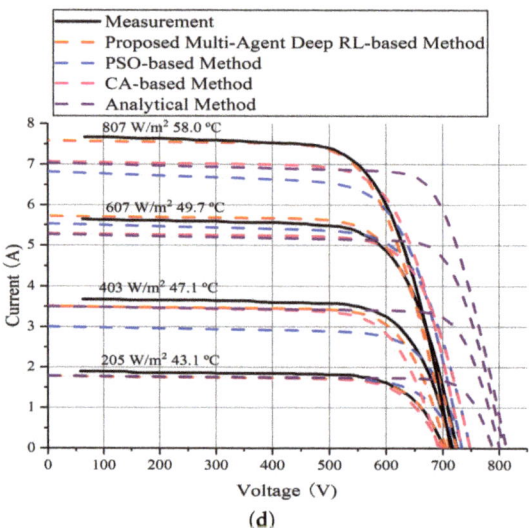

(d)

Figure 7. Comparison of measured and model estimated I–V characteristics in typical days in four seasons: (**a**) 28 September 2018, autumn; (**b**) 17 January 2019, winter; (**c**) 1 May 2019, spring; and (**d**) 22 July 2019, summer.

Table 4. Comparison of MAE (A) for different methods in Figure 8.

Date	Ambient Condition	Proposed Multi-Agent Deep RL-Based Method	PSO-Based Method	CA-Based Method	Analytical Method
28 September 2018	245 W/m^2 29.2 °C	0.36	0.37	0.25	0.31
	405 W/m^2 34.5 °C	0.20	0.26	0.11	0.25
	611 W/m^2 32.3 °C	0.09	0.16	0.35	0.36
	805 W/m^2 49.7 °C	0.29	0.46	0.35	0.69
17 January 2019	222 W/m^2 10.1 °C	0.04	0.14	0.14	0.07
	452 W/m^2 16.9 °C	0.09	0.16	0.31	0.14
	600 W/m^2 26.3 °C	0.14	0.19	0.29	0.29
1 May 2019	214 W/m^2 29.7 °C	0.06	0.13	0.04	0.12
	402 W/m^2 30.5 °C	0.14	0.34	0.12	0.20
	602 W/m^2 39.5 °C	0.05	0.31	0.34	0.59
	772 W/m^2 43.9 °C	0.34	0.62	0.49	0.75
22 July 2019	205 W/m^2 43.1 °C	0.09	0.13	0.11	0.19
	403 W/m^2 47.1 °C	0.20	0.62	0.29	0.36
	607 W/m^2 49.7 °C	0.10	0.25	0.43	0.64
	807 W/m^2 58.0 °C	0.12	0.80	0.57	1.01

Additionally, the PSO-based and CA-based method both obtain greater MAE or MAPE. Similar conclusions can also be observed from Figure 7. The reason is that, for these meta-heuristic methods, the model parameters are extracted using the measured I–V curve at the latest time step. The assumption that the model parameters would not change significantly between two adjacent time steps is a necessary precondition. However, for the actual outdoor circumstance, the ambient irradiance may vary randomly according to the actual meteorological conditions. Thus, the above assumption is not always valid, which causes the lower accuracy of the meta-heuristic methods. For the proposed multi-agent deep RL-based method, the RL agents attempt to regulate the model parameters towards more suitable values, according to the residuals of I–V characteristics. Once the DDQN is trained with enough samples, then better accuracy can be obtained.

Table 5. Comparison of MAPE (%) for different methods in Figure 7.

Date	Ambient Condition	Proposed Multi-Agent Deep RL-Based Method	PSO-Based Method	CA-Based Method	Analytical Method
28 September 2018	245 W/m^2 29.2 °C	20.52	44.27	57.24	58.51
	405 W/m^2 34.5 °C	7.87	26.36	19.57	47.42
	611 W/m^2 32.3 °C	3.51	23.92	9.63	47.38
	805 W/m^2 49.7 °C	7.23	29.26	7.54	68.38
17 January 2019	222 W/m^2 10.1 °C	2.94	25.20	29.27	5.16
	452 W/m^2 16.9 °C	3.49	18.41	52.84	4.86
	600 W/m^2 26.3 °C	8.98	18.33	7.38	12.93
1 May 2019	214 W/m^2 29.7 °C	4.04	20.34	5.33	23.37
	402 W/m^2 30.5 °C	5.60	18.90	5.45	42.26
	602 W/m^2 39.5 °C	2.11	23.91	12.76	62.05
	772 W/m^2 43.9 °C	7.57	18.66	15.84	44.77
22 July 2019	205 W/m^2 43.1 °C	5.52	20.05	7.82	42.38
	403 W/m^2 47.1 °C	7.71	32.11	10.30	73.67
	607 W/m^2 49.7 °C	2.64	32.22	46.55	93.07
	807 W/m^2 58.0 °C	3.32	23.85	22.54	69.43

Figure 8 shows the time consumption of model parameter extraction using the proposed multi-agent deep RL-based method and other methods. The parameter extraction programs are executed on the same PC with Intel(R) Core(TM) i7-6700HQ CPU (@2.60 GHz, eight cores) and 8 GB memory, without GPU acceleration. The PSO-based method is faster than other methods. The average time cost of the proposed multi-agent deep RL-based method is approximately 2.343 s, which is similar to that of the CA-based method. The most time is consumed by computing the DDQN. However, it should be pointed out that the computation of DDQN can be accelerated using the GPUs, and the time cost of the proposed multi-agent deep RL-based method can be further reduced.

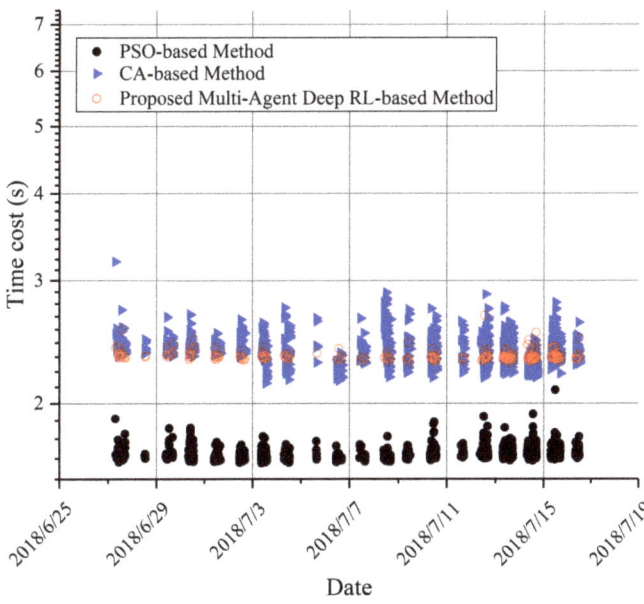

Figure 8. Time cost of parameter extraction for different methods.

5. Conclusions

In this paper, a multi-agent deep RL framework is proposed for estimating the model parameters and modeling the PV array in the next time step. The environment state based on the high-dimensional residuals of I–V characteristics and a corresponding cooperative reward is presented for the RL agents. The actions of each agent considering the damping amplitude are designed. Then, the entire framework of modeling of PV array based on multi-agent deep RL is presented. The feasibility and accuracy of the proposed method are verified by the one year measured data of a PV array. The experimental results show that the higher modeling accuracy of the next time step is obtained by the extracted model parameters using the proposed method, compared with that using the conventional meta-heuristic algorithms and the analytical method. The daily root mean square error (RMSE) is approximately 0.5015 A in the first day, and converges to 0.1448 A in the last day of training. The time consumption of model parameter extraction using the proposed multi-agent deep RL-based method is approximately 2.343 s by using a PC without GPU acceleration. The time cost could be further reduced if the GPU acceleration is utilized.

Future research should focus on enhancing the convergence speed of the proposed multi-agent deep RL-based method. Another aspect would be to optimize the network structure and corresponding hyper-parameters. The proposed modeling approach would be considered to embed in the existing FDD platform for the intelligent operation and maintenance of the PV array.

Author Contributions: Conceptualization, J.Z. and Z.Y.; methodology, J.Z.; software, J.Z. and Z.Y.; validation, J.Z. and Z.Y.; formal analysis, J.Z. and L.F.; investigation, X.C. and L.C.; resources, Y.L.; data curation, J.Z. and Z.Y.; writing—original draft preparation, J.Z. and Z.Y.; writing—review and editing, J.Z., K.D. and F.H.; visualization, J.Z. and Z.Y.; supervision, K.D. and F.H.; project administration, K.D. and F.H.; funding acquisition, J.Z., X.C., K.D. and F.H. All authors have read and agreed to the published version of the manuscript.

Funding: This research was supported by Changzhou Sci & Tech Program (Grant No. CJ20200074), Natural Science Foundation of Jiangsu Province (Grant No. BK20201163), the Fundamental Research Funds for the Central Universities (Grant No. B210204005), Bundesministerium für Bildung und Forschung PV Digital 4.0 (Grant No. 13FH020PX6), and Postgraduate Research & Practice Innovation Program of Jiangsu Province (Grant No. KYCX21_0464).

Institutional Review Board Statement: The study did not require ethical approval.

Informed Consent Statement: Not applicable.

Data Availability Statement: Not applicable.

Conflicts of Interest: The authors declare no conflict of interest.

Nomenclature

Abbreviations
ABC	artificial bee colony
ADAM	adaptive moment estimation
CA	culture algorithm
DDM	double-diode model
DDQN	double deep Q network
FDD	fault detection and diagnosis
IEA	International Energy Agency
MAE	mean absolute error
MAPE	mean absolute percentage error
MDP	Markov decision process
PSO	particle swarm optimizer
PV	photovoltaic
ReLU	rectified linear unit
RL	reinforcement learning
RMSE	root mean square error
SDM	single-diode model
STC	standard test conditions

Symbols

I_{ph}	photocurrent
I_s	saturation current of diode
a	ideal factor of diode
R_s	equivalent series resistance
R_{sh}	equivalent parallel resistance
E_g	band gap energy
$P_{mpp,stc}$	maximum power
$V_{mpp,stc}$	voltage at maximum power point
$I_{mpp,stc}$	current at maximum power point
$V_{oc,stc}$	open-circuit voltage
$I_{sc,stc}$	short-circuit current
K_i	temperature coefficient of current
K_v	temperature coefficient of voltage
q	electronic charge
k	Boltzmann constant
T	temperature of solar cell

References

1. IEA. *Global Energy Review 2021*; IEA: Paris, France, 2021. Available online: https://www.iea.org/reports/global-energy-review-2021 (accessed on 17 June 2022).
2. Ahmadi, M.; Samet, H.; Ghanbari, T. A New Method for Detecting Series Arc Fault in Photovoltaic Systems Based on the Blind-Source Separation. *IEEE Trans. Ind. Electron.* **2020**, *67*, 5041–5049. [CrossRef]
3. Ahmadi, M.; Samet, H.; Ghanbari, T. Series Arc Fault Detection in Photovoltaic Systems Based on Signal-to-Noise Ratio Characteristics Using Cross-Correlation Function. *IEEE Trans. Ind. Inform.* **2020**, *16*, 3198–3209. [CrossRef]
4. Karmakar, B.K.; Pradhan, A.K. Detection and Classification of Faults in Solar PV Using Thevenin Equivalent Resistance. *IEEE J. Photovoltaics* **2020**, *10*, 644–654. [CrossRef]
5. Ding, H.; Ding, K.; Zhang, J.; Wang, Y.; Gao, L.; Li, Y.; Chen, F.; Shao, Z.; Lai, W. Local outlier factor-based fault detection and evaluation of photovoltaic system. *Sol. Energy* **2018**, *164*, 139–148. [CrossRef]
6. Lu, X.; Lin, P.; Cheng, S.; Lin, Y.; Chen, Z.; Wu, L.; Zheng, Q. Fault diagnosis for photovoltaic array based on convolutional neural network and electrical time series graph. *Energy Convers. Manag.* **2019**, *196*, 950–965. [CrossRef]
7. Piliougine, M.; Guejia-Burbano, R.A.; Petrone, G.; Sánchez-Pacheco, F.J.; Mora-López, L.; Sidrach-de-Cardona, M. Parameters extraction of single diode model for degraded photovoltaic modules. *Renew. Energy* **2021**, *164*, 674–686. [CrossRef]
8. Li, Y.; Ding, K.; Zhang, J.; Chen, F.; Chen, X.; Wu, J. A fault diagnosis method for photovoltaic arrays based on fault parameters identification. *Renew. Energy* **2019**, *143*, 52–63. [CrossRef]
9. Wang, H.; Zhao, J.; Sun, Q.; Zhu, H. Probability modeling for PV array output interval and its application in fault diagnosis. *Energy* **2019**, *189*, 116248. [CrossRef]
10. Harrou, F.; Taghezouit, B.; Sun, Y. Improved kNN-Based Monitoring Schemes for Detecting Faults in PV Systems. *IEEE J. Photovoltaics* **2019**, *9*, 811–821. [CrossRef]
11. Huang, J.M.; Wai, R.J.; Yang, G.J. Design of Hybrid Artificial Bee Colony Algorithm and Semi-Supervised Extreme Learning Machine for PV Fault Diagnoses by Considering Dust Impact. *IEEE Trans. Power Electron.* **2020**, *35*, 7086–7099. [CrossRef]
12. Ma, T.; Gu, W.; Shen, L.; Li, M. An improved and comprehensive mathematical model for solar photovoltaic modules under real operating conditions. *Sol. Energy* **2019**, *184*, 292–304. [CrossRef]
13. Qais, M.H.; Hasanien, H.M.; Alghuwainem, S. Identification of electrical parameters for three-diode photovoltaic model using analytical and sunflower optimization algorithm. *Appl. Energy* **2019**, *250*, 109–117. [CrossRef]
14. Jiao, S.; Chong, G.; Huang, C.; Hu, H.; Wang, M.; Heidari, A.A.; Chen, H.; Zhao, X. Orthogonally adapted Harris hawks optimization for parameter estimation of photovoltaic models. *Energy* **2020**, *203*, 117804. [CrossRef]
15. Nunes, H.G.G.; Pombo, J.A.N.; Mariano, S.J.P.S.; Calado, M.R.A. Suitable mathematical model for the electrical characterization of different photovoltaic technologies: Experimental validation. *Energy Convers. Manag.* **2021**, *231*, 113820. [CrossRef]
16. Vankadara, S.K., Chatterjee, S., Balachandran, P.K. An accurate analytical modeling of solar photovoltaic system considering R_s and R_{sh} under partial shaded condition. *J. Syst. Assur. Eng. Manag.* **2022**. [CrossRef]
17. Liu, G.; Qin, H.; Tian, R.; Tang, L.; Li, J. Non-dominated sorting culture differential evolution algorithm for multi-objective optimal operation of Wind- Solar-Hydro complementary power generation system. *Glob. Energy Interconnect.* **2019**, *2*, 368–374. [CrossRef]
18. Chen, X.; Xu, B.; Mei, C.; Ding, Y.; Li, K. Teaching–learning–based artificial bee colony for solar photovoltaic parameter estimation. *Appl. Energy* **2018**, *212*, 1578–1588. [CrossRef]
19. Chen, Z.; Lin, Y.; Wu, L.; Cheng, S.; Lin, P. Development of a capacitor charging based quick I–V curve tracer with automatic parameter extraction for photovoltaic arrays. *Energy Convers. Manag.* **2020**, *226*, 113521. [CrossRef]

20. Chen, Z.; Chen, Y.; Wu, L.; Cheng, S.; Lin, P.; You, L. Accurate modeling of photovoltaic modules using a 1-D deep residual network based on I–V characteristics. *Energy Convers. Manag.* **2019**, *186*, 168–187. [CrossRef]
21. van Hasselt, H.; Guez, A.; Silver, D. Deep Reinforcement Learning with Double Q-learning. *arXiv* **2015**, arXiv:1509.06461v3.
22. Mnih, V.; Kavukcuoglu, K.; Silver, D.; Graves, A.; Antonoglou, I.; Wierstra, D.; Riedmiller, M. Playing atari with deep reinforcement learning. *arXiv* **2013**, arXiv:1312.5602.
23. Zhang, J.; Liu, Y.; Li, Y.; Ding, K.; Feng, L.; Chen, X.; Chen, X.; Wu, J. A reinforcement learning based approach for online adaptive parameter extraction of photovoltaic array models. *Energy Convers. Manag.* **2020**, *214*, 112875. [CrossRef]
24. Mathworks Help Center. PV Array. Available online: https://ww2.mathworks.cn/help/physmod/sps/powersys/ref/pvarray.html (accessed on 26 June 2022).
25. Akbarimajd, A.; Hoertel, N.; Hussain, M.A.; Neshat, A.A.; Marhamati, M.; Bakhtoor, M.; Momeny, M. Learning-to-augment incorporated noise-robust deep CNN for detection of COVID-19 in noisy X-ray images. *J. Comput. Sci.* **2022**, *63*, 101763. [CrossRef] [PubMed]
26. Pang, Y.; Hao, L.; Wang, Y. Convolutional neural network analysis of radiography images for rapid water quantification in PEM fuel cell. *Appl. Energy* **2022**, *321*, 119352. [CrossRef]
27. Hong, Y.Y.; Rioflorido, C.L. A hybrid deep learning-based neural network for 24-h ahead wind power forecasting. *Appl. Energy* **2019**, *250*, 530–539. [CrossRef]

Article

A Horse Herd Optimization Algorithm (HOA)-Based MPPT Technique under Partial and Complex Partial Shading Conditions

Sajid Sarwar [1], Muhammad Annas Hafeez [1], Muhammad Yaqoob Javed [1,*], Aamer Bilal Asghar [1,*] and Krzysztof Ejsmont [2,*]

1. Department of Electrical and Computer Engineering, COMSATS University Islamabad, Lahore 54000, Pakistan; engrsajidsarwar@gmail.com (S.S.); m.annas13@yahoo.com (M.A.H.)
2. Faculty of Mechanical and Industrial Engineering, Warsaw University of Technology, 02-524 Warsaw, Poland
* Correspondence: yaqoob.javed@cuilahore.edu.pk (M.Y.J.); aamerbilal@cuilahore.edu.pk (A.B.A.); krzysztof.ejsmont@pw.edu.pl (K.E.)

Abstract: The inconsistent irradiance, temperature, and unexpected behavior of the weather affect the output of photovoltaic (PV) systems, classified as partial or complex partial shading conditions. Under these circumstances, obtaining the maximum output power from PV systems becomes problematic. This paper proposes a population-based optimization model, the horse herd optimization algorithm (HOA), inspired by natural behavior, to solicit the maximum power under partial or complex partial shading conditions. It is an intelligent strategy inspired by the surprise pounce-chasing style of the horse herd model. The proposed technique outperforms the standard in different weather conditions, needs less computational time, and has a fast convergence speed and zero oscillations after reaching a power point's maximum limit. A performance comparison of the HOA is achieved with conventional techniques, such as "perturb and observe" (P&O), the bio-inspired adaptive cuckoo search optimization (ACS), particle swarm optimization (PSO), and the dragonfly algorithm (DA). The following comparison of the presented scheme with the other techniques shows its better performance with respect to fast tracking and efficiency, as well as stability under disparate weather conditions and the ability to obtain maximum power with negligible oscillation under partial and complex shading.

Keywords: photovoltaic (PV); incremental conductance (InC); dragonfly (DA); maximum power point tracking (MPPT); perturb and observe (P&O); adaptive cuckoo search optimization (ACS); particle swarm optimization (PSO); local maxima (LM); complex partial shading (CPS); partial shading (PS)

Citation: Sarwar, S.; Hafeez, M.A.; Javed, M.Y.; Asghar, A.B.; Ejsmont, K. A Horse Herd Optimization Algorithm (HOA)-Based MPPT Technique under Partial and Complex Partial Shading Conditions. *Energies* 2022, 15, 1880. https://doi.org/10.3390/en15051880

Academic Editors: Fouzi Harrou, Ying Sun, Bilal Taghezouit and Dairi Abdelkader

Received: 6 February 2022
Accepted: 26 February 2022
Published: 3 March 2022

Publisher's Note: MDPI stays neutral with regard to jurisdictional claims in published maps and institutional affiliations.

Copyright: © 2022 by the authors. Licensee MDPI, Basel, Switzerland. This article is an open access article distributed under the terms and conditions of the Creative Commons Attribution (CC BY) license (https://creativecommons.org/licenses/by/4.0/).

1. Introduction

As stated by the International Energy Agency (IEA), about 28% of worldwide electricity generation in 2020 is based on renewable energy, and 90% of the new installed power capacity is generated using renewable sources [1]. Photovoltaic (PV) generated power capacity has increased by a factor of 18 since 2010. The most significant parameters of PV systems are their ease of availability, low maintenance cost, eco-friendly production, and the system's renewable nature. PV systems may be used as either grid-connected or standalone alternative energy sources [2]. A maximum power point (MPP) searching technique is critical in order to achieve the efficient operation of any PV system, which enables the maximum conversion of solar energy to power. The MPPT performance in PV energy systems is compromised due to the various shading conditions of PV panels; these shading conditions can be classified into partial and complex partial shading. In the literature, various works are available that deal with optimization techniques to mitigate these shading conditions [3,4]. Therefore, advanced PV systems are proposed in the literature, and a block diagram of such a system is shown in Figure 1 that includes sensors for voltage and current measurement and a DC-DC Cuk converter, using the MPPT technique, which, in turn, controls the Cuk converter and drives the switch for the DC-DC converter [5].

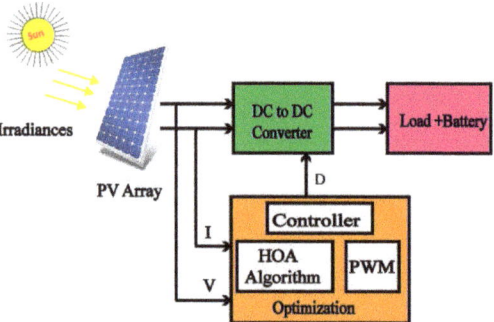

Figure 1. An optimized PV system diagram.

In this article, we focus on an optimization technique for the efficient operation of a PV system in partial shading (PS) and complex partial shading (CPS) conditions. Therefore, we will now briefly discuss recent works relevant to this field.

1.1. Prior Works

Regarding the current-voltage and power-voltage characteristics of PV, the characteristics curves of the power-voltage (P-V) and current-voltage (I-V) of photovoltaic cells are non-linear, due to changes in weather conditions. However, to deal with nonlinearities, the MPP technique is employed to predict and harvest the MPP in rapidly changing and variable weather conditions and also to optimize the system to run at MPP. Many conventional, as well as soft-computing, MPPT algorithms have been introduced to upgrade the effectiveness of photovoltaic energy systems through PS and uniform irradiance (UI) conditions. Several techniques are suggested in the published literature that deals with uniform irradiance to achieve MPPT, while more recent research works refer to optimization techniques that are applied for PS conditions [5], although few discuss CPS conditions.

Some of the classical techniques for MPPT in PV systems are briefly discussed here. The fractional short circuit current (FSCC) technique makes it quick and simple to harvest the maximum power point, although the drawback is that it cannot track the exact MPP and works in offline mode [5]. The fractional open-circuit voltage (FOCV) technique is a direct, simple, offline, and easy to implement technique similar to FSCC; however, it is unable to track the exact MPP [5]. Similarly, "perturb and observe" (P&O) is an extensively exploited technique for the finding of MPP. Its working technique is the same as that in hill-climbing algorithms, and it is able to track the MPP in both offline and online modes, but its performance decreases when a PS condition occurs [5]. Incremental conductance (InC) performs better than P&O; however, it does not extract the exact MPP. It also works on the principle of the hill-climbing algorithm [6].

The classical techniques are simple and have a very fast response time; however, these techniques are not effective for attaining global maxima (GM) in the online mode and for dynamically changing PS conditions. Therefore, to achieve MPP in non-uniform environmental conditions, many soft computing techniques have been introduced in the literature. Several of these are based on fuzzy logic and artificial intelligence [7]. Hybrid techniques can be used in combination with other techniques like InC and P&O, in order to improve the system's efficiency under PS conditions [8]. In [9], the author presents a new MPPT control for PV systems that depends on the search and rescue (SRA) optimization method. The suggested approach improves PV system efficiency by decreasing the oscillations at the global maximum (GM) and monitoring the GM quickly and efficiently. Other notable aspects of the proposed SRA control technique include robustness, power tracking performance in a steady state, and implementation simplicity. Many evolutionary algorithms, such as the particle swarm optimization (PSO) algorithm, the genetic method (GA), etc., are stochastically based methods that are efficient for optimization. However, these are unable to track MPP under CPS and give optimal performance, in terms of convergence and tracking speed, to harvest GM. Adaptive cuckoo optimization (ACO) is another technique that is inspired by an animal model, the aggressive reproduction behavior of the cuckoo. ACO gives improved performance, has good convergence speed and approximate accuracy, and requires a smaller number of parameters for tuning, although it is unable to track MPP under CPS conditions [10,11].

In [12], the authors present a paper using an HOA with a boost converter and battery load installed within the PV system. When the battery load provides a constant voltage, the boost converter performs better, but in a grid-tied PV system, where battery load is not installed as part of the PV system, the boost converter is unable to provide the desired performance. In the grid-tied PV system, the output fluctuates because the boost converter cannot provide a constant voltage, because of which the performance of the PV system deteriorates; therefore, a bidirectional Cuk converter is used in the current research work. A Cuk converter is used to overcome output fluctuations when the PV system is grid-tied (without a battery load) in combination with an intelligent technique, which can harvest GM under PS and CPS conditions.

1.2. Contribution

In this article, we propose the application of the horse herd optimization algorithm (HOA) method, which is a nature-inspired technique with the characteristic of harvesting energy under PS and CPS conditions. The performance of the HOA is evaluated in terms of various parameters, such as settling time, convergence speed, and fewer iterations to find the GM. Furthermore, an intensive comparison of the HOA is presented that can track the maximum energy under PS and CPS conditions. The HOA is tested in terms of different scenarios for PS and CSP, and its performance is compared with that of other optimization techniques.

The motivation for utilizing HOA for MPPT in PS and CPS is due to a number of factors. These include fewer iterations while tracking GM, with close to zero oscillations, an almost 100% tracking efficiency, the lowest settling time, and its efficiency in terms of tracking speed in addition to a steady-state response with the bidirectional Cuk converter. The structure of the Cuk converter is that of a boost converter, involving a buck converter as well. It converts one voltage level to another voltage level, having zero-ripple current. It can produce either step-up or -down voltages, a property that makes its use desirable for a wide range of voltage applications. In the majority of prior works, boost converters and battery loads are used. Boost converters perform better when a battery load is installed with the PV system since batteries provide a constant output voltage; however, when battery load is not installed with the PV system, the output voltage fluctuates. The main motivation here for using the Cuk converter is that it exhibits both the properties of step-down and step-up voltages and gives a continuous output, even when no battery load is installed with a PV system.

The design of the Cuk converter allows a continuous current flow through the input side, regardless of the state of the switch. The circuit in Figure 2 depicts a Cuk converter, which shows that the application of LC filters at the input and output sides facilitates a smooth current waveform.

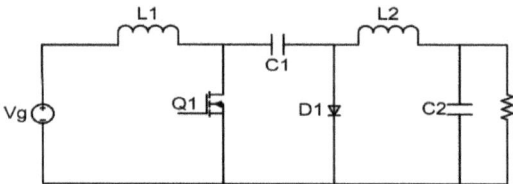

Figure 2. Circuit diagram of the Cuk converter.

The Cuk converter also produces a very low output voltage ripple, due to the presence of a second-order low-pass filter. This filter is a combination of inductors and capacitors found in the converter. The design of the inductor ensures zero-ripple behaviour and a reduction in electromagnetic interference. Therefore, the overall impact of this converter's utilization is inherently low noise and the greater efficiency of the PV energy system.

The analysis in this article is carried out in the context of HOA applications and highlights the following contributions.

Under different weather circumstances, the performance of the chosen approach is contrasted to that of some other techniques.

- Its superiority is underlined by the experimental results and, since only one parameter is used for the exploration and exploitation phase it results, in terms of quick tracking, in almost zero oscillations.
- The HOA particles are able to remain stationary and the oscillation becomes equal to zero when a cycle of iteration ends, and the power converging efficiency is approximately 99.1%. The absence of this characteristic in PSO and ACS, etc. results in the loss of power and unwanted oscillations.
- The comparison between the HOA and the existing scheme is performed under four different scenarios of weather conditions. The HOA technique can harvest maximum energy under PS and CPS. Moreover, the results of tracking the MPP under different PS and CPS scenarios are represented in the experimental part of this paper, which clearly shows that the HOA technique performs better with respect to convergence rate and zero oscillation, as well as fast-tracking in comparison to P&O, InC, PSO, ACS, and DFO. The HOA technique does not oscillate on GM and will successfully reach a steady state, resulting in the increase in efficiency of the overall system.

1.3. Organization

This paper comprises the following sections. The PS and CPS are discussed in Section 2. Sections 3 and 4 present the mathematical model and the tracking mechanism of the HOA algorithm, respectively. A detailed comparative analysis of the HOA algorithm with the other optimization algorithms is illustrated in Section 5. Finally, our conclusions are presented in Section 6.

2. Partial and Complex Partial Shade

When one portion of the PV module receives an inconsistent irradiance that is different from the rest of the PV area, the PV system fails to provide a uniform output; as a result, PS or, in the worst-case scenario, CPS occurs. Under these conditions, whether PS or CPS, different irradiance levels are received by the PV modules [13].

The shaded modules are unable to provide the desired voltage, degrading its efficiency, and as a result, mismatching effects occur. To counter a bypass diode, the mismatching effects can be reduced [14]. Figure 3 shows a set of four PV modules, joined in a series, with a bypass diode in the reverse direction. In uniform irradiance conditions, all diodes receive an equal amount of irradiance, 1000 W/m^2, and there is no drop in voltage. Under PS conditions, PV modules receive various levels of irradiance, which are 1000 W/m^2, 600 W/m^2, 300 W/m^2, and 800 W/m^2, as shown in Figure 3. The P-V curves are demonstrated in Figures 4 and 5, and Figure 6 shows the UIC, PS, and CPS conditions.

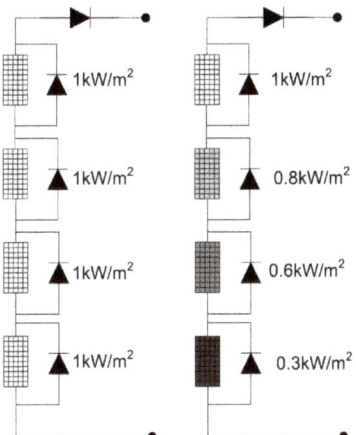

Figure 3. Cases of uniform irradiance and partial shading.

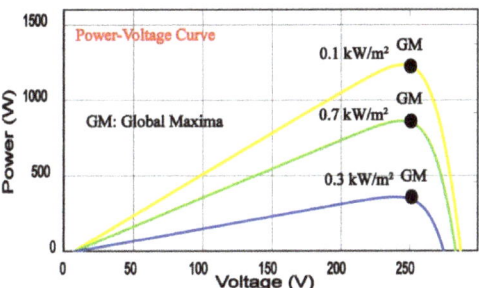

Figure 4. The voltage–power curve under UIC.

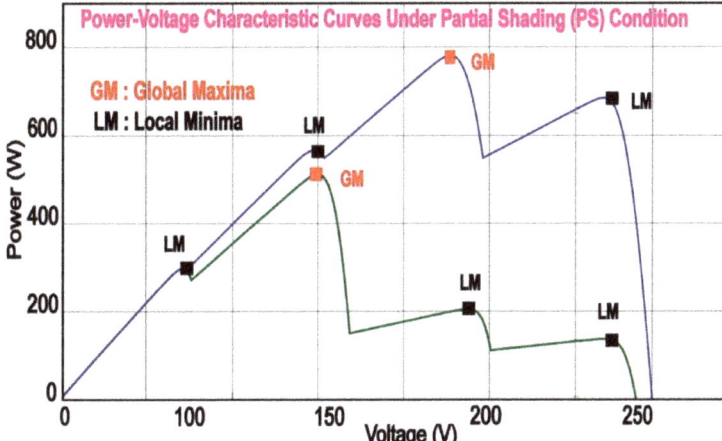

Figure 5. The voltage–power curve under PSC.

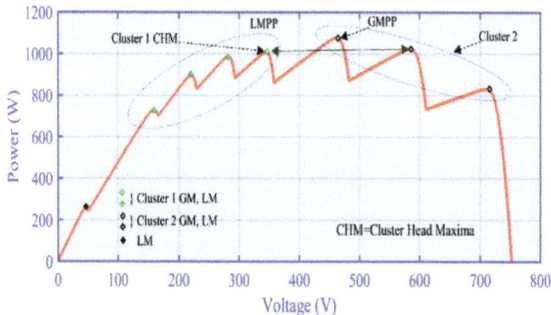

Figure 6. Cluster formulation of the CPS scenario.

PV modules are connected in series, and, in PS conditions, each module has an effect on the PV system. Figure 7 shows the IV curve of the PV system. There are four PV modules used for PS scenarios. PV modules 1, 2, 3, and 4 have irradiance (G) values of 800, 250, 700, and 400, respectively, and their currents are 1.6 A, 2.4 A, 4.2 A, and 4.8 A, respectively. The individual modules have only single global maxima (GM). However, when combinations of four PV modules are used, a single GM and three local maxima (LM) appear on the IV curves.

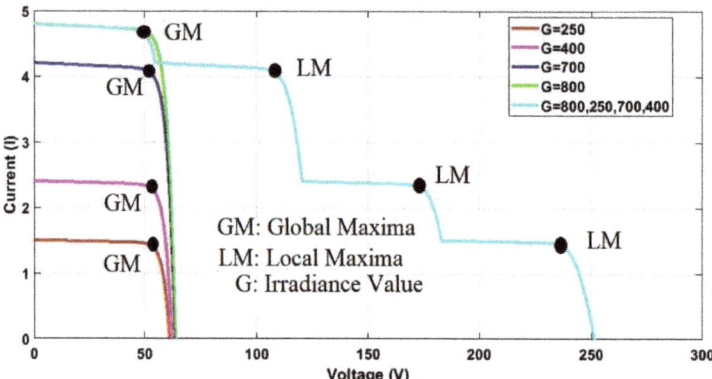

Figure 7. IV curves under PS conditions.

Figure 8 illustrates the power voltage curves of the PV system. Each PV module has its own power rating. Individually, PV modules 1, 2, 3, and 4 give a power of 70 W, 120 W, 220 W, and 250 W, respectively. Moreover, in the case of a combination of four PV modules, only one GM and three LM appear on the PV curve. When all the PC modules are connected in series, they give a power of 449.8 W at the GM.

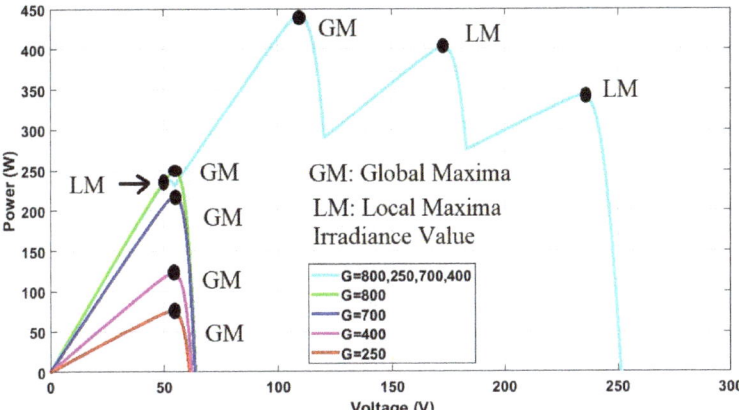

Figure 8. PV curves under PS conditions.

3. Mathematical Model of the HOA Algorithm

The behavioral patterns of horses in their natural habitat are the basis for this study. The grazing, hierarchy, sociability, imitation, defense mechanism, and roaming behaviors are the most common behavioral patterns seen in horses [15]. As a result, the six general behaviors of horses of various ages provide the inspiration for this method. At each step, the horses are moved in accordance with Equation (1).

$$P_m^{iter,age} = Vel_m^{iter,age} + P_m^{(iter-1),age}, \quad age = \alpha,\ \beta,\ \gamma,\ \delta \quad (1)$$

In this equation:

- $P_m^{iter,age}$ denotes the *mth* horse position.
- *age* shows the range of each horse.
- *iter* describes the current number of iterations.
- $Vel_m^{iter,age}$ illustrates the velocity of the vector of that horse.

At various times in their lives, horses demonstrate different behaviors. A horse's total lifespan is around 25–30 years [16]. In this case, δ represents horses between the ages of 0 and 5, γ represents horses between the ages of 5 and 10, β represents horses between the ages of 10 and 15, and α denotes horses older than 15 years. To determine the age of the horses, each iteration should have a thorough matrix of answers. In this case, the matrix could be ordered based on the best replies, with the first 10% of the horses from the top of such an ordered matrix being chosen as α horses. The β group is made up of the next 20% of the population. The γ and δ groups are responsible for 30% and 40% of the remaining horses, correspondingly. To determine the velocity vector, the methods to imitate the six actions of the various groups of horses are quantitatively executed.

Taking into account the following behavior patterns [15–17], Equations (2)–(5) may be represented as the motion vectors of horses of various ages throughout each cycle of the method.

$$Vel_m^{iter,\alpha} = Gra_m^{iter,\alpha} + DefMec_m^{iter,\alpha} \quad (2)$$

$$Vel_m^{iter,\beta} = Gra_m^{iter,\beta} + H_m^{iter,\beta} + Soc_m^{iter,\beta} + DefMec_m^{iter,\beta} \quad (3)$$

$$Vel_m^{iter,\gamma} = Gra_m^{iter,\gamma} + H_m^{iter,\gamma} + Soc_m^{iter,\gamma} + Imt_m^{iter,\gamma} + Ro_m^{iter,\gamma} + DefMec_m^{iter,\gamma} \quad (4)$$

$$Vel_m^{iter,\delta} = Gra_m^{iter,\delta} + Imt_m^{iter,\delta} + Ro_m^{iter,\delta} \quad (5)$$

These are the major phases in individual and social intelligence for horses.

3.1. Grazing (Gra)

Horses are roaming animals that eat grasses, plants, and other forage. They graze in pastures for between 16 and 20 h per day, with only a few hours of rest. Continuous eating is the term for this type of gradual grazing—you may have seen mares grazing in pastures when carrying their foals [17].

The grazing area for each horse is modeled using the HOA technique. As a result of the coefficient g, each horse grazes in certain locations, as shown in Figure 9. Horses graze at any age and for the rest of their lives. Grazing is implemented mathematically, in line with Equations (6) and (7).

$$Gra_m^{iter,age} = g_{iter}(low + r * upp)(P_m^{(iter-1)}), \quad age = \alpha, \beta, \gamma, \delta \tag{6}$$

$$g_m^{iter,age} = w_g \times g_m^{(iter-1),age}, \tag{7}$$

Here, $Gra_m^{iter, age}$ denotes the parameter of motion of the ith horse and illustrates the related horse's ability to graze. The grazing variable lowers linearly at w_g for each iteration. The variable "r" is an arbitrary value of between 0 and 1, while "low" and "upp" are the lower and upper boundaries of the grazing space, respectively. For all age groups, it is advised that "low" and "upp" should be set to 0.95 and 1.05, respectively. The coefficient g value is set to 1.5 in all range ages.

3.2. Hierarchy (H)

Horses are not self-sufficient [18]. They live their lives following a leader, and this is something that humans will do frequently. According to the rule of dominance [18], a mature stallion or a filly is likewise responsible for management in groups of wild horses.

The inclination of a group of horses to follow the lead of the most trained and powerful horse is regarded as the coefficient h_m in HOA and is shown in Figure 9. So, at the middle ages of β and γ (aged 5–15 years), studies have demonstrated that horses follow the law of hierarchy [17]. Equations (8) and (9) can be used to define this (Section 3.6).

$$H_m^{iter,age} = h_m^{iter,age}(P_{lbh}^{(iter-1)} - P_m^{(iter-1)}) \tag{8}$$

$$h_m^{iter,age} = h_m^{(-1+iter),age} \times w_h \tag{9}$$

Here, $H_m^{iter,age}$ illustrates the location of the best horse with the variable of velocity. The value $P_{lbh}^{(iter-1)}$ indicates the position of the best horse.

3.3. Sociability (Soc)

Horses need social interaction and may coexist with other animal species. Because wild horses may be hunted by predators, life in a group ensures their safety. Pluralism improves their survival odds and makes it easier to flee. Horses frequently fight each other owing to their social characteristics, and their very uniqueness is a cause of their anger. Some horses appear to enjoy being with other animals such as cattle and sheep, but they dislike being alone [17].

This behavior is depicted by element s as a movement toward the average location of other horses, as seen in Figure 9. Horses between the ages of 5 and 15 years are primarily interested in being with the herd, as shown by the given formulas:

$$Soc_m^{iter,age} = soc_m^{iter,age}\left[\left(\frac{1}{N}\sum_{j=1}^{N} P_j^{(-1+iter)}\right) - P_m^{(-1+iter)}\right] \quad age = \beta, \gamma \tag{10}$$

$$soc_m^{iter,age} = soc_m^{(-1+iter),age} \times \omega_{soc} \tag{11}$$

In the above equations:

- $Soc_m^{iter,age}$ describes the vector of social motion that is presented by the ith horse.
- $soc_m^{iter,age}$ shows the orientation of that horse in the direction of group ith.
- $iter$, the iteration is reduced in every cycle, has a parameter of ω_s.
- N expresses the total number of horses.
- age represents the age range of each horse.

From an evaluation of these factors, the s coefficient for γ and β horses is derived.

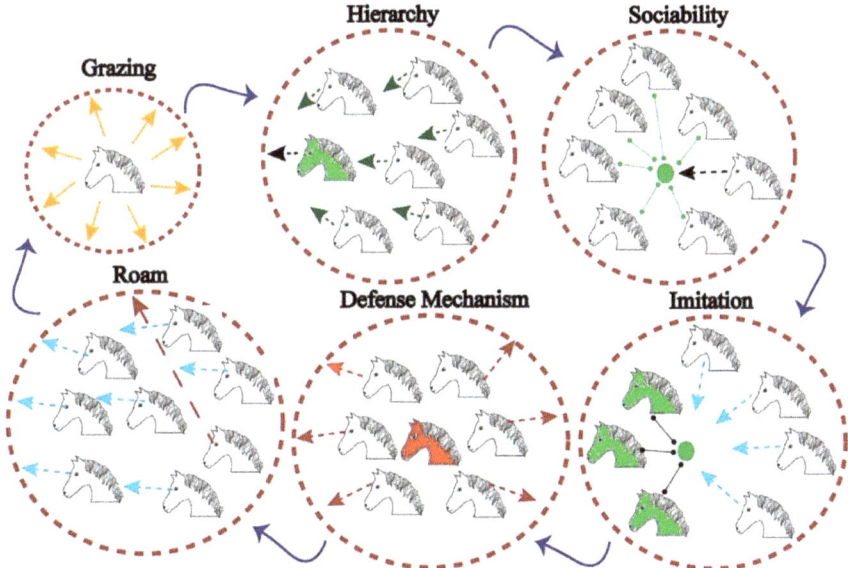

Figure 9. Diagram representing grazing, hierarchy, sociability, imitation, defense mechanisms, and roam of the HOA.

3.4. Imitation (Im)

Horses copy one another and pick up on each other's positive and negative habits, such as locating the best grazing spot [17]. In the current method, the imitation behavior of horses is also taken into account as the factor i. Young horses tend to imitate older ones, and this trait persists throughout their lives (see Figure 9, as explained in Equations (12) and (13)).

$$Im_m^{iter,age} = im_m^{iter,age}\left[\left(\frac{1}{pN}\sum_{j=1}^{pN} P_j^{(-1+iter)}\right) - P^{(-1+iter)}\right] age = \gamma \quad (12)$$

$$im_m^{iter,age} = im_m^{(-1+iter),age} \times \omega_{im} \quad (13)$$

In the above equations:

- $Im_m^{iter,age}$ expresses the vector of motion that represents the ith horse around the average of the best horse at P position.
- $im_m^{iter,age}$ shows the orientation of that horse in the direction of the group on the ith iteration. This is reduced in every cycle, with a parameter of ω_{im}.
- pN represents the number of horses in the best positions, where p is 10% of the selected horses.
- ω_{im} is a reduction factor per cycle for i_{iter}.

3.5. Defense Mechanism (DefMec)

The attitude of horses reflects the fact that they have historically been preyed upon [17]. They use the fight-or-flight reaction to defend themselves. Their initial impulse is to flee. In addition, when trapped, they will buck. Horses battle for food and water to keep rivals at bay and to avoid dangerous locations where adversaries such as wolves may lurk [15–18].

In the HOA method, the horses' defense mechanism works by fleeing away from those horses who exhibit improper or suboptimal behaviors, as illustrated in Figure 9. This factor characterizes their primary defense mechanism. As previously stated, horses must either run from or battle their foes. When possible, such a defensive system exists throughout the lifecycle of a young or adult horse. A negative coefficient in Equations (14) and (15) represents the horse's defensive system, which keeps the animal away from dangerous situations.

$$DefMec_m^{iter,age} = defmec_m^{iter,age}\left[\left(\frac{1}{qN}\sum_{j=1}^{qN} P_j^{(-1+iter)}\right) - P^{(-1+iter)}\right] \quad age = \alpha, \beta, \gamma \quad (14)$$

$$defmec_m^{iter,age} = defmec_m^{(-1+iter),age} \times \omega_{defmec} \quad (15)$$

In the above equations:

- $DefMec_m^{iter,age}$ describes the escape vector of the ith horse, based around the average position of a horse in the worst P position.
- qN shows the number of horses in the worst positions, where q is 20% of the total horses.
- ω_{defmec} represents the reduction factor per cycle for iIter that was calculated earlier.

3.6. Roam (Ro)

In the pursuit of food, horses move and graze across the countryside, moving from pasture to pasture [17]. The majority of horses are maintained in stables, although they preserve the aforementioned trait. A horse may abruptly change its grazing site. Horses are incredibly curious, and they frequently visit different pastures and get to know their surroundings. The horses may see each other through the side walls of their enclosures, and their desire for sociability is satisfied in an adequate stable [17,18].

The factor r is used to imitate this behavior in the algorithm, as nothing more than a random movement. Roaming is virtually never seen in horses while they are young, and it progressively fades as they mature. This process is depicted in Figure 9. Equations (16) and (17) show the roam variables. The flowchart of the HOA algorithm is given in Figure 10.

$$Ro_m^{iter,age} = ro_m^{iter,age} \partial P^{(-1+iter)} \quad age = \gamma, \delta \quad (16)$$

$$ro_m^{iter,age} = ro_m^{(-1+iter),age} \times \omega_{ro} \quad (17)$$

Here, $Ro_m^{iter,age}$: is the arbitrary velocity vector of the ith horse for just a local area search and an escape from local minima.

ω_{ro} represents a reduction factor of $ro_m^{iter,age}$ per cycle.

By putting the results from Equations (6)–(17) into Equations (2)–(5), we can establish the generic velocity vector.

Velocity of δ horses at the age of 0–5 years:

$$\begin{aligned}Vel_m^{iter,\delta} = &\left[w_g \times g_m^{(iter-1),\delta}(low + r*upp)[P_m^{(iter-1)}]\right] \\ +&im_m^{(-1+iter),\delta} \times \omega_{im} \times \left[\left(\frac{1}{pN}\sum_{j=1}^{pN} P_j^{(-1+iter)}\right) - P^{(-1+iter)}\right] \\ +&ro_m^{(-1+iter),\delta} \times \omega_{ro} \times \partial P^{(-1+iter)}\end{aligned} \quad (18)$$

Velocity of γ horses at the age of 5–10 years:

$$Vel_m^{iter,\gamma} = \left[w_g \times g_m^{(iter-1),\gamma}(low + r*upp)[P_m^{(iter-1)}]\right]$$
$$+h_m^{(-1+iter),\gamma} \times w_h \times [P_{lbh}^{(iter-1)} - P_m^{(iter-1)}]$$
$$+soc_m^{(-1+iter),\gamma} \times \omega_{soc} \times \left[\left(\frac{1}{N}\sum_{j=1}^{N} P_j^{(-1+iter)}\right) - P_m^{(-1+iter)}\right]$$
$$+im_m^{(-1+iter),\gamma} \times \omega_{im} \times \left[\left(\frac{1}{pN}\sum_{j=1}^{pN} P_j^{(-1+iter)}\right) - P^{(-1+iter)}\right] + ro_m^{(-1+iter),age} \times \omega_{ro} \times \partial P^{(-1+iter)} \quad (19)$$

Velocity of β horses at the age of 10–15 years:

$$Vel_m^{iter,\gamma} = \left[w_g \times g_m^{(iter-1),\beta}(low + r*upp)[P_m^{(iter-1)}]\right]$$
$$+h_m^{(-1+iter),\beta} \times w_h \times [P_{lbh}^{(iter-1)} - P_m^{(iter-1)}]$$
$$+soc_m^{(-1+iter),\beta} \times \omega_{soc} \times \left[\left(\frac{1}{N}\sum_{j=1}^{N} P_j^{(-1+iter)}\right) - P_m^{(-1+iter)}\right]$$
$$-defmec_m^{(-1+iter),\beta} \times \omega_{defmec}$$
$$\times \left[\left(\frac{1}{qN}\sum_{j=1}^{qN} P_j^{(-1+iter)}\right) - P^{(-1+iter)}\right] \quad (20)$$

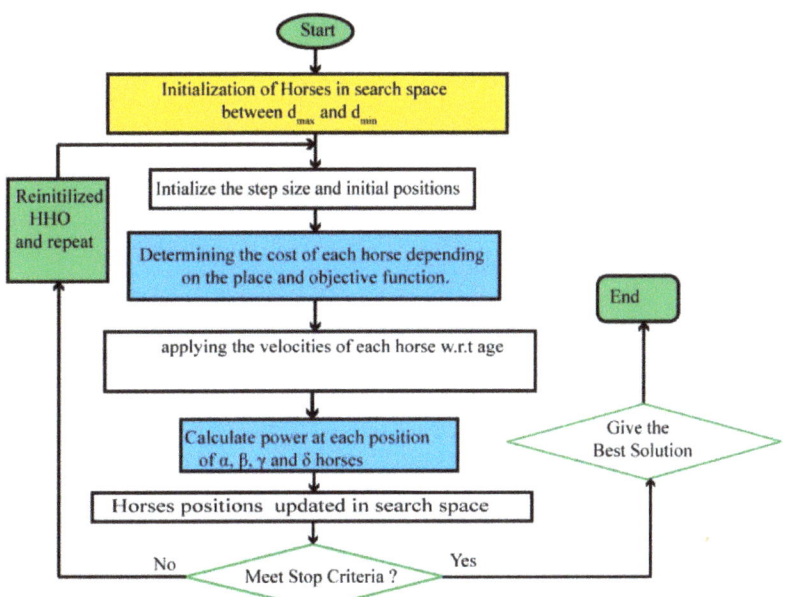

Figure 10. Flowchart of the HOA algorithm.

Velocity of α horses at the age of 10–15 years:

$$Vel_m^{iter,\alpha} = \left[w_g \times g_m^{(iter-1),\alpha}(low + r*upp)[P_m^{(iter-1)}]\right]$$
$$-defmec_m^{(-1+iter),\alpha} \times \omega_{defmec}$$
$$\times \left[\left(\frac{1}{qN}\sum_{j=1}^{qN} P_j^{(-1+iter)}\right) - P^{(-1+iter)}\right] \quad (21)$$

Some observations on how the HOA algorithm might be advantageous are as follows:
- The α horses will get the best reactions and also serve as role models for the rest. They take over the coaching role as they begin their hunt for the optimum reaction

and develop an exploited strategy. When the characteristics of grazing and defensive mechanisms must be used, this behavior occurs.
- The β horses diligently look for the most likely ideal locations, paying great attention to α.
- The γ horses are created using all their inherent behaviors. They seem to be useful for both the explorative and exploitative phases, even though they exhibit both strong and arbitrary movements.
- Young horses seem to be more rambunctious and livelier, making them more suited to the exploring period.

The following are the main characteristics of our HOA method:
1. The horse herd optimization algorithm (HOA) is a novel MPPT approach that has been developed.
2. To collect the GM, the proposed approach needed fewer iterations.
3. In PS and CPS situations, the proposed approach shows almost no oscillation and can collect GM.
4. Experiments and findings show that the proposed approach with interims of rapid searching and minimal oscillation is preferable.
5. A statistical study is performed to determine the algorithm's efficiency, detecting speed, and steady-state reaction.

The HOA technique's pseudo-code is shown in the box below.

(a) Basic configuration: providing variables with a boundary limit and other factors.
(b) Initializing: creating a suitable space with a uniform random selection of horses.
(c) Checking fitness level: determining the cost of each horse, depending on the place and objective function.
(d) Evaluating age: assessing the ages of (α, β, γ, and δ) horses.
(e) Implement the velocity: with respect to every horse's age, apply the velocity.
(f) Revise the position: updating the position of all horses in the search space.
(g) End: if the stop criteria are not met, go to step (c).

4. Tracking Mechanism of HOA

The tracking mechanism is illustrated in the flow chart of HOA in Figure 10. By using the transient value of the voltage at the output and the duty cycle (dc), the tracking behavior of HOA is presented. The partially shaded power-voltage curve is illustrated at the top right corner, shown in Figure 11b, in which there exists only one point; this point is GM, while the remaining three points are LM. In Figure 11b, HOA is initialized with four horses, named P1, P2, P3, and P4. The efficiency of the PV system is affected by increasing or decreasing the number of horses; therefore, four horses are used here to achieve good performance from the HOA. The fitness is calculated for each horse by using the magnitude of power. The corresponding power of each horse at a distinct location determines the movement of a horse, and the expression (4) in Section 3 is used to update the movement of each horse. As illustrated in Figure 11b, point P2 has the highest fitness value; therefore, the output is given to P2. In the initial 45–55 milliseconds, the sudden increase in power is due to its highly efficient explorative/searching performance, controlled by (10) and (11). At the start, the exploration phase remains dominant until the 201-millisecond point. Therefore, it is difficult to track the GM. In Figure 11b, at 50 milliseconds, P2 encounters LM2. The remaining horses demonstrate lower fitness, and the controlled output remains unchanged for a few milliseconds in terms of the dc of the selected converter. However, other horses start searching for the best solution. When the horse is wedged in at LM, this indicates the minima of its personal best; in addition to this, it keeps searching, until and unless the horses explore an improved solution. It can be noticed that P3 is the best solution and the horses have left the P2 point, as shown in Figure 11b. The convergence of horses begins in the next 80 to 125 milliseconds. In the meantime, P4 starts searching for the new, fittest solution, resulting in a little surge at around 125 milliseconds. Now, *P3* overtakes *P4*. Once more, LM3 is encountered, and the output of HOA becomes stagnant at LM3. In the meantime, the mechanism breaks the LM3 trap. The GM is obtained within 141 milliseconds, and it can be observed that all the horses settle at the GM successfully and the HOA reaches a state of equilibrium. During the searching process, large fluctuations of voltage transients are observed as an initial phase effect; finally, the oscillations produced by the voltage are considerably reduced and the HOA successfully tracks the GM. The power and voltage are tracked by HOA, present in Figure 11a,c, respectively.

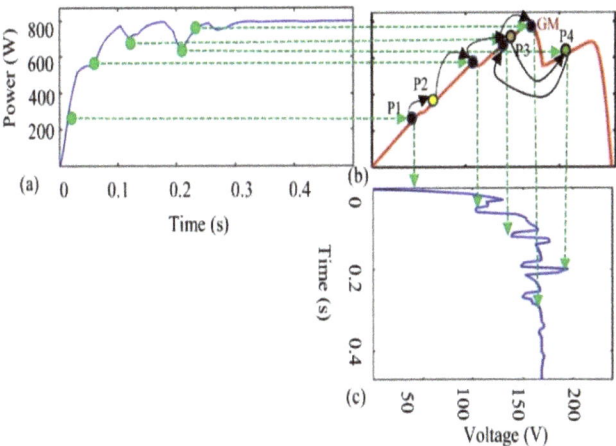

Figure 11. The tracking mechanism of the HOA through P-V curve (**a**) power-time curve, (**b**) GM tracking curve and (**c**) voltage-time curve.

HOA under Complex Partial Shading (CPS) Conditions

Most optimization algorithms for MPPT are unable to track the GM under CPS conditions. As mentioned earlier, HOA is proposed here specifically for this purpose. Therefore, we will proceed to discuss the CPS conditions in detail and the consequent impact of the HOA's application. CPS occurs when myriad modules of PV cells, connected in series, are subjected to PS55. This extreme situation results in the formation of multiple close peaks of LM. Such a collection of local maxima is known as a cluster. Every cluster has its own maxima, named the cluster head maxima (CHM) [19,20].

A specific CPS case is shown in Figure 6, hereafter referred to as case 4. which will be later utilized to acquire the GM, using HOA, for the research work presented in this paper. The left half of the curve of P-V presents a cluster, including 4 MPPs. The corresponding power of LM, starting from left to right, is observed as 729.6 W, 898.3 W, 989.8 W, and 1080 W, respectively. The computed maximum power value of the cluster is 1080 W. Three MPPs exist in a cluster on the right half-curve. Their respective powers are observed as 1080 W, 1025 W, and 831 W, respectively, from right to left. At the extreme left peak, the maxima of the cluster head occur, which gives the global MPP.

It is clear that the cluster values of CHM1 and LM2 are quite close to each other, 1010 W and 1025 W, having a minor difference of 14.5 W that comprises less than 2% of the maximum power. Consequently, this algorithm does not re-initialize the next epoch to track the MPP, due to being wedged in, and the horses may not find the area between CHM2 and GM. Additionally, in previous iterations, the vectors of velocity intentionally slow down the motion of the horses. For improved convergence and minimum oscillations, the slower motion in the previous iteration cycle is convenient. Undetected GM causes a remarkable 5.7% loss of attainable power, due to a complicated PS. For GMPP tracking, which is present in the middle areas of the power and voltage characteristics curves, the HOA method is useful.

To resolve the abovementioned problem, a common search with a huge number of horses is used; however, by increasing the number of horses, there is an exponential increase in the resources needed for completing the communal interactivity. This causes an increase in cost, as well as computational complexity, while reducing the application range. Generally, when applying MPPT, 4 to 6 particles are used, and empirical outcomes are achievable by this efficient process [17]. Effective solutions are obtained in HOA by creating efficient groups, maintaining the space among adjacent horses, as well as initializing the process again. The procedure can be made even more efficient by initializing and moving the HOA particles, such that the scanned areas are skipped effectively. The highest exploration can be ensured via the horses' mobility utilizing HOA.

5. Experimental Results

This section discusses four different scenarios, in which three cases represent four conditions of operation and one case represents twelve conditions of operation. For formulating the problem comprehensively, the different scenarios are chosen for comparing the results of HOA with those found using PSO, ACS, P&O, and DFO techniques. Case 1 presents the fast-changing nature of irradiance, Cases 2 and 3 pertain to the PS conditions, while Case 4 deals with the CPS condition. The final conclusions are drawn, based on the attained performance. Table 1 presents a detailed analysis of the results.

Table 1. Techniques for comparing the power, tracking, and efficiency with that of the HOA.

Method	Irradiance Scheme	Convergence Time (s)	GM Settle Time (s)	GM Existed	Power at GM	Power Tracking (W)	Energy Value (kWh)	Efficiency (%)
DFO	Case 1	0.24	0.28	Yes	1260	1259	1.66	99.9
	Case 2 PS	0.26	0.43	Yes	450	448.7	0.85	99.5
	Case 3PS	0.19	0.21	Yes	796	793.5	1.55	99.7
	Case 4CPS	0.19	0.22	Yes	1078	1075	2.12	99.8
HOA	Case 1	0.16	0.20	Yes	1260	1259.9	1.66	99.9
	Case 2 PS	0.19	0.37	Yes	450	449.7	0.86	99.8
	Case 3PS	0.19	0.22	Yes	796	795.8	2.12	99.9
	Case 4CPS	0.17	0.25	Yes	1078	1077	1.65	99.8
P&O	Case 1	0.12	0.12	Yes	1260	1237	0.46	98.1
	Case 2 PS	LM	LM	No	450	220	0.47	67.7
	Case 3PS	LM	LM	No	796	238	0.51	32.0
	Case 4CPS	LM	LM	No	1078	262	1.64	24.7
PSO	Case 1	0.47	0.70	Yes	1260	1257	0.83	94.6
	Case 2 PS	0.41	0.81	Yes	450	439.2	1.48	97.6
	Case 3PS	0.68	0.70	Yes	796	791.5	2.10	99.4
	Case 4CPS	0.42	0.50	Yes	1078	1068	1.65	99.2
ACS	Case 1	0.46	0.69	Yes	1260	1258	0.83	99.8
	Case 2 PS	0.30	0.84	Yes	450	420	1.49	95.5
	Case 3PS	0.35	0.45	Yes	796	778.6	2.10	97.8
	Case 4CPS	0.40	0.56	Yes	1078	1067	3.10	99.2

The performance analysis depends on different factors, including the time required for tracking, the convergence of power, the settling time, oscillations while in steady-state, transience in the voltage, currents, efficiency, and obtained power, as well as the energy used by the techniques to obtain the power. The results verify the conjecture that the HOA performs more efficiently compared to other optimization techniques. Table 2 shows the UIC and PS conditions, and the corresponding irradiance level received by the PV panels.

Table 2. Case 1 to Case 3: levels of irradiance.

Cases	Irradiance $S_i \left(\frac{kW}{m^2}\right)$				P_{max}
C_{1-4}	PV1	PV2	PV3	PV4	(W)
Case1 Fast Changing	1, 0.7, 0.3	1, 0.7, 0.3	1, 0.7, 0.3	1, 0.7, 0.3	1260, 880, 380
Case2 (Partial Shading)	0.8	0.25	0.7	0.4	449.7
Case3 (Partial Shading)	0.5	0.8	1.0	0.9	796.1

5.1. Case 1: Fast-Changing Irradiance

All the modules of the PV cells are provided in Case 1 with equal irradiances, but the level of irradiance changes with respect to time, which is called fast-changing irradiance. Table 2 shows the irradiances' pattern. The MPP is shifted by the change in irradiance, as shown in Figure 4. The power comparison of HOA with the existing techniques is shown in Figure 12. HOA achieves a maximum value of efficiency in terms of power in the initial interval, when it reaches 1260 W. For comparison with the power efficiencies achieved by HOA, note that DFO, PSO, ACS, and P&O are 1259.5 W, 1257 W, 1239 W, and 1210 W, respectively. These values show that HOA achieved 99.98% efficiency. Case 1 exhibits 3 different regions, based on the values of irradiance. Considering the mean value is more suitable for measuring the efficiency of the competing techniques, since the value of irradiance changes with reference to time [2]. The mean values of the powers attained by HOA, DFO, PSO, ACS, and P&O are 834.2 W, 822.9 W, 820.1 W, 828 W, and 819.4 W, respectively, indicating the greatest attained average value was achieved with the HOA. The HOA generates about 6–33 W more, compared with the other algorithms. The total achievable efficiency by HOA, DFO, PSO, ACS, and P&O, which is the ratio of average to the highest power value, is 99.27%, 97.96%, 97.91%, 97.95%, and 98.79%, respectively. The ranking of these techniques in terms of power is as follows: HOA > DFO > PSO > ACS > P&O. The measured time of tracking of HOA, DFO, PSO, ACS, and P&O is 0.14 s, 0.18 s, 0.45 s, 0.47 s, and 0.33 s, respectively. The value of the settling time is calculated as 0.25 s, 0.25 s, 0.38 s, 0.62 s, and 0.70 s for HOA, DFO, PSO, ACS, and P&O, respectively. The HOA tracking and settling time is 50% faster for attaining the GM. The overshoot response in HOA is faster and aids in the prevention of unwanted oscillations, which may result in power loss. There is a convergence of P&O with GM, although it does not stop at the GM because of the continuously produced oscillations due to perturbations. The value of oscillations produced by P&O is 21 W; in the initial 0–2 s interval, there is an oscillation between 1259 W and 1238 W.

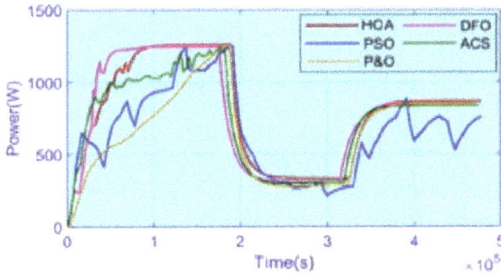

Figure 12. Comparison of HOA power for Case 1.

The dc or the duty ratio is the parameter to be controlled, as shown in Figure 13. The HOA successfully reduces the oscillation value to less than or equal to 1 W, resulting in a 95.24% reduction in the value of oscillations. The arbitrary oscillations by ACS and PSO remain quite high. Figure 12 indicates that PSO demonstrated the highest oscillations. ACS also produced random fluctuations. The transience caused by the voltage is shown in Figure 14.

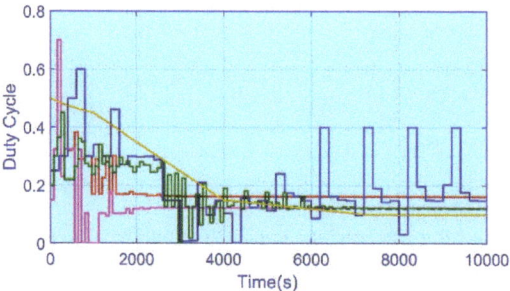

Figure 13. Comparison of the HOA duty-cycle for Case 1.

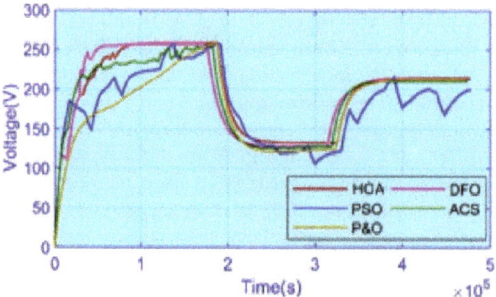

Figure 14. Comparison of HOA voltage for Case 1.

5.2. Case 2: PS Scenario 1

The value of global MPP lies at 450 W in Case 2. Figure 5 shows the curves of P-V and Table 2 gives the order in which the irradiance follows. The duty cycle comparison is presented in Figure 15. Some MPPT techniques utilize the method of making selections on a random basis to search the particles for breaking LM [15]. ACS and PSO algorithms show a high level of random behaviour. For generating unwanted variations, both methods employ arbitrary increases in the step size of the dc. The settling time of the ACS and PSO algorithms is large compared to that of the HOA. The HOA demonstrates almost zero oscillations in the equilibrium state at the global MPP. Figure 15 compares the power obtained by the HOA, DFO, PSO, ACS, and P&O algorithms. The calculations of the efficiency and the power are made against the global MPP, which is located at 450 W. The HOA demonstrates 99.94% efficiency, compared to 99.77% for DFO, 99.55% for PSO, 97.93% for ACS, and P&O, 99.90%; thus the HOA could reliably be called the most efficient technique for tracking the global MPP so far. The GM rapid-tracking and ordered settling time indicates the robustness of the MPPT method. Simulation results, based on the experiments, indicate that on average, the HOA, DFO, PSO, ACS, and P&O take 0.14 s, 0.19 s, 0.68 s, 0.30 s, and 0.22 s, respectively. Figures 16 and 17 show the stable power and voltage produced by the HOA.

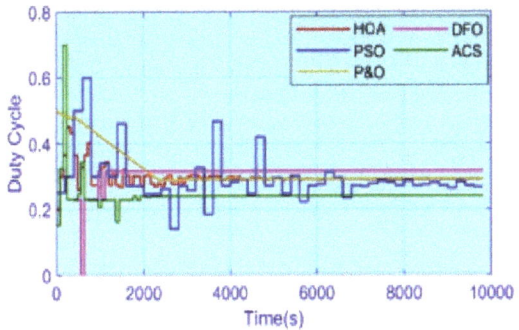

Figure 15. Comparison of HOA duty cycles for Case 2.

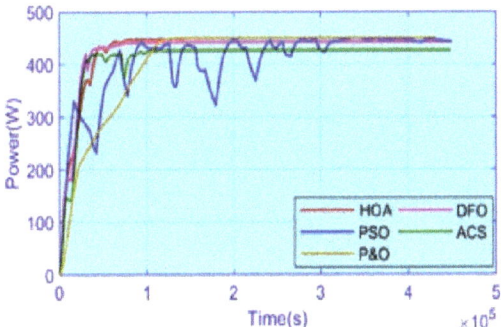

Figure 16. Comparison of the HOA power for Case 2.

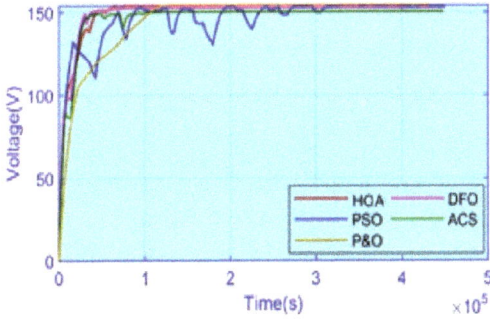

Figure 17. Comparison of HOA voltage for Case 2.

5.3. Case 3: PS Scenario 2

Table 2 shows the values of irradiance under the PS, while Figure 5 displays the equivalent curves of P-V, respectively. Three LMs and one GM are shown in the red curve, with a value of 796 W. P&O fails in tracking the GM by getting stranded in the area that is on the left of the P-V curves, thus limiting its efficiency value by the LM's corresponding power.

Figure 18 shows the resultant power values, while Figure 19 demonstrates the control that the duty cycle provides. Figure 20 shows the voltage values. The peak value of power under the condition of PS, obtained by HOA, DFO, PSO, ACS, and P&O, is 795.1 W, 794.4 W, 785 W, 794.6 W, and 580 W, respectively. The maximum value of efficiency obtained is

99.88% and 99.80% by HOA and DFO, respectively; however, P&O obtains the minimum efficiency at around 49.40% and is stuck at LM1. The HOA, DFO, PSO, ACS, P&O have tracking times of 0.18 s, 0.18 s, 0.41 s, 0.39 s, and 0.45 s, respectively, while 0.40 s, 0.46 s, 0.56 s, 0.81 s, and 0.84 s are their times to settle, respectively. The HOA and DFO algorithm's performances are almost equivalent while tracking the GM. The HOA tracks faster by 19%, thus settling in less than 455 ms for the GM. Due to rapid tracking, the unwanted oscillations are removed, while increasing the robustness. The P&O time for tracking is neglected here because it falls into the LM and is thus unable to locate the GM. This exceptional performance capability of HOA is shown in Case 3, which is followed by DFO, PSO, ACS, and P&O. Although the efficiency achieved by PSO is 97.61%, arbitrary oscillations can be seen in the values of voltage and current. ACS exhibits the same behavior, which in a normal operating situation is undesirable. Power converges 1–4% more in the case of the HOA algorithm, having less than a 1 W ripple, and, in the iteration cycles in the upcoming stages, the oscillations become zero. There are negligible oscillations in the curves of voltage as the output becomes stable under the HOA, as depicted in Figure 20. The duty cycle updates during every epoch, as shown in Figure 17, demonstrating the detection and convergence of HOA to GM with the fewest iterations and showing its superiority.

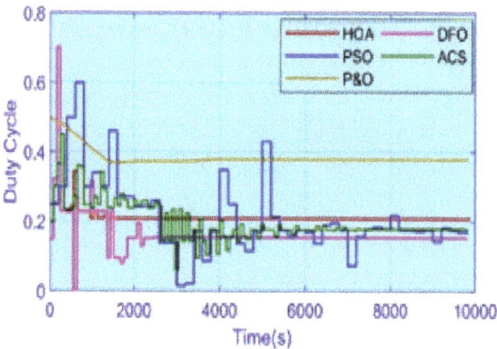

Figure 18. Comparison of the HOA duty-cycle for Case 3.

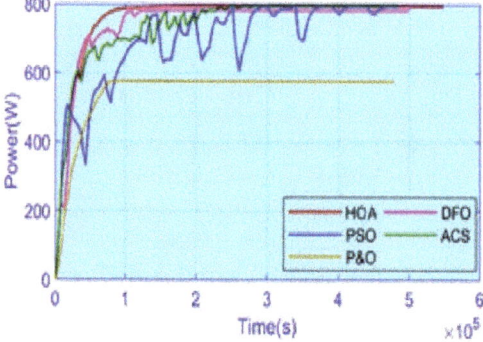

Figure 19. Comparison of the HOA power for Case 3.

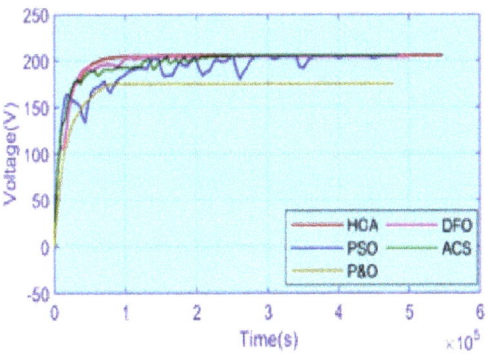

Figure 20. Comparison of the HOA voltage for Case 3.

5.4. Case 4: Complex Partial Shading

This case discusses the CPS situation presented in Figure 6, where arrays of PV cells are serially joined together in the scenario mentioned in Table 3. Figure 21 compares the results of the power comparison. The DC-DC Cuk converter duty cycle measures the controlling activity depicted in Figure 21. The tracked power by the HOA, DFO, PSO, ACS, and P&O is 1079.3 W, 1079.1 W, 1060 W, 890 W, 510 W, respectively. The HOA achieved 99.93% efficiency, while the DFO was 99.92%, PSO 98.7, and ACS 94.7; P&O achieved the lowest power conversion efficiency of 67.4% among all the algorithms. Figure 22 shows that, as desired, the HOA can track the global MPP by utilizing the minimum iterations. Under the HOA and DFO models, there are minimal oscillations; the comparison between voltages is shown in Figure 23. The HOA exhibits the advantages of stable output and steady current.

Table 3. Irradiance level of CPS Cases.

Cases	Irradiance $S_i \left(\frac{kW}{m^2} \right)$				P_{max} (W)
Case4	PV1 = 0.4 PV5 = 0.5 PV9 = 1.00	PV2 = 0.2 PV6 = 0.4 PV10 = 0.8	PV3 = 0.6 PV7 = 0.2 PV11 = 0.7	PV4 = 0.3 PV8 = 0.3 PV12 = 1.0	1078

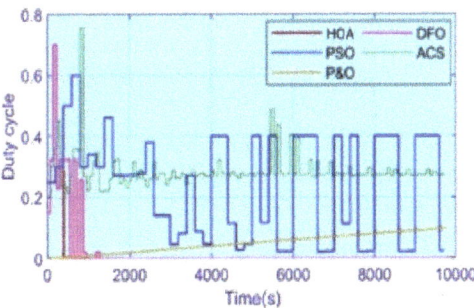

Figure 21. Comparison of the HOA duty-cycle for Case 4.

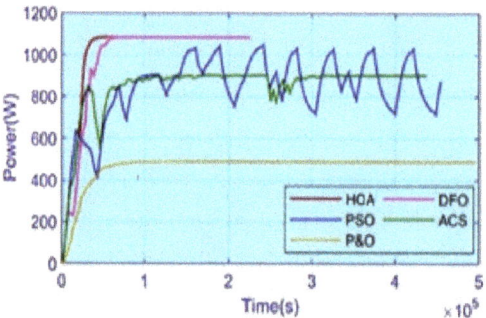

Figure 22. Comparison of the HOA power for Case 4.

For tracking or trailing the GM, the HOA, PSO, ACS, and DFO take 0.15 s, 0.42 s, 0.40 s, and 0.19 s, respectively, while the time to settle is 0.22 s, 0.31 s, 0.51 s, and 0.19 s, respectively. Comparing the results of the demonstration shows that the shortest settling time is from the HOA, followed by the DFO. The HOA settled at 0.22 s and under CPS conditions, and it was faster by 56 ms–300 ms on average, compared to the remaining methods. The performance rating of these techniques is HOA > DFO > ACS > PSO > P&O.

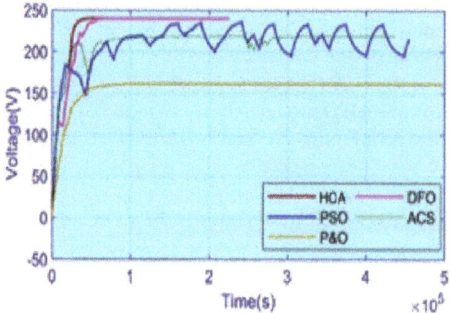

Figure 23. Comparison of the HOA voltage for Case 4.

5.5. Efficiency and Performance Evaluation

On the basis of a statistical evaluation of HOA with competing algorithms, a performance evaluation has been carried out that helped to examine the common characteristics among the techniques. Conventionally, the P&O technique is rapid and easily implementable, as control depends on the gradient. Due to the oscillations, LM achieved and power wastage in the surroundings of MPP was created, thus making P&O an inconvenient choice for high-efficiency applications. PSO can locate GMPP with 99% efficiency under the conditions of PS, which was less in the case of CPS. ACS caused undesirable fluctuations while achieving an efficiency of 93–98%. The ACS took 820 ms to find the GM. The HOA successfully equipped the transient and steady-state oscillations. The overshoot offered by the HOA in response is the lowest compared to the other techniques and the efficiency value outperforms in every operating condition, up to 98%.

The novel HOA technique presented herein can track the global MPP in 95–310 ms in comparison to the time required by the other computing techniques. The HOA achieves 99.4% efficiency, on average, and performs very well among the rest of the competing techniques. Under the HOA, the oscillations decrease to less than 1 W, thus increasing the efficiency of re-tracking. Table 1 summarizes the results of all the respective techniques. According to Case 1, HOA outperforms during the transient phase, when it is exploring the optimum result, confirming it has the best ability to re-track. In Cases 2 to 3, other techniques are less efficient for converging power, while bio-inspired methods are more successful in locating the GM. Case 4 demonstrates the capability of the HOA to tackle the CPS scenario. There is a compromise in the PSO's performance due to random initialization, as in other techniques, even after reaching the global MPP.

6. Conclusions

An MPPT method that is based on the HOA is presented in this paper with a Cuk converter. The assessment analysis of the HOA method has been performed qualitatively and quantitatively, versus the DFO, ACS, P&O, and PSO algorithms. Experimental results based on simulations are presented for four distinct scenarios that represent rapidly changing irradiance, in terms of the PS, along with CPS conditions. The outcomes confirm the effectiveness of the HOA method and show that it outperforms other optimization algorithms, in terms of the searching time of GM, the efficiency of power consumption, and oscillation reduction. Therefore, it is concluded that for increasing the performance of PV systems in different operating conditions related to PS and CPS, it is efficient to employ the MPPT method, which is based on an HOA with a Cuk converter.

Author Contributions: Conceptualization, M.A.H., S.S., A.B.A. and M.Y.J.; methodology, M.A.H., S.S., M.Y.J. and A.B.A.; software, M.A.H., S.S. and M.Y.J.; validation, M.A.H., S.S., M.Y.J. and A.B.A.; formal analysis, M.A.H., S.S., M.Y.J. and A.B.A.; investigation, M.A.H., S.S., A.B.A., K.E. and M.Y.J.; resources, M.A.H., S.S., M.Y.J. and A.B.A.; data curation, S.S. and M.Y.J.; writing—original draft preparation, M.A.H. and S.S.; writing—review and editing, M.A.H., S.S., M.Y.J., A.B.A. and K.E.; visualization, M.A.H., S.S., M.Y.J., A.B.A. and K.E.; supervision, A.B.A. and K.E.; project administration, A.B.A. and K.E.; funding acquisition, K.E. and A.B.A. All authors have read and agreed to the published version of the manuscript.

Funding: This research was funded by the Polish National Agency for Academic Exchange, under grant no. PPI/APM/2018/1/00047, entitled "Industry 4.0 in Production and Aeronautical Engineering" (International Academic Partnerships Program). The APC was funded by the Polish National Agency for Academic Exchange. The authors also want to offer their thanks for the substantive support provided by the KITT4SME (platform-enabled KITs of artificial intelligence for an easy uptake by SMEs) project. The project was funded by the European Commission H2020 Program, under GA 952119.

Institutional Review Board Statement: Not applicable.

Informed Consent Statement: Not applicable.

Data Availability Statement: Not applicable.

Conflicts of Interest: The authors declare no conflict of interest.

References

1. Capuano, L. *U.S. Energy Information Administration's International Energy Outlook 2020*; US Department of Energy: Washington, DC, USA, 2020; p. 7. Available online: https://www.Eia.Gov/Outlooks/Ieo/ (accessed on 20 September 2021).
2. Eldin, A.H.; Refaey, M.; Farghly, A. A Review on Photovoltaic Solar Energy Technology and its Efficiency. In Proceedings of the 17th International Middle-East Power System Conference (MEPCON'15), Mansoura, Egypt, 15–17 December 2015; pp. 1–9.
3. Sarwar, S.; Javed, M.Y.; Jaffery, M.H.; Arshad, J.; Rehman, A.U.; Shafiq, M.; Choi, J.-G. A Novel Hybrid MPPT Technique to Maximize Power Harvesting from PV System under Partial and Complex Partial Shading. *Appl. Sci.* **2022**, *12*, 587. [CrossRef]
4. Javed, M.Y.; Hasan, A.; Rizvi, S.T.H.; Hafeez, A.; Sarwar, S.; Telmoudi, A.J. Water Cycle Algorithm (WCA): A New Technique to Harvest Maximum Power from PV. *Cybern. Syst.* **2021**, 1–23. [CrossRef]
5. Javed, M.Y.; Mirza, A.F.; Hasan, A.; Rizvi, S.T.H.; Ling, Q.; Gulzar, M.M.; Safder, M.U.; Mansoor, M. A Comprehensive Review on a PV Based System to Harvest Maximum Power. *Electronics* **2019**, *8*, 1480. [CrossRef]
6. Radjai, T.; Rahmani, L.; Mekhilef, S.; Gaubert, J.P. Implementation of a modified incremental conductance MPPT algorithm with direct control based on a fuzzy duty cycle change estimator using dSPACE. *Sol. Energy* **2014**, *110*, 325–337. [CrossRef]
7. Mohanty, P.; Bhuvaneswari, G.; Balasubramanian, R.; Dhaliwal, N.K. MATLAB based modeling to study the performance of different MPPT techniques used for solar PV system under various operating conditions. *Renew. Sustain. Energy Rev.* **2014**, *38*, 581–593. [CrossRef]
8. Krishna, K.S.; Kumar, K.S. A review on hybrid renewable energy systems. *Renew. Sustain. Energy Rev.* **2015**, *52*, 907–916. [CrossRef]

9. Zafar, M.H.; Khan, N.M.; Mirza, A.F.; Mansoor, M.; Akhtar, N.; Qadir, M.U.; Khan, N.A.; Moosavi, S.K.R. A novel meta-heuristic optimization algorithm based MPPT control technique for PV systems under complex partial shading condition. *Sustain. Energy Technol. Assess.* **2021**, *47*, 101367. [CrossRef]
10. Mohapatra, A.; Nayak, B.; Das, P.; Mohanty, K.B. A review on MPPT techniques of PV system under partial shading condition. *Renew. Sustain. Energy Rev.* **2017**, *80*, 854–867. [CrossRef]
11. Mirza, A.F.; Ling, Q.; Javed, M.Y.; Mansoor, M. Novel MPPT techniques for photovoltaic systems under uniform irradiance and Partial shading. *Sol. Energy* **2019**, *184*, 628–648. [CrossRef]
12. Mansoor, M.; Mirza, A.F.; Ling, Q. Harris Howk optomization-Based MPPT Control for PV Systems under Partial Shading Conditions. *J. Clean. Prod.* **2020**, *274*, 1–19. [CrossRef]
13. Farh, H.M.H.; Eltamaly, A.M. Maximum Power Extraction from the Photovoltaic System under Partial Shading Conditions. *Smart Energy Grid Des. Isl. Ctries* **2020**, 107–129. [CrossRef]
14. Rezk, H.; Al-Oran, M.; Gomaa, M.R.; Tolba, M.A.; Fathy, A.; Abdelkareem, M.A.; Olabi, A.; El-Sayed, A.H.M. A novel statistical performance evaluation of most modern optimization-based global MPPT techniques for partially shaded PV system. *Renew. Sustain. Energy Rev.* **2019**, *115*, 109372. [CrossRef]
15. Mills, D.S.; McDonnell, S.M.; McDonnell, S. (Eds.) *The Domestic Horse: The Origins, Development and Management of Its Behaviour*; Cambridge University Press: Cambridge, UK, 2005.
16. Krueger, K.; Heinze, J. Horse sense: Social status of horses (*Equus caballus*) affects their likelihood of copying other horses' behavior. *Anim. Cogn.* **2008**, *11*, 431–439. [CrossRef] [PubMed]
17. MiarNaeimi, F.; Azizyan, G.; Rashki, M. Horse herd optimization algorithm: A nature-inspired algorithm for high-dimensional optimization problems Knowledge-Based. *Systems* **2021**, *213*, 106711. [CrossRef]
18. Bogner, F. A Comprehensive Summary of The Scientific Literature on Horse Assisted Education in Germany. Ph.D. Thesis, Van Hall Larenstein, Leeuwarden, The Netherlands, 2011.
19. Mansoor, M.; Mirza, A.F.; Ling, Q.; Javed, M.Y. Novel Grass Hopper optimization based MPPT of PV systems for complex partial shading conditions. *Sol. Energy* **2020**, *198*, 499–518. [CrossRef]
20. Mirza, A.F.; Mansoor, M.; Ling, Q.; Yin, B.; Javed, M.Y. A Salp-Swarm Optimization based MPPT technique for harvesting maximum energy from PV systems under partial shading conditions. *Energy Convers. Manag.* **2020**, *209*, 112625. [CrossRef]

Article

A Parameter Estimation Method for a Photovoltaic Power Generation System Based on a Two-Diode Model

Chao-Ming Huang [1,*], Shin-Ju Chen [1] and Sung-Pei Yang [2]

1. Department of Electrical Engineering, Kun Shan University, Tainan 710, Taiwan; sjchen@mail.ksu.edu.tw
2. Department of Green Energy Technology Research Center, Kun Shan University, Tainan 710, Taiwan; spyang@mail.ksu.edu.tw
* Correspondence: cmhuang@mail.ksu.edu.tw; Tel.: +886-6-205-0518

Abstract: This study presents a parameter estimation method that uses an enhanced gray wolf optimizer (EGWO) to optimize the parameters for a two-diode photovoltaic (PV) power generation system. The proposed method consists of three stages. The first stage converts seven parameters for the two-diode model into 17 parameters for different environmental conditions, which provides more precise parameter estimation for the PV model. A PV power generation model is then established to represent the nonlinear relationship between inputs and outputs. The second stage involves a parameter sensitivity analysis and uses the overall effect method to remove the parameters that have smaller effect on the output. The final stage uses an enhanced GWO that is associated with measurement data to optimally estimate the parameters that are selected in the second stage. When the parameters are estimated, the predicted value for the PV power output is calculated for specific values of solar irradiation and module temperature. The proposed method is verified on a 200 kWp PV power generation system. To confirm the feasibility of the proposed method, the parameter estimation before and after optimization are compared, and these results are compared with other optimization algorithms, as well as those for a single-diode PV model.

Keywords: two-diode model; parameter estimation; gray wolf optimizer

1. Introduction

Photovoltaic (PV) power output is changeable and unpredictable, since it is only generated during the day and not at night. For a large power grid, PV power generation is an uncontrollable power source, therefore there is restricted dispatching. However, the power output from a PV has less inertia than that from traditional units. When an accident occurs in the system, the frequency response decreases as there is a decrease in the inertia of the system, which becomes unstable. Accurately estimating PV power output gives an accurate reference for auxiliary services, such as frequency modulation and rapid response of backup capacity, but the random nature of the output makes estimation difficult.

Estimating parameters for PV power generation involves statistical methods and physical methods. Statistical methods use a black-box model to establish a nonlinear relationship between inputs and outputs. The inputs that are used are the historical PV power output, irradiance, and weather information, and the output is the estimated value for PV power generation. This method uses either indirect or direct forecasting. Indirect prediction [1–3] predicts future irradiance using historical irradiance data and other weather variables, and uses a conversion formula to convert irradiance into PV power output. The curves for irradiance and PV power output are quite similar, thus this method usually accurately estimates PV power output if the irradiance prediction is accurate. Direct prediction [4–10] uses the historical PV power output and weather variables (including irradiance) as input variables, and the prediction results for PV power generation are the output. This method requires an accurate weather forecast to produce good forecast results.

Physical methods establish a physical model for PV power generation between the input and output to convert environmental variables, such as irradiance and temperature, into a power output. Physical model involves either an ideal model [11], a simple power model [12], an experimental model [13], a single-diode model [14–24], a two-diode model [22–27], or a three-diode model [28,29]. The single-diode model with five parameters has a simpler architecture, and has been widely used to simulate the electrical behavior of solar cells. To produce more accurate estimate, the two-diode model with seven parameters is developed to enhance the simulation performance in low irradiance. The three-diode model adds another diode to improve the defects of the recombination process in two-diode model [28]. However, the addition of a diode makes the model more complicated. Considering the accuracy and complexity, this study uses a two-diode model to simulate the electrical behavior of solar cells. When the PV power generation model is created, it is difficult to estimate parameters because there is a nonlinear relationship between these parameters. In addition, after a period of operation, the PV module parameters that are provided by the manufacturer change due to aging and deterioration of the solar cell, therefore these must be corrected.

Some parameters affect the output only slightly and will be eliminated in the parameter selection process. When the parameters that affect the output are selected, an optimization tool is used to accurately estimate the parameters. Several optimization algorithms have been used to estimate the parameters of solar cells, such as the hybrid charged system search algorithm [15], the particle swarm optimization (PSO) method [18], the differential evolution algorithm (DE) [19], the chaos-embedded gravitational search algorithm [21], the bonobo optimizer [22], the improved cuckoo search algorithm [23], the chaotic improved artificial bee colony algorithm [24], the ranking-based whale optimizer (WO) [28], and the grasshopper optimization algorithm [29]. As mentioned above, most studies use different optimization tools to solve the parameter estimation problem. The estimation accuracy depends heavily on the chosen optimization algorithm. In addition, the five-parameter and seven-parameter methods, which are respectively used for single-diode and two-diode models, are still imprecise. To solve this problem, a novel approach is proposed in this study. The proposed method consists of three stages. The first stage converts seven parameters for the two-diode model into 17 parameters and establish a PV power generation model in the MATLAB/SIMULINK environment. The second stage combines sensitivity analysis and the overall effect method to remove the parameters that have a smaller effect on the output. The final stage uses an EGWO to optimally estimate the parameters.

The differences compared to the previous studies and the contributions of this study are highlighted as follows:

- A PV power generation system based on a two-diode model is established in the MATLAB/SIMULINK environment, which can be used for parameter estimation of PV power plants of different types and scales.
- Converting the seven parameters of the two-diode model into 17 parameters according to different environmental conditions provides more precise parameter estimates for the PV model.
- A parameter elimination technique that combines parameter sensitivity analysis and the overall effect method is used to remove the parameters that have little effect on the output.
- To enhance the global search ability of GWO, a dynamic crowding distance (DCD) algorithm is used to eliminate the agents with higher density region in the optimization process.

The remainder of this paper is organized as follows. Section 2 details the PV power generation models. Section 3 describes the proposed parameter estimation method. Section 4 presents the simulation results for a 200 kWp PV power generation system and conclusions are offered in Section V.

2. The PV Power Generation Models

2.1. Single-Diode Model

Figure 1 shows the circuit of a single-diode model which is composed of a photo current source, a diode, a shunt resistance, and a series resistance. The output current of the model is expressed as [14,15]:

$$I = I_L - I_o \left[exp\left(\frac{V + IR_s}{n_I V_t}\right) - 1 \right] - \frac{V + IR_s}{R_{sh}} \qquad (1)$$

where I is the output current for the solar cell, I_L is the photo current, R_{sh} is the parallel resistance, R_s is the series resistance, I_o is the saturation currents for the diode, V_t is the thermal voltage, and n_I is the ideal factor. Since $exp\left(\frac{V+IR_s}{n_I V_t}\right) \gg 1$, Equation (1) can be simplified as [16]:

$$I = I_L - I_o \left[exp\left(\frac{V + IR_s}{n_I V_t}\right) \right] - \frac{V + IR_s}{R_{sh}} \qquad (2)$$

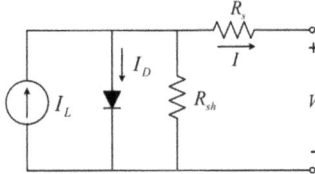

Figure 1. The circuit of a single-diode model.

2.2. Two-Diode Model

For a two-diode model, the saturation current is generated by two diodes. Figure 2 shows the circuit of a two-diode model. The output current for this model is expressed as [25–27]:

$$I = I_L - I_{o1}\left[exp\left(\frac{V + IR_s}{n_{I1} V_{t1}}\right)\right] - I_{o2}\left[exp\left(\frac{V + IR_s}{n_{I2} V_{t2}}\right)\right] - \frac{V + IR_s}{R_{sh}} \qquad (3)$$

where I_{o1} and I_{o2} are the saturation currents for the two diodes, V_{t1} and V_{t2} are the thermal voltage, and n_{I1} and n_{I2} are the ideal factors. In Equation (3), I_{o2} is used to compensate for the compound loss in the depleted area. This model produces more accurate estimates than a single-diode model if there is low irradiance or shading, but the addition of a diode makes the model more complicated.

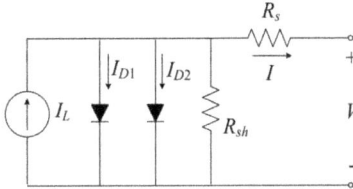

Figure 2. The circuit of a two-diode model.

Equation (3) shows that seven parameters must be estimated for the two-diode model: I_L, I_{o1}, I_{o2}, n_{I1}, n_{I2}, R_s, and R_{sh}. These parameters change for different irradiance and temperature values as [17,25–27]:

$$I_L = \frac{G}{G_{ref}}\left[I_{L,ref} + \alpha_{Imp}\left(T - T_{ref}\right)\right] \qquad (4)$$

$$I_{o1} = I_{o1,ref} \left(\frac{T}{T_{ref}}\right)^3 \exp\left(\frac{qE_g}{k}\left(\frac{1}{T_{ref}} - \frac{1}{T}\right)\right) \quad (5)$$

$$I_{o2} = I_{o2,ref} \left(\frac{T}{T_{ref}}\right)^{\frac{3}{2}} \exp\left(\frac{qE_g}{n_{I2}k}\left(\frac{1}{T_{ref}} - \frac{1}{T}\right)\right) \quad (6)$$

$$n_{Ii} = n_{I,ref}, \ i = 1, 2 \quad (7)$$

$$R_s = R_{s,ref} \quad (8)$$

$$R_{sh} = R_{sh,ref}\left(\frac{G_{ref}}{G}\right) \quad (9)$$

$$E_g = E_{g,ref}\left[1 - 0.0002677\left(T - T_{ref}\right)\right] \quad (10)$$

where G is the solar irradiance (kW/m^2), G_{ref} is the solar irradiance under standard test condition (STC), T is the surface temperature of the solar cell (K), T_{ref} is the surface temperature under STC, $\alpha_{I_{mp}}$ is the temperature coefficient at the maximum power point, and $E_{g,ref}$ (eV) is the gap energy for the material under STC. STC defines a test environment with 1000 (W/m^2) irradiance, a temperature of 298 (K) and a 1.5 air mass.

Under any environmental conditions, the short-circuit current I_{sc} and the open-circuit voltage V_{oc} are expressed as [17,25–27]:

$$I_{sc} = \frac{G}{G_{ref}}\left[I_{sc,ref} + \alpha_{I_{sc}}\left(T - T_{ref}\right)\right] \quad (11)$$

$$V_{oc} = V_{oc,ref} + \beta_{oc}\left(T - T_{ref}\right) \quad (12)$$

At the maximum power operating point, the current I_{mp} and the voltage V_{mp} are expressed as [17,25–27]:

$$I_{mp} = I_{mp,ref}\left(\frac{G}{G_{ref}}\right) \quad (13)$$

$$V_{mp} = V_{mp,ref} + \beta_{oc}\left(T - T_{ref}\right) \quad (14)$$

where $\alpha_{I_{sc}}$ is the temperature coefficient at short-circuit current, and β_{oc} is the temperature coefficient at open-circuit voltage.

Combining Equation (4) to Equation (14), the nonlinear relationship between the seven parameters and the related parameters is briefly expressed as:

$$A(Y) = B(X) \quad (15)$$

where $Y = [I_L, I_{o1}, I_{o2}, n_{I1}, n_{I2}, R_s, R_{sh}]$ and $X = [I_{L,ref}, I_{sc,ref}, V_{oc,ref}, I_{mp,ref}, V_{mp,ref}, G_{ref}, T_{ref},$ $n_{I1,ref}, n_{I2,ref}, R_{s,ref}, R_{sh,ref}, I_{o1,ref}, I_{o2,ref}, \alpha_{I_{mp}}, \alpha_{I_{sc}}, \beta_{oc}, g_{,ref}]$. As shown in Equation (14), the seven parameters in Y are controlled by the 17 parameters in X, which are optimized to provide a more accurate estimation of parameters.

3. The Proposed Method

The proposed parameter estimation method establishes a PV power generation model, selects parameters using a sensitivity analysis, and the overall effect method and optimizes parameters using an EGWO. Figure 3 shows a schematic diagram of the proposed method.

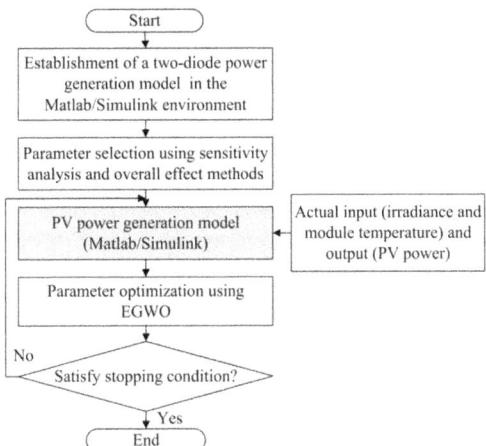

Figure 3. The schematic diagram of the proposed method.

3.1. Establishment of PV Power Generation Model

Using the two-diode equivalent circuit, the PV power generation model is established using Matlab/Simulink software. The model inputs are the solar irradiance and the module temperature, and the outputs are the current and power generated. Figure 4 shows the establishment of a PV power generation model, where subsystem1 is used to calculate seven parameters, including I_L, I_{o1}, I_{o2}, n_{I1}, n_{I2}, R_s and R_{sh}, and subsystem2 is used to calculate the current and power output.

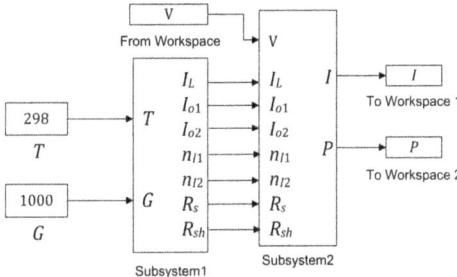

Figure 4. Establishment of a PV power generation model.

3.2. Parameter Selection

To allow more accurate parameter estimation, the original seven parameters in the PV model are converted into 17 parameters for this study. The parameters that are provided by the manufacturer change due to natural degradation of the solar cell. Some parameters have little effect on the output, and can be removed from the model. Parameters are selected to reduce the calculation time for the optimization process.

The parameter selection method for this study uses a parameter-output sensitivity matrix at a specific steady-state operating point. A principal component analysis (PCA) [30] is then used to evaluate the effect on the overall outputs. The magnitude of the parameter effect is evaluated by the sensitivity coefficient $\overline{S}_{ij}$ [30]:

$$\widetilde{S}_{ij} = \frac{\widetilde{\theta}_j}{\widetilde{y}_i} \frac{\partial y_i}{\partial \theta_j} = \frac{\widetilde{\theta}_j}{\widetilde{y}_i} \overline{S}_{ij} \qquad (16)$$

where $\widetilde{\theta}_j$ is the jth parameter, and $\widetilde{y}_i$ is the ith output. In Equation (6), j = 1, 2, ... , Q, Q is the number of parameters.

There is a disturbance on the jth parameter, such that $\Delta\theta = \theta_j - \widetilde{\theta}_j$, the ith output changes (i.e., $\Delta y_i = y_i - \widetilde{y}_i$) and the sensitivity coefficient is approximated as [30]:

$$\overline{S}_{ij} = \frac{\partial y_i}{\partial \theta_j} \approx \frac{\Delta y_i}{\Delta \theta_j} \tag{17}$$

Equation (17) is a dimensionless sensitivity matrix that expresses the relationship of each parameter with respect to each output. The parameters that have smaller effect on the output are removed in the first step, and the PCA is then used to evaluate the effect of each parameter on the overall outputs.

Combining Equations (16) and (17), the overall effect of the jth parameter is expressed as:

$$E_{eff,j} = \frac{\sum_{i=1}^{n_o} |\lambda_i P_{ij}|}{\sum_{i=1}^{n_o} |\lambda_i|} \tag{18}$$

where $E_{eff,j} \in [0, 1]$ is the effect of the jth parameter on the overall variables, λ_i is the eigenvalue for the ith output, P_{ij} represents the degree of contribution for the jth parameter on the ith output, and n_o is the number of outputs. The parameters with a larger value of E_{eff} are then optimized using an EGWO algorithm.

3.3. Enhanced Gray Wolf Optimizer (EGWO)

The GWO was proposed by Mirjalili and Lewis [31]. Wolves have very strict social behaviors, which are roughly classified into four categories: α, β, δ, and Ω in order of fitness value. The Ω is the lowest gray wolf, which is dominated by other wolves. The GWO uses surrounding prey, attacking prey, and searching for other prey strategies to model the social behavior of wolves. To enhance the global search ability of GWO, a dynamic crowding distance (DCD) [32] algorithm is used to eliminate the agents with higher density region in the optimization process. Figure 5 shows the pseudocode for the EGWO to optimize the parameters [33], which is described as follows.

```
Initial setting (max number of iteration, population size, coefficients a, A and C)
Initial agents
Fitness value calculation of each search agent
call subroutine (PV power generation model created in SIMULINK)
P̄α=the location of α wolf
P̄β=the location of β wolf
P̄δ=the location of δ wolf
while (t < max number of iteration)
    for each search agent
        Update the location of each wolf according to surrounding strategy
    end for
    Update coefficients a, A, and C
    Fitness value calculation of all search agents
    call subroutine (PV power generation model created in SIMULINK)
    use DCD to eliminate the agents with higher density region
    Update P̄α, P̄β and P̄δ
    t=t+1
end while
return P̄α
```

Figure 5. The pseudocode for the EGWO to optimize the parameters [33].

3.3.1. Surrounding Prey

The wolves usually use surrounding strategy to hunt prey, which is expressed as [31]:

$$\vec{X}(t+1) = \vec{X}_p(t) - \vec{A} \cdot \vec{D} \tag{19}$$

$$\vec{D} = \left|\vec{C}\vec{X}_p(t) - \vec{X}(t)\right| \tag{20}$$

where t is the present iteration step, $\vec{A}$ and $\vec{C}$ are coefficients, and $\vec{X}$ and $\vec{X}_p$ denote the location of wolves and the location of the prey, respectively. In Equations (19) and (20), $\vec{A} = 2\vec{a} \cdot \vec{r} - \vec{a}$ and $\vec{C} = 2 \cdot \vec{r}$, $\vec{a}$ decreases linearly from 2 to 0 along the optimization process, and $\vec{r} \in [0, 1]$ is a random vector.

3.3.2. Attacking Prey

After the surrounding is finished, the wolves stop moving and start attacking their prey. In this stage, Ω wolves change their location based on the best location of α, β, and δ as [31]:

$$\vec{D}_\alpha = \left|\vec{C}_1 \cdot \vec{P}_\alpha - \vec{P}\right|, \vec{D}_\beta = \left|\vec{C}_2 \cdot \vec{P}_\beta - \vec{P}\right|, \vec{D}_\delta = \left|\vec{C}_3 \cdot \vec{P}_\delta - \vec{P}\right| \tag{21}$$

$$\vec{P}_1 = \vec{P}_\alpha - \vec{A}_1 \cdot \vec{D}_\alpha, \vec{P}_2 = \vec{P}_\beta - \vec{A}_2 \cdot \vec{D}_\beta, \vec{P}_3 = \vec{P}_\delta - \vec{A}_3 \cdot \vec{D}_\delta \tag{22}$$

$$\vec{P}(t+1) = \frac{\vec{P}_1 + \vec{P}_2 + \vec{P}_3}{3} \tag{23}$$

where $\vec{P}$ is the location of the wolves, and $\vec{P}_\alpha$, $\vec{P}_\beta$ and $\vec{P}_\delta$ denote the respective locations of the α, β, and δ wolves.

3.3.3. Search for Other Prey

To achieve a global search, GWO allows $\vec{A}$ to set randomly greater than 1 or less than -1. This forces an exploratory search and allows the agents to search for the other prey so that the optimization process can run away the local minimum values.

3.3.4. Dynamic Crowding Distance (DCD)

DCD [32] is a diversity maintenance strategy for retaining a certain number of solutions uniformly distributed in the space of feasible solution. In this paper, DCD is employed to eliminate adjacent feasible solutions as follows [32]:

$$d_i = \frac{\sum_{j=1, j \neq i}^{C} |fit_i - fit_j|}{fit_{max} - fit_{min}} \tag{24}$$

where fit_i is the fitness value of the ith feasible agent, fit_j is the fitness value of the jth feasible agent, C is the number of feasible agents, and fit_{max} and fit_{min} are the maximum and minimum fitness values, respectively.

Equation (24) states that if the value of d_i is small, the ith feasible agent is in a higher density area and has a higher probability to be eliminated. The deprecated agents will be replaced by randomly generated agents.

In Equation (24), the fitness value is calculated as:

$$fit_j = \sum_{j=1}^{C} (O_{j,est} - O_{j,mea})^2 \tag{25}$$

Where $O_{j,est}$ is the estimated value of the jth agent, and $O_{j,mea}$ is the measured value of the jth agent. The feasible agent with lower fitness value is better in the iteration process.

4. Numerical Results

The proposed method was tested using a 200 kWp PV power generation system. The data were collected from January 2019 to December 2019, which consists of the hourly historical PV power output and the associated irradiance and module temperature. Due to sunshine, the data in summer season (from June to September) were collected from 06:00 a.m. to 19:00 p.m. at a total of 14 points; in the non-summer season, data were collected at a total of 12 points from 06:00 a.m. to 17:00 p.m. To verify the feasibility of the proposed method, the proposed EGWO was compared with the other swarm optimization algorithms such as PSO and WO. To evaluate the accuracy of the forecast, the mean relative error (MRE) is used as follows [15]:

$$\text{MRE} = \frac{1}{N} \sum_{i=1}^{N} \frac{|P_{fore} - P_{true}|}{P_{cap}} \times 100\% \qquad (26)$$

where P_{fore} is the estimated value, P_{true} is the actual value, P_{cap} is the capacity of the PV power generation, and N is the number of data points. As shown in Equation (26), the MRE is calculated by dividing the estimation error by the capacity of PV power generation in order to reduce the weight of the lower power generation to the error percentage.

4.1. Establishment of PV Power Generation Model

Table 1 indicates the reference values for the 17 parameters under STC. These parameter values are obtained by the manufacturer or by experience. A PV power generation model is then created using the 17 parameters in the MATLAB/SIMULINK environment. Figure 6 shows the current–voltage (I-V) and power–voltage (P-V) characteristic curves for diverse irradiance values. The higher the irradiance, the larger is the output current and power, but the effect on the maximum voltage is small. Figure 7 shows the I-V and P-V curves under different temperatures. The greater the module temperature, the less is the output current and power, and there is a significant effect on the maximum voltage. As observed in Figures 6 and 7, irradiance affects current and power output more than module temperature.

Table 1. The reference values for related parameters under STC.

No	Parameter	Reference Value	No	Parameter	Reference Value
1	$I_{L,ref}$ (A)	3.45	10	$I_{o1,ref}$ (A)	1.16×10^{-15}
2	$V_{oc,ref}$ (V)	66.4	11	$I_{o2,ref}$ (A)	1.07×10^{-15}
3	$I_{sc,ref}$ (A)	3.66	12	$n_{I1,ref}$	1.8609
4	$V_{mp,ref}$ (V)	52.0	13	$n_{I2,ref}$	1.8609
5	$I_{mp,ref}$ (A)	3.51	14	$\alpha_{I_{sc}}$ (A/K)	6.81×10^{-4}
6	G_{ref} (W/m^2)	1000	15	$\alpha_{I_{mp}}$ (A/K)	6.50×10^{-4}
7	T_{ref} (K)	298	16	β_{oc} (V/K)	-0.166
8	$R_{s,ref}$ (Ω)	2.4089	17	$E_{g,ref}$ (eV)	1.121
9	$R_{sh,ref}$ (Ω)	150			

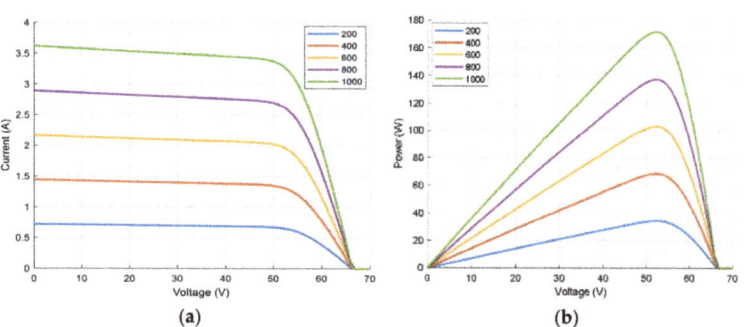

Figure 6. The (**a**) I–V and (**b**) P–V characteristic curves for different irradiance values.

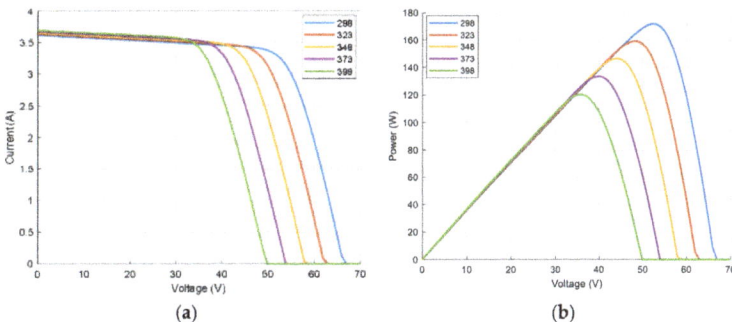

Figure 7. The (**a**) I–V and (**b**) P–V characteristic curves for different temperatures.

4.2. Parameter Selection for Optimization

To determine the effect of individual parameters on the outputs, a parameter sensitivity analysis with ±5% disturbance is used, and the results are shown in Table 2. The results for the overall effect value show that parameters $I_{L,ref}$, $V_{oc,ref}$, $I_{sc,ref}$, $V_{mp,ref}$, $I_{mp,ref}$, G_{ref}, T_{ref}, $R_{s,ref}$, $R_{sh,ref}$, $n_{I1,ref}$, $\alpha_{I_{mp}}$, and β_{oc} have a greater effect on the output, parameters $I_{o1,ref}$, $I_{o2,ref}$, $\alpha_{I_{sc}}$, and $E_{g,ref}$ have little effect on the output. Furthermore, $n_{I2,ref} = n_{I1,ref}$, therefore $n_{I2,ref}$ can be removed. Obtained from this table that in the optimization process, the five parameters $I_{o1,ref}$, $I_{o2,ref}$, $\alpha_{I_{sc}}$, $n_{I2,ref}$, and $E_{g,ref}$ will remain unchanged, and only 12 parameters are used for optimization.

Table 2. Parameter sensitivity matrix and overall effect value for individual parameters for a ±5% disturbance.

No.	Parameter	Power	Current	Voltage	E_{eff}
1	$I_{L,ref}$ (A)	0.6210	0.0312	4.2×10^{-6}	0.9532
2	$V_{oc,ref}$ (V)	0.001	0.002	0.0098	0.3440
3	$I_{sc,ref}$ (A)	−0.120	−0.0025	−0.0001	0.8031
4	$V_{mp,ref}$ (V)	0.004	0.00075	5.1×10^{-5}	0.4680
5	$I_{mp,ref}$ (A)	0.052	0.001	3.2×10^{-5}	0.7865
6	G_{ref} (W/m^2)	−0.194	−0.0038	−0.0025	0.9425
7	T_{ref} (°K)	0.490	0.0125	0.14525	0.8821
8	$R_{s,ref}$ (Ω)	−0.1155	−0.02201	−0.0000	0.7971
9	$R_{sh,ref}$ (Ω)	0.0015	1.3×10^{-5}	0.0011	0.3635
10	$I_{o1,ref}$ (A)	3.5×10^{-6}	1.2×10^{-6}	4.8×10^{-5}	0.0806
11	$I_{o2,ref}$ (A)	2.9×10^{-6}	0.6×10^{-6}	1.6×10^{-5}	0.0912
12	$n_{I1,ref}$	0.0410	0.0023	8.5×10^{-5}	0.3131
13	$n_{I2,ref}$	0.0410	0.0023	8.5×10^{-5}	0.3131
14	$\alpha_{I_{sc}}$ (A/K)	5.1×10^{-6}	1.8×10^{-6}	1.2×10^{-7}	0.0112
15	$\alpha_{I_{mp}}$ (A/K)	0.00067	0.00032	2.9×10^{-7}	0.2302
16	β_{oc} (V/K)	0.00024	0.00011	-9.3×10^{-7}	0.2031
17	$E_{g,ref}$ (eV)	5.1×10^{-6}	1.8×10^{-6}	0.8×10^{-5}	0.0633

4.3. Parameter Optimization

This paper uses an EGWO to optimize the 12 parameters that are selected in the parameter selection stage. Table 3 shows the reference parameters and the parameters after optimization. The ranges for parameters are set in terms of operator experience. In total, four different weather types, including sunny, rainy, cloudy, and slightly cloudy, are used to study the estimation results. Table 4 shows a comparison of the estimation results before and after parameter optimization for different weather types. An optimized parameter gives a smaller value for MRE than one that is not optimized. To verify the performance of the proposed EGWO method, the similar swarm optimization algorithms, such as PSO [18,34] and WO [28,35], are also used to optimize the 12 parameters. The numerical results are shown in Table 5. The proposed EGWO outperforms PSO and WO for different weather types. This table also shows that optimized estimates produce more accurate results than the parameters that are not optimized. The average computation time of the PSO and WO methods through 10 different runs is 12.5 min. and 10.5 min., respectively, while the proposed EGWO takes approximately 9.1 min.

Table 3. Reference parameters and optimized values using EGWO.

No.	Parameter	Reference	Range	Optimization
1	$I_{L,ref}$ (A)	3.45	3.4~3.5	3.42
2	$V_{oc,ref}$ (V)	66.4	63~69	66.35
3	$I_{sc,ref}$ (A)	3.66	3.5~5.4	3.71
4	$V_{mp,ref}$ (V)	52.0	41~55	51.62
5	$I_{mp,ref}$ (A)	3.51	3.43~3.65	3.508
6	G_{ref} (W/m^2)	1000	950~1050	1015.3
7	T_{ref} (K)	298	282~310	295.6
8	$R_{s,ref}$ (Ω)	2.4089	2.3~2.5	2.424
9	$R_{sh,ref}$ (Ω)	150	130~170	148
10	$n_{I1,ref}$	1.8609	1.75~1.95	1.86
11	$\alpha_{I_{mp}}$ (A/K)	6.50×10^{-4}	4.50×10^{-4}~8.50×10^{-4}	4.93×10^{-4}
12	β_{oc} (V/K)	-0.166	-0.145~-0.185	-0.171

Table 4. Estimation results before and after parameter optimization using EGWO.

Weather Types	Optimization	MRE (%)
Sunny day	Before optimization	3.7532
	After optimization	1.2542
Rainy day	Before optimization	1.1991
	After optimization	0.6931
Cloudy day	Before optimization	1.7640
	After optimization	0.9277
Slightly cloudy day	Before optimization	1.9742
	After optimization	1.7337

Table 5. Estimation results using different optimization algorithm.

Weather Type	Method	MRE (%)
Sunny day	Before optimization	3.7532
	PSO [18,34]	1.8321
	WO [28,35]	1.6235
	EGWO [31,33]	1.2542
Rainy day	Before optimization	1.1991
	PSO [18,34]	0.9125
	WO [28,35]	0.9012
	EGWO [31,33]	0.6931
Cloudy day	Before optimization	1.7640
	PSO [18,34]	0.9936
	WO [28,35]	0.9312
	EGWO [31,33]	0.9277
Slightly cloudy day	Before optimization	1.9742
	PSO [18,34]	1.7452
	WO [28,35]	1.7545
	EGWO [31,33]	1.7337

Table 6 shows the estimation results for different PV models using EGWO. The single-diode model with nine parameters produces lower MRE than the single-diode model with five parameters. Similarly, the proposed two-diode model with 12 parameters allows better estimate than the two-diode model with seven parameters. The results in this table show that using Equation (15) to convert the original model to a more refined model according to different environmental conditions can provide more accurate parameter estimation.

Table 6. Estimation error (MRE%) for different PV models using EGWO.

Weather Type	Single-Diode Model [1]	Two-Diode Model [2]	Single-Diode Model [3]	Two-Diode Model [4]
Sunny day (25–26 July)	2.8521	2.8011	2.2951	1.7487
Rainy day (8–9 December)	1.8922	1.8910	1.7973	1.7869
Cloudy day (1–2 November)	2.2324	2.2025	2.0390	1.7340
Slightly cloudy day (21–22 June)	2.8865	2.6698	2.6538	2.0996

[1] Five parameters ($I_L, I_0, n_1, R_s, R_{sh}$) are optimized. [2] Seven parameters ($I_L, I_{o1}, I_{o2}, n_{J1}, n_{J2}, R_s, R_{sh}$) are optimized. [3] 9 parameters ($I_{L,ref}, V_{oc,ref}, I_{sc,ref}, V_{mp,ref}, I_{mp,ref}, G_{ref}, T_{ref}, R_{s,ref}, R_{sh,ref}$) are optimized. [4] 12 parameters ($I_{L,ref}, V_{oc,ref}, I_{sc,ref}, V_{mp,ref}, I_{mp,ref}, G_{ref}, T_{ref}, R_{s,ref}, R_{sh,ref}, n_{J1,ref}, \alpha_{I_{mp}}, \beta_{oc}$) are optimized.

Figures 8–11 respectively show a comparison of the estimation results for a two-diode model and a single-diode model for sunny, rainy, cloudy, and slightly cloudy days. In total, nine parameters are optimized for the single-diode model, which are selected from the original 13 parameters. The curves show that the two-diode model produces better estimation results than the results for a single-diode model. Table 7 compares the estimation performance of the two models for different time periods. The two-diode model gives better estimation results in the morning and afternoon periods if irradiance is low. The two models give similar results for the higher irradiance period at noon. The average error for the two-diode model shows that it gives better estimation results than the single-diode model.

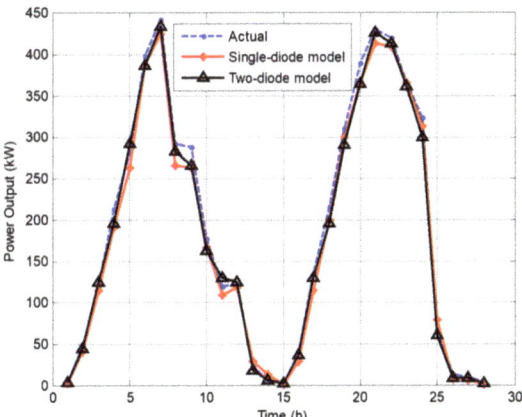

Figure 8. Estimation results for a sunny day (25–26 July).

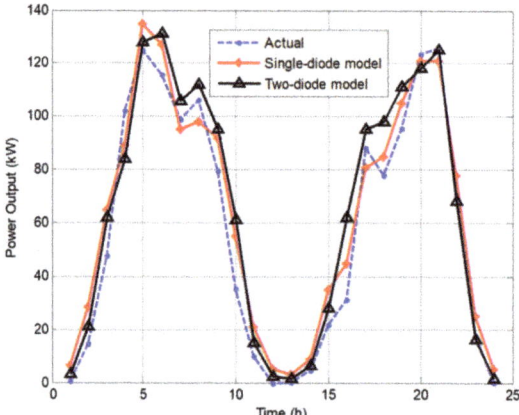

Figure 9. Estimation results for a rainy day (8–9 December).

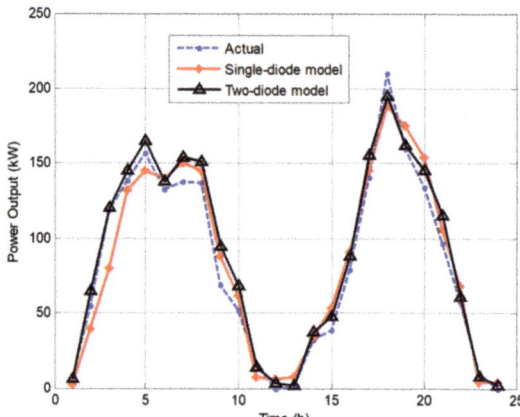

Figure 10. Estimation results for a cloudy day (1–2 November).

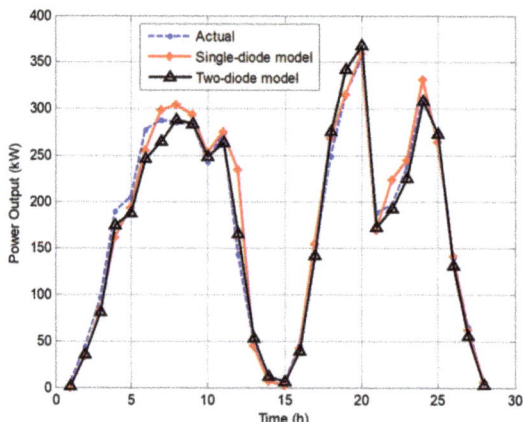

Figure 11. Estimation results for a slightly cloudy day (21–22 June).

Table 7. Comparison results of single-diode and two-diode models for different time periods.

Weather Type	Time Period	Single-Diode Model MRE (%)	Two-Diode Model MRE (%)
Sunny day (25–26 July)	Morning [1]	2.1855	1.3590
	Noon [2]	3.2484	2.4492
	Afternoon [3]	1.4296	1.3600
	Average error	2.2951	1.7487
Rainy day (8–9 December)	Morning [1]	2.0953	2.0278
	Noon [2]	1.4920	1.9675
	Afternoon [3]	1.8045	1.3655
	Average error	1.7973	1.7869
Cloudy day (1–2 November)	Morning [1]	2.4880	1.0525
	Noon [2]	2.5213	2.1633
	Afternoon [3]	1.8313	1.8188
	Average error	2.0390	1.7340
Slightly cloudy day (21–22 June)	Morning [1]	2.3463	2.0363
	Noon [2]	2.6648	2.9756
	Afternoon [3]	2.8888	1.2744
	Average error	2.6538	2.0996

[1]: Morning: 06:00–09:00 a.m.; [2]: Noon: 10:00–15:00 for June–September and 10:00–14:00 for other months; [3]: Afternoon: 16:00–19:00 for June–September and 15:00–17:00 for other months.

4.4. Discussion

The following observations are yield from the above results:

- A photovoltaic power generation system based on a two-diode model is established in the MATLAB/SIMULINK environment, which can be applied to PV power plants of different types and scales only by changing the number of modules in series and parallel.
- As observed in Tables 4 and 5, the proposed algorithm combining GWO and DCD allows better global search ability and lower estimation error than the PSO and WO methods.
- As shown in Table 6, whether a single-diode model or a two-diode model is used, it is more accurate to convert the original model to a more refined model with more parameters according to different environmental conditions.
- Although the proposed EGWO takes approximately 9 min to complete the parameter optimization, it only needs to be executed offline, and usually needs to be performed once a month or when a new PV array is installed.

5. Conclusions

This study creates a PV power generation system based on a two-diode model in the MATLAB/SIMULINK environment. A sensitivity analysis and the overall effect are then used to eliminate the parameters that have a smaller effect on the outputs. An enhanced GWO algorithm is employed to optimize the 12 parameters that are selected from the original 17 parameters. Testing on a 200 kWp PV power generation system shows that optimized parameters produce better estimation results than parameters that are not optimized for four different weather types. When compared with PSO and WO algorithms, the proposed EGWO allows for better optimization performance in terms of estimation error and computation time. Whether a single-diode model or a two-diode model is used, it is more accurate to convert the original model to a more refined model with more parameters according to different environmental conditions. Furthermore, a two-diode model gives better estimation results than a single-diode model in the morning and afternoon when irradiance is lower. The two modes give similar results during the high irradiance period at noon. The average error values show that the two-diode model gives better estimation results. Although the proposed method allows more accurate estimate than previous works, the estimation error caused by the shading effect is still unsolved, which is the limitation of the proposed method. A future work to improve the estimation error due to shading is under study. In addition, the weather information, such as wind speed and wind direction, which affect heat dissipation from the PV module, can be considered as input to increase the estimation accuracy.

Author Contributions: This paper is a collaborative work of all authors. Conceptualization, C.-M.H. and S.-J.C.; methodology, C.-M.H.; validation, C.-M.H. and S.-P.Y.; writing—original draft preparation, C.-M.H. All authors have read and agreed to the published version of the manuscript.

Funding: This research was funded by the Ministry of Science and Technology, Taiwan, ROC, under the grants MOST 110-3116-F-006-001.

Institutional Review Board Statement: Not applicable.

Informed Consent Statement: Not applicable.

Data Availability Statement: Not applicable.

Conflicts of Interest: The authors declare no conflict of interest.

Nomenclature

$\alpha_{I_{mp}}$	Temperature coefficient at the maximum power point
$\alpha_{I_{sc}}$	Temperature coefficient for the short-circuit current
β_{oc}	Temperature coefficient for the open-circuit voltage
λ_i	Eigenvalue of the ith output
$\widetilde{\theta}_j$	The jth parameter
$\vec{A}$	Coefficient vector
C	Number of feasible agents
$\vec{C}$	Coefficient vector
d_i	Diversity of the ith agent
DCD	Dynamic crowding distance
DE	Differential evolution
EGWO	Enhanced gray wolf optimizer
$E_{eff,j}$	The effect of the jth parameter with respect to the overall variables
E_g	Gap energy
$E_{g,ref}$	Gap energy under STC
fit_i	Fitness value of the ith feasible agent
fit_j	Fitness value of the jth feasible agent
fit_{max}	Maximum fitness value
fit_{min}	Minimum fitness value
G	Solar irradiance
G_{ref}	Solar irradiance under STC
GWO	Gray wolf optimizer
I	Output current
I_L	Photo current
$I_{L,ref}$	Photo current under STC
I_{mp}	Maximum output current
$I_{mp,ref}$	Maximum output current under STC
$I_o\ (I_{o1},\ I_{o2})$	Saturation current
$I_{o1,ref}\ \left(I_{o2,ref}\right)$	Saturation current under STC
I_{sc}	Short-circuit current
$I_{sc,ref}$	Short-circuit current under STC
k	Boltzmann constant (1.38×10^{-23} J/K)
$n_I\ (n_{I1},\ n_{I2})$	Ideal factor
$n_{I1,ref}\ \left(n_{I2,ref}\right)$	Ideal factor under STC
n_o	Number of outputs
N	Number of data points
$O_{j,est}$	Estimated value of the jth agent
$O_{j,mea}$	Measured value of the jth agent

P_{cap}	Capacity of the PV power generation
P_{fore}	Estimated value
P_{true}	Actual value
PSO	Particle swarm optimization
PV	Photovoltaic
$\vec{P}$	Location of the gray wolf
P_{ij}	Principal component element for the jth parameter of the ith output
$\vec{P}_\alpha$	Positions of α wolf
$\vec{P}_\beta$	Positions of β wolf
$\vec{P}_\delta$	Positions of δ wolf
Q	Number of the parameter
q	Electron charge $(1.60 \times 10^{-19}\ C)$
R_s	Series resistance
$R_{s,ref}$	Series resistance under STC
R_{sh}	Parallel resistance
$R_{sh,ref}$	Parallel resistance under STC
$\overline{S}_{ij}$	Sensitivity coefficient in the steady state
STC	Standard test condition
t	Current iteration
T	Surface temperature
T_{ref}	Surface temperature under STC
V	Output voltage
V_{mp}	Maximum output voltage
$V_{mp,ref}$	Maximum output voltage under STC
V_{oc}	Open-circuit voltage
$V_{oc,ref}$	Open-circuit voltage under STC
$V_t\ (V_{t1}, V_{t2})$	Thermal voltage
WO	Whale optimizer
$\vec{X}$	Location vector of agent
$\vec{X}_p$	Location vector of the prey
$\tilde{y}_i$	The ith output

References

1. Liu, J.; Fang, W.; Zhang, X.; Yang, C. An Improved Photovoltaic Power Forecasting Model with the Assistance of Aerosol Index Data. *IEEE Trans. Sustain. Energy* **2015**, *6*, 434–442. [CrossRef]
2. Wang, F.; Yu, Y.; Zhang, Z.; Li, J.; Zhen, Z.; Li, K. Wavelet Decomposition and Convolutional LSTM Networks Based Improved Deep Learning Model for Solar Irradiance Forecasting. *Appl. Sci.* **2018**, *8*, 1286. [CrossRef]
3. Ramli, A.M.; Makbui, B.; Houssem, R.E.H. Estimation of Solar Radiation on PV Panel Surface with Optimum Tilt Angle Using Vortex Search Algorithm. *IET Renew. Power Gener.* **2018**, *12*, 1138–1145. [CrossRef]
4. Sun, Y.; Szucs, G.; Brandt, A.R. Solar PV Output Prediction from Video Streams Using Convolutional Neural Networks. *Energy Environ. Sci.* **2018**, *11*, 1811–1818. [CrossRef]
5. Zang, H.; Cheng, L.; Ding, T.; Cheung, K.W.; Liang, Z.; Wei, Z.; Sun, G. Hybrid Method for Short-Term Photovoltaic Power Forecasting Based on Deep Convolutional Neural Network. *IET Gener. Transm. Distrib.* **2018**, *12*, 4557–4567. [CrossRef]
6. Zhang, X.; Li, Y.; Lu, S.; Hamann, H.F.; Hodge, B.M.; Lehman, B. A Solar Time Based Analog Ensemble Method for Regional Solar Power Forecasting. *IEEE Trans. Sustain. Energy* **2019**, *10*, 268–279. [CrossRef]
7. Lee, W.; Kim, K.; Park, J.; Kim, J.; Kim, Y. Forecasting Solar Power Using Long-Short Term Memory and Convolutional Neural Networks. *IEEE Access* **2018**, *6*, 73068–73080. [CrossRef]
8. Agoua, X.G.; Girard, R.; Kariniotakis, G. Probabilistic Models for Spatio-Temporal Photovoltaic Power Forecasting. *IEEE Trans. Sustain. Energy* **2019**, *10*, 780–789. [CrossRef]
9. Aprillia, H.; Yang, H.T.; Huang, C.M. Short-Term PV Power Forecasting Using a Convolutional Neural Network-Salp Swarm Algorithm. *Energies* **2020**, *13*, 1879. [CrossRef]
10. Lateko, H.; Yang, H.T.; Huang, C.M.; Aprillia, H.; Hsu, C.Y.; Zhong, J.L.; Phuong, N.H. Stacking Ensemble Method with the RNN Meta-Learner for Short-Term PV Power Forecasting. *Energies* **2021**, *14*, 4733. [CrossRef]
11. Pavan, A.M.; Mellit, A.; Lughi, V. Explicit Empirical Model for General Photovoltaic Devices: Experimental Validation at Maximum Power Point. *Sol. Energy* **2014**, *101*, 105–116. [CrossRef]

12. Mattei, M.; Notton, G.; Cristofari, C.; Muselli, M.; Poggi, P. Calculation of the Polycrystalline PV Module Temperature Using a Simple Method of Energy Balance. *Renew. Energy* **2006**, *31*, 553–567. [CrossRef]
13. Jadli, U.; Thakur, P.; Shukla, R.D. A New Parameter Estimation Method of Solar Photovoltaic. *IEEE J. Photovolt.* **2018**, *8*, 239–247. [CrossRef]
14. Sabudin, S.N.M.; Jamil, N.M. Parameter Estimation in Mathematical Modeling for Photovoltaic Panel. *Mater. Sci. Eng.* **2019**, *536*, 1–11.
15. Huang, Y.C.; Huang, C.M.; Chen, S.J.; Yang, S.P. Optimization of Module Parameters for PV Power Estimation Using a Hybrid Algorithm. *IEEE Trans. Sustain. Energy* **2020**, *11*, 2210–2219. [CrossRef]
16. Hou, J.; Xu, P. The Matlab/Simulink Simulation Model of the PV Array Based on the Four-Parameter Model. *Renew. Energy Resour.* **2013**, *31*, 10–19.
17. Chouder, A.; Silvestre, S.; Sadaoui, N.; Rahmani, L. Modeling and Simulation of a Grid Connected PV System Based on the Evaluation of Main PV Module Parameters. *Simul. Model. Pract. Theory* **2012**, *20*, 46–58. [CrossRef]
18. Ye, M.; Wang, X.; Xu, Y. Parameter extraction of solar cells using particle swarm optimization. *J. Appl. Phys.* **2009**, *105*, 094502. [CrossRef]
19. Cárdenas-Bravo, C.; Barraza, R.; Sánchez-Squella, A.; Valdivia-Lefort, P.; Castillo-Burns, F. Estimation of Single-Diode Photovoltaic Model Using the Differential Evolution Algorithm with Adaptive Boundaries. *Energies* **2021**, *14*, 3925. [CrossRef]
20. Stornelli, V.; Muttillo, M.; de Rubeis, T.; Nardi, I. A New Simplified Five-Parameter Estimation Method for Single-Diode Model of Photovoltaic Panels. *Energies* **2019**, *12*, 4271. [CrossRef]
21. Valdivia-González, A.; Zaldívar, D.; Cuevas, E.; Pérez-Cisneros, M.; Fausto, F.; González, A. A Chaos-Embedded Gravitational Search Algorithm for the Identification of Electrical Parameters of Photovoltaic Cells. *Energies* **2017**, *10*, 1052. [CrossRef]
22. Al-Shamma'a, A.A.; Omotoso, H.O.; Alturki, F.A.; Farh, H.M.H., Alkuhayli, A.; Alsharabi, K.; Noman, A.M. Parameter Estimation of Photovoltaic Cell Modules Using Bonobo Optimizer. *Energies* **2022**, *15*, 140. [CrossRef]
23. Kang, T.; Yao, J.; Jin, M.; Yang, S.; Duong, T. A Novel Improved Cuckoo Search Algorithm for Parameter Estimation of Photovoltaic (PV) Models. *Energies* **2018**, *11*, 1060. [CrossRef]
24. Oliva, D.; Ewees, A.A.; Aziz, M.A.E.; Hassanien, A.E.; Cisneros, M.P. A Chaotic Improved Artificial Bee Colony for Parameter Estimation of Photovoltaic Cells. *Energies* **2017**, *10*, 865. [CrossRef]
25. Kurobe, K.I.; Matsunami, H. New Two-Diode Model for Detailed Analysis of Multicrystalline Silicon Solar Cell. *Jpn. J. Appl. Phys.* **2005**, *44*, 8314–8322. [CrossRef]
26. Chin, V.J.; Salam, Z.; Ishaque, K. An Accurate and Fast Computational Algorithm for the Two-Diode Model of PV Module Based on Hybrid Method. *IEEE Trans. Ind. Electron.* **2017**, *64*, 6212–6222. [CrossRef]
27. Ishaque, K.; Salam, Z.; Taheri, H. Accurate MATLAB Simulink PV System Simulator Based on a Two-Diode Model. *J. Electron.* **2011**, *11*, 179–187. [CrossRef]
28. Mohamed, A.B.; Reda, M.; Attia, E.F.; Sameh, S.A.; Mohamed, A. Efficient Ranking-Based Whale Optimizer for Parameter Extraction of Three-Diode Photovoltaic Model: Analysis and Validations. *Energies* **2021**, *14*, 3729.
29. Elazab, O.S.; Hasanien, H.M.; Alsaidan, I.; Abdelaziz, A.Y.; Muyeen, S.M. Parameter Estimation of Three Diode Photovoltaic Model Using Grasshopper Optimization Algorithm. *Energies* **2020**, *13*, 497. [CrossRef]
30. Dunteman, G.H. *Principal Components Analysis*; Sage: Newbury Park, CA, USA, 1989.
31. Mirjalili, S.; Mirjalili, S.M.; Lewis, A. Grey Wolf Optimizer. *Adv. Eng. Softw.* **2014**, *69*, 46–61. [CrossRef]
32. Luo, B.; Zheng, J.; Wu, X.J. Dynamic crowding distance: A new diversity maintenance strategy for MOEAs. In Proceedings of the 2008 Fourth International Conference on Natural Computation, Jinan, China, 18–20 October 2008; pp. 580–585.
33. Mirjalili, S. Grey Wolf Optimizer (GWO), Version 1.6, 2018. Available online: https://www.mathworks.com/matlabcentral/fileexchange/44974-grey-wolf-optimizer-gwo (accessed on 25 September 2021).
34. Biswas, P. Particle Swarm Optimization (PSO), Version 1.5.0.2. Available online: https://www.mathworks.com/matlabcentral/leexchange/43541-particle-swarm-optimization-pso (accessed on 8 February 2022).
35. Mirjalili, S. The Whale Optimization Algorithm, Version 1.0.0.0. Available online: https://www.mathworks.com/matlabcentral/_leexchange/55667-the-whale-optimization-algorithm (accessed on 8 February 2022).

MDPI
St. Alban-Anlage 66
4052 Basel
Switzerland
www.mdpi.com

Energies Editorial Office
E-mail: energies@mdpi.com
www.mdpi.com/journal/energies

Disclaimer/Publisher's Note: The statements, opinions and data contained in all publications are solely those of the individual author(s) and contributor(s) and not of MDPI and/or the editor(s). MDPI and/or the editor(s) disclaim responsibility for any injury to people or property resulting from any ideas, methods, instructions or products referred to in the content.

www.ingramcontent.com/pod-product-compliance
Lightning Source LLC
LaVergne TN
LVHW070417100526
838202LV00014B/1474